Message from the WISQ Workshop Chairs

The number of Web information systems (WIS) has grown phenomenally. This in turn has triggered specific research and development focusing on WIS, i.e., information systems (IS) that are integrated in the Web. Also recently new paradigms have evolved such as Web services. The openness of WIS implies that the system developers at development time tend to know the anticipated users of WIS much less well than would be the case for traditional (i.e., non-Web) IS. Determining the functional and non-functional requirements for WIS thus becomes virtually impossible. The functional requirements (at least to some extent) can be considered as being constituted by the key services the vendor wants to have on offer. However, the non-functional requirements have to be replaced by WIS quality. That turns quality into a particular concern with respect to WIS.

From a user's perspective quality can be defined as the suitability for intended or practical use. However, this notion of suitability is subjective and cannot be applied easily in a system under study. A number of quality aspects have been defined already for software systems (and for IS in particular), for simplifying quality related investigations. Competition has led to the fact that for a particular business there are a number of WIS available that implement the key operations. Therefore customers have a choice as to whether to continue using what is not satisfactory or trying something new. New technologies such as Web services seem additionally to suggest that WIS quality should be considered from a different angle or with different concepts, methods and tools than IS in general.

WISQ 2005 was a forum for discussing and disseminating research regarding the quality of WIS and Web services from a holistic point of view and in a comprehensive manner. WISQ 2005 was the third in a series of workshops that commenced in 2003 as the Web Services Quality Workshop (WQW 2003) and continued on in 2004 as the Web Information Systems Workshop (WIS 2004). All three editions of the workshop were held in conjunction with the Web Information Systems Engineering (WISE) conference series.

This year, we received 12 submissions of which 7 papers were accepted. All papers were independently peer-reviewed by the international Program Committee of WISQ 2005.

September 2005

Roland Kaschek
Shonali Krishnaswamy

Message from the WBL Workshop Chair

Recent advances in Internet technologies have rapidly changed our life in various ways. Especially the Web has many positive effects on education. It overcomes the time and space limitations of traditional schools. Teachers and students are now using the Web to access vast amounts of information and resources in the cyberspace. The Web also allows educators to implement a range of new teaching and learning practices, which redefine classroom-learning experiences.

The aim of this workshop was to invite researchers from various fields to present and discuss their ideas on Web-based learning. Areas of interest include various aspects of Web-based learning such as user interface design, learning and content management system, quality management in Web-based learning, the infrastructure of the Web-based learning environment, curriculum design in Web-based learning, assessment strategy in Web-based learning, instructional design methods for Web-based learning, collaborative Web-based learning, and virtual university, etc.

A total of 14 research papers were submitted from 8 countries and were reviewed through 12 program committees. Each paper was reviewed by two internationally renowned program committee members. Papers were rigorously examined and selected based on their significance, originality, technical quality, relevance, and clarity of presentation. Finally 10 papers were selected to be presented at the workshop.

I would like to take this opportunity to thank all the authors who submitted papers to the workshop. I also thank the Program Committee members. Thanks also go to the conference organizers for their support.

September, 2005   Woochun Jun

Message from the SSWS Workshop Chairs

The Semantic Web is an extension of the World Wide Web which seeks to provide data and metadata in a format more amenable for use by intelligent agents and other computer programs. Recent W3C Recommendations for the Semantic Web include the Resource Description Framework (RDF) and the OWL Web Ontology Language. These standards define a graph data model and provide formal semantics for reasoning and inferring additional content. The scale and open world nature of the Semantic Web impose additional challenges beyond those addressed by earlier knowledge base systems.

As deployment of the Semantic Web progresses, scalability becomes increasingly important. The SSWS 2005 workshop seeks to bring together researchers and practitioners to present and discuss recent ideas and results addressing scalability challenges.

Of 21 submitted papers 11 were accepted. These cover a range of topics including existing implementations, benchmarking, interoperability, optimization techniques, approximation methods, experimental results, and lessons learned.

September, 2005

Mike Dean
Yuanbo Guo
Zhengxiang Pan

Organization

WISE 2005 Workshop Chair

Alexandros Biliris   Columbia University, USA

WISQ Program Chairs

Roland Kascheck   Massey University, New Zealand
Shonali Krishnaswamy   Monash University, Australia

WBL Program Chair

Woochun Jun   Seoul National University of Education, Korea

SSWS Program Chairs

Mike Dean   BBN Technologies, USA
Yuanbo Guo   Lehigh University, USA
Zhengxiang Pan   Lehigh University, USA

WISE05 Publication Chair

Quan Z. Sheng   The University of New South Wales, Australia

WISQ Program Committee Members

Boualem Benatallah   The University of New South Wales, Australia
Frada Burstein   Monash University, Australia
Stephane Bressan   National University of Singapore, Singapore
Coral Calero   University of Castille-La Manch, Spain
Fabio Casati   HP Labs, USA
Oscar Diaz   University of the Basque Country, Spain
Gill Dobbie   University Auckland, New Zealand
Ulrich Frank   University of Essen, Germany
Sven Hartmann   Massey University, New Zealand
Annika Hinze   University of Waikato, New Zealand
Klaus P. Jantke   FIT Leipzig, Germany
Christian Kop   University of Klagenfurt, Austria
Seng Loke   Monash University, Australia

Kinshuk	Massey University, New Zealand
Michael Maximilien	IBM Almaden, USA
George Eby Matthew	Infosys Technologies, India
Massimo Mecella	University of Rome, Italy
Heinrich C. Mayr	University of Klagenfurt, Austria
Mario Piattini	University of Castille-La Manch, Spain
Gustavo Rossi	La Plata National University, Argentina
Demetrios Sampson	University of Piraeus, Greece
Graeme Shanks	Monash University, Australia
Amit Sharma	Infosys Technologies, India
Alexei Tretiakov	Massey University, New Zealand
Jian Yang	Macquarie University, Australia
Arkady Zaslavsky	Monash University, Australia
Yanchun Zhang	Victoria University of Technology, Australia
Xiaofang Zhou	University of Queensland, Australia

WBL Program Committee Members

Ralf Klamma	RWTH Aachen, Germany
Whakyung Rim	Busan National University of Education, Korea
Feng-Hsu Wang	Ming-Chuan University, Taiwan
Seongbin Park	Korea University, Korea
John Shepherd	University of New South Wales, Australia
Sean W.M. Siqueira	Catholic University of Rio de Janeiro, Brazil
Hanil Kim	Cheju National University, Korea
Li Yang	Western Michigan University, USA
Oksam Chae	Kyunghee University, Korea
Le Gruenwald	University of Oklahoma, USA
Nalin K. Sharda	Victoria University, Australia
Ilkyeun Ra	University of Colorado at Denver, USA

SSWS Program Committee Members

Grigoris Antoniou	University of Crete & ICS FORTH, Greece
Dave Beckett	University of Bristol, UK
Pierre-Antoine Champin	Lyon 1 University, France
Oscar Corcho	University of Manchester, UK
Ying Ding	University of Innsbruck, Austria
Jeff Heflin	Lehigh University, USA
Atanas Kiryakov	Ontotext Lab, Sirma AI, Bulgaria
Brian McBride	HP Laboratories, UK
Peter F. Patel-Schneider	Bell Laboratories, USA
Dennis Quan	IBM Watson Research Center, USA
Paulo Pinheiro da Silva	Stanford University, USA

Heiner Stuckenschmidt   Vrije University, The Netherlands
York Sure   University of Karlsruhe, Germany
David Wood   University of Maryland, USA
Takahiro Yamaguchi   Keio University, Japan

Table of Contents

Workshop on Web Information Systems Quality

Workshop on Web-Based Learning

Tools

Session 2: Models

Session 3: Innovative Applications

Workshop on Scalable Semantic Web Knowledge Base Systems

Session 1: Scalable Repository and Reasoning Services

Session 2: Practical Semantic Web Applications

Session 3: Query Handling and Optimization Techniques

Ontology for the Selection of e-Processes

Frina Albertyn

Eastern Institute of Technology, Private Bag 1201, Napier, New Zealand
falbertyn@eit.ac.nz

Abstract. Creating an e-Commerce Information System (eCIS) also creates its quality. The development process used to develop an eCIS thus impacts on the quality of the resulting systems. Developers need to select a development process to be followed from a number of available processes. Their choice might be flawed as a result of insufficient knowledge regarding development processes, the quality characteristics of the processes, or a selection methodology. This paper defines an ontology for development processes of eCIS (e-Processes). It provides characteristics and for each a scale and thus a conceptual framework for quantitatively assessing e-Processes. Furthermore a selection methodology and the architecture of a prototype e-Process selection tool are discussed.

1 Introduction

Computer and cognitive science researchers have been trying to find an answer to the question on how to represent knowledge. In order to represent knowledge it needs to be structured. The philosophical elaborations focus on how knowledge is structured and reasoning occurs. [1] The ontological nature of an IS is that it should be true representations of the world. Initially the computational ontologies were taxonomy systems for the presentation of knowledge but the need arose to have a theoretical basis for knowledge representation. Ontology thus provides us with generic models of the real world [1].

Information Systems consist of functional or non-functional system requirements. Functional requirements address the operations the system implements. Non-functional requirements, however, address the way system operations are accessed and executed. Creating systems with given quality characteristics is therefore an approach to the controlled implementation of non-functional requirements. The e-Process selection method that is introduced in this paper focuses largely on system quality and the extent to which the different e-Processes address that quality.

Different companies use the Web differently. The buying and selling of goods electronically is known as E-commerce. Companies are required to use E-commerce in order to enhance the competitiveness of their businesses and increase the efficiency of their operations, [2]. Web development, especially eCIS development, requires quick completions of the project, while delivering quality software, [3]. E-Processes are different from traditional development processes. Even though none of the features required for development are completely new, development processes that focus specifically on e-Commerce systems are not completely defined [4].

M. Dean et al. (Eds.): WISE 2005 Workshops, LNCS 3807, pp. 1 – 10, 2005.

The development process used to develop an eCIS impacts on the quality of the resulting system. Numerous development processes are available for the development of an eCIS and the developers need to choose, preferably, the most suitable one for the project at hand. System quality is threatened if an inadequate eProcess is followed. This paper introduces an e-Process Selection Ontology and Methodology. Even if the eProcess identified by our methodology is not used this methodology may be beneficial, as it may identify an education need if it repeatedly recommends the use of an eProcess that differs from the in-house standard. The methodology can also be used to make the developers aware of those eProcess characteristics for which the selection is sensitive. This sensitivity information may be used to focus attention on critical development issues regardless of the eProcess that is actually used. Weak point analysis may have the same effect. Spending time to select the best suited e-Process for a system under development requires resources. The author believes that spending these resources is justified as the quality of the system under development is affected. The minimum outcome of following our methodology is increased awareness of critical development issues and of reasons that lead to a particular e-Process being selected.

Paper Outline. See in Section 2 the conceptual background of the work and in section 3 the eProcess ontology. Section 4 discusses the selection methodology and section 5 the architecture of the eProcess selection tool. In conclusion future work is discussed and the references listed.

2   Related Work

Quantification of the software process followed, see e.g., [5] is a well-known approach to controlling the efficiency of IS development. Such quantification can take the form of firstly providing scales, i.e., ordered sets of values, for sensibly chosen dimensions that are supposed to represent the views most relevant for the quantification case at hand. Secondly, the software process is scored in each dimension, i.e., a scale value is associated to the process that expresses the extent to which the particular process has the quality defined by that particular view. In particular with respect to software processes for object-oriented target languages or the comparison of such processes several proposals for lists of dimensions, also called features, are known, see, e.g., [5]. The functionality of software processes is often used for comparison (i.e., the type and number of specified development artifacts) while the quality of the processes (i.e., the particular aid provided for creating the specified artifacts and the quality thereof) is often neglected, [5].

WIS development is a growing part of IT activities within most organizations. The process of WIS development within organizations is still largely uncertain, [6]. This paper publishes the results of a research exercise involving 25 UK companies researching the way that WIS are currently developed within UK based organizations.

Research into the selection of an appropriate e-Process has created a number of approaches. A taxonomy regarding various classification features of methodologies for workflow systems development is discussed in [7]. The E-Processes selection approach in [8] relies on identification of situation patterns that best supported a particular process. This qualitative approach may become inconclusive as at the same time several patterns might apply to a lesser or higher degree.

We employ quantification as the main idea for e-Process selection. According to [8] the quality aspects to be considered are organization, project, and team[1]. We integrate these into an approach extending the one in [9] that we are going to present in the next section. eCIS development requires web site development techniques (such as user profiling) as well as the traditional IS development competencies [10, 11]. In [12] the authors conceptualize the term WIS as opposed to IS. The e-Process selection methodology and tool builds on that conceptualization - which have been applied to select the e-Process best suited for developing a business process assembler, i.e., a software component for associative retrieval of business processes [13].

3 Ontology Based Selection of e-Processes

According to Gruber's frequently used definition (see, e.g. [14, 15, 16] an ontology [17] is "an explicit specification of a conceptualisation" that is shared by a number of people and is created for a particular purpose. For a critical discussion of that definition refer to [18] where the definition is discussed as "... a logical theory accounting for the intended meaning of a formal vocabulary". We prefer Gruber's definition because it will be difficult to define a logical theory of software processes with a formal vocabulary. Another alternative conception of IS ontology is a hermeneutic enterprise [19]. We believe that with the time- and resource limitations of a not too innovative system a strictly followed ontology is necessary. We concede that defining the requirements of non-standard projects (to the extent to which the project is highly innovative) or for very difficult to design systems the hermeneutic approach is preferable.

The purpose for creating our ontology is to enable the identification of one, best suited eProcess from a set by quantifying the e-Processes. The conceptualization we use is a list of views on e-Processes. We define a concept representing each view. The concept list, with the provided scale for each view, allows the representation of each e-Process as point in a multi-dimensional, real vector space. We model the extent to which an e-Process is suited for the current project by a norm of that e-Process. A norm on a vector space is a mapping that associates to each vector x a real number $\| x \|$ such that (1) $\| x + y \| \leq \| x \| + \| y \|$, (2) $\| ax \| = | a | \| x \|$, and (3) $\| x \| = 0$, only if x = (0, ..., 0). Vector spaces on which a norm is defined are called normed linear space. For more detail regarding such spaces see, e.g. [20]. The norm gives us a concept of nearness in the space. The process representations, sufficiently near to each other can then be grouped into one cluster. This means they appear similar to the users of our approach. Clustering techniques might be used for organizing e-Processes into clusters. The normed linear space we have in mind might offer the potential for addressing the e-Process selection task in terms of a case-based approach.

3.1 Our e-Processes Ontology

We associate scales with each of the e-Process quality aspects and then interpret the e-Processes as points in a number space, the dimension of which is the number of

---

[1] Rather than quality aspect the source uses the term "methodology variable".

quality aspects used. In order to aggregate or decompose the dimensions in this space a scale up or drill down is possible. Considering super spaces of that space allows the further inclusion of quality aspects if that should be required. Considering subspaces of that space essentially means to ignore certain quality aspects, which may be done for reducing the complexity of the choice among a number of e-Processes.

At the highest level of abstraction groups are introduced to describe e-Processes. The groups considered are: Application, conception, documentation, methodology, modeling system, organization and tool support. We use these groups to address e-Process aspects assumed to be important in order to choose one of them for a particular development task. The groups are:

Application, i.e., the intended system, its quality, its size, the available budget, running cost, benefit and amortization time.

Conception, i.e., the domain of e-Process application, the activity- and artifact life-cycles recommended by the e-Process.

Documentation, i.e., the availability and quality of education - and documentation material including cases studies and the e-Process definition. Furthermore we subsume under documentation the market share of the e-Process.

Methodology, i.e., support for creating and analyzing the prescribed or recommended deliverables, for developing in teams and for a controlled evolution of deliverables.

Modeling system, i.e., the concepts proposed for systems development including explanations of how to use and represent these concepts.

Organization, i.e., the enterprise culture, business strategy followed, the technology used as well as project objectives, requirements, users and implementation, staff skills, their education and experience, team composition, staff work-load and organization temporal aspects - development time.

Tool support, i.e., the availability and quality of tools to carry out the e-Process and the vendor trustworthiness.

Refining our characteristics, grouping or naming them differently, or adding some may impact on a particular choice being made but will not invalidate our method.

The e-Process selection methodology described is based on the use of a multi-dimensional real vector space. Each factor considered as relevant for the e-Process selection is represented by a dimension of that space. Each e-Process is then represented by a point in that space and for each of the space's dimension a weighting factor is introduced. Presupposing we consider n e-Process characteristics then each e-Process p can be encoded as an n-tuple, i.e., as a vector (s_1, ..., s_n) of scores s_i for the i-th characteristic. Furthermore with respect to a project at hand the vector (w_1, ..., w_n) of weighting factors w_i is relevant where w_i is the weighting factor of the i-th characteristic. This encoding allows us to quantitatively compare e-Processes and chose the one that appears as most appropriate. To further refine our selection process, sensitivity analysis, as well as weak-point analysis is applied to identify the kind of improved e-Process that would be suitable with respect to a development task at hand.

3.2 Characteristics Used for e-Process Comparison

Defining a concept of quality for IS and measuring that quality with respect to a given IS though clearly important tasks appear not to be a very common practice. Likewise, a quality concept for e-Processes could play an important role in systems development but is hard to define and seems to be out of scope of practitioners. Obviously, a project control that is aware of both system- and process quality is even harder to realize. However, it must be expected to have significant potentials. We approach the quality problem for e-Processes by first briefly referring to the work of the international standardization organization ISO, see [21]. The concept of a system's quality by ISO was roughly defined as the consistency of that system that makes it suitable for its intended (or implied) use. This definition's advantages are its closed form, that it focuses on system use, and that it is universally applicable. However, it involves the somewhat dark concept of "system consistency" that would need further elaboration. With the use of an IS quite a lot of views on that system's so-called quality aspects or characteristics, may be relevant. Consequently measuring and maintaining system quality according to the ISO definition is not really practical.

It appears more promising to use the approach sketched above, i.e., to use prioritized lists of quality aspects see, e.g. [22]. These may be more or less aggregated, for example, focusing on correctness and efficiency, see, e.g. [23]. We believe that the following statements are true with respect to e-Process selection: No list of quality aspects for information systems can ever be complete for all projects; for a given development task some of the quality aspects may be important while others are less important and; for a given project certain quality aspects may not or must not affect the selection process. The weighting factors of the respective quality aspects may then be set to zero.

In terms of the multi-dimensional vector spaced mentioned above this means considering only a subspace as framework for eProcess selection. As we propose in total 54 quality aspects and thus deal with a 54-dimensional space, it must be considered desirable to reduce the dimensionality of the space. We propose doing that with a sensitivity analysis of the quality aspects with respect to the norm of the e-Processes in our space. One can, for example, omit (by zeroing their weight) from a current consideration the quality aspects with low weight (for example lesser than half of the maximum or the average weight) and low sensitivity (for example lesser than half of the maximum or average of a threshold value). Obviously this simple approach cannot guaranty the consideration being focused at the smallest dimensional subspace suitable. However, in some cases the number of dimensions to be used in an e-Process selection task might be reducible to a considerable degree. One can gain some further impact on the number of dimensions to be considered in an e-Process selection case by using a threshold value specification for eliminating dimensions that differs from the ones mentioned above, i.e., average and maximum.

Currently our selection tool is configured to address all the quality aspects listed below. (Definitions are not included because of space limitations.)

Application: Adaptability, Availability, Completeness, Correctness, Cost, Ergonomics, Interoperability, Maintenance, Performance, Precision, Safety, Security, Development Budget, Running Costs, Amortization Time.

Conception: Domain of Method Application, Recommended Life Cycle Activities.

Documentation: Documents, Apply methodology.

Methodology: Maturity, Accuracy, Reliability, Understandability, Ease of use, Ease of learning, Acceptable, Change Management.

Modeling System: Development for re-use, Documentation and Deliverables.

Organization: Infrastructure, Enterprise Culture, Technology, Current Level of Business, External Exposure, Current Client Base, Personnel Internet Experience, Geographic Interaction, IT Strategy, Business Strategy, Future Plans, Objectives, Requirements, Implementation Strategies, Skills, Education, Team Experience, Knowledge, Other Project Involvement, Development Time.

Tool Support: Availability of Tools, Modeling Tool Quality, Vendor Support, Robustness.

To standardize and normalize the sum of the weights of quality aspects is 1 and all these weights are values between 0 and 1. These weights express the relevance of a quality aspect regarding a given development task. A "best guess" is needed here. The scale value scoring an e-Process with respect to a quality aspect expresses the degree to which this process meets the definition of that aspect and therefore might contribute to the developed system having the respective quality. Also, in this respect, a "best guess" is needed. Apparently, validation of both of the "best guesses" mentioned here, is a very difficult task. We believe the respective figures are characteristics of the selection process. Defining and documenting these values will be of some benefit to the developers. The tool represents the range of the scale values internally as the interval [0, 1]. The value range, as available to the tool-user, is essentially unrestricted.

4   The e-Processes Selection Methodology

The key parts of our selection methodology are represented using a programming language type pseudo code notation. We use structured programming concepts which are self-explaining therefore no references are given.

Our selection method is model-based with a number of pre-defined e-Process quality aspects used as a conceptual framework within which e-Processes can be quantified and compared. This method only indirectly allows incorporation into the selection process experiences obtained by applying a given e-Process. We provide a top-level meta-procedure for reusing e-Process application experiences. Initially a formally computed score is awarded to each e-Process. The UPDATE operation in the procedure below multiplies the currently obtained score with a value u ∈ [0, 1]. This may allow an experience-based choice among e-Processes that are not sufficiently distinguished from each other by our main selection method. The complete update history of individual e-Processes is stored. We believe there is a potential of using case-based selection and model-based selection for the same case. The idea is to identify a number of suitable e-Processes and hope that the intersection of these sets is not empty.

```
DECLARE P ENUMERATION TYPE,
DECLARE e-Processes := {RUP, AM/XP, OSP, SBU }
DECLARE score( e-Processes ) REAL STATIC;
FOR ALL p IN e-Processes
        DO   score( p ) := || p ||; ENDFOR;
LOOP
        ON (no case at hand ) EXIT;
        CHOOSE p IN e-Processes;
```

```
        APPLY p;
        ASSESS p's success;
        UPDATE score( p );
ENDLOOP; END;
```

Symbolic names are introduced for two key parts of the procedure, namely weak point analysis (WPA) and sensitivity analysis (SA). WPA is a procedure that can be applied at a system S with input channels $I_1, ..., I_m$ and an output channel O. We do not discuss the system concept or its use here. Respective information can be found in [24]. The current values at these channels are denoted as $v(I_1) = v_1, ..., v(I_m) = v_m$, and $v(O) = v_O$, respectively. Associate with each input channel J a pair (s_J, i_J) of a score s_J (i.e., the ratio current channel value divided by maximum channel value) and the impact i_J (i.e., the percentage to which v_O is determined by s_J) of J. Let furthermore T, T' $\in$ [0 , 1] be threshold values. WPA(S , T , T') is then the set of weak points of S, i.e., the subset of input channels of S for which holds that their score is below T and their impact is above T'. That means that weak points are the input channels of a system with high impact and small value. More detail regarding using weak point analysis can be found in [25]. Currently we cannot aid in choosing the threshold values. The same goes for the estimation of the impact factors. We hope, however, that experience with tool and methodology will help making a sensible choice.

Sensitivity analysis works in the same setting of a system S with input channels I_1, ..., I_m and an output channel O. Again the current values at these channels are denoted as $v(I_1) = v_1, ..., v(I_m) = v_m$, and $v(O) = v_O$, respectively. Let to each input channel J be associated an interval D_J. Let s be an integer such that starting at the lower boundary l of D_J one can step through this interval with s steps and reach its upper boundary u. The step length thus is $(u - l) / s$. Let the relative absolute maximum deviation from v_O produced by stepping through D_J be the real number $r_J \in [0, 1]$ when all other input channels values apart from J are kept constant at or close to their expected value (or a guess of it). SA(S , s , T) is the set of sensitive input channels, i.e., those input channels J for which $r_J \geq T$. The systems we are applying these forms of analysis to are eProcesses - their characteristic scores (see below) are considered as input channel values and their weighted score sum as the output channel value.

The initial heuristics use some conventions. Let there be m characteristics $c_1,...,c_m$ and n e-Processes $P_1, ... , P_n$. Then each e-Process can be represented by an m-tuple of numbers between 0 and 1. For each characteristic c_i, $i \in \{1, ... , m\}$, and each process P_j, $j \in \{1, ... ,n\}$, we ask an enterprise staff, who is an expert in the field, to determine the weight $w_1, ..., w_m$ of characteristic $c_1, ..., c_m$ and the performance $p(1,j), ..., p(m,j)$ of process P_j with respect to characteristic $c_1, ..., c_m$ respectively. The j-th row of the matrix $(p[u, v])_{\{1 \leq u \leq m, 1 \leq v \leq n\}}$ is denoted as p[* , j]. That row contains the scores of process P_j. We chose the numbers w_i such that $\sum w_i = 1$ and $0 \leq w_i \leq .1$, $\forall i \in \{1, ...,m\}$. Our initial heuristics is then:

```
DECLARE C, W REAL, winner INTEGER
DECLARE P, s, S, T, T' STATIC REAL ARRAY
SET ( P , s , S , T , T' );
LOOP  FOR j ∈ { 1 , … , n }
   W = w[ 1 ] * p[ 1 , j ] + … + w[ m ] * p[ m , j ] ;
```

```
IF ( C < W ) THEN { winner := j ; C := W ; };
END LOOP;
SA( P_winner , s[ winner ] , T[ winner ]  );
WPA( P_winner  , T[ winner ] , T'[ winner ]  ); END;
```

At algorithm termination, the value of the variable winner, is the index of one of those processes with maximal weighted score-sum. Sensitivity analysis and weakpoint analysis are then performed for that eProcess. The sensitivity analysis identifies the characteristics that might lead to another eProcess to be selected using the methodology. The weakpoint analysis identifies those eProcess characteristics which are considered important but in which the winning eProcess scores low. Additional guidance can be sought for these characteristics.

5 Selection Tool Architecture

The architecture (see Fig. 1) of the prototype (described here) implements the ontology and the selection methodology. It involves a multi-tier integration of browsers, applets, servlets, application servers, and back-end services which includes the databases. Our solution will use Visual InterDev to create and manage the HTML and Active Server Pages. As seen in our logical services it includes User Interface, Web Services, Business Rules, Data and Utility Services. Currently the prototype has incorporated into the ontology the following e-Processes: Rational Unified Process (RUP), Agile modeling with extreme programming (AM/XP), Open Source System Development (OSP), Storyboarding with user profiling (SBU). The prototype can easily extend the base of modeled e-Processes. The key functions offered by the e-Process selection tool to the process experts are to add/edit the values used for assessment, add/edit the characteristics and groups as well as add new e-Processes. The user of the system will only be able to apply the selection tool which will calculate the results and recommend an e-Process. The developer is thus assisted to make a decision on the e-Process that will best suit their needs.

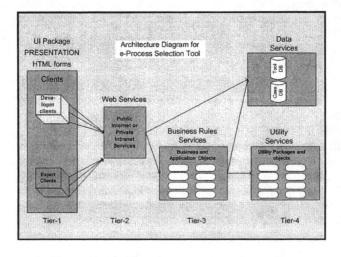

Fig. 1. Architecture Diagram for e-Process Selection Tool

6 Future Research

A subspace of the vector space, with its dimensions as small as possible while still enabling a sensible selection, will be used to make the selection process more transparent to developers. Further ideas will be defined and incorporated into the tool. Similarly, the extent to which the tool can support experience based eProcess selection shall be increased. A case-based database is in the process to be incorporated into the tool to store the selection cases with reasoning support. The good points in our methodology that can be identified will be introduced, see [5], a metrics-based evaluation of object-oriented software development methods. The prototype will be elaborated. The prototype has been applied on a few projects and this will be expanded. The tool will be placed on the web for feedback.

References

1. Michael Rosemann, Iris Vessey, Ron Weber and Boris Wyssusek (2004). On the Applicability of the Bunge-Wand-Weber Ontology to Enterprise Systems Requirements. ACIS 2004, Hobart, Tasmania.
2. Kurt A. Pflughoeft, K. Ramamurthy, Ehsan S. Soofi, Masoud Yasai-Ardekani and Fatemeh Zahedi (2003). "Multiple Conceptualizatins of Small Business Web Use and Benefit." Decision Sciences 34(3): p. 467 - 512.
3. Srinarayan Sharma, Vijayan Sugumaran and Balaji Rajagopalan (2002). "A framework for creating hybrid-open source software communities." Information Systems Journal 12(1): 7.
4. Volker Gruhn and Lothar Schope (2002). "Software processes for the development of electronic commerce systems." Information and Software Technology 44(2002): 891 - 901.
5. Reiner R. Dumke and Eric Foltin (1996). Metrics-based Evaluation of Object-Oriented Software Development Methods. Magdeburg, The Software Measurement Laboratory of Magdeburg (SMLAB). 2004.
6. M.J. Taylor, J. McWilliams, H. Forsyth and S. Wade (2002). "Methodologies and website development: a survey of practice." Information and Software Technology 44(2002): 381 - 391.
7. Fahad Al-Humaidan and B.N. Rossiter (2000). A taxonomy and Evaluation for System Analysis Methodologies in a Workflow Context: SSADM, UML,SSM,OPM., Newcastle University. 2003.
8. Linda V. Knight, Theresa A. Steinbach and Vince Kellen (2001). System Development Methodologies for Web-Enabled E-Business: A Customization Paradigm. 2003.
9. Roland Kaschek and Heinrich C. Mayr "Characteristics of Object Oriented Modeling Methods." EMISA Forum 1998(2): 10-39.
10. Richard Vidgen (2002). "Constructing a web information system development methodology." Info Systems Journal 2002(12): 247-261.
11. Richard Vidgen, David Avison, Bob Wood and Trevor Wood-Harper (2002). Developing Web Information Systems, Butterworth-Heinemann.
12. Roland Kaschek, Klaus-Dieter Schewe, Catherine Wallace and Claire Matthews (2004). Story Boarding for Web-Based Information Systems. Chapter 1. Taniar D., Wenny Rahayu J.: *Web Information Systems,* IDEA Group Publishing. Hersey, PA. 2004.

13. Frina Albertyn and Sergiy Zlatkin (2004). The process of developing a business processes assembler. ISTA 2004: 3rd International Conference on Information Systems Technology and Its Applications., Salt Lake City, Utah, USA July 15-17, 2004.
14. Peter Fettke and Peter Loos (2003). Ontological evaluation of reference models using the Bunge-Wand-Weber model. Ninth Americas Conference on Information Systems.
15. A.L. Opdahl, B. Henderson-Sellers and F. Barbier (2001). "Ontological analysis of whole-part relationships in OO-models." Information and Software Technology 43(2001): 387 - 399.
16. Yair Wand, Veda C. Storey and Ron Weber (1999). "An ontological analysis of the relationship contruct in conceptual modeling." ACM Transactions on Database Systems 24(4): 494 - 528.
17. T. R. Gruber. Toward principles for the design of ontologies used for knowledge sharing. Presented at the Padua workshop on Formal Ontology, March 1993.
18. Gloria L. Zuniga. "Ontology: Its transformation from philosophy to information systems". Proceedings of FOIS 2001.
19. Frederica T. Fonseca, and James E. Martin. ""Toward an alteranative notion of information systems ontologies: Information engineering as a hermeneutic enterprise". Journal of the American Society for Information Science 56, 1 (2005): pp 46 – 57.
20. Walter Rudin. "Real and complex analysis". McGraw-Hill Book Company. New York et al. 2nd printing of 3rd edition. 1987.
21. ISO-Standard (1991). Information Technology - Software product evaluation - Quality characteristics and guidelines for their use: International Standard 9126. 1991 (E). SO/IEC Copyright Office,Case Postal 56,CH-1211, Geneva, Switzerland.
22. Mario Barbacci, Thomas H. Longstaff, Mark H. Klein and Charles B. Weinstock (1995). Software Quality Attributes. Pittsburgh, Pennsylvania, Carnegie Mellon University: 1-53.
23. Stephen R. Schach (2002). Object-Orientated and Classical Software Engineering, McGraw Hill.
24. Niv Ahituv, and Seev Neumann (1990). Principles of information systems for management. Wm. C. Brown Publishers. Dubuque, IA. 3rd edition. 1990.
25. Rolf Böhm, and Sven Wenger (1996). Methods and techniques of system development; (In German). Hochschulverlag AG an der ETH Zürich. 2nd edition.1996.

Managing Web GIS Quality

Yassine Lassoued and Omar Boucelma

LSIS-UMR CNRS 6168 and Université Paul Cézanne,
Avenue Escadrille Normandie-Niemen, F-13397 Marseille
first.last@lsis.org

Abstract. Data quality descriptions play a key role in Geographic Information Systems (GIS). With the availability of geographic data sources over the internet, there is a real issue to be addressed, that is how to ensure quality of web-based heterogeneous GIS. The issue is threefold: first, we have to perform data integration, second we have to manage the quality information if any, and third, we have to provide a mechanism that mixes two technologies, which, to the best of our knowledge has not yet been fully addressed.

1 Introduction

Data quality descriptions are crucial for the development of Geographic Information Systems (GIS). With the availability of geographic data sources on the internet, there is a big issue to be addressed, that is the manipulation of multiple heterogeneous data sources, each of them providing (or not) some quality criteria. The issue is threefold: first, we have to perform data integration, second we have to manage the information quality if any, and third, we have to provide a mechanism that mixes two technologies, which, to the best of our knowledge has not yet been fully addressed.

The database (DB) community has extensively studied and developed data integration systems leading to, among others, mediation systems [12]. As for the GIS community, the work was focused on interoperability aspects, see [9] for instance. Most of the approaches propose to enrich the data models in order to conform to a "unified model", and the creation of the OpenGIS consortium (OGC) is the most visible output of this trend. Several geographic data quality models have been also proposed such as FGDC [11], IGN [10], or the ISO/TC 211 model [2].

In this paper we describe a *quality mediation* approach that allows a community of users to access a set of autonomous and heterogeneous data sources with different qualities. A user of our system poses a query over the global schema. She models her needs, in terms of data quality, as quality conditions conforming to the proposed quality model. The system uses the data sources as well as their data quality information and quality aggregation operations in order to provide a solution of "good" quality.

This paper is organized as follows. Section 2 introduces the problem through a concrete example. Section 3 describes the quality mediation system, while Section 4 details the query rewriting process. Finally we conclude in section 5.

M. Dean et al. (Eds.): WISE 2005 Workshops, LNCS 3807, pp. 11–20, 2005.

2 Motivating Example

The example results from a real geographic data integration problem being studied in the REV!GIS project [3].

2.1 Data Sources and Schemas

We are using OGC's abstract feature model with its GML encoding [8]. A GML data source provides two main elements: an XML Schema Description (XSD) and a GML document. The XSD describes the structure of the GML document that represents a source schema. We also use a tree representation of an XSD, this means that a schema is viewed as a tree whose nodes correspond to XSD elements. A non-terminal node corresponds to a class (a complex-type element) and a leaf corresponds to an attribute (a simple type element or a geometric property).

The example used in this article consists of three real data sources referred to as BDTQ-21ee201 (TQe), BDTQ-31hh202 (TQh) (Bases de Données Topographique du Québec) [4] and NTDB-21e05 (NT) the National Topographic DataBase [1] as represented by their spatial covers and schemas in Figure 1, and their quality metadata in Figure 2.

TQ1 and TQ2 sources have the same schema which consists initially of 25 classes covering several geographic themes at the scale of 1/20 000. For sake of simplicity, we consider only classe *vCommL* which represents linear objects belonging to the transportation network: roads, railways, bridges, etc.

NT has another schema which consists of 196 classes that cover several features at a scale of 1/50 000. Here again, for sake of simplicity we consider only class *roadL* that represents linear roads.

2.2 Schema Mappings

The problem is to seamlessly access the various data sources described above. Our solution consists in a mediation system that supplies a *mediation schema* or *global schema*. Example of such global schema is given in Figure 3, where Class *Road* represents linear roads. TQ1, TQ2 and NT source schemas are semantically linked to the global schema by means of schema mapping rules. Mappings identify portions of a source schema

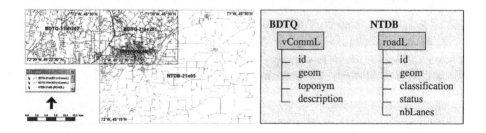

Fig. 1. Spatial Covers of Data Sources with their Schemas

Quality parameter	BDTQ–21ee201 & BDTQ–31hh202	NTDB–21e05
Scale	1/20 000	1/50 000
Spatial cover	21ee201 : [(−72°, 45°22'30''),(−71°30', 45°30')]	[(−72°, 45°15'),(−71°, 45°30')]
	31hh202 : [(−72°30', 45°22'30''),(−72°, 45°30')]	
Provider	Ministry of Natural Resources – Québec	Topographic Information Center – Sherbrooke
Validation date, date of validity	1995	1996
Geometric accuracy	4m	10m
Nomenclature source	Québec Toponym Commission	
Roads classification source	Transportation Ministry	
Frequency of updates	5 years	
deficit, surplus, classification error	1%	5%

Fig. 2. Data Sources Metadata

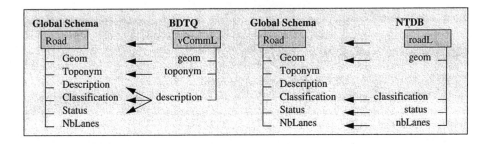

Fig. 3. Mappings between sources BDTQ and NTDB with the global schema

and the global schema that correspond (totally or partially). Figure 3 shows part of the mappings between TQ1 (or TQ2) and the global schema and those between NT and the global schema.

Note that correspondances between elements are not usually trivial (e.g., one-to-one). They may need restrictions (in case of partial mappings between classes, such as between *vCommL* and *Road* for example) or conversion functions (in case of attribute mappings with heterogeneous representations such as for *classification* and *Classification* for example)

2.3   Problem Sketch

Consider a user who is interested in information about highways of a given region b with a given quality condition. She may express a SQL like query Q_0:

Q_0: **Select** *all information about road objects of type Highway **such that** data cover region b and have been validated during the last 10 years (i.e., 1995–2005), with a deficit rate of road objects that is less than 1%, a geometric accuracy of at most 5 meters and a high semantic accuracy of the operational state of the roads.*

First of all, query processing may be different depending on the choice of the spatial cover b. For example, if we respectively choose region B, B' or B'' of Figure 4, the number of data sources that will participate in query processing is respectively two, three or zero. The case of B'' is trivial since the query has no answer. Examples with B and B' are more complicated for the reasons explained below.

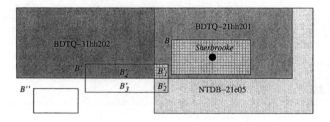

Fig. 4. Two sources do participate with B as spatial cover, three sources with B', and none with B''

Case of region B: Both TQh and NT are eligible over the whole surface B. Both sources satisfy the condition for the validation date. The deficit rate of the first source (1%) is sufficient; that of the second is higher (i.e., worse) than required (5% > 1%), however we cannot reject the data source because, when considered with the first one it will improve (decrease) the total deficit rate. According to the quality conditions, the geometric property must be extracted from TQe, information about the operational state must be extracted from NT, while the rest of information can be extracted from any source.

Note that in modifying the quality conditions we may also modify the origins of attributes. For example, requiring a validation date between 1996 and 2004 instead of requiring a geometric accuracy of at most $5m$ implies that the geometric property should be extracted from NT instead of TQe.

Suppose now that the deficit rate required by the user is 0.5% (instead of 1%). In this case, even though both data sources do not satisfy the condition with the deficit rate, they are still interesting and, if used together, they may lead to a good result. In fact, the probability that an object is absent from both data sources is $1\% * 5\%$, i.e., 0.05%, which is less than 0.5%.

Case of region B': In region B', TQh and NT cover different zones. Zones B_1', B_2', B_3' and B_4' (see Figure 4) do not involve the same data sources. However each of them is homogeneous and can be treated in the same way we did above for B and B''.

3   Quality Mediation System

3.1   Integration System

Definition 1 (Integration System). *An integration system is defined as a tuple* $\mathcal{I} = (G, \mathcal{S}, \mathcal{M}, \mathcal{Q}, key)$, *where G is a global schema, $\mathcal{S} = \{S_i, i \in [1..n]\}$ is a set of source schemas (also called local schemas), $\mathcal{M} = \{M_i, i \in [1..n]\}$ is the set of their respective descriptions, i.e., for each $i \in [1..n]$, M_i is the set of mapping rules between S_i and G. The term $\mathcal{Q}$ denotes a quality model and function key associates to each class of the global schema a global key.*

For object identifiers, we are using a global key mechanism similar to the one described in [5]. This mechanism is a simplified version of the *XML keys* defined in [6], for XML documents. We suppose that each class C of the global schema has a *global key*. This global key is an attribute or a tuple of attributes of class C allowing identification of class instances (i.e., from which the values of the remaining attributes depend), independently of the data source from which they are extracted. For example, we suppose that the key attribute of classes *Road* is its geometric property. Note that the *id* attribute cannot be used as a global key, because it allows to identify only objects of the same data source. Hence it is called a local key [5].

3.2   Quality Model

A *quality model* allows the representation of various data quality parameters. It is mainly composed of quality criteria called *quality parameters* or *quality elements*. Several geographic quality models have been proposed by standard or public institutions such as FGDC [11], the ISO/TC 211 model [2], or the IGN [10] that we adopted as our quality reference model.

Quality Parameters. The IGN quality model we have adopted is composed of the following parameters:

$$\mathcal{Q}_0 = B_b : \text{ Spatial cover} \qquad \mathcal{Q}_1 = P_1 : \text{ Lineage}$$
$$\mathcal{Q}_2 = P_2 : \text{ Currentness} \qquad \mathcal{Q}_3 = P_3 : \text{ Geometric accuracy}$$
$$\mathcal{Q}_4 = P_4 : \text{ Semantic accuracy} \qquad \mathcal{Q}_5 = C_1 : \text{ Completeness}$$
$$\mathcal{Q}_6 = C_2 : \text{ Consistency}$$

Each of the parameters $\mathcal{Q}_i, i \in [0..6]$, is evaluated through a tuple of sub-parameters $(\mathcal{Q}_i^1, \cdots, \mathcal{Q}_i^{k_i})$. For sake of simplicity, we only consider the IGN sub-parameters listed

Table 1. Quality Parameters and Sub-parameters

Parameter	Applicable to	Sub-parameter	Significance	Type
$\mathcal{Q}_0$	Geographic classes	$\mathcal{Q}_0^1 = B_b$	Bounding box	*BoundingBox*
$\mathcal{Q}_1 = P_1$	Geometric properties	$\mathcal{Q}_1^1 = P_1^1$	Scale	*Float*
	Classes, attributes	$\mathcal{Q}_1^2 = P_1^2$	Provider	*String*
		$\mathcal{Q}_1^3 = P_1^3$	Source	*String*
		$\mathcal{Q}_1^4 = P_1^4$	Source organization	*String*
$\mathcal{Q}_2 = P_2$	Classes, attributes	$\mathcal{Q}_2^1 = P_2^1$	Validation date	*Date*
		$\mathcal{Q}_2^2 = P_2^2$	Date of validity	*Date*
		$\mathcal{Q}_2^3 = P_2^3$	Expiry date	*Date*
		$\mathcal{Q}_2^4 = P_2^4$	Frequency of updates	*Integer*
$\mathcal{Q}_3 = P_3$	Geometric properties	$\mathcal{Q}_3^1 = P_3^1$	Position accuracy	*Float*
		$\mathcal{Q}_3^2 = P_3^2$	Shape accuracy	*Float*
$\mathcal{Q}_4 = P_4$	Attributes	$\mathcal{Q}_4^1 = P_4^1$	Semantic accuracy	*Enumeration / Float*
$\mathcal{Q}_5 = C_1$	Classes, attributes	$\mathcal{Q}_5^1 = C_1^1$	Deficit rate	*Percentage*
		$\mathcal{Q}_5^2 = C_1^2$	Surplus rate	*Percentage*
$\mathcal{Q}_6 = C_2$	Classes	$\mathcal{Q}_6^1 = C_2^1$	Accordance rate	*Percentage*
	Attributes	$\mathcal{Q}_6^2 = C_2^2$	Violation rate	*Percentage*

in Table 1. Because Q_5 and Q_6 have a different behavior, they are denoted respectively by C_1 and C_2. In fact, as explained later, these are percentages which can be improved or degraded by combining data sets.

The quality model is attached to the global schema, each parameter applies to one or more types in the global schema. Column 2 of Table 1 indicates to which type of elements each parameter (or sub-parameter) is applicable. Each quality sub-parameter, when applied to a global schema element, is evaluated using a value of a given type. The last column of Table 1 represents the type of each sub-parameter.

Quality Assertions

Definition 2 (Quality Assertion). *A quality assertion κ associates to each quality sub-parameter Q_i^j, $i \in [0..6], j \in [1..k_i]$, and an element E of the global schema (such as Q_i^j is applicable to E) a quality value $\kappa(Q_i^j, E)$. For ordered quality sub-parameters, κ returns an interval (a rectangle in case of the spatial cover), whereas for others it returns a finite set of values.*

For example, if κ_{vr} denotes the quality assertion that describes the element *vCommL* of data source TQe that corresponds to class *Road* of the global schema, then we have:

$$\kappa_{vr}(Q_0^1, Road) = [-72, -71.5] \times [45.375, 45.5],$$
$$\kappa_{vr}(Q_1^2, Road) = \{ \text{'Ministry of Natural Resources of Québec'} \},$$
$$\ldots,$$
$$\kappa_{vr}(Q_6^2, Road) = [0, 1\%].$$

The advantage of such representation is that it allows the expression of implicit preference relationships without having to define them. For example, to express that the deficit rate of a class E is better than 1% according to a quality assertion κ, we use the expression:

$$\kappa(C_1^1, E) = [0, 1\%].$$

3.3   Source Description

A source description specifies the mappings between the global schema and the source schema. Source descriptions are used by the mediator during query rewriting. In order to ensure expressive and generic correspondences between schemas, we use *mapping functions* (such as restrictions, concatenation, conversion functions, geometrical or topological functions, specific administrator defined functions, etc.).

Definition 3 (Mapping). *We define a mapping as a couple $(E \longleftarrow e, \kappa)$, where E is an element of the global schema, e is an element or a tuple of elements of the source schema (identified by their absolute or relative paths), and κ is a quality assertion describing element E.*

E is called *target* of the mapping, e is its *source* and κ is its *quality assertion*. The quality assertion κ of the mapping describes the quality of element E as being corresponding to *e*. For example, mapping between classes *Road* and *vCommL* of TQe can be expressed as follows:

$$(Road \longleftarrow vCommL, \kappa_{vr}),$$

where κ_{vr} is the quality assertion defined in section 3.2.

4 Query Processing

4.1 Query Language and Representation

We are using GQuery [7], a spatial query language, extended by a clause SUCH THAT to express quality constraints. A query expression is defined as a bloc FOR-LET-WHERE-SUCH THAT followed by a RETURN clause. We assume that clause WHERE contains conditions with only an attribute, an operator ($=$, $<$, $\leq$, $\neq$, etc.) and a constant; it does contain no joins and no attribute comparison. For example, query Q_0, defined in section 2.3, can be written as follows:

```
FOR $x in document("Region/Road")
WHERE $x/Type = "Highway"
SUCH THAT
    Bb(Road) = [-71.95, -71.65]*[45.38, 45.44]
    AND P.2.2(Road) = [1994, 2004]
    AND P.3.1(Road/lineStringProperty) = [0,5m]
    AND P.4.1(Road/Operational) = [High,VHigh]
    AND C.1.1(Road) = [0, 1%]
RETURN
<Sherbrooke>
    <Road> $x </Road>
</Sherbrooke>
```

4.2 Query Rewriting

Query rewriting is done in four steps: (1) decomposition of a query into *elementary sub-queries*, this leads to a *Global Execution Plan* (GEP), (2) correspondence discovery and subquery reformulation over local sources, (3) space partitioning which leads to *Sectoral Execution Plans* (SEP), and (4) construction of the Final Execution Plan (FEP). In the next sub-sections, we shortly describe these steps.

Query Decomposition. A query is decomposed into elementary sub-queries (EQ), each of them returns an attribute or a key together with the key it depends on. In doing so, we can rewrite the initial query as the join of these EQ, hence building the *Global Execution Plan* (GEP). For example, query Q_0 can be decomposed into 5 EQ ($q_0 \cdots q_4$) returning respectively attributes *Toponym, Description, Classification, Status* and *NbLanes* together with the geometric property *Geom*.

Extraction of Correspondences. The goal of this phase is to explore source descriptions in order to identify the relevant sources and the interesting mappings for each elementary sub-query. The result is a *source evaluation* for each sub-query and data source, showing how to express the sub-query over the source schema and specifying the quality of the corresponding result.

Given q (an EQ) and a source description M of S, we define the evaluation of q over S as the set of mappings $E \longleftarrow e$, where E traverses the whole set of elements required by q. The quality assertion associated with this evaluation, is calculated as the union of the quality assertions of the mappings composing it.

Example. Consider query Q_0 and its sub-queries q_i, $i \in [0..4]$, and suppose that the required coverage is rectangle B of Figure 4. Consider the descriptions M_1, M_2 and M_3 of TQe, NT and TQh respectively. Let $\mathcal{R}_1$, $\mathcal{R}_2$ and $\mathcal{R}_3$ be the mapping rules for element *Road* respectively with elements *vCommL* of TQe, *roadL* of NT and *vCommL* of TQh, as illustrated in Figure 5, where nodes of the left-side trees represent mappings.

Consider q_2 which extracts attribute *Classification* together with key *Geom* of class *Road*. Only rules $\mathcal{R}_1$ and $\mathcal{R}_2$ allow a full evaluation of q_2. In fact, according to $\mathcal{R}_1$, each element of q_2 has a correspondent with satisfactory quality. According to $\mathcal{R}_2$, each element of q_2 has a correspondent. Despite the geometrical accuracy of property *Geom* is not satisfied, the evaluation is taken into account because *Geom* is a global key. Element *Road* has a mapping in $\mathcal{R}_3$, but its quality is not that good because the spatial covers do not overlap. Consequently, we can reject this mapping. Since it is not useful anymore to use this rule for the rest of the elementary queries, we can prune it.

In the same way, we proceed with the rest of elementary queries without taking account of the pruned branches of the mapping rules. Figure 5 depicts, respectively in white and gray, the branches that are kept and those that are pruned; while black cells show the quality values that are violated.

Elementary Query Reformulation. Once the elementary sub-queries (ESQs) evaluations are performed, it is possible to reformulate them in terms of the source schemas. This is done in replacing sub-query elements by their correspondents while adding the restrictions resulting from the mappings. For each sub-query evaluation, there corresponds a reformulated query having the same quality assertion as the evaluation.

Sectoral Execution Plans. Each elementary sub-query of a query Q may involve a set of different data sources that play a certain role in different regions of the space, see for instance example of rectangle B' of Figure 4. This leads to the creation of different sectors, each of them generating a different way for evaluating sub-queries. Sectorisation is motivated by two main reasons: (i) it avoid useless computations (while trying to join information of an area to those of a disjoined area) and (ii) it allows to estimate the quality of the final execution plan. For each region, we compute a *Sectoral Execution Plan* (SEP), together with its quality assertion.

Final Execution Plan. The *Final Execution Plan* (FEP) of a query Q corresponds to the selection of a SEP for each sector. The goal of the query rewriting process is to obtain a FEP with a *good quality*, i.e., each of its SEP has a good quality. Our goal is to know which of the reformulated queries will participate to the FEP in a way that guarantees a satisfying quality. The difficulty of making such a choice comes from the fact that quality parameters are often contradictory. For example, improving the deficit rate means degrading the surplus rate and the logical consistency. Thus, the problem is to obtain a compromise leading to a rather complete result without affecting its surplus rate or its logical consistency.

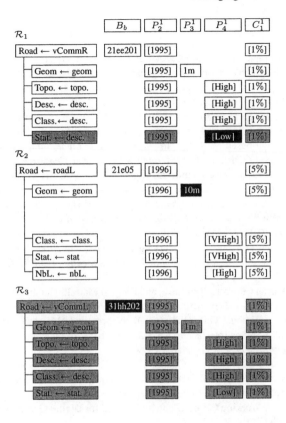

Fig. 5. Mapping rules for *Road* element

5   Conclusion

In this paper, we described a quality mediation approach that we developed in the context of GIS integration project. Besides the well known semantic heterogeneities, we also had to address the very difficult problem that is of assessing data quality of the mediated geographic system.

One of the problems of this approach is related to the complexity of query rewriting. Incorporating quality information in the rewriting algorithm increases the complexity. For instance, some quality criteria are contradictory: improving the deficit rate implies the degradation of the surplus or the violation rate. The trade-off is to deliver a rather complete result without affecting its consistency.

We believe our approach has three main advantages. First, it allows dynamic combination of mapping rules accordingly with the quality requirements, leading to quality rating of the result before data extraction. Second, it takes into account other metadata such as the spatial cover in the query rewriting process, leading to a significant reduction of useless operations (join of information related to different areas). Finally, it ensures system extensibility: adding or removing a data source does not significantly affect the global schema, and may result in some new mapping rules to be inserted in the system.

References

1. Centre for topographic information. www.cits.rncan.gc.ca.
2. ISO/TC 211 Geographic Information/Geomatics. www.isotc211.org/.
3. The REV!GIS project. www.lsis.org/REVIGIS/, 2000-2004.
4. Base de données topographiques du Québec (BDTQ), 1:20,000.
   felix.geog.mcgill.ca/heeslib/bdtq_20000.html, July 2001.
5. Bernd Amann, Catriel Beeri, Irini Fundulaki, and Michel Scholl. Querying XML Sources Using an Ontology-based Mediator. In *On the Move to Meaningful Internet Systems 2002: CoopIS, DOA, and ODBASE: Confederated International Conferences CoopIS, DOA, and ODBASE 2002. Proceedings*, volume 2519, pages 429 – 448, Evry, January 2002. Springer-Verlag Heidelberg.
6. Peter Buneman, Susan Davidson, Wenfei Fan, Carmem Hara, and Wang-Chiew Tan. Keys for XML. In *WWW '01: Proceedings of the tenth international conference on World Wide Web*, pages 201–210. ACM Press, 2001.
7. F-M. Colonna and O. Boucelma. Querying GML Data. In *Proc. 1ère Conférence en Sciences et Techniques de l'Information et de la Communication (CoPSTIC'03), Rabat*, 11–13 décembre 2003.
8. Simon Cox, Adrian Cuthbert, Ron Lake, and Richard Martell. Geography Markup Language (GML) 2.0. www.opengis.net/gml/01-029/{GML}2.html, February 20th 2001.
9. C.B. Cranston, F. Brabec, G.R. Hjaltason, D. Nebert, and H. Samet. Interoperability via the Addition of a Server Interface to a Spatial Database: Implementation Experiences with OpenMap. In *interop99*, Zurich, March 1999.
10. Benoît David and Pascal Fasquel. Qualité d'une Base de Données Géographique : Concepts et Terminologie. LIV 67, IGN, Direction Technique, Service de La Recherche, 2-4 Av. Pasteur, F-94165 Saint-Mandé Cedex, février 1997.
11. Metadata Ad Hok Working Group. Content Standard for Digital Geospatial Metadata. Technical report, FGDC, 1998.
12. G. Wiederhold. Mediators in the architecture of future information systems. *IEEE Computer*, pages 38–49, March 1992.

A Reusability Model for Portlets[*]

Mª Ángeles Moraga[1], Coral Calero[1], Iñaki Paz[2],
Oscar Díaz [2], and Mario Piattini[1]

[1] Alarcos Research Group, University of Castilla-La Mancha, Spain
{MariaAngeles.Moraga, Coral.Calero, Mario.Piattini}@uclm.es
[2] ONEKIN Research Group, University of the Basque Country, Spain
inaki.paz@ehu.es, oscar@si.ehu.es

Abstract. By means of portals, a company can give each person the information that responds to their specific needs. Nowadays, portals tend to be
constructed by means of portlets. So, if we want "good" portals, we must select
the most appropriate portlets for their construction. This requires the existence
of appropriate quality models to assess portlet's diverse characteristics. Perhaps
one of the most important non-functional characteristics (from the point of view
of the portlet consumer) is reusability.This work aims to define a reusability
model for portlets that will allow the assessment of the portlet reusability level.
As an example of application, we have applied the reusability model to a
concrete portlet in order to know its level of reusability.

1 Introduction

In the last decade, portals have evolved from being simple providers of access web
pages and corporate databases to become a support for intelligent management,
application integration and collaborative processing (Collins, 1999). The advantage of
portals is their ability to integrate and personalize several technologies (groupware,
databases, data-warehouses, e-mail, meta-data, intelligent management systems, etc.)
within a single business management tool (Kvitka, 2002). Aligned with this
integration imperative, portlets have recently been proposed to integrate third-party
applications into the portal realm. A portlet is a multi-step, user-facing application to
be delivered through a Web application. So, if we want "good" portals, we must select
the most appropriate portlets for constructing the portal. For this reason, the portlet
market requires the existence of quality models. Quality, however, is a wide concept
that must be defined according to other sub-characteristics. In the portlet context,
there are two fundamental quality characteristics namely, usability, defined as the
capability of the portlet to be understood, learned or used under specified conditions,
and reusability, defined as the capability of the portlet to be used in different portals

---

[*] This work was conducted when the first author was in stage at the University of the Basque
Country and is part of the DIMENSIONS project (PBC-05-012-1) supported by FEDER and
la Consejería de Educación y Ciencia de la Junta de Comunidades de Castilla-La Mancha.
and the CALIPO project (TIC 2003-07804-C05-03) supported by the Ministerio de Ciencia y
Tecnologia.

M. Dean et al. (Eds.): WISE 2005 Workshops, LNCS 3807, pp. 21 – 32, 2005.
© Springer-Verlag Berlin Heidelberg 2005

by several developers. We have already defined a portlet usability model (Diaz et al., 2004). So this paper, focuses on the reusability characteristic.

This paper is structured as follows. Section 2 gives a brief on portlets. Section 3 explains the portlet reusability model. Section 4 shows the assessment of the portlet reusability level. Section 5 applies this model to a specific portlet. Last section summarizes this paper and proposes future work.

2 Portlets: A Brief Summary

A portlet is a multi-step, user-facing application to be delivered through a Web application (e.g. a portal). Its novelties could be best assessed by comparing portlets with a technology which is already well-known, such as Java Servlets. As with Servlets, Java portlets run in a portlet container, a server container that provides portlets with a running environment. Servlet generates HTML pages as a result of a browser invocation. Likewise, a portlet also generates XHTML fragments (or other markup language) to be framed by the invoker.

There are however, two main differences between these two technologies. Firstly, a Servlet is a one-step process, while a portlet comprises a multi-step process. A portlet comprises the state-handling and navigation logic that supports the multi-step process. Secondly, a Servlet can generate a full page. By contrast, a portlet generates fragments which are to be arranged along with fragments from other portlets to build up the final portal's page. Hence, a portal page can contain a number of portlets that users can arrange into columns and rows, minimizing, maximizing or customising to suit their individual needs. So far however, the lack of a common model prevents portlet interoperability. This hinders a portlet which has been developed in, let´s say, Oracle Portal, being deployed at a Plumtree portal and vice-versa. However, the delivery of the Web Services for Remote Portlets (WSRP) specification overcomes this problem. WSRP defines four interfaces (OASIS, 2005), Service Description Interface, Markup Interface, Registration Interface and Portlet Management Interface, and also other characteristics that will be used to define the several attributes that affect the reusability characteristic. For example, the WSRP standard defines modes and window states. Additional modes can be introduced at developer's risk. A mode states a way of behaving. Depending on the portlet mode, the portlet renders different content and performs different activities.

3 Portlet Reusability Model

In this work we are attempting to obtain the dimensions that affect portlet reusability. Reusability is "the degree to which a software module or other work product can be used in more than one computing program or software system" (IEEE, 1990). But portlet reusability is "the capability of the portlet to be used in different portals by several developers". It is important not to get reusability mixed up with interoperability. In the context of WSRP-compliant portlets, judging interoperability does not make sense as these portlets are interoperable by definition. Our model is based on the component reusability model of (Washizaki et al., 2004). In this model, component reusability is broken down into three dimensions: understandability, adaptability and portability (selected from the ISO/IEC 9126 standard, (ISO, 2001) and adapted on the basis of an analysis of the activities carried out when reusing a black-box component. When reusing a portlet, we carry out the same activities as when reusing a component, hence, the dimensions that affect reusability are the same in both cases. However, these dimensions need to be adapted to account for the peculiarities of the portlet notion. In (Washizaki et al., 2004) adaptability is considered to be a dimension of reusability. However, the ISO/IEC 9126 standard contemplates adaptability as a sub-dimension of portability. Therefore in line with the ISO/IEC 9126 standard, we consider adaptability as a sub-dimension of portability. Furthermore, it should be noticed that reusability can be seen from two points of view: the perspective of the end-user - the person who uses the portlet (end-user issues)- and that of the portal administrator - the one who integrates the portlet into the portal (portal administrator issues)-. Therefore reusability, and hence understandability and portability, must be studied from both perspectives (table 1).

Table 1. Dimensions and sub-dimensions proposed for reusability

| CHARACTERISTIC | DIMENSION | SUB-DIMENSIONS | |
		End-user issues	Portal Administrator issues
Reusability	Understandability	--------------	---------------
	Portability	Customizability	Installability
			Empathy
		Personalizability	Replaceability

3.1 Study of the Reusability Dimensions

Basing our study on the characteristics of a portlet and taking into account the dimensions described for portlet reusability and the two stakeholders identified for a portlet, we are going to present in this section, several attributes for reusability.

UNDERSTANDABILITY (table 2) affects portlet reusability because we must understand a portlet's functionality in order to reuse it: the end-user needs to understand it to be able *to use it*. The portal administrator needs to understand the portlet functionality in order *to integrate it* correctly into the portal.

Table 2. Attributes identified in the understandability dimension for each role

| DIMENSION | ATTRIBUTES | |
	End-user issues	Portal Administrator issues
Understandability	User manuals	Documentation
	Description	Documentation language
	Preview mode	Keywords
		Data types of properties

Table 3. Attributes proposed for the sub-dimensions of portability

Dimension	Point of view	Subdimensions	Attribute		
Portability	End-user issues	Customizability	*Edit* mode		
		Personalizability	Complexity user profile		
			Locales		
	Portal Administrator	Installability	Documentation		
		Empathy	*Mime-Type*		
			Modes	*wsrp:config*	
				custom modes	
			WindowStates	*wsrp: minimized*	
				wsrp:maximized	
				wsrp: solo	
				custom windowStates	
			Locales		
			clonePortlet/setPortletProperties		
			CSS		
		Replaceability	"mode" ad hoc		
			"extensions" ad hoc		
			"Window State" ad hoc		

Attributes for both end-user and portal administrator are described as follows:

− User manuals: related to the existence of user manuals that help the end-user to understand the portlet easily.
− Description: this refers to the existence of a description of the portlet functionality, helping the end-user to understand it. This information can be obtained through the method *getPortletDescription*.
− Preview mode: in this mode, the portlet should provide a rendering of its standard *wsrp:view* mode content, as a visual sample of how this Portlet will appear on the end-user's page with the current configuration.
− Documentation: the portlet provides information related to the portlet that can help the portal administrator to understand the portlet.
− Documentation language: the documentation is provided in several languages.
− Keywords: it refers to the keywords that describe the portlet.
− Data types of properties: it is advisable to obtain information related to the data types of properties, because the more complex data types are, the more difficult it is to understand the properties. This information can be obtained through the method *getPortletProperties*.

PORTABILITY affects portlet reusability because a portlet must be capable of being transferred from one environment to another without problems. In Table 3, we set out the subdimensions and attributes that affect portability.

The following subdimensions for portability have been proposed:

− Customizability: capability of the portlet to adapt to itself to the end-user.
− Personalizability: capability of a portlet to allow the end-user to adapt it to his/her preferences.
− Installability: capability of the portlet to be installed.

Table 4. Measures proposed for the attributes of the understandability dimension

Dimension: UNDERSTANDABILITY			
Attribute		*Measure*	*Measure domain*
End-user issues	User manuals	The portlet vendor provides user manuals.	Boolean (True/False)
	Description	The portlet specifies its functionality.	Boolean (True/False)
	Preview mode	The portlet supports *preview* mode	Boolean (True/False)
Portal Adminis-trator issues	Documenta-tion	The portlet vendor provides additional documentation.	Boolean (True/False)
	Documenta tion language	Number of languages in which the documentation is written.	Natural number
	Keywords	Number of keywords provided by the portlet.	Natural number
	Data types of properties	Complexity of the data types of properties	Val.: 3=non-complex, 2=normal, 1= complex

- Empathy: capability of the portlet to harmonise with other independent portlets, both aesthetically and functionally.
- Replaceability: capability of the portlet to be used instead of another portlet for the same purpose and in the same environment.
  The meaning of the attributes is explained as follows:
- Edit mode: the portlet provides content and logic that let a user customize the behaviour of the Portlet.
- Complexity user profile: information stored on the portlet related to the end-user.
- Locales: this is, the different languages that the interface supports.
- Documentation: that specifies the additional requirements for running the portlet.
- Mime-Type: mime types supported by the portlet.
- Modes: modes that the portlet supports for this mime-type. A portlet will be more adaptable if it supports the modes: Wsrp: config (the *config* portlet mode should be used by the portlet to display one or more configuration views that allow administrators to configure portlet preferences. It is defined in the JSR 168 standard) and Custom modes (it allows the declaration of additional custom modes)
- windowStates: it refers to additional window states that the portlet supports for this mime-Type. They can be: wsrp:minimized (the portlet should not render visible markup, but is free to include non-visible data) , wsrp:maximized (the portlet is likely to be the only portlet being rendered in the aggregated page, or to have more space compared to other portlets in the aggregated page), wsrp:solo (the portlet is the only one being rendered in the aggregated page) and custom windowStates (it allows additional custom window states to be declared).
- locales: the locale of the returned markup, that is, the language in which returned markup is written.
- clonePortlet/setPortletProperties: this refers to the chance of creating a new portlet from a existing portlet and of modifying the properties of the cloned portlets.

Table 5. Measures proposed for portability dimension

Dimension: PORTABILITY				
Sub-dimensions	Attribute		Measure	Measure domain
End-user iss. / Customi-zability	Edit mode		The portlet supports *edit* mode	Boolean (T/F)
End-user iss. / Persona-lizability	Complexity of the user profile		Number of user profile characteristics that the portlet stores.	Natural number.
	Locales		Number of locales supported by the portlet	Natural number
Portal Administrator issues / Installa-bility	Documentation		Exist documentation	Boolean (T/F)
Portal Administrator issues / Empathy	*mime-Type*		Number of different mime-Type supported.	Natural number
	Modes	*wsrp:edit*	The portlet supports *edit* mode/custom modes	Value among 0 and 2^2
		custom modes		
	Window-states (WS)	*minimized*	Number of additional window states supported by the portlet.	Natural number
		maximized		
		solo		
		custom WS		
	locales		Number of locales supported by the portlet	Natural number
	clonePortlet/setPortletPro perties		The portlet implements *clonePortlet()* method and *setPortletProperties()* method.	Boolean (T/F)
	CSS		The portlet supports style sheets.	Boolean (T/F)
Portal Administrator issues / Replacea bility	"Mode" ad hoc		Number of additional modes supported by the portlet.	Natural number
	"Extensions" ad hoc		Number of structures extended by the portlet.	Natural number
	"Window State" ad hoc		Number of additional window states supported by the portlet	Natural number

- CSS: a common style sheet permits a common look-and-feel across the portlets contained on the page.
- "mode" ad hoc: additional modes exist. Additional modes reduce the portlet replaceability.
- "extensions" ad hoc: extensions exist for the structure.
- window state" ad hoc: additional window states exist. These additional window states are not mandatory.

3.2 Measures and Values

Now that we have identified the attributes that affect the reusability, we can define measures for each one of them. In Table 4, we show the measures defined for the

---

[1] The measure "the portlet supports *edit* mode/custom modes" can take the value 0 when the portlet does not support any of these modes, 1 when the portlet supports one of these modes and 2 when the portlet supports both modes.

UNDERSTANDABILITY and in Table 5 for the *PORTABILITY* dimension together with their domain.

4 Assessment of the Portlet Reusability

Once the measures for each one of the identified attributes have been determined, the portlet reusability level must be ascertained. To do this, we first need to assess the portlet understandability and portability levels.

In order to assess the portlet *UNDERSTANDABILITY LEVEL* (Table 6), we have defined a tuple of seven elements.

Table 6. Values proposed for portlet understandability

Understanda-bility	Set of values						
	user manuals	functio-nality	*preview* mode	additional documen-tation	Number of languages supported	Number of key words	Complexi-ty of the data types
Excellent	1	1	1	1	2^+	4^+	3
High	1	1	1	1	2	[2-3]	[2-3]
Middle	1	1	1	1	1	[2-3]	[2-3]
Acceptable	1	1	0	1	1	2^+	1^+
Non-accep.	Rest						

Each element of the tuple represents one of the measures presented in Table 4 (in the same order). Having done this, we assess the portlet *understandability* level as this depends on the values of each vector's element. We have taken into account the following considerations in order to assess the values: first, the Boolean measures acquire the value one if they are true and zero if they are false, second, the maximum number of languages in which the documentation is written will normally be two but we also consider the possibility of obtaining a larger number, third, although the number of keywords provided by a portlet is a natural number, we consider that portlets provide 4 keywords, at most; finally, the data types of properties are non-complex and the measure acquires the value 3. When we specify a "+" as superscript of the number, the value for this element is this or greater.

From the *PORTABILITY* point of view, we first need to assess the level of each one of the sub-dimensions which have this as their end: customizability, personalizability, installability, empathy and replaceability.

In the *customizability sub-dimension* we have defined only one measure (Table 5) that will take the value 1 if the portlet supports the edit mode (very acceptable level) and 0 if not (non-acceptable level).

In the *personalizability sub-dimension*, we have established two different measures (Table 5). As a following step, we have assessed the different personalizability levels (Table 7).

Table 7. Personalizability levels

Personalizability levels	Set of values
Very acceptable	$(22^+,1); (18^+,2^+)$
Acceptable	$([17\text{-}21],1); ([14,17],2^+)$
Non-acceptable	Rest

Therefore *Very acceptable* is when the portlet stores 22 or more user profile characteristics (that is, more than one-quarter of the total) and it supports one locale, or the portlet stores 18 or more user profile characteristics (that is, more than one-fifth of the total) and it supports two or more locales, *Acceptable* is when the portlet stores between 17 and 21 user-profile characteristics (that is, between one-fifth and one-quarter of the total) and it supports one locale, or the portlet stores among 14 and 17 user profile characteristics (that is, between one-sixth and one-fifth of the total) and it supports two or more locales and *Non-acceptable* is the rest of the cases.

In the ***installability sub-dimension,*** we have defined only one measure (Table 5) that acquires the value 1 (very acceptable level) when the portlet provides documentation related to the installation and 0 in other case (non-acceptable level).

In the ***empathy sub-dimension***, we have set out the measures presented previously (Table 5) and have taken into account the following considerations to assess the level of empathy: first, normally the maximum number of mime-type supported by the portlet is 2 (nevertheless, we consider the possibility of obtaining a greater number), second, we consider that the measure "number of additional window states supported by the portlet" normally acquires a value between 0 and 4 (in the worst case, the portlet does not implement any additional window state and in the best case, the portlet implements the 4 additional window states. It is also possible that the portlet may provide more than one *custom* mode. We consider this possibility, but it is not usual), third, the usual maximum number of languages supported by the interface is 2 (in spite of this, here too we consider the possibility of obtaining a larger number), finally, the measure "the portlet implements *clonePortlet()* method and *setPortletProperties()* method" acquires the value one when it implements both methods and it acquires the value zero when it does not implement any method.

Table 8 outlines the output where each level is characterised as follows: *Very acceptable* (when the portlet supports two mime-types, it supports the *edit* mode and it defines one or more *custom* modes. It also supports the *minimized, maximized, solo* window states. The portlet defines one or more *custom* window states and it can be rendered in one or more locales. It implements the *clonePortlet()* and *setPortletProperties()* methods and it supports style sheets.), *Acceptable* (if the portlet supports one mime-type; it supports the *edit* mode but it does not define *custom* modes. The portlet supports the *minimized, maximized, solo* window states, but it does not define *custom* window state. The portlet can be rendered in one or more locales; it implements the *clonePortlet()* and *setPortletProperties()* methods and it supports style sheets) and *Non-acceptable* (all other cases).

Table 8. Empathy level

Empathy level	Set of values					
	number of different mime-Type supported	the portlet supports *edit* mode/cus-tom modes	number of additional window states supported by the portlet	number of locales supported by the portlet	the portlet implements *clonePortlet()* method and *setPortletPropert ies ()* method	the portlet support s style sheets
Very Acc.	2	2^+	4^+	1^+	1	1
Acceptable	1	1	3	1^+	1	1
Non-Acc.	Rest					

Table 9. Replaceability levels

Replaceability level	Set of values		
	number of additional modes supported by the portlet	number of structures extended by the portlet	number of additional WS supported by the portlet
VeryAcceptable	0	0	0
Acceptable	Rest		
Non-acceptable	4^+	1^+	4^+

We have taken into account the considerations seen below in assessing the *replaceability sub-dimension* level (Table 9): first, for the measure "number of additional modes supported by the portlet" (Table 5): if the portlet supports additional modes it reduces its replaceability, because the consumer may not support additional modes, second, for the measure "number of extended structures by the portlet": if the portlet extends the predefined structures, it reduces its replaceability because it is possible that the consumer does not support the extended structures, finally, for the measure "number of additional window states supported by the portlet": if the portlet supports window states different to *normal* window state it reduces its replaceability, because the consumer may not support additional window states.

Where: *Very acceptable (*means that the portlet only supports the *view* mode; it does not extend the predefined structures and it only supports the *normal* window state), *Acceptable* (means the rest of cases) and *Non-acceptable* (means that the portlet either supports all the additional modes (*edit, help* or *preview*) but does not define *custom* modes or, on the other hand, supports some additional modes and defines *custom* modes. The portlet extends one or more structures. The portlet supports all the additional window states: *minimized, maximized* or *solo* but it does not define *custom* window states or, on the other hand, supports some additional window states and defines *custom* window states.).

Once we have determined the portlet level for each of the sub-dimensions, we could assess the portlet *PORTABILITY LEVEL* on the basis of the obtained values for each sub-dimension. The different portability levels are summarized in Table 10[2].

---

[2] Two of the five sub-dimensions which make up the portability, acquire the *very acceptable* or *non-acceptable* value. For this reason, the portability level is *acceptable* when those sub-dimensions obtain the *very acceptable* value.

We can assess the portlet *REUSABILITY LEVEL* according to the understandability and portability level that the portlet has obtained. The different levels defined for the portlet reusability are set out in Table 11.

Table 10. Portability levels

Portability levels	Set of values
Excellent	All the sub-dimensions have obtained the *very acceptable* level.
High	One sub-dimension has obtained acceptable and the rest the *very acceptable* level.
Middle	Two sub-dimensions have obtained *acceptable* and the rest the *very acceptable* level.
Acceptable	Three sub-dimensions have obtained *acceptable* and the rest the *very acceptable* level.
Non-acceptable	Rest of the cases.

Table 11. Reusability levels

Reusability level	Set of values
Excellent	The two dimensions (understandability and portability) have obtained the *Excellent* value.
High	One dimension has obtained the *Excellent* value and the other has obtained the *High* value. One dimension has obtained the *Excellent* value and the other has obtained the *Middle* value. The two dimensions have obtained the *High* level.
Middle	One dimension has obtained the *Excellent* value and the other has obtained the *Acceptable* value. One dimension has obtained the *High* value and the other has obtained the *Middle* value. One dimension has obtained the *High* value and the other has obtained the *Acceptable* value. The two dimensions have obtained the *Middle* value.
Acceptable	One dimension has obtained the *Middle* value and the other has obtained the *Acceptable* value. The two dimensions have obtained the *Acceptable* value.
Non-Acc.	Rest of cases.

5 Applying the Reusability Model for Portlets to a Specific Portlet

In order to illustrate our portlet reusability model, we have applied it to a specific portlet. The goal of this portlet is to carry out a search for cars, but it is not a commercial portlet. It is used for research and more specifically, for performing tests. For this reason, part of its capabilities is not implemented and the portlet is not available to the rest of the community. This portlet has been developed using the JSR168 standard. Table 12 shows the results for the *UNDERSTANDABILITY* dimension. Following our model and taking into account the values shown in Table 12, the portlet understandability is not acceptable.

Table 12. Results for understandability

Measure	Value
The portlet vendor provides user manuals.	False
The portlet specifies its functionality.	True
The portlet supports *preview* mode	False
The portlet vendor provides additional documentation.	False
Number of languages in which the documentation is written.	0
Number of keywords provided by the portlet.	1
Complexity of the data types of properties	1

Table 13. Results for subdimensions of portability

Subdimension	Measure	Value
Customizability	The portlet supports *edit* mode	True
Personalizability	Number of user profile characteristics that the portlet stores.	0
	Number of locales supported by the portlet	1
Installability	Exist documentation	False
Empathy	Number of different mime-Type supported.	1
	The portlet supports *edit* mode/custom modes	1
	Number of additional window states supported by the portlet.	0
	Number of locales supported by the portlet	1
	The portlet implements *clonePortlet()* method and *setPortletProperties()* method.	False
	The portlet supports style sheets.	False
Replaceability	Number of additional modes supported by the portlet.	0
	Number of structures extended by the portlet.	0
	Number of additional window states supported by the portlet	0

We assess the values for the *PORTABILITY* dimension as the next step (Table 13). To do this, we assess the values for each sub-dimension. According to the results, the portlet customizability is very acceptable, the personalizability is not acceptable, the installability is non-acceptable, the empathy is non-acceptable and the replaceability is very acceptable.

Therefore, taking into account levels of the portability sub-dimensions, the portlet portability is non-acceptable because, although there are two sub-dimensions of portability that have obtained the value of very acceptable, there are three that have obtained the value non-acceptable.

Finally, according to the portlet understandability and portability levels, we can affirm that the portlet *REUSABILITY* is non-acceptable. This result is coherent because the portlet is not a commercial portlet and as such it does not implement all the possible characteristics. It does not provide additional documents which are necessary to obtain a good value for portlet reusability. Having assessed the portlet reusability level we are in a position to improve the obtained reusability level, implementing those characteristics necessary for portability and understandability dimensions to obtain a higher level such the inclusion of user manuals, or the implementation of the clonePortlet and setPortletProperties methods.

6   Conclusions and Future Work

Second-generation portals are far from being monolithic pieces of software. Their complexity calls for a component-based approach where portlets are the technical enabler. The proposal and ample support for the WSRP portlet standard predict an emergent portlet market. A main requirement for the blooming of this market is the existence of portlet quality models that assess portal developers in selecting the appropriate portlet.

This works provides some insights on a reusability model for portlets based on the WSRP standard. As a first attempt, the model has been applied to a sample portlet. The output serves not only to indicate the adequacy of the portlet but to guide the portlet developer to detect the weaknesses of the portlet as far as reusability is concerned.

In future work, we have to validate through surveys done by experts, both the dimensions and the measures proposed for the usability, but especially the set of values used to assess the portlet usability.

Also, we plan to define other models for the rest of the portlet quality characteristics until we will have dealt with all characteristics that affect that quality. These characteristics are: functionality, reliability and efficiency.

The final goal is to have a quality model that could be used, on one hand, to decide on the best portlet and, on the other hand, to identify possible improvements in the quality of a given portlet.

Bibliography

Collins, D. (1999). Datawarehouses, enterprise information portal and the SmartMart meta directory. Information Builders Systems Journal. Vol. 12(2) pp. 53-61.

Diaz, O., C. Calero, M. Piattini and A. Irastorza (2004). Portlet usability model. IBM Research Report. RA221(W0411-084). ICSOC 2004.,pp. 11-15.

IEEE (1990). Institute of Electrical and Electronics Engineers. IEEE Standard Computer Dictionary: A Compilation of IEEE Standard Computer Glossaries., New York

ISO (2001). ISO/IEC 9126. Software Engineering-Product Quality. Partes 1 a 4., International Organization for Standardization/International Electrotechnical Commission.

Kvitka, C. (2002). Profiting with portals.May/June. 21. Available in: http://www.oracle.com/technology/oramag/oracle/02-may/o32news_portals.html. Accessed: Septiembre, 2004.

OASIS (2005). Web Service for Remote Portals (WSRP) Version 2.0. Available in: http://www.oasis-open.org/commitees/wsrp/. Accessed: June.

Washizaki, H., H. Yamamoto and Y. Fukazawa (2004). A Metrics Suite for Measuring Reusability of Software Components. Software Metrics Symposium. Ninth International.,pp. 211-223.

Towards Using Simulation for Enhancing Web Information Systems' Utility

Phuong Nguyen and Sergiy Zlatkin

Department of Information Systems,
Massey University, New Zealand
{N.P.Nguyen, S.Zlatkin}@massey.ac.nz

Abstract. The awareness for quality of Web information systems is increasing. Utility is a quality aspect that is of particular importance with respect to the economical sustainability of Web information systems. Like other quality aspects, utility can be focused at a priori, at run-time, or a posteriori. A priori and runtime considerations of utility appear as not really appropriate with respect to utility. An a posteriori focus on utility however is dangerous, as maintaining an already deployed system is particularly expensive. We therefore suggest using simulation as a quasi a posteriori approach for utility enhancement. In the paper, we discuss a generic model of Web information system use. We furthermore discuss an algorithm for generating a simulation model out of that usage model. We also discuss the foundations of a heuristic for analysing the respective simulation model.

1 Introduction

An information system (IS) that is integrated into the World Wide Web (WWW) is called Web information system (WIS). The introduction of WIS has pushed systems development to a different level. Challenges, opportunities and also threads for IS development and use were created [Ka04]. WIS typically are available to everyone who can access the Web at any time, anywhere and for virtually any purpose. [Ka04] indicated the benefits that WIS could bring to the parties who use it, including the vendor of the WIS and the customers. The customers using the services offered by a WIS would no longer suffer from the limitations of staff, regarding availability and prejudices against certain customer types, and physical resources with respect to available office space and printed documents, etc. Using WIS to achieve their goals, the customers do not have to commit to certain business hours as they have to do traditionally since direct staff-customer interaction would not be needed. The organizations employing WIS, on the other hand, may benefit greatly from using WIS for their business: (1) virtually unlimited business periods might increase the business volume carried out by customers; (2) the cost of business cases in average might be reduced since they need less staff time allocated to them; (3) the quality of business cases can be increased as well as their documentation; (4) business cases can be adapted better to the customers' needs; (5) new customers might be attracted; and (6) customer-relationship management can be simplified and made more efficient. WIS eventually may increase the return on investment.

M. Dean et al. (Eds.): WISE 2005 Workshops, LNCS 3807, pp. 33–42, 2005.

With the above potentials, WIS currently have become a dominant type of IS. However, ensuring that WIS satisfy the expectations of their users in terms of the quality of service usage experience is not an easy thing, as the users' expectations evolve and might not have been taken care of properly in the first place. We aim at contributing to the provisioning of procedures, methods and tools for measuring and managing the utility of WIS. There are a number of quality aspects that throughout WIS-development should be considered. Among these are usability, quality of services, security and privacy. A successful WIS requires a close and deep investigation into the business objectives and the users' needs. It also requires an in-depth understanding of the communication aspects relevant to customer behaviour as the user navigates through a WIS, [Wa03]. The capability to forecast the behaviour of WIS users is very important for WIS-development.

Paper Outline: We discuss related work in section 2. In section 3 we discuss utility and why it deserves consideration and discuss in section 4 our generic WIS usage model. We focus on utility enhancement in section 5 and conclude the paper with a future work section.

2 Related Work

This paper is a revised and extended version of [Ng04]. It is still research in progress. For recent proposals regarding WIS development, we refer the reader to [Ga93], [Ga95], [At98], and [Sc05]. Obviously a development method is only sustainable if it puts both vendor and user in a win-win situation. Intuitively it is clear that context is important for utility. Realizing that context-awareness appears to be a promising idea for increasing usability of WIS, [Bi04] proposed an approach to context-awareness of WIS. In this approach, there are four main contexts identified. They are customer's scenario context, vendor's context, developer's context, and WIS's scene context. In-depth understanding of these contexts, according to [Bi04], is essential to designing a WIS that can meet high quality expectations concerning usability, performance and maintainability.

Focusing on the customer's scenario context, [Ka03] proposed an approach to context modelling for WIS. In their work, they investigated on how contexts of WIS can be modelled in order to avoid customers getting lost or confused while navigating through the information space implemented by a WIS. Based on the notion of context space, the source suggests "...depending on the location of a customer in the information space of the WIS, the usage history and a corresponding user type, a suitable continuation will be suggested to a customer, which will allow him or her to regain the possibility of using the respective WIS efficiently".

Also focusing on the quality and performance of WIS, some other studies have proposed different approaches and tools to improve the performance of WIS from technical aspects. [Se03] presented a collection of tools that allow individuals to experience realistic network delays. These tools, referred to as wide-area network delay simulator (WANDS), demonstrate how simulations could provide a realistic experience on network delays through a variety of network conditions. Such tools could bring benefits to different groups of people including practitioners, researchers and educators. Practitioners would more effectively assess usability in the context of realistic network delays in order to evaluate and improve the materials that will be delivered via the WWW while researchers would more effectively investigate the factors that affect the usability of information and web applications. Educators, on the other hand, would effectively convey the importance of design decisions in the context of World Wide Web.

Considering the process of controlling performance of Web site and back-end systems a key factor for every Web-enabled company, [Ca01] has researched on approaches to web performance testing and measurement. Their research aims at analysing fast characterisation of system and user's behaviour in order to give fast feedback on any issues. In order to test and measure web performance, these researchers presented two tools: WEBSAT (WEB Server Application Time) and BMPOP (BenchMark Point of Presence). WEBSAT is a system that uses web server log files to produce a table containing the users, and the IP addresses, of the users and, mainly the execution time of every object requested by the browser. BMPOP, on the other hand, is a system that is able to simulate a user who uses a connection to an Internet service provider to download a web page. These tools help to study the performance of a web site through a log file that records the execution time as well as the response time of the system as to per user's request. This information would allow web developer to know how and where to develop a better WIS that meets the user's expectations.

3 Utility of WIS

Throughout WIS-development a focus on WIS-quality is needed. WIS-quality has been addressed among others by [Ne00], [Fi00], and [Zh01]. For a discussion of software quality see, e.g. [Gh04]. [Fi00] defined WIS-quality from the perspectives of end users and WIS-providers as good performance; high levels of availability, security, and accessibility, and as the capability of WIS to convey organisational images, to attract customer and to effectively support the business respectively.

[Fi00] also identified the WIS-quality factors including visibility (the site is easy to communicate with), intelligibility (the content is easy to assimilate and interpret), credibility (level of user confidence), engagibility (extent of user experience), and differentiation (speciality and identity of owner organisation). [Fi00] argues that these factors are very helpful to any organisations that are engaged in E-commerce since they will help designing a WIS that could assure high return on investment.

However, the users may change their views of the quality that is desired. Some users may cease using the WIS and others may join the user community. Competing WIS may come up and impact the users' expectation. A change of the appraisal of the quality of a WIS is thus likely if the focus is on its lifetime. The constant in that changing perception of quality is utility if understood as in economics, where it means the level of happiness or satisfaction gained from the consumption of a package of goods or services [Ga03]. In the area of information system, utility is considered as the match between user functional- and non-functional requirements and WIS functionality and quality, respectively [Ne00]. We think that utility is directly proportional to the degree to which customers continue using a WIS for a given portfolio of tasks. It is, however, possible that utility cannot be fully covered by observing the user behaviour or by analyzing the usage log. Rather, it might be necessary to ask users for their opinion regarding the utility of the WIS they are using.

4 A Generic WIS-Usage Model

We aim at using simulation as a quasi a posteriori approach to enhancing WIS utility. For being capable of constructing a respective simulation model we need to understand the user-WIS interaction. Thus we are going to work out a generic WIS-usage model. Our idea in that respect is that for each user type a small number of test users are observed while they interact with the WIS prior to its deployment. The respective findings are then invested in that generic WIS-usage model. We derive a simulation model from it and use the simulation run for simulating a real load scenario. That way, findings, as observed for individual users, may be used for studying the interdependency resulting from many users using the WIS at the same time. That is then what potentially makes simulation beneficial for utility enhancement. In the sequel of this section we presuppose a fixed user type to be given. The following considerations until further notice concern that user type.

4.1 WIS Service – A High Level Classification

Providers implement WIS because they want key services[1] being used by a public. WIS can be reasonably complex. Potential customers don't need to be expert in the respective business. Therefore providers implement supporting services. These shall make it easier to identify, access, and invoke the most appropriate key services available. We therefore group the services into the classes "key service" and "supporting service", see Fig. 1. Each rectangle shown in the diagram represents a particular group or class of services. Upwards directed arrows ("a kind of ") indicate that the service group close to the arrow head has subgroups as indicated at the bottom of the arrow.

Key services are the services the vendor wants the public to use. These are the services for which users would pay a fee. These services are not limited to simple database retrieval or update operations. Key services may require user involvement, as inputting parameters quite often are compulsory to executing this kind of services. Take making a payment online for an example. In order for the transaction to be carried out, the user at first needs to enter his username and password to log in to the system, then enter the account number of payee and the amount to be transferred etc.

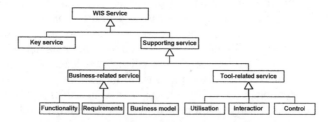

Fig. 1. High-level classification of WIS services

If this information is not provided by the user, the transaction then will never be successfully executed. Online registration, online banking, electronic shopping are some examples of the services that fall in this category.

---

[1] Please note that these not necessarily are Web services.

Supporting services are the services that provide users with the information to effectively and efficiently employ the key services. The business-related supporting services provide users with information regarding (1) the functionality of the key services; (2) the requirements that need to be met for successfully launching the key services; and (3) the business model that governs the usage of the key service. The tool-related supporting services provide users with information regarding (1) how to launch individual services; (2) how to identify and tailor the most suitable service; and (3) how to adapt and control the WIS for getting the best out of it with least effort.

To validate the proposed classification of WIS services and a WIS-user behavior model we consider the example of on-line services of The National Bank, New Zealand (Fig. 2) (http://www.nationalbank.co.nz/online/onlinebanking/default.asp).

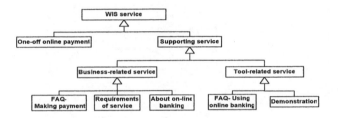

Fig. 2. Classification of online banking service

We particularly focus on accomplishing One-off payments. One-off on-line payment is the actual key service. Though the business model for this service is quite obvious, i.e. to transfer money from customer's account into any account within New Zealand, The National Bank WIS provides business-related services describing the business core of the One-off payment. Particularly the "Making payments" sub-section of the FAQ section gives answers to such questions about (1) activating/disabling one-off payment (Functionality); (2) the difference between one-off payments and bill payments; (3) the structure of bank account record (Business Model); and (4) information required to accomplish the one-off payment (Requirements). Furthermore, the "About Online Banking" section provides additional information regarding the business model, such as the list of all functions provided and the fees for each of those functions. The "Using Online Banking" sub-section of the FAQ section of that WIS provides information that we would classify as "Utilization" of the service as it answers such questions like (1) what the customer may do with Online Banking WIS, (2) what are the hardware and software required to use the key services of WIS, (3) what kind of software may be used together with the given WIS (e.g., spreadsheets, MS Money, etc.). The "Demonstration" section provides a step-by-step guide explaining how the customer may/should use the WIS to accomplish different tasks. It provides guidelines to interact and to control over the WIS.

4.2   The WIS-Usage Model

The model (Fig. 3) basically represents the cognitive tasks, or mental states of the user when invoking WIS services. There are four mental states identified, i.e. identifying need resolution, identifying solution, tailoring solution and executing solution.   In addition, there are two other special states, which are the start state and the final state. These states are connected by transitions, representing a change of states caused by an event.

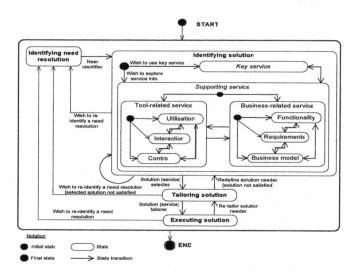

Fig. 3. WIS-usage model

As can be seen from Fig. 3, the four main states that users might experience when using WIS services are nested in another state. This means that the user does not necessarily have to go through these four states in order to get his/her need satisfied. State-by-pass is possible. In fact, one could start at any state and end the whole process any time that s/he wants. For example, once knowing clearly what needs to be done and being familiar with the WIS, one could go directly to the state of executing the solution/service without having to go through all of the other states.

Identifying need resolution: This is the state where the user decides what they want to do. Initially, the user might not understand what s/he really wants, or might not know how to satisfy what s/he needs. Navigating through a web site might help to find appropriate solutions. For example, a bank offers internet banking services to users. Some users might know about the advantage of this service and want to learn more about it in terms of everyday banking needs. Other users might not know that they need the service until they read about it. There are other users who already have chosen a service, have registered for it, and want to use it to solve their needs.

Identifying solution: Having identified the need, the user moves to the second state, i.e. the state of finding solution to his or her needs. Following the scenario of internet banking services, depending on the needs identified in the previous state, the user could choose to explore the information about some supporting services or key services (Fig. 3). Identifying solution is considered as one of the user's states that should be further explored and investigated. A self-transition attached to this state means that the behaviour represented by this state could be repeated by the user. Also from the model, there are some other nested states representing invocations of different services. The separation of these services based on the classification of WIS services discussed previously.

Tailoring solution: At this state, the user, to the best of his/her knowledge achieved from previous states, will tailor the selected solution in order to match it with his/her need.

Executing solution: This is the final state where the selected solution after being tailored will be executed and completed. One of the main actions at this state could be providing all parameters needed for a solution to be executed. The user might then exit the system if satisfying with the results, or restart the whole process if the results do not quite meet initial expectations.

For validating the WIS-usage model, we carried out some experiments again on the National Bank website. We asked a representative of each of two different user types to visit the web site of the bank and make an online payment. We, at this stage, distinguish only two types of WIS-users: the experienced users who are experienced in using the WIS, and the novice users. After logging in, the first user, which is an experienced user, immediately navigated straight to the "One-off payment location", provided all required data and completed the payment. The navigation path in that case looks like: Start→Executing Solution→End. Before logging in, the novice user on the other hand had to read information about On-line banking to define that he/she is interested in one-off payment rather than bill or automatic payments. By reading "Making payments" sub-section of the FAQ section the user identified the requirements for and the procedures of one-off payment. To be completely sure the user decided to watch the Demonstration on how to use the WIS to establish the payment. Unfortunately there was no link from the business-related service to the tool-related service. Therefore the user had to guess where to navigate to view the Demonstration about one-off payment. The navigation path in that case looks like: Start→Identify need resolution→Identifying solution→Tailoring solution→Executing solution→End.

5   Enhancing the Utility of Web Information System

We intend to do our simulation studies with Arena [Ke02]. To save space we only sketch the generation of the simulation model from the generic usage model in figure 3. The simulation model has the servers "identifying need resolution", "Tailoring solution", "Executing solution", "Key services"[2], "Utilization", "Interaction", "Control", "Functionality", "Requirements", and "Business model". For each of these a user type depending retention time distribution is obtained. Furthermore a user type

---

[2] Obviously, for obtaining more expressive simulation results, one needs to refine the key services.

depending arrival distribution is obtained that describes the log in of customers into the WIS. Furthermore user type depending relative frequencies of state transitions are obtained. These frequencies are used as approximations for the transition probabilities in such way that for each state the probabilities of the transitions sums up to 1 that start in that state. That includes the loops.

We now sketch our preliminary ideas for an analysis heuristic. Obviously, one can now –analytically or by simulation- observe the genesis of input queues for each server that represents a WIS-service. The length of these queues together with the arrival distribution can be used for defining a scaling policy, i.e., a policy for adding servers or even hardware to the WIS.

Furthermore, for each server that represents a WIS-service, one can estimate the probability of a server request, i.e., for a WIS-service execution and use that information as input in an WIS-architecture redesign such as to achieve a more adequate relationship between the number of key service executions and the number of supporting services executions. One can similarly assess the probability of the occurrence of long navigation paths until key service execution. If that probability is "large", WIS design changes could be considered in order that the probability of the occurrence of long paths is reduced. Note, that what counts as a "long" path or as a "large" probability depends on the case at hand.

Provided the data obtained throughout the simulation is logged one can consider the relative frequency of key service invocation in relation to the length of the respective navigation paths and try to change the WIS-design such that the more frequently used key services are accessed via the shorter navigation paths. Similarly, a significant number of navigation paths not leading to a key service being invoked can be used as a motive of a system redesign. Similarly time to completion can be used as a design goal. A more sophisticated WIS-usage model would even allow making the reduction of the number of complaints to be a design goal.

We consider the possibility of guessing and validating a formula for the WIS-utility as observed by users of a given type. If we can manage the formula to be such that it can be evaluated based on the data available during the simulation then it becomes even possible to experiment with the system design such as to increase the utility.

The simulation model shows how to simulate the behaviour of a potentially large number of users concurrently accessing the WIS. We consider the WIS as a media in which users compete for resources they need for achieving their goals. Simulating that competition for a number of users helps studying the utility of WIS. Respective practical experiments are expensive and cannot be conducted often. Anticipating this competition based on the WIS-usage model, without actually simulating it, is hard to do. Parameters of simulation runs are for each request type, the number of user requests, the resources needed for each of the requests, whether the resources available could satisfy the users' demands, and utilisation of WIS resources at all times. Respectively, the results obtained from this simulation model would be analysed and weakpoints of the WIS, such as bottlenecks, would be identified. Once weakpoints are identified, suggestions on how to overcome them can be made. The suggested solution can involve a redesign the WIS for triggering a change of the user's behaviour. Alternatively, the provisioning of additional resources may be part of the solution such as more disk space, main memory, a larger number of servers, or a faster network connection.

6 Future Work

We are going to implement a system for the automatic generation of the simulation model. The input for the respective function will be the WIS-usage model for a case at hand together with the empirical data needed for a simulation study, as obtained by a small number of experiments involving test persons. The output will be the Arena simulation model. The WIS-usage model, compared to what we have by now, has to be enhanced such as to incorporate a realistic number of user types. Also priorities of user5 types should be built into the simulation model. Furthermore, a WIS architecture model shall be developed. It is supposed to become an input for the simulation model generation as well. Having such a model as an input component would allow simulating the effect of architecture changes and additional resource provisioning. That would significantly increase the impact of the approach outlined in this paper. Obviously, for such a simulation approach to be practical, one needs to be capable of generating the WIS-usage model from the WIS code.

An analysis heuristic has to be developed and validated. Such a heuristic can focus on patterns of sequences of service invocations and be similar in spirit to what we have sketched above.

References

[At98]   Atzeni, P., Gupta, A. and Sarawagi, S. Design and maintenance of data-intensive web-sites. In Proceeding EDBT'98, Springer-Verlag, Berlin, 1998.

[Bi04]   Bineman-Zdanovicz, A., Kaschek, R., Schewe, K-D. and Thalheim, B. Context-Aware Web Information Systems. APCCM Conference, Dunedin, New Zealand, 2004.

[Ca01]   Cassone, G., Elia, G., Gotta, D., Mola, F. and Pinnola, A. Web Performance Testing and Measurement: a complete approach. Available at: http://www.cmgitalia.it/download/seminario_marzo_2004/web_complete_approach_cassone.pdf, 2001. Accessed at Dec 12th, 2004.

[Fi00]   Fitzpatrick, R. Additional Quality of Factors for the World Wide Web. In Proceedings of the Second World Congress For Software Quality, Yokohama, Japan, Union of Japanese Scientists and Engineers (JUSE), Tokyo, Japan, 2000.

[Ga03]   Gans, J. S., King, S. P., Stonecash, R. E. and Mankiw, N. G. Principles of Economics (2nd ed.). Thomson, Nelson Australia Pty Limited, 2003.

[Ga93]   Garzotto, F., Paolini, P. and Schwabe, D. HMD – a model-based approach to hypertext application design. ACM Transactions on Information Systems, 11(1):1-26, January, 1993.

[Ga95]   Garzotto, F., Mainetti, L. and Paolini, P. Hypermedia design, analysis and evaluation issues. Communications of the ACM, 58(8):74-76, August 1995.

[Gh04]   Ghezzi, C., Jazayeri, M., and Mandrioli, D. Software Qualities and Principles. Ch. 101 of Tucker, A. B. (Ed.) Computer Science Handbook. Chapmann & Hall/CRC, 2004.

[Ka03]   Kaschek, R., Schewe, K-D., Thalheim, B. and Zhang, L. Context Modelling for Web Information Systems. CAiSE03 workshop 2003.

[Ka04]   Kaschek, R., Schewe, K-D., Wallace, C. and Matthews, C. Story Boarding for Web-based Information Systems. In Taniar, D. and Rahayu, J. W. (Eds.) Web Information Systems: Idea Group Inc, 2004, pp. 1 – 33.

[Ne00]   Nielsen, J. Designing Web Usability. Indianapolis, Ind.: New Riders, 2000.

[Ng04] Nguyen, P. Simulating User Behavior – A Proposed Approach to Improving Web Information Systems, In Kaschek, R., Mayr, H. C., and Liddle, S. (Eds.) Proceedings of the 4th International Conference on Information Systems Technology and its Application, Lecture Notes in Informatics Vol. P-63, Gesellschaft für Informatik, Bonn, 2005, pp. 191 – 195.

[Sc05] Schewe, K.-D., Thalheim, B. Conceptual Modelling of Web Information Systems. Data & Knowledge Engineering, 54: 147 – 188, 2005.

[Se03] Sears, A. Simulating Network Delays: Applications, Algorithms, and Tools. International Journal of Human-Computer Interaction, 16(2): 301-323, 2003.

[Wa03] Wallace, C., Kaschek, R., Matthews, C. and Schew, K-D. Factors Constituting Successful Online Communication: Human or Technical. ANZCA3 Conference, Brisbane, July 2003.

[Zh01] Zhang, P., Von Dran, G. M., Blake, P. and Pipithsuksunt, V. Important Design Features in Different Website Domains: an empirical study of user perception. E-service Journal, 1910: 77-91, 2001.

[Ke02] Kelton, D. W., Sadowski, R. P. and Sadowski, D. A. Simulation with Arena (2nd ed.). McGraw-Hill, New York, NY 10020.

Adaptive Multimedia Content Delivery in Ubiquitous Environments*

SeungMin Rho[1], JeongWon Cho[2], and EenJun Hwang[2,**]

[1] Graduate School of Information and Communication, Ajou University, Suwon, Korea
anycall@ajou.ac.kr
[2] Department of Electronics and Computer Engineering, Korea University, Seoul, Korea
{jwcho, ehwang04}@korea.ac.kr
Tel.: +82-2-3290-3256, fax: +82-2-921-0544

Abstract. Due to the dramatic technology development in Internet and wireless communication, it becomes possible to access multimedia contents and services using handheld devices. However, most multimedia contents and services on the Web are optimized for desktop computing environment. Even though multimedia contents can represent rich semantics, they are not suitable for handheld devices with limited resources and computing capabilities. Moreover, depending on user preference or usage scenarios, not all the data are relevant or critical to the application. In this paper, we present an adaptation scheme of multimedia contents on the wireless devices for QoS-aware delivery. Especially, we seek to adapt multimedia contents based on available system and network resources, client terminals, user preferences and some other environmental characteristics.

1 Introduction

Over the past few years, the volume of multimedia contents has increased a lot. Similarly, mobile devices such as PDA and mobile phone have grown in popularity and performance. Along this trend, people have become enthusiastic about watching multimedia contents through their handheld or mobile devices. The capabilities of such devices vary widely but are usually limited in terms of network bandwidth, processor speed, screen display, and decoding capabilities. As a result, there are many restrictions in viewing multimedia contents through mobile devices. Therefore, there is a growing need for delivering multimedia data to a variety of devices while adjusting its quality based on the resources available.

Ubiquitous computing is the ability to extend applications and services normally conducted on personal computers to handheld and wireless devices, which eventually enables any where, any time, and with any device access to multimedia information systems. Ubiquitous computing environment involves a variety of devices with different capabilities in terms of processing power, screen display, input facilities and network connectivity which can vary between wired and different types of wireless

---

* This research is supported by the MIC (Ministry of Information and Communication), Korea, under the ITRC (Information Technology Research Center) support program supervised by the IITA (Institute of Information Technology Assessment).
** Corresponding author.

M. Dean et al. (Eds.): WISE 2005 Workshops, LNCS 3807, pp. 43–52, 2005.
© Springer-Verlag Berlin Heidelberg 2005

links. The diversity of these devices will make it difficult and expensive to tailor multimedia contents separately for each individual type of device. Therefore, adapting multimedia contents to such diverse client devices becomes critical in this heterogeneous environment. Multimedia information needs to be customized according to user preference, client capabilities, network and natural environment characteristics. This customization process includes transcoding (format conversion – e.g. XML to WML), scalable coding (spatial and temporal resolution reduction – e.g. bit-rate reduction) and transmoding (modality conversion – e.g. video to image, video to audio). In general, adaptive multimedia content delivery systems have been focusing on specific problems such as varying network conditions and devices [1, 2]. The purpose of such adaptive systems is to deliver multimedia contents to users any time, any where on any device. In order to achieve this kind of adaptation, we exploit both MPEG-7 [3] and MPEG-21 [4] standards under the heterogeneous environment.

The organization of the rest of this paper is as follows. In section 2, we briefly introduce several related adaptation schemes. In section 3, we describe the overall system architecture for our QoS adaptive multimedia delivery. In section 4, we show the profiles for the content adaptation. In section 5, we present the implementation details of the system, and in section 6, we conclude the paper.

2 Related Work

Content adaptations can be classified into two main types depending on when these different content variants are created [5]. In the static adaptation, for example, when the client requests the video, the server analyzes the context and selects the best alternative form of the multimedia content and sends it to the client. With the static adaptation approach, the content provider can have a tight control over what is transcoded and how the result is presented [6]. In the dynamic adaptation, desired multimedia contents are adapted and delivered on the fly according to the dynamic requirements presented to the server which could be based on the current characteristics of the client environment [7]. For example, when network bandwidth is unstable, we can reduce the frame rate, resolution or color depth of the video delivered.

In regarding to the location where the adaptation is performed, many researchers describe three possible places for implementing adaptation in computer networks [5, 8]. Adaptation operations can take place in the server, the client or the proxy. So far, fewer examples are reported in the server-based adaptation [9]. Although server or sender as content providers have full control over the content quality and have more computational power to make reliable adjustment on the content quality, this adaptation has a major drawback that additional computation and resource consumption are required on the server which lacks in scalability. There are many systems that implement their own adaptation scheme separately in a proxy between the server and the client. The advantages of this approach are scalability, cost effectiveness and transparent design. Although this approach has many advantages, it still has efficiency problems affected by computation resource and time. Finally, in the client-based adaptation, the client device is responsible for adaptation and uses the device information and its capability to guide the adaptation process. In the Odyssey system [10], all the adaptation processes are done by the client which is the receiver of data from a remote data sender. Such a receiver-initiated adaptation strategy has a benefit of scalability, since servers do not need to be changed when there are new applications requesting for adaptation.

3 System Architecture

Fig. 1 shows the overall system architecture to deliver multimedia content in a QoS adaptive way over wired and wireless connections. We have considered different types of client devices such as Laptop and Pocket PC (PDA). When the client device connects to the server under various network conditions, the server determines whether it is possible to display multimedia contents on the client device. If the server decides that the client device is not adequate for displaying, then it contacts the client to get the device features and current network information. The information may include client hardware, software, browser (or media player), and network condition. When the server receives this information, it assigns a unique ID to the client device and store the device, network and media content descriptions as a XML document in the MPEG-7 content description database.

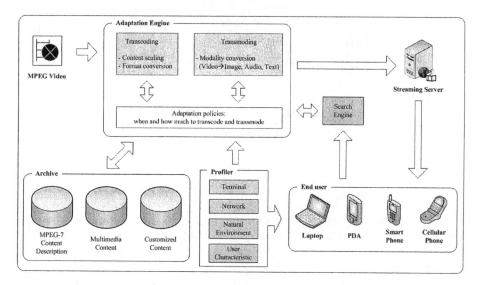

Fig. 1. Overall system architecture

The search and adaptation engines are the core components in the system. The search engine finds semantically meaningful segments from video using keywords with their start time and duration which are passed over from the adaptation engine. As we mentioned, the physical adaptation is a quality driven adaptation. The adaptation engine takes device description (terminal profile), network condition information (network profile), natural environment information (natural environment profile), and users request or their preference (user characteristics profile) for quality parameters. The parameters include start and end time of the video, bit rate, picture quality, frame rate, and frame size. The MPEG-7 content description for original content in multimedia content database is based on the high quality format (i.e., high resolution, high picture quality and high frame rate). However, when this description does not match with the parameters produced by the adaptation engine, we need to transcode/transmode the video from the original description to a new adapted profile.

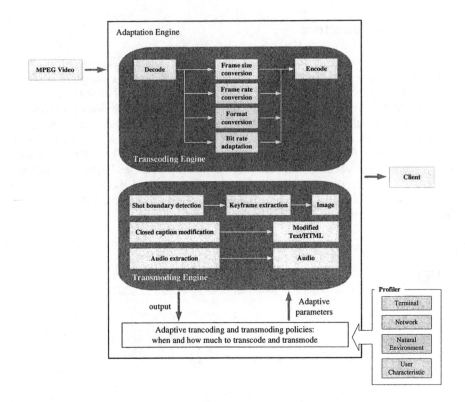

Fig. 2. Processes in the adaptation engine

Fig. 2 illustrates the overall steps in the adaptation engine to determine when and how much to transcode and transmode. Multimedia content adaptation proceeds in the three steps. In the first step, the profiler produces adaptive parameters for that particular context of device, network condition and user characteristics. In the second step, the profiler determines whether the content should be transcoded or transmoded and then sends the adaptive parameters into the transcoding or transmoding engine, respectively. In the third step, the encoder takes the adaptive parameters and produces an adapted multimedia content for streaming through the transcoding engine. On the other hand, transmoding engine converts video into other modality such as image, audio and text/html using key-frame extraction from each detected video shot, audio extraction and closed caption modification, respectively. The adaptive multimedia contents are sent to the client device by the streaming server.

4   Profiles for Adaptation

The adaptation describes the terminal capabilities as well as network characteristics, natural environment, and user preference [4]. We outline more detailed information below with sample terminal and network descriptions.

- *Terminal capabilities*: User can adapt various formats of multimedia for viewing on a particular terminal by the terminal-side capabilities such as codec and I/O capabilities. Codec capability specifies the format that particular terminal is capable of encoding or decoding. I/O capability includes a description of display characteristics and audio output capabilities.
- *Network characteristics*: Network capabilities and network conditions affect multimedia adaptation for transmission efficiency and robustness. For instance, we can lower the network bandwidth of a video stream if the available bandwidth is insufficient. Network capabilities define the maximum capacity of a network and the minimum guaranteed bandwidth and network conditions describe network parameters such as the available bandwidth and delay characteristics.
- *Natural environment*: Natural environment pertains to the physical environmental conditions around a user such as lighting condition and noise level, or a circumstance such as the time and location.
- *User characteristics*: User characteristics include a description of user information, usage preferences and history. User preferences define preferences related to the user hardware such as PDA and handheld PC. For audio, the specification describes preferred audio power and equalizer settings. For visual information, the specification defines display preferences such as the preferred color temperature, brightness, saturation, and contrast.

5 Implementation

In this paper, we have implemented a prototype system for delivering multimedia content in a QoS adaptive way. The system selects appropriate multimedia contents through the adaptation engine based on the evaluation of various multimedia content alternatives to adapt the client device. The client platform is developed by Microsoft Embedded Visual Tools with the DirectX Platform Adaptation Kit (DXPAK). We have tested streaming video files encoded in Windows Media Video Format (*.wmv*), Advanced Streaming Format (*.asf*), and Audio Video Interleave Format (*.avi*) as in [11].

Fig. 3 shows a content adaptation process on the PDA client based on the device capability and user preference. According to the client's profile, the requested video is transcoded and displayed into different formats such as different frame rate and frame size. An adaptation example considering the network characteristics (mainly the bandwidth of the connection) is shown in Fig. 4. We evaluated the adaptation performance under various networking conditions. We first obtained the terminal and network profiles for each modality by monitoring the network condition. Then, the collected adaptive parameters can be fed into the adaptation engine for determining any degradation. When the network bandwidth is enough, the PDA client can display the video. However, under the scarce bandwidth, the adaptation engine might decide content degradation by transmoding. During this degradation stage, the user can still listen to the audio with key frame images or read the closed caption.

Fig. 5 and Fig. 6 illustrate cpu and memory usage when running a Windows file format such as *.asf*, *.avi* and *.wmv*. Files were encoded using both RGB and YUV.

Fig. 5 shows that avi file format needs more processing power compared to other format such as asf or wmv. From the figure, we can see that the average cpu time of avi format file is around 40 percent loading time while the average cpu times for rendering asf and wmv file format exhibit 20 and 17 percent on the average, respectively. As shown in Fig.5, three different curves are fluctuated between 6 and 26 seconds. This is because there is a peak in cpu time for each shot change in the video sequence. Fig. 6 shows the client memory usage for both asf and wmv format. Both used 50% of available memory on the average while rendering the file to the screen; however, the avi file format demonstrates a slight rise in memory usage towards the closing stages of the sampling period.

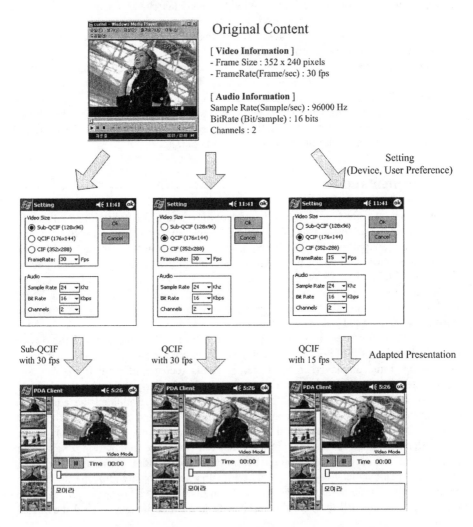

Fig. 3. Adaptation based on the device capabilities and user preferences

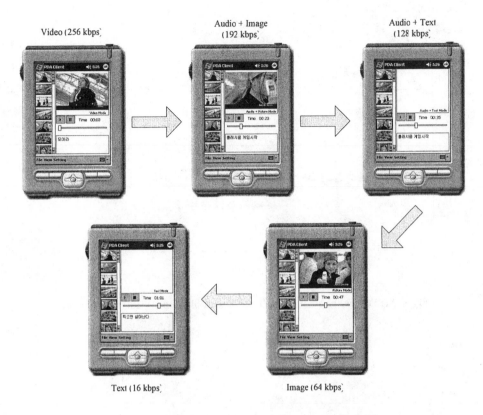

Fig. 4. Adaptability of the system by the network conditions

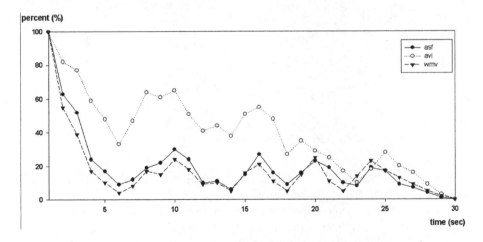

Fig. 5. CPU usage among the YUV encoded file formats (asf, avi and wmv)

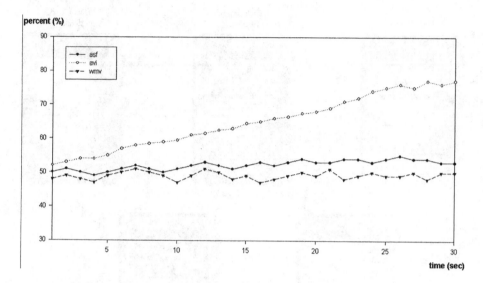

Fig. 6. Memory usage among the YUV encoded file formats (asf, avi and wmv)

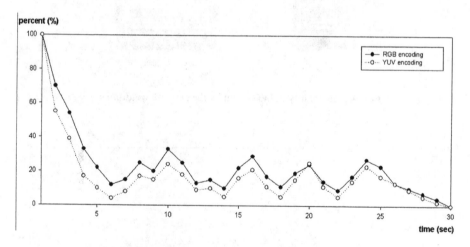

Fig. 7. CPU usage of RGB and YUV encodings for wmv format

Small video size such as 352 × 240 would be inappropriate for the most desktop and laptop platform and would be the most appropriate for the PDA. Fig. 7 and Fig. 8 compare the cpu and memory usage when rendering files with RGB encoding format and YUV encoding format. From these figures, we can conclude that the most bandwidth-friendly format is *.wmv* because it saved both memory and cpu usage while rendering the file to the PDA screen.

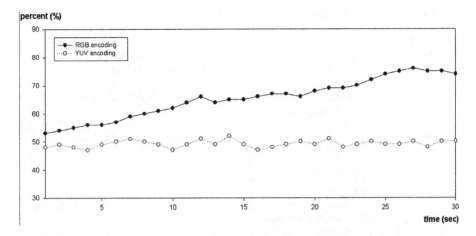

Fig. 8. Memory usage of RGB and YUV encodings for wmv format

6   Conclusion

In the coming ubiquitous computing environment, same multimedia contents may have to be transcoded or transmoded into different forms according to network condition and device capabilities. Content adaptation is one of the key issues that need to be dealt with for developing an adaptive multimedia delivery system. Towards this, we present a QoS aware adaptation scheme for ubiquitous applications. For the adaptation, the scheme considers various factors such as current system and network condition, client device, user preference and natural environmental characteristics. In this paper, we use the dynamic multimedia content adaptation to reduce bandwidth required for delivery. We also design an adaptation engine and implement the framework for adaptation driven by user perceived quality rather than just bit-rate reduction. Our system support media adaptation not for video only but cross-media adaptation using other media components such as audio, image and text.

References

1. W. Y. Ma, I. Bedner, G. Chang, A. Kuchinsky, and H.J. Zhang, "A framework for adaptive content delivery in heterogeneous network environments," SPIE Multimedia Computing and Networking, San Jose, California, USA, 2000.
2. R. S. Ramanujan, J. A. Newhouse, M. N. Kaddoura, A. Ahamad, E. R. Chartier, and K. J. Thurber, "Adaptive Streaming of MPEG Video over IP Networks," Proceedings of the 22nd IEEE Conference on Computer Networks (LCN 97), November 1997.
3. ISO/IEC JTC1 SC29/WG11 N3465, "MPEG-7 Multimedia Description Schemes WD," Beijing, 2000.
4. MPEG Requirements Group, "MPEG-21 Multimedia framework, Part 1: Vision, technologies and strategy," Proposed Draft Technical Report, 2nd Edition, Doc. ISO/MPEG N6269, MPEG Waikaloa Meeting, USA, December 2003.

5. Anthony Vetro, Charilaos Christopoulos, and Huifang Sun, "Video Transcoding Architectures and Techniques: An Overview," IEEE Signal Processing Magazine, pp. 19-29, March 2003.
6. Surya Nepal and Uma Srinivasan, "Adaptive video highlights for wired and wireless platforms," in Proc. Int. Conf. on Multimedia & Expo (ICME), pp. 269-272, 2003.
7. Noble, B.D., Price, M., and Satyanarayanan, M., "A Programming Interface for Application-aware Adaptation in Mobile Computing", Proc. 2nd USENIX Symposium on Mobile and Location-Independent Computing, Ann Arbor, MI, USA, Apr. 1995.
8. Han, R., Bhagwat, P., LaMaire, R., Mummert, T., Perret, V., and Rubas, J., "Dynamic Adaptation in an Image Transcoding Proxy for Mobile WWW Browsing". IEEE Personal Communication, 5(6): pp. 8-17, 1998.
9. Lei, Z., Georganas, N.D., "Context-based media adaptation in pervasive computing", Proceedings of IEEE Canadian Conference on Electrical and Computer (CCECE'01), Toronto, May 2001.
10. C.G.M. Snoek, M. Worring, "Multimodal video indexing: A review of the state-of-the-art," in Multimedia Tools and Applications, 2004.
11. Kevin Curran and Stephen Annesley, "Transcoding media for bandwidth constrained mobile devices," International Journal of Network Management, vol. 15, pp. 75-88, 2005.
12. R. Mohan, J. Smith, C.-S. Li, "Adapting multimedia internet content for universal access," IEEE Trans. Multimedia 1(1), pp. 104–114, March 1999.
13. Sumi Halal, Latha Sampath, Kevin Birkett and Joachim Hammer, "Adaptive delivery of video data over wireless and mobile environments," Wireless Communications and Mobile Computing Vol. 3, pp. 23-36, 2003.
14. K. Nagao, Y. Shirai, K. Squire, "Semantic annotation and transcoding: making web content more accessible," IEEE Multimedia 8(22) pp. 69–81. 2003.
15. J. Magalhaes, F. Pereira, "Using MPEG standards for multimedia customization," Signal Processing: Image Communication Vol. 19, pp. 437-456, 2004.
16. Surya Nepal and Uma Srinivasan, "DAVE: a system for quality driven adaptive video delivery," Proc. of the 5th ACM SIGMM international workshop on Multimedia information retrieval, pp. 223-230, 2003.

Incorporating the Timeliness Quality Dimension in Internet Query Systems

Sandra de F. Mendes Sampaio, Chao Dong, and Pedro R. Falcone Sampaio

School of Informatics, University of Manchester,
Manchester M60 1QD
{S.Sampaio, P.Sampaio}@Manchester.ac.uk
Chao.Dong@Postgrad.Manchester.ac.uk

Abstract. Internet Query Systems (IQS) are information systems used to query the World Wide Web by finding data sources relevant to a given query and retrieving data taking into account issues such as the unpredictability of access and transfer rates, infinite streams of data, and the ability to produce partial results. Despite the wide availability of research focusing on query processing for IQS, there are surprisingly few contributions addressing data quality issues such as timeliness and accuracy of data resulting from Internet query processing. This paper provides an overview of an ongoing research effort to extend IQS with a data quality component to ensure timeliness of data resulting from Internet query processing. In particular, we illustrate the quality model, data source layer design and the quality aware algebraic query processing framework adopted in our implementation effort.

1 Introduction

Over the past few years, a set of new demands for advanced information management tools have appeared, as the Internet became ubiquitous. Mainstream information management applications such as Bioinformatics [1], and e-Science [2] typically consume data from a variety of web sources and apply a multitude of tools for querying, collecting, formatting, and comparing web data. The complex data retrieval and processing requirements posed by these applications demand information management components that can speedily, simply and accurately deal with the chaos of query processing across heterogeneous and distributed web sources. From a user's point of view, the key functionality is to compose information requests and expect high quality results without needing to understand the idiosyncrasies relating to each data source.

Within the portfolio of Internet information management tools available, Internet Query Systems (IQS) have combined the capabilities of search engines, mediators and database management systems enabling DBMS-like query processing and data management over multiple Internet data sources, allowing users to query a global information system without being aware of the site structure, query languages, and semantics of the data repositories that store the relevant data for a given query [3].

Despite the advanced capabilities for querying, combining, integrating and collating data supported by IQS, assessing and measuring trust levels, accuracy and timeliness of information processed from the different data sources is still an elusive goal. The

M. Dean et al. (Eds.): WISE 2005 Workshops, LNCS 3807, pp. 53–62, 2005.
© Springer-Verlag Berlin Heidelberg 2005

lack of application semantic support (e.g., ontologies) and the low levels of data quality obtained from using IQS have often driven potential users to adopt domain specific tools (e.g., specialized Bioinformatics query and retrieval systems such as TAMBIS [4]), instead of generic DBMS-like query processing and data management approach for multiple Internet data sources typically supported by an IQS. More recently, there is a new stream of research on information quality for Internet information systems that seeks to buck this trend by developing quality aware query processing approaches and systems. Within the core issues being tackled we can point out the concepts of timeliness [5, 7] and accuracy [5, 7]. The first deals with the degree to which the data is up-to-date; the second deals with the degree of correctness and precision with the data to the object in the real world.

This paper addresses the timeliness quality dimension of data retrieved from remote internet data sources in the context of Internet Query System architectures. The proposed approach is based on the incorporation of a data quality module into an existing Internet Query System. In particular, we illustrate the quality model, data source layer design and the quality aware algebraic query processing framework adopted in our implementation effort.

This paper is structured as follows. Section 2 discusses background research into Internet Query Systems and data quality dimensions. Section 3 introduces the timeliness data quality model adopted. Section 4 presents the data source layer design. Section 5 presents the Timeliness quality aware query processing framework. Section 6 illustrates an example of timeliness query processing. Section 7 discusses related work, and Section 8 summarizes the work and discusses future directions.

2   Internet Query Systems and Data Quality

Internet Query Systems (IQS) are being developed to enable DBMS-like query processing and data management over multiple Internet data sources, shielding the user from complexities such as heterogeneity. The intelligent query processing approach supported by IQS allows users to query a global information system without being aware of the sites, structure, query languages, and semantics of the data repositories that store the relevant data for a given query [3]. IQS research is primarily focused on query processing techniques, e.g., query engines for producing partial results, query optimization of XML-based languages, search engines and techniques for indexing data sources. There are also two widely known systems available, such as Niagara [3] and WebFormulate [6]. However, a major drawback in existing IQS has been the absence of awareness of the quality of data retrieved from remote data sources, hence affecting the overall quality of the information obtained from the IQS. Typical examples of data quality issues arising in IQS generated query results are [7]:

- *Accuracy of data:* Data can have errors or inconsistencies in its representation. For example, the data values "ST Louis" and "Saint Louis" may not be matched in a Join between different relational tables despite referring to the same address instance, due to the different representation formats.
- *Timeliness of data:* Data can be of poor quality when it is not timely enough for the intended use. For example, a data source containing sales information is used to compute sales bonus due on the 15th of the following month. However, some units

of the company may take several days to send in updated sales information reducing the quality of the computed results.

- *Completeness of data:* Data can be incomplete. For example, a data source containing information on repairs done on capital equipment is used as a base for evaluating information about warranty satisfaction. However, repairs are often done and the information about repairs is not entered into the data source.

Despite the significant progress achieved by research on database integration and ontology-based query processing, the data quality issues above are challenges that still demand solutions both at the database architecture and query processing research fronts.

3   Timeliness Quality Model Underpinning the Query System

Timeliness in data quality is a contextual, task-dependent dimension and refers to the extent to which data is up-to-date for the task at hand. Timeliness data quality models have been previously developed in the management science domain to assess data unit quality levels throughout the information processing value chain based on the *Currency* and *Volatility* of the data [10].

In a data quality Timeliness model, *Currency* is defined as the age of a data unit when it is delivered to the user. It is dependent upon three key factors: (i) the time when the data is delivered to the user (*Delivery time*), (ii) the time when the data was entered into the Storage System (*Input Time*), and (iii) how old the data was when entered into the Storage System (*Age*). Factor iii represents the time interval between the occurrence of the real-world event that determined the state of the data and the time when the data was entered into the Storage System. The formal definition of *Currency* is described as follows [10]:

$$Currency = (Delivery\ Time - Input\ Time) + Age. \tag{1}$$

When bridging the above definitions towards the context of Internet Query Systems, we regard a storage system as a data source, and we define *Delivery Time* as the time when the data unit arrives at the site of the Internet Query System. Factors *Input Time* and *Age* are defined exactly as above and should be provided by the data source as information that will be used by the Internet Query System to measure the Timeliness of each data unit fetched from the data source (data quality policy assumption). Note that the Timeliness measure of a data unit can not be known until the data unit arrives at the site of the Internet Query System. *Volatility* is defined as the length of time during which the data unit remains valid. This information should also be provided by the data source to be used when measuring the Timeliness of each data unit by the Internet Query System. From the above definitions, the Timeliness measurement formula articulated in [10] is also applicable to the Internet Query System context:

$$Timeliness = \{max[(1 - Currency/Volatility),\ 0]\}^s \tag{2}$$

Formula (2) develops an absolute measure for Timeliness, rather than a relative one, on a continuous scale from 0 to 1, where 1 represents the highest Timeliness measure and is appropriate for data that meet the most strict Timeliness standard, and

0 represents the lowest Timeliness measure and is appropriate for data that are unacceptable from the Timeliness perspective. The exponent s is a parameter that allows control of the sensitivity of Timeliness to the Currency-Volatility ratio, and its value should be chosen depending upon the context in which data is being judged. For example, having this ratio equal or close to zero is desirable, and as the ratio increases, Timeliness can be slightly ($s = 0.5$) or significantly affected ($s = 2$), or neither ($s = 1$).

4   Data Source Layer: Using Tags to Compute Timeliness

To enable quality aware query processing, data sources should provide quality information relating to each data unit stored, including the *Input time* of the data, the *Age* and the *Volatility* as discussed in the data quality model. The information needs to be tagged and delivered to the IQS mediator so that quality assessment query processing takes place. To attach timeliness tags to data, we have adapted the mechanism proposed in [11] for tagging data quality factors to relational data. The tagging is done at attribute level, i.e. each attribute of a tuple in a relation is tagged with quality information that is taken into consideration during query processing. The quality factors associated with a particular attribute are stored in a Information Quality Relation (IQR) and each tuple in the IQR refers to a particular instance of the attribute. The attributes of the IQR (or Information Quality Attributes) are composed of the identifier of the attribute instance and a number of quality indicators. Figure 1 shows the mechanism.

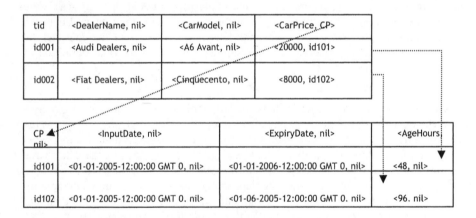

Fig. 1. Tagging Mechanism

With the mechanism, it is also possible to derive aggregate quality indicators from a basic quality indicator and associate information from different IQRs. Figure 1 also illustrates an IQR (CP, InputDate, ExpiryDate, Age) associated with a relation (tid, DealerName, CarModel, CarPrice) via the identifier CP of attribute CarPrice. Each tuple in the IQR describes the available data quality information for a tuple in the relation. For example, for attribute CarPrice of tuple id001, the available quality information is described in tuple id101 of the IQR, where id101 is the identifier of attribute CarPrice for tuple id001.

```
Currency = (Delivery Time - Input Time) + Age.
Age = 48 hours
Currency = (01-06-2005-12:00:00 GMT 0  -  01-01-2005-12:00:00 GMT 0) + 48 hours
Currency = (4320 hours) + 48 hours
Currency = 4368 hours
```

> Note that Delivery Time and Input Time are shown in hours, however, other fine-grained time scales are also addressed in our approach

```
Volatility = Expiry Time - Input Time + Age.
Volatility = 8640 hours  +  48 hours
Volatility = 8688 hours
```

> Volatility is measured by adding the interval during which the data will remain stored in the system (unchanged) since it has been input to the system (Expiry Time - Input Time) and the age of the data before it was input to the system. This result indicates the total amount of data validity time.

```
Timeliness = {max[(1 - Currency/Volatility), 0]}¹
Timeliness = {max[(1 - 4368/8688), 0]}¹
Timeliness = {max[0.49, 0]}¹
Timeliness = 0.49
```

Fig. 2. Timeliness measurement using IQR tags

Also note that the attributes of the IQR shown in Figure 1 are Timeliness quality factors and can be used to measure the Timeliness quality of attribute CarPrice for each of the instances of the relation. For example, assuming that the Delivery Time is 01-06-2005-12:00:00 GMT 0, for tuple id001 the Timeliness measure is obtained as described in Figure 2. The interpretation of the result (0.49) as being "sufficient" or "not enough" for the task is left to the user.

```
<carDealerInformation>
  <dealer id="id001">
    <name>Audi Dealers</name>
    <car>
      <model>A6 Avant</model>
      <price>
        <value>26000</value>
        <dataQuality>
          <timeliness>
            <inputDate>01-01-2005-12:00:00 GMT 0</inputDate>
            <expiryDate>01-01-2006-12:00:00 GMT 0</expiryDate>
            <ageHours>48</ageHours>
          </timeliness>
        </dataQuality>
      </price>
    </car>
  </dealer>
</carDealerInformation>
```

Fig. 3. Tagging Mechanism for XML Data

In the context of the Internet Query System adopted in our implementation (Niagara), to cooperate with the IQS, data sources need to export data in XML, therefore IQR tags and the associated data should be mapped into an XML schema where data quality factors are defined as child elements of an XML element, as shown in Figure 3.

5 Quality Aware Algebraic Query Processing Framework

The quality aware query processing implementation framework described in this paper is being developed as an extension to the Niagara IQS algebraic operators. When a query is submitted to Niagara as an XML-based query expression, it is transformed into two sub-queries, a search engine query and a query engine query. While the former is used by the search engine to select the data sources that are relevant to answer the query, the latter is optimized and ultimately mapped into a quality aware algebraic query execution plan that incorporates algebraic operators addressing timeliness information. Following data source selection, the process of fetching data takes place and streams of data start flowing from the data sources to the site of the Internet Query System for query execution. This process is illustrated in Figure 4.

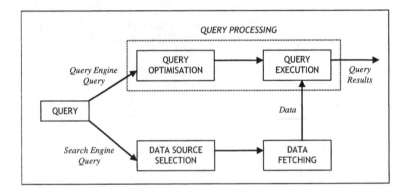

Fig. 4. Query Processing and Data Search in Niagara

The Timeliness algebra whose operators compose a query execution plan is an XML algebra extended with an operator that encapsulates the capability of measuring the Timeliness quality of XML data based on Timeliness factors tagged on the data. The algebraic query processing framework adopted in our implementation extends algebraic quality operators developed for relational systems [11] to devise an XML-based algebra for the Niagara IQS that can take into account Timeliness quality information during query execution.

The quality aware algebraic framework is described in Table 1. In essence, the Timeliness algebra is similar to an XML-algebra, but it has an additional operator, the Timeliness operator, which encapsulates the capability of measuring, inserting and propagating Timeliness information in XML data, provided the data has Timeliness factors associated with it (IQR tags). Note that IQS complexities relating to the ability to deal with streams of data, produce partial results and issues in synchronization are out of the scope of our approach, therefore, are not reflected in Table 1.

Table 1. Timeliness Algebra

Logical Operators	Description
Scan (inputData)	Receives the data coming from the network (inputData), builds a data structure for each unit of data (input) and passes each structure to the next operator. Data containing Timeliness information (input time, expiry time and age elements) are treated as any other XML element, but are associated with a specific element in the structure by being treated as children elements to this element.
Select (input, pred)	Receives an input containing a number of values for XML elements and attributes, applies a predicate (pred) over the input and either discards or retains the input depending on whether the predicate evaluates to false or true.
Project (input, listElem)	Receives an input containing a number of values for XML elements and attributes, and discards all the elements that are not specified in listElem (list of elements). For each discarded element, all the Timeliness elements are also discarded
Join (inputLeft, inputRight, pred)	Receives two inputs, each containing a number of values for XML elements and attributes, "concatenates" both inputs, retaining all their elements, applies a predicate (pred) over the result and either discards or retains the result depending on whether the predicate evaluates to false or true.
Timeliness (input)	Receives an input containing a number of values for XML elements and attributes, calculates the Timeliness measure for each element in the input, attach each measure to the corresponding element (as a child element).

6   Timeliness Query Processing: An Example

In this section we provide an example of a query expressed in Niagara's query language (XML-QL) and the results obtained when running queries according to the quality aware query processing framework. The query is based on the DTD shown in Figure 5 and the XML data schema discussed in Figure 3.

Figure 6 illustrates a query which lists the model and the price of each car that has a price greater than or equal to 20K submitted to the Niagara system. Figure 7 shows the query execution plan generated for query 1, based on the physical XML-algebra implemented within the Niagara system, extended to deal with Timeliness information.

According to the plan (from bottom up) each car element is scanned, has its price value element tested by Select on (value >= 20K), has some of its attributes projected by Construct (Construct is the counterpart of Project in the Physical algebra), as well as restructured according to how the user specified the structure of the query result, and, finally, has Timeliness measured and added to the result by the Timeliness operator.

```
<!ELEMENT carDealerInformation (dealer)*>
<!ELEMENT dealer (name, car*)>
<!ATTLIST dealer id ID #REQUIRED>
<!ELEMENT name (#PCDATA)>
<!ELEMENT car (model, price)>
<!ELEMENT model (#PCDATA)>
<!ELEMENT price (value, dataQuality)>
<!ELEMENT value (#PCDATA)>
<!ELEMENT dataQuality (timeliness)>
<!ELEMENT timeliness (inputDate, expiryDate, ageHours)>
<!ELEMENT inputDate (#PCDATA)>
<!ELEMENT expiryDate (#PCDATA)>
<!ELEMENT ageHours (#PCDATA)>
```

Fig. 5. Example DTD

```
WHERE
<carDealerInformation>
 <dealer>
  <car>
   <model>$v4</>
   <price>
    <value>$v6</>
   </>
  </>
 </>
</>
IN"*"conform_to "file:/home/mcassss/MyFiles/Research/NiagaraSystem/Data/Timeliness/data.dtd",
$v6 >= "20000"
CONSTRUCT
<result>
 <model>$v4</>
 <value>$v6</>
</>
```

Fig. 6. Query 1: Car Price Query

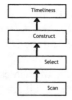

Fig. 7. Query plan for query 1

Fig. 8. Expected results for query 1

The calculation of the Timeliness measure for this example is shown in Figure 2. Figure 8 shows the results for Query 1, when executed according to the plan described in Figure 7.

7 Related Work

In [8], data quality is incorporated into schema integration by answering a global query using only queries that are classified as high quality and executable by a subset of the data sources. This is done by assigning quality scores to queries based on previous knowledge about the data to be queried, considering quality dimensions such as completeness, timeliness and accuracy. The queries are ranked according to their scores and executed from the highest quality plan to the lowest quality plan until a stop criteria is reached. The described approach, however, does not use XML as the canonical data model and does not address physical algebraic query plan implementation issues.

In [9] an approach for data quality management in Cooperative Information Systems is described. The architecture has as its main component a Data Quality Broker, which performs data requests on all cooperating systems on behalf of a requesting system. The request is a query expressed in the XQuery language along with a set of quality requirements that the desired data have to satisfy. A typical feature of cooperative query systems is the high degree of data replication, with different copies of the same data received as responses. The responses are reconciled and the best results (based on quality thresholds) are selected and delivered to users, who can choose to discard output data and adopt higher quality alternatives. All cooperating systems export their application data and quality data thresholds, so that quality certification and diffusion are ensured by the system. The system, however, does not adopt an algebraic query processing framework and is not built on top of a mainstream IQS.

8 Conclusions and Future Work

With the advent of the Internet and the exponential growth in the availability of data on the web, the need for systems and tools to query and retrieve high quality information from Internet data has become paramount. Despite the significant amount of work in the development of search engines and other Internet technologies for retrieving and processing Internet data, Internet Query Systems (IQS) still have a long way before becoming widely accepted and as effective as Database Management Systems (DBMS) in providing information systems with high quality data.

Despite the advanced capabilities for querying, combining, integrating and collating data supported by IQS; assessing, measuring and enforcing information quality factors such as accuracy and timeliness during query processing is still an elusive goal.

This paper provides an overview of an ongoing research effort to extend IQS with a data quality component to ensure timeliness and accuracy of data resulting from Internet query processing. In particular, we illustrate the quality model, data source layer design and the quality aware algebraic query processing framework adopted in our effort to engineer a timeliness quality aware query processor. The algebraic framework for adding data quality operations enables the seamless integration of established algebraic query optimization techniques in the database literature and also builds upon the authors' successful previous experience in using the algebraic approach for implementing parallel database algebras [12] and deductive object-oriented database algebras [13] for the Polar and DOQL database management systems, respectively.

Future work for this project includes the incorporation of the data accuracy quality dimension into the query processing framework and a cost model that takes quality factors into consideration during query plan optimization.

References

[1]   Arthur M. Lesk, Introduction to Bioinformatics, Oxford University Press, 2002
[2]   The UK e-Science Programme, http://www.rcuk.ac.uk/escience
[3]   Jeffrey F. Naughton, David J. DeWitt, David Maier, et al. The Niagara Internet Query System. IEEE Data Eng. Bull. 24(2): 27-33 (2001)
[4]   Baker, P., Brass, A., Bechhofer, S., Goble, C., Paton, N., and Stevens, R. (1998). TAMBIS: An Overview. In Proc. of Conf. on Intelligent Systems for Molecular Biology, pages 25-34.
[5]   Jack Olson, Data Quality: the Accuracy Dimension, Morgan Kauffmann, 2003
[6]   J. Leopold, M. Heimovics, T. Palmer, WebFormulate: A Web-Based Visual Continual Query System, WWW 2002, May 7-11, Hawaii, 2002
[7]   M. Gertz, T. Ozsu, G. Saake, K. Sattler, Data Quality on the Web, Dagstuhl Seminar , 2003
[8]   F. Naumann, U. Lesser; J. Freytag, Quality-driven Integration of Heterogeneous Information Systems; Proceedings of the 25th VLDB Conference, Scotland, 1999
[9]   M. Mecella, M. Scannapieco, A. Virgillito, R. Baldoni, T. Catarci, C. Batini, The DaQuinCIS Broker: Querying Data and Their Quality in Cooperative Information Systems. LNCS 2800. Pages: 208-232. 2003.
[10] Ronald Ballou; Richard Wang; Harold Pazer; Giri Kumar Tayi, Modeling Information Manufacturing Systems to Determine Information Product Qaulity, Management Science, 44, 4; ABI/INFORM Global, Pages.462-464, 1998
[11] Richard Y. Wang; M.P. Reddy; Henry B. Kon, Toward Quality data: An attribute-based approach, Decision Support Systems 13 (1995), 349-372, 1995
[12] J. Smith, Sandra de F. Mendes Sampaio, Paul Watson, Norman W. Paton: The Design, Implementation and Evaluation of an ODMG Compliant, Parallel Object Database Server. Distributed and Parallel Databases 16(3): 275-319 (2004)
[13] Pedro R. Falcone Sampaio, Norman W. Paton: Query processing in DOQL: A deductive database language for the ODMG model. Data & Knowledge Eng. 35(1): 1-38 (2000)

SOAP Request Scheduling for Differentiated Quality of Service

Ching-Ming Tien[1], Cho-Jun Lee[2], Po-Wen Cheng[2], and Ying-Dar Lin[1]

[1] Department of Computer and Information Science,
National Chiao Tung University, 1001, Ta Hsueh Road,
Hsinchu, Taiwan 300
{cmtien, ydlin}@cis.nctu.edu.tw
[2] Computer and Communications Research Laboratories,
Industrial Technology Research Institute, 195 Chung Hsing Road,
Section 4, Chu Tung, Hsinchu, Taiwan 310
{ChoJunLee, sting}@itri.org.tw

Abstract. This paper presents a SOAP request scheduling algorithm for differentiated quality of service. The scheduling algorithm can be deployed on a Web services server or any server that processes SOAP requests. Due to the resource-intensive security processing of SOAP messages, this research implements the scheduling algorithm on a QoS security server. The security server schedules the requests forwarded from the Web services server for the security processing and then sends the valid requests back to the Web services server for executing the Web services. The design of the scheduling algorithm is derived from the traditional deficit round-robin scheduling. However, the scheduling algorithm schedules requests according to the probed CPU resource consumption of requests. In the evaluation, the scheduling algorithm reveals the service differentiation on the throughput and response time and the little scheduling overhead. The resource utilizations are measured to prove the security processing is much more resource-intensive than the Web services execution.

1 Introduction

Web services are self-describing and modular business applications that expose the business logic as services over the Internet through programmable interfaces and standard Internet protocols. A Web services can be invoked by different service requesters; thus, a service provider may wish to offer different Service Level Agreements (SLAs) to different consumers to guarantee different levels of Quality of Service (QoS) [1]. The QoS issues of Web services can be discussed from two perspectives: service consumers and service providers. From the service consumer perspective, a Web services potentially could be provided by many service providers with different SLAs. A service consumer can invoke one or more Web services to accomplish a task after the discovery of the Web service. Many researches have presented QoS brokers and middlewares between service providers

M. Dean et al. (Eds.): WISE 2005 Workshops, LNCS 3807, pp. 63–72, 2005.

and consumers for service selection and composition [2][3][4][5][6]. However, these help a service provider little to guarantee the service levels described in the SLAs. From the service provider perspective, requests for a Web services should be controlled in order to meet the guarantees in the negotiated SLAs. Some researches have proposed request scheduling and resource allocation algorithms to allow a service provider to provide service differentiation to multiple classes of service consumers [7][8][9][10]. Through prioritizing a request or estimating the resource requirement of a request, the throughput or response time can be differentiated among service classes.

In this paper, a SOAP (Simple Object Access Protocol) request scheduling algorithm that manages the system resource for differentiated quality of service is presented. The scheduling algorithm can be deployed on a Web services server or any server that processes SOAP requests. This research chooses to implement the scheduling algorithm on a security server because the security processing of SOAP messages, such as message integrity, message confidentiality, and message authentication, often consume more system resources than the Web services execution. The security server accepts SOAP requests forwarded from the Web services server. Then the request scheduling algorithm schedules the requests to determine the order and time of forwarding requests to the security processing. The Deficit Round Robin (DRR) scheduling [11] is emulated by the scheduling algorithm. However, the presented scheduling algorithm differs from the traditional DRR scheduling in that the former schedules requests but the latter schedules packets. The DRR scheduling requires packet size to be known, whereas the presented scheduling algorithm requires the amount of the server resource consumed by a request to be known. Another difference is that the traditional DRR scheduling is work-conservative, it never idles a link if it has a packet. The presented scheduling algorithm is also work-conservative in order to keep the server busy. However, it is non-work-conservative because it chooses to remain idle when there is no enough server resource, even if it has requests to service.

The presented QoS security server is implemented using the open source packages of the Apache XML project [12]. The security server has a request thread pool and a security thread pool for accepting requests from the Web services server and performing the tasks of the security processing, respectively. In the evaluation, the throughput and response time of each service class are measured to demonstrate the effectiveness of the service differentiation. The CPU and memory resource utilizations of the Web services server and security server are measured during the evaluation to prove the security processing actually consume much more resource than the Web services execution.

The rest of this paper is organized as follows. Section 2 introduces the related work regarding the Web services differentiation. Section 3 presents the architecture of the QoS security server and the design of the request scheduling algorithm. Section 4 describes the implementation and the evaluation of the presented solution. Section 5 finally gives the conclusion and the future work of this research.

2   Related Work of Web Services Differentiation

If a service provider wants to offer differentiated levels of services to multiple classes of service consumers, the SOAP requests destined to a server should be controlled for service differentiation. The general way to achieve this is to deploy a QoS broker or middleware in front of a server to determine the number, order, or time of requests to be forwarded to the server. The following introduces some researches related to Web service differentiation.

A QoS architecture consisting of a broker and proxies to map the QoS requirements from higher layers onto the underlying network layer has been presented in [9]. The proxies mark priorities of requests and responses in the IP packets and let underlying transporting technologies control the QoS. Although this solution can close the gap between the Web services layer and network layer, the prerequisite of success is the underlying transport technology must support QoS. However, the fact is QoS technologies are not widely deployed in the practical networks.

A smartware for according scheduling priorities to requests has been presented in [7]. Its scheduling algorithm adjusts the priorities accorded to requests dynamically to maintain the ratio of the request throughputs, measured by the number of requests per second, with respect to the incoming request traffic. A lower than normal arrival of a request category will penalize the priority, while the greater than expected arrivals will reinforce the priority positively. A concern of this solution is that the overhead of encoding service priority levels in the request header is high. This would affect the performance of the middleware.

A QoS broker that manages the server resource to be allocated to requests has been presented in [10]. The broker employs two resource allocation algorithms, homogenous resource allocation (HQ) and non-homogenous resource allocation(RQ), for legacy and QoS servers respectively. The HQ algorithm sets many threshold points and a step size and calculates the amount of the server resource to be allocated to a client. The RQ algorithm allocates different amounts of resources to different clients according to their requirements. It creates a virtual client to reserve some unused resource to reduce instability. If the reserved resource is not enough, it reconfigures the resource allocation among some existing clients to let the incoming client receive a satisfactory service quality. The purposes of the algorithms is to achieve a high average system utility and avoid making frequent resource reconfigurations. Nevertheless, the nature of the resource reconfiguration is not good for the scheduling. The scheduling algorithms should accurately allocate needed resource to a request rather than correcting the allocation after a reconfiguration.

An architecture and prototype implementation of a performance management for cluster-based Web services has been presented in [8]. The management tasks of the system include resource allocation, load balancing, and server overload protection. Its global resource manager periodically computes the number of concurrent requests to be sent to a server. It uses a simple queuing model to predict the response time of request for different resource allocation values. However, the omitted fact of this research is that different types of requests bring different amounts of resource consumptions. Only counting the number of concurrent requests processed on a server would lead to a bottlenecked or a non-fully-utilized resource.

3   QoS Security Server and Request Scheduling Algorithm

Web services security offers message integrity, message confidentiality, and message authentication in SOAP communications. All XML Web services security functions, such as XML schema validation, XML encryption, XML signature, Web services security and others, require extensive XML processing. If all these security functions are executed on a Web services server, the performance of the Web services would be downgraded seriously. Therefore, the secure XML processing should be offloaded from the Web services server. Here a QoS security server and a SOAP request scheduling algorithm are presented to offload the security processing of SOAP messages and provide service differentiation to Web services consumers.

The architecture of the QoS security server is shown in Fig. 1. The Web services server accepts requests from the Internet. The requests are then forwarded to the security server for the security processing. The request classifier classifies the requests into different service classes according to the pre-defined QoS policies and puts the requests into the corresponding class queues. The request scheduler checks the availability of the CPU resource. If the available resource is enough for the requirement of a request, the request scheduler fetches the request from the queue and determines the order and time the request being sent to the security processor. The security processor performs the security processing for the request. The valid requests will be sent back to the Web services server for executing the Web services, whereas the invalid ones will be dropped. The Web services server returns the response to the requester. The detailed design of the QoS security server is discussed as follows.

Request Profiling. A service provider may assign different security levels to different requesters. Hence, securing SOAP requests could go through different steps. XML schema validation, XML encryption, and XML signature are possible steps. A request could go through one step only, whereas another request could go through two or more steps. This means different requests would lead to different resource consumptions when being processed. In order to manage

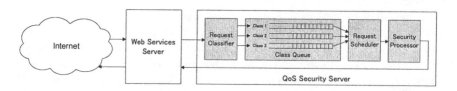

Fig. 1. Architecture of the QoS security server

the resource of the security server for the service differentiation, the resource consumption of the security processing of a request has to be known. The request profiling is a process to profile the resource requirement of a request. The resource consumption of every security function is measured. The amount of the resource requirement of a request is derived from summing all the resource consumptions of the needed security functions. The profiled information is stored in a resource requirement table. The request classifier refers to this table when estimating the resource requirement for a request.

Request Classification. The SLAs of the service provider and its clients define the service treatments the service provider should provide. The service provider therefore defines QoS policies for the request classifier to classify clients into different service classes. The QoS policies are defined in a QoS policy table that describes the rules of classifying requests and the service weights of the service classes. The request classifier accepts a request from the Web services server and inspects the HTTP header and the metadata contained in the SOAP request, such as user id, subscriber id and service name, etc. The header information and metadata are compared with the rules in the QoS policy table. If matched, the request will be classified into a service class; otherwise, it will be dropped. Once a request is classified, the request classifier lookups the resource requirement of the request from the resource requirement table. The request classifier then tags the resource requirement onto the request and puts the request into an appropriate class queue. The requests in the classes queue will wait for being scheduled to the security processor.

Request Scheduling. The key idea of designing the request scheduler is derived from the Deficit Round Robin (DRR) scheduling. A traditional DRR scheduler schedules packets to manage the bandwidth of a link. Whereas in this research, the request scheduler schedules SOAP requests to manage the resource of the security server. The request scheduler determines which request to be fetched next from the class queues and when to forward a request to the security processor for the security processing.

The operation of the request scheduler is shown in Fig. 2. The numbers in the blocks in the queues represent the amounts of resource requirements of the queued requests. The request scheduler uses a deficit counter to record the unused service quantum of a class and a round-robin pointer to point to the class queue to be serviced. It services the request at the head of each non-empty class queue which the value of the deficit counter is greater than the resource requirement of the request. In addition, the request scheduler checks the amount of the available resource for deciding whether to forward a request to the security processor or not. If the available resource is enough for the requirement of the request to be serviced, the request scheduler forwards the request to the security processor; otherwise, the request scheduler stops the scheduling and waits for the resource released from the finish of the security processing of a request. A deficit counter is decremented by the resource requirement of a request being serviced. When the value of the deficit counter is lower than the resource requirement of

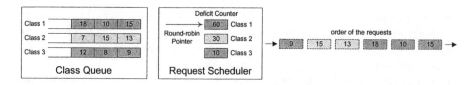

Fig. 2. Operation of the request scheduler

the request that at the head of the queue, this means the service quantum in this round is already not enough for the requirement of this class. The round-robin pointer at this time moves to the next queue and the next deficit counter is incremented by the defined quantum size. Through the request scheduling, the resource of the security server is shared among the classes according to the ratio of the quantum sizes assigned to the classes.

The presented request scheduler and the traditional DRR scheduler are different in several aspects. First, the presented scheduler schedules requests instead of packets. Then, the presented scheduler schedules requests according to the resource requirement of a request, not packet size. Finally, the presented scheduler is work-conservative to the security server; that is, it keeps the security server busy at any time. On the other hand, the presented scheduler is non-work-conservative to the class queues because it may choose to remain idle if there is no enough resource. However, the traditional DRR scheduler is work-conservative. The DRR scheduler keeps scheduling packets if there is any packet in the queues.

4   Implementation and Evaluation

4.1   Implementation

The implementation of the QoS security server is based on the open source packages of the Apache XML project, including XML Security, Xerces, Xalan, Log4j, Jakarta Discovery, and Jakarta HttpClient. The security server has two thread pools, the request thread pool and security thread pool. The threads in the request thread pool perform the tasks of accepting requests from the Web services server; whereas those in the security thread pool perform the tasks of the security processing. Each thread pool is given some fixed number of threads to use. The request thread pool size is larger than the security thread pool size so as to make the class queues accumulate enough requests for the request scheduling. The purpose of using the thread pools is to increase the performance through multi-threading and avoid too much thread switching overhead. When the Web services server forwards a request to the security server, the request thread pool assigns the request to one of its threads. The request classifier classifies the request and puts the request into an appropriate class queue. The request thread is released to accept a new request. Similarly, the security thread pool assigns a security thread to perform the security processing for a scheduled request. Once the security processing of the request is finished, the security thread is released for an upcoming request.

4.2   Evaluation

Evaluation Environment. The evaluation environment consists of three SOAP request generators, a Web services server, a database server, and a QoS security server. The platform of each generator and server is an Intel Pentium 4 2GHz system with 2GBytes of main memory and a 100 Mbps Ethernet network adaptor. Each request generator emulates 50 service requesters to sends a large amount of requests to the Web services server. Therefore the total number of the emulated service requesters is 150. Each request generator sends a new request to the Web services server after the generator has received a response. More request generators put more load on the Web services server. The Web services server forwards the requests to the security server for the security processing and service differentiation. The valid requests are sent back to the Web services server to execute the Web services, whereas the invalid ones are dropped. The Web services server submits queries to the database server and response to the service requesters.

In the evaluation, the QoS disabled and QoS enabled scenarios are compared. The QoS disabled scenario is that the security server processes the requests immediately without any request scheduling mechanism, whereas the QoS enabled scenario is that the security server performs the presented request scheduling algorithm to manage the CPU resource. In the QoS enabled scenario, three services classes are defined and the ratio of the quantum sizes is set to 6:3:1. The throughput, response time, resource utilization of the Web services server and security server of the both scenarios are recorded for analyzing the results.

Service Differentiation. The effectiveness of the service differentiation can be observed mainly from the throughput of the Web services server and the average processing time of requests. Fig. 3(a) shows the throughputs in the QoS disabled and QoS enabled scenarios. In the QoS disabled scenario, it is obvious that there is no service differentiation among the three classes because the throughput of each class is almost the same, i.e. 86 requests per second. The throughputs of the three classes in the QoS enabled scenarios are 148, 75, and 26 requests per second respectively, and the ratio of the throughputs is 5.75:2.92:1, very close to the defined ratio of 6:3:1. The QoS enabled scenario demonstrates the effectiveness of the service differentiation. On the other hand, the total throughput in the QoS enabled scenario (248 requests per second) is a little bit lower than that in the QoS disabled scenario (258 requests per second). This reveals the overhead of the presented scheduling algorithm is very little.

Another result that can demonstrate the effectiveness of the service differentiation is the response time of processing a request. The response time is the time interval between the time a client issues a request and the time the client finishes receiving a response. The duration of the response time may contain the transmission delay, classification delay, queuing delay, and security processing delay, and Web services execution delay. Fig. 3(b) shows the response times in the QoS disabled and QoS enabled scenarios. In the QoS disabled scenario,

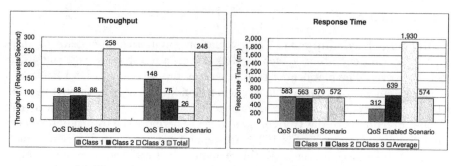

(a) Throughput.   (b) Response time.

Fig. 3. Throughput and response time in the QoS disabled and QoS enabled scenarios

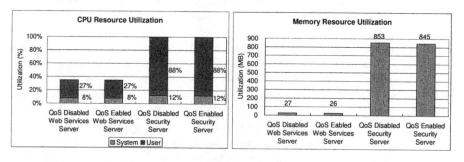

(a) CPU resource utilizations.   (b) Memory resource utilizations.

Fig. 4. Resource utilizations in the QoS disabled and QoS enabled scenarios

the three classes of clients perceive about 572 ms of response time. There is no service differentiation on response time in the QoS disabled scenario. However in the QoS enabled scenario, the three classes of clients perceive 312, 639, and 1930 ms of response time respectively. The response time in the QoS enabled scenario is differentiated among the three classes, even through the ratio of the response times of the three classes is not 6:3:1. Comparing the average response times of the three classes in the QoS enabled scenraio, the response time of the class 1 is rewarded, whereas the response times of the class 2 and class 3 are penalized. The average response time in the QoS enabled scenario (574 ms) is almost the same as that in the QoS disabled scenario (572 ms). This tells the presented scheduling algorithm only make the response time a little bit longer.

Resource Utilization. The need of offloading the security processing from the Web services server is based on the prerequisite that the security processing actually consumes more resource than the Web services execution. Fig. 4 compares the CPU and memory resource utilizations of the Web services server and security server. The majority of the CPU resource utilization is spent in the user space due to the Web services execution and security processing. Both the CPU and memory resource utilizations reveal the security processing is very resource intensive. An interesting finding is that there is no obvious difference on the resource utilization between the QoS disabled and QoS enabled scenarios. However, the QoS enabled scenario has demonstrated its effectiveness of the service differentiation and the little overhead.

5   Conclusion and Future Work

Quality of service of Web services allows a service provider to offer different service level agreements to different consumers. This paper presents a SOAP request scheduling algorithm to manage the system resource for differentiated QoS. The presented scheduling algorithm can be deployed on a Web services server or any server that processes SOAP requests. This research chooses to implement the scheduling algorithm on a QoS security server to offload the security processing of SOAP messages from the Web services server and provide service differentiation to Web services consumers. The security server schedules the requests forwarded from the Web services server for the security processing and then sends the valid requests back to the Web services server for executing the Web services. The design of the scheduling algorithm is derived from the traditional deficit round-robin scheduling. However, it schedules requests according to the probed CPU resource consumption of requests.

The QoS security server is implemented based on the open source packages of the Apache XML project. It uses a request thread pool and a security thread pool to perform the tasks of accepting requests from the Web services server and security processing, respectively. The request thread pool size is larger than the security thread pool size so as to make the class queues accumulate enough requests for the request scheduling. In the evaluation, the presented scheduling algorithm reveals the service differentiation on the throughput and response time and the little scheduling overhead. The CPU and memory resources of the Web services server and security server are measured to prove that the security processing is much more resource-intensive than the Web services execution and it is necessary to offload the security processing from the Web services server.

The presented scheduling algorithm only manages one server resource for the service differentiation. Actually, the requests accessing Web services may consume multiple server resources. Hence, a future direction of this research is on multiple-resource request scheduling. The scheduling algorithm should be capable of managing multiple resources to maximum the resource utilizations and at the same time provide service differentiation. Another future direction is enforcing QoS on compositive Web services. The execution of a Web service may rely on executing several related Web services or tasks on different servers. Therefore, the scheduling algorithm should keep a Web services differentiated when a request is processed sequentially or parallelly on several servers.

References

1. Schmietendorf, A., Dumke, R., Reitz, D.: SLA Management - Challenges in the Context of Web-Service-Based Infrastructures, Proceedings of the 2004 IEEE International Conference on Web Services (2004) 606–613
2. Zeng, L., Benatallah, B., Dumas, M.: Quality Driven Web Services Composition, Proceedings of the 12th International Conference on World Wide Web (2003) 411–421
3. Zeng, L., Benatallah, B., et al.: QoS-Aware Middleware for Web Services Composition, IEEE Transaction of Software Engineering, Vol. 30, No. 5 (2004) 311–327
4. Liu, Y., Ngu, A. H. H., Zeng, L.: QoS Computation and Policing in Dynamic Web Service Selection, Proceedings of the 13th international World Wide Web Conference (2004) 66–73
5. Yu, T., Lin, K. J.: Service Selection Algorithms for Web Services with End-to-End QoS Constraints, Proceedings of the 2004 IEEE International Conference on E-Commerce Technology (2004) 129–136
6. Maximilien, E. M., Singh, M. P.: Toward Autonomic Web Services Trust and Selection, Proceedings of the 2nd International Conference on Service Oriented Computing (2004) 212-221
7. Sharma, A., Adarkar, H., Sengupta, S.: Managing QoS through Prioritization in Web Services, Proceedings of the 4th International conference on Web Information Systems Engineering Workshops (2003) 140–148
8. Levy, R., Nagarajarao, J., Pacifici, G., Spreitzer, M., Tantawi, A. , Youssef, A.: Performance Management for Cluster Based Web Services, Proceedings of the 8th International Symposium on Integrated Network Management (2003)
9. Tian, M., Gramm, A., Naumowicz, T., Ritter, H., Schiller, J.: A Concept for QoS Integration in Web Services, Proceedings of the Fourth International Conference on Web Information Systems Engineering Workshops (2003) 149–155
10. Yu, T., Lin, K. J.: The Design of QoS Broker Algorithms for QoS-Capable Web Services, Proceedings of the 2004 IEEE International Conference on e-Technology, e-Commerce and e-Service (2004) 17–24
11. Shreedhar, M., Varghese, G.: Efficient Fair Queuing Using Deficit Round-Robin, IEEE/ACM Transaction on Networking, Vol. 4, Issue 3 (1996) 375–385
12. Apache XML Project, http://xml.apache.org/

Portraying Algorithms with Leonardo Web[*]

Vincenzo Bonifaci[1,4], Camil Demetrescu[1], Irene Finocchi[2],
Giuseppe F. Italiano[3], and Luigi Laura[1]

[1] Dipartimento di Informatica e Sistemistica,
Università di Roma "La Sapienza",
Via Salaria 113, 00198 Roma, Italy
{bonifaci, demetres, laura}@dis.uniroma1.it
[2] Dipartimento di Informatica,
Università di Roma "La Sapienza",
Via Salaria 113, 00198 Roma, Italy
finocchi@di.uniroma1.it
[3] Dipartimento di Informatica, Sistemi e Produzione,
Università di Roma "Tor Vergata",
Via del Politecnico 1, 00133 Roma, Italy
italiano@disp.uniroma2.it
[4] Department of Mathematics and Computer Science,
Technical University of Eindhoven, Den Dolech 2 - PO Box 513,
5600 MB Eindhoven, The Nederlands
v.bonifaci@tue.nl

Abstract. In this paper we describe our own experience in preparing animated presentations of computer science concepts with Leonardo Web, a Java-based animation system that we have previously developed. Our discussion is aimed at highlighting how different visualization tools and techniques turned out to be useful in realizing effective Web-based teaching material. Our experience culminated in the preparation of an on-line repository of animated illustrations for a textbook on algorithms and data structures edited by McGraw-Hill in 2004.

1   Introduction

Algorithm animation is related to the use of dynamic graphics and visual metaphors to illustrate the methodology and the run-time behavior of computer algorithms at different abstraction levels [31]. Such animations offer great potentialities to enhance teaching and understanding of basic programming and algorithmic concepts, from simple statements such as variable assignments, branching or iteration to the design of recursive programs and the analysis of correctness and running time of algorithms and data structures. For these reasons, algorithm animation tools appear to be well-suited for use in fundamental courses of the computer science curriculum, such as "Introduction to programming" and "Algorithms and data structures", and much research has been focused on developing tools that could be used in academic environments: see, e.g., [2, 5, 6, 7, 10, 11, 17, 33] and the systems reviewed in [13, 15, 31].

[*] Work supported in part by the Italian Ministry of University and Research (Project "ALGONEXT - Algorithms for the Next Generation Internet and Web").

M. Dean et al. (Eds.): WISE 2005 Workshops, LNCS 3807, pp. 73–83, 2005.
© Springer-Verlag Berlin Heidelberg 2005

However, even with the help of algorithm animation tools, there remain many technical and pedagogical challenges in creating effective, interactive visualizations. Preparing animated presentations may be time-consuming and boring for the instructor, and the students may be unable to use them due to platform-dependency issues. There is a general consensus that the World Wide Web provides an ideal medium for overcoming some of these drawbacks and for delivering algorithm animations [4, 24, 23]: not only HTML and JAVA technologies do not suffer from system dependency problems, but they also offer the possibility of combining animations with other supplementary hypertext material that turns out to be very important to help learners interpret the graphical representation. More in general, the use of the Web for education and distance learning can be naturally considered as a valid support for improving the cooperation between students and instructors.

Related work. A popular approach to algorithm animation over the Web consists of writing Java applets that display the desired visualizations (see, e.g., [1, 19, 28, 32]). With this ad-hoc and typically cumbersome approach, highly customized and interactive presentations can be obtained by annotating an implementation of a specific algorithm with hooks to Java visualization methods. A few Web-based systems can be also found in the literature with the aim of automating (or at least simplifying) the process of creating visualizations, but the quest for simple, light, general-purpose, and easy-to-use tools still demands for further efforts. JEliot [17] is well-suited at illustrating basic programming concepts: it parses the Java code and allows the user to choose a subset of variables to visualize according to built-in graphical interpretations. JDSL [2] is a Java library of data structures that features a visualizer for animating operations on abstract data types such as AVL trees, heaps, and red-black trees [9]: the visualization of these data types is embedded into the library. VEGA [18] is a C++ client/server visualization environment especially targeted to portraying geometric algorithms. WAVE [14] hinges upon a publication-driven approach: algorithms run on a developer's remote server and their data structures are published on blackboards held by the clients, that attach visualization handlers to the public data structures.

Most of the Web-based algorithm animation tools described in the literature assume the existence of an underlying running program written in a specific programming language. These tools receive as input the implementation of an algorithm, an input instance, and a specification of the visualization; their output is a visual trace of the algorithm execution, i.e., a sequence of moving images that describe the evolution of the data at-run-time. Some efforts towards language-independent and more general solutions can be found in systems such as JSamba [29], which exploits a scripting-based approach, and JAWAA [26], which features an editor to generate animation traces. In a previous work [3], we have introduced Leonardo Web, which integrates WYSIWYG editing capabilities with the traditional batch generation based on the program-driven animation approach.

Leonardo Web. Leonardo Web offers a collection of Java-based tools for creating and delivering general-purpose animated presentations. The *Library* makes it possible to generate animations in a batch fashion directly from Java code according to an imperative specification style. These batch-generated animations can be considered as a visualization skeleton and can be later refined by adding comments, explanations, and by orchestrating the overall graphical layout using a graphical editor (the *Builder*). A viewer for Leonardo Web presentations (the *Player*) can be used both as a Java stand-alone application and over the Web as a Java applet. Up to date information about the Leonardo Web tools can be found at the Web site http://www.dis.uniroma1.it/~leoweb [21].

Our contributions. In this paper we describe how we have been using the Leonardo Web tools to prepare animated presentations of computer science concepts. Our experience culminated in the preparation of a repository of animated illustrations for a textbook on algorithms and data structures edited by McGraw-Hill in 2004 [12]. The textbook is currently being used in undergraduate courses on algorithms and data structures in several Italian universities, and the animations are available at the textbook website http://www.ateneonline.it/demetrescu/.

We have been using our repository as a teaching aid both in face-to-face and in on-line introductory courses on computer science subjects, including Java Programming and Algorithms and Data Structures, at the Universities of Rome "La Sapienza" and "Tor Vergata". According to these preliminary experiments, the use of animations proved itself to be a valuable teaching and learning aid, confirming the trend reported in more extensive studies such as [16, 20, 25, 27, 30].

Since preparing effective teaching material is a complex task that involves several design, pedagogical and technological issues, in our discussion we try to highlight how different visualization tools and techniques turned out to be useful at this aim. In particular, we address the methodology that we have followed in producing the animations, discussing key aspects such as the choice of meaningful input instances and the techniques used for generating the algorithm's execution trace and the graphical illustration of its run-time behavior.

2   An Overview of Leonardo Web

In this section we briefly recall some of the key aspects of Leonardo Web. The interested reader can find architectural details and implementation issues in [3]. Leonardo Web animations are stored as plain text files written in a simple *scripting language*, which specifies the incremental changes between key frames. The incremental nature of the scripting language makes presentation scripts small and compact, and thus amenable, together with the 100 KB applet version of the Player, to a quick access even on slow network connections.

The Builder. Presentations in Leonardo Web can be easily created using the Builder, a visual editor for building animations. The tool, shown in Figure 1, allows the user to design and maintain a sequence of key frames (or scenes), which are the backbone of the presentation. Each frame can contain bitmapped images,

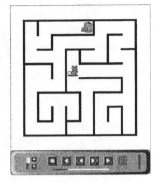

Fig. 1. Screenshots of the Builder and the Player

text and 2D graphical objects drawn from a vocabulary of elementary geometric shapes, including circles, ellipses, lines, rectangles, and arbitrary polygons. The user can interact with the Builder's GUI in order to add, resize, move, hide, group, align and delete graphical objects. The sequence of key frames in the presentation is shown as a list of numbered *thumbnails*, which provide a graphical storyboard that helps the user control the big picture of the presentation and select individual frames for editing. Since the number of intermediate frames between consecutive scenes is an attribute of the graphical objects themselves, it possible to animate them in the same scene at different speeds. Interestingly, the Builder can also open and modify presentations created in some other way (e.g., directly writing a script or using the Library): this allows the users to create and refine presentations via the combined use of different tools, using the most appropriate one in different stages of the animation specification process.

The Player. The Leonardo Web Player has been designed as a light and easy-to-use presentation viewer. It is able to interpret text files created by the Builder, and can be used both as a stand-alone Java application and as an applet inside a Web page. The graphic user interface of the Player, shown in Figure 1, is clean and simple, resembling to a standard VCR control tool. The user can start, stop, rewind, and play the presentation both forward and backward. Playing is supported either in a step-by-step fashion, or continuously. Animated transitions of graphical objects, including movements and color changes, are smoothly rendered by the system by generating sequences of interpolating interframes. To support effective on-line deployment even on slow network connections, the Player is fully multi-threaded, allowing it to start playing a presentation even if it has not been completely downloaded from the remote peer.

The Library. While the Builder appears to be flexible enough to support common user's needs, sometimes presentations include complex animations that portray some technical aspect of a topic of interest, which might be difficult to specify visually. In this scenario, it might be easier to write a program whose execution produces the desired animation script, rather than having to specify it directly in the Builder. Still, a script generated in this way can be later refined and completed using the Builder. To support this scenario Leonardo Web provides a Java library (JLeoScript) that provides primitives for creating presentation scripts. Available primitives supported by the class JLeoScript include adding graphical objects to the scene, deleting existing graphical objects, moving, grouping and resizing objects, and changing color.

3   A Repository of Algorithm Animations

In this section we describe our own experience in preparing animated presentations of computer science concepts with Leonardo Web. Our discussion is aimed at highlighting how different visualization tools and techniques turned out to be useful in realizing effective teaching material. Our experience culminated in the preparation of AnimASD-1.0, a repository of animated illustrations for a textbook on algorithms and data structures edited by McGraw-Hill in 2004 [12]. The textbook is currently being used in undergraduate courses on algorithms and data structures in several Italian universities. The animations, listed in Table 1, were generated with Leonardo Web and can be browsed online at the textbook website http://www.ateneonline.it/demetrescu/ (student area).

We have been using the repository as a teaching aid in computer science in the following 2004 and 2005 introductory undergraduate courses:

- Introductory courses on Java Programming and Fortran Programming, University of Rome "La Sapienza". The use of animated presentations included graphical explanations of basic sorting procedures such as BubbleSort, Merge-Sort and QuickSort.
- Introductory course on Algorithms and Data Structures, University of Rome "Tor Vergata". Several fundamental topics covered by the course were presented using the AnimASD-1.0 repository.

In all the courses above, we have shown the animations using the Leonardo Web Player in combination with classical blackboard explanations and Microsoft Powerpoint slides. The availability of our repository over the Web allowed students to browse them on their own from home, enhancing the learning process.

In the remainder of this section we discuss some animation design issues and how our system helped us to support them. In particular, we will focus on integration aspects between different visualization tools and animation design techniques.

3.1   Animation Design Methodology

Preparing effective teaching material is a complex task that involves several design, pedagogical and technological issues. In the particular case of illustrating concepts in algorithms and data structures, the dynamic aspects of a computation play a crucial role, and therefore most of the work involves portraying the runtime behavior of algorithmic procedures. In the rest of this section, we describe the methodology that we have followed in producing the animations in the AnimASD-1.0 repository. We will sometimes assume that the reader has some

Table 1. The core of `AnimASD-1.0`, a repository of animations realized with Leonardo Web for the McGraw-Hill textbook on Algorithms and Data Structures [12]

Exponential growth of Fibonacci Numbers
Linear-time algorithm for computing Fibonacci numbers
Binary search algorithm
Breadth-first traversal of a binary tree
Iterative and recursive depth-first traversals of a binary tree
BubbleSort algorithm
MergeSort algorithm
QuickSort algorithm
Linear-time algorithm for computing the median of a sequence
Successful and unsuccesful search in a binary search tree
Rotations in AVL trees
Insertions in a hash table based on the chaining technique
Operations on a d-heap data structure
Operations on a (quick-union) union-find data structure
Illustration of a greedy algorithm for change management of a vending machine
Breadth-first traversal of a graph
Kruskal's algorithm for computing the minimum spanning tree of a graph
Dijkstra's algorithm for computing the shortest paths tree of a graph

familiarity with elementary algorithmic concepts. To design our animations, we have worked in three main phases:

1. choice of the algorithm's input instance
2. generation of the algorithm's execution trace
3. graphical illustration of the algorithm's behavior

We now address these three phases, discussing the most relevant aspects of our work.

Choosing the input instance. The choice of input instances is often a fundamental step in designing an effective animation. The goal of a meaningful test set is to highlight relevant aspects of a computation, such as situations that force a worst case in the algorithm's performance, or boundary cases that require special actions of the algorithm. We now exemplify some situations where these issues were especially relevant in the design of our animations:

Seeking for a key in a binary search tree. In the animation of a search operation in a binary search tree, we have chosen to consider both the cases of successful and unsuccessful search.

Bubblesort algorithm. This is a classical algorithm whose performance depends upon the particular configuration of the input data. As two extreme cases, the algorithm on a sequence already sorted terminates in one pass, while the execution on a sequence in reverse order requires a linear number of passes.

In some cases, however, the particular input instance is irrelevant, since the actions performed by the algorithm do not depend on the actual data configuration. A relevant example is the following:

Rotations in AVL trees. AVL trees are classical data structures that support efficient search of items by key. To understand how AVL trees work, it is fundamental to understand the so-called "rotation" operations, whose behavior can be explained in a very high-level way, independently of the actual input data (see Figure 2).

Generating the algorithm execution trace. Once the input data has been chosen, a crucial step is to determine the correct sequence of actions that an algorithm performs on that input. For very small test sets, we could do it by hand, producing an execution sketch typically in the form of a graphical storyboard on a piece of paper. In the case of larger inputs, we found this method to be very long and error-prone. In this case, we found it more convenient to use the classical post-mortem event-driven algorithm animation approach [31]. In particular, we wrote a Java implementation of the algorithm annotated with calls to graphical commands provided by the Leonardo Web Library. Running this annotated implementation on the desired input produces as output a raw Leonardo Web visualization that portrays the program's execution. This kind of batch-generated animation can be considered as a visualization skeleton and can be later refined by adding comments, explanations, and by orchestrating the overall graphical layout using the Leonardo Web Builder.

Graphical illustration of the algorithm's behavior. The final stage in producing animations in the repository was the graphical illustration of algorithmic execution traces using the Leonardo Web Builder. This stage involved different design aspects:

1. *Defining the graphical guidelines.* To ensure graphical coherence of different animations in the repository, we have designed a set of common stylistic guidelines. In particular, we have defined a standard palette of colors for text and graphical objects, as well as a template for the animation canvas, including a standard title bar.
2. *Choosing the visual representation.* For each animation, we have chosen an appropriate visual metaphor. For instance, in the case of sorting algorithms we have used the classical sticks representation to portray the sequences

Fig. 2. Portraying AVL tree rotations in Leonardo Web

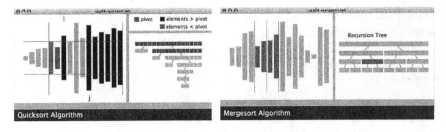

Fig. 3. Portraying Quicksort and Mergesort in Leonardo Web

of items being processed. In this kind of structural representation, items are abstractly depicted as sticks of size proportional to their values (see Figure 3).

3. *Integrating simultaneous views.* In some cases, the combined use of simultaneous views can be very useful to portray different aspects of a computation. For instance, in the case of recursive algorithms such as QuickSort and MergeSort we have added to the sticks view also a representation of the recursion tree. This turned out to be very useful to portray the recursive nature of the algorithms, helping students to keep track of the execution state (see Figure 3).

4. *Choosing the animated transition styles.* The smooth animation capabilities of Leonardo Web helped us define appropriate graphical transitions between different key frames of the animation.

5. *Choosing the right level of details.* To highlight different aspects of a computation, we have tuned the level of details of the animation by picking different levels of abstraction at different stages of the execution.

6. *Complementing visualizations with textual explanations.* While graphical metaphors can effectively portray several aspects of the algorithmic behavior of a piece of code, we integrated several textual explanations as a valuable tool to enhance the student's comprehension.

While the Builder provides fine control on editing animations scripts, occasionally we found it useful to specify some details of the animation by directly editing the animation script. This is a common practice in professional Web authoring applications, where complex Web pages are typically developed with a combined use of WYSIWYG tools and textual programming.

4   Other Applications of Leonardo Web

Besides algorithm animation, the Leonardo Web tools can be useful in several scenarios. For example, the MicroOpGen [22] is a Java application that allows users to write and execute assembly programs for the PD32 processor [8], a modern (didactical) processor used in computer architecture courses in several Italian universities. Most notably, the MicroOpGen is able to export the trace of a PD32 program as a Leonardo Web animation (also shown in Figure 4) that

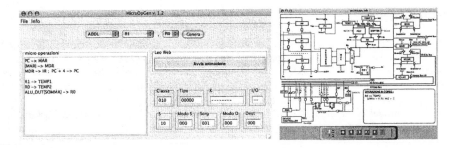

Fig. 4. The MicroOpGen interface (left) and the produced circuital animation (right) (by courtesy of Paolo Romano)

details the program execution in terms of the operations performed by the micro circuital components inside the PD32 processor.

5 Exporting Leonardo Web Animations

A key aspect in the effective deployment of animated illustrations in class lectures is the smooth integration of different presentation tools. While task switching between slide-oriented applications such as Powerpoint and Leonardo Web can be easily achieved with keyboard shortcuts, we found it quite useful to import some animations directly inside Powerpoint slides so as to help students maintain focus on the topic. This motivated us to extend Leonardo Web with the capability to export animations in standard formats. In particular, the system currently features exporting presentations as animated GIFs, which are widely supported by modern graphical applications and can be visualized by any Web browser. While this allowed us to import animations in our Powerpoint course slides, the main drawback of this method is that speed/direction playback control turns out to be less flexible than in the Leonardo Web Player and the resulting file size is much larger than the original text-based animation script. Other ongoing projects include exporting Leonardo Web presentations as:

1. *Macromedia Flash scripts.* Very flexible and well suited for Web-based deployment.
2. *LaTeX graphical commands.* Especially useful for creating storyboards to be included in handouts.
3. *Microsoft Powerpoint macros.* Allows it to read animation scripts directly from Powerpoint slides.

Acknowledgments. We wish to thank Benedetto Colombo, Paolo Colecchia, Mauro Guerrieri, Marco Longano, and Erin Mulla for their contribution to Leonardo Web. We also thank Paolo Romano for his help with the MicroOpGen application.

References

1. Algorithma. Department of Computer Science, California State University, 2000. URL: http://web.csusb.edu/public/class /cs455_1/winter2000/index.html.
2. R.S. Baker, M. Boilen, M.T. Goodrich, R. Tamassia, and B. Stibel. Testers and Visualizers for Teaching Data Structures. *SIGCSE Bulletin (ACM Special Interest Group on Computer Science Education)*, 31, 1999.
3. V. Bonifaci, C. Demetrescu, I. Finocchi, and L. Laura. A Java-based system for building animated presentations over the Web. *Science of Computer Programming*, 53(1):37–49, 2003.
4. C.M. Boroni, F.W. Goosey, M.T. Grinder, and R.J. Ross. A Paradigm Shift! The Internet, The Web, Browsers, Java, and the Future of Computer Science Education. *SIGCSE Bulletin: Proc. 29th SIGCSE Technical Symposium on Computer Science Education*, 30(1):145–149, 1998.
5. M.H. Brown and M. Najork. Collaborative Active Textbooks: a Web-Based Algorithm Animation System for an Electronic Classroom. In *Proc. 12th IEEE Int. Symposium on Visual Languages (VL'96)*, pages 266–275, 1996.
6. M.H. Brown and R. Sedgewick. A System for Algorithm Animation. In *Proceedings of ACM SIGGRAPH'84*, pages 177–186, 1984.
7. G. Cattaneo, U. Ferraro, G.F. Italiano, and V. Scarano. Cooperative Algorithm and Data Types Animation over the Net. In *Proc. XV IFIP World Computer Congress, Invited Lecture*, pages 63–80, 1998.
8. G. Cioffi, A. Jorno, and T. Villani. *Il processore PD32 (in italian)*. Masson, 1994.
9. T.H. Cormen, C.E. Leiserson, R.L. Rivest, and C. Stein. *Introduction to Algorithms*. McGraw-Hill, 2001.
10. P. Crescenzi, C. Demetrescu, I. Finocchi, and R. Petreschi. Reversible Execution and Visualization of Programs with Leonardo. *Journal of Visual Languages and Computing*, 11(2), 2000. System home page: http://www.dis.uniroma1.it/~demetres/Leonardo/.
11. C. Demetrescu and I. Finocchi. Smooth Animation of Algorithms in a Declarative Framework. In *Proceedings of the 15th IEEE Symposium on Visual Languages (VL'99)*, pages 280–287, 1999.
12. C. Demetrescu, I. Finocchi, and G. F. Italiano. *Algorithms and Data Structures (in Italian)*. McGraw Hill, 2004.
13. C. Demetrescu, I. Finocchi, G.F. Italiano, and S. Naeher. Visualization in algorithm engineering: Tools and techniques. In R. Fleisher, B. Moret, and E. Meineche Schmidt, editors, *Dagstuhl Seminar on Experimental Algorithmics 00371*, LNCS 2547, chapter 2, pages 24–50. Springer Verlag, 2002.
14. C. Demetrescu, I. Finocchi, and G. Liotta. Visualizing Algorithms over the Web with the Publication-driven Approach. In *Proc. of the 4-th Workshop on Algorithm Engineering (WAE'00)*, LNCS 1982, pages 147–158, 2000.
15. S. Diehl, editor. *Software Visualization*. LNCS 2269. Springer Verlag, 2001.
16. I. Finocchi and R. Petreschi. Hands on algorithms: an experience with algorithm animation in advanced computer science classes. In *Proc. of the 2nd Program Visualization Workshop (PVW'02)*, pages 93–102, 2002.
17. J. Haajanen, M. Pesonius, E. Sutinen, J. Tarhio, T. Teräsvirta, and P. Vanninen. Animation of User Algorithms on the Web. In *Proceedings of the 13th IEEE International Symposium on Visual Languages (VL'97)*, pages 360–367, 1997.
18. C.A. Hipke and S. Schuierer. VEGA: A User Centered Approach to the Distributed Visualization of Geometric Algorithms. In *Proceedings of the 7-th International Conference in Central Europe on Computer Graphics, Visualization and Interactive Digital Media (WSCG'99)*, pages 110–117, 1999.

19. L. Kucera. Homepage. URL: http://www.ms.mff.cuni.cz/acad/kam/kucera.
20. A.W. Lawrence, A.N. Badre, and J.T. Stasko. Empirically Evaluating the Use of Animations to Teach Algorithms. In *Proceedings of the 10th IEEE International Symposium on Visual Languages (VL'94)*, pages 48–54, 1994.
21. Leonardo Web, 2005. URL: http://www.dis.uniroma1.it/~leoweb.
22. MicroOpGen, 2005. URL: http://www.dis.uniroma1.it/~ciciani/microopgen/.
23. T. Naps. Algorithm Visualization Served Off the World Wide Web: Why and How. *ACM SIGCSE Bulletin*, 28:66–71, 1996.
24. T. L. Naps, R. Fleisher, M. McNally, G. Rößling, C. Hundhausen, S. Rodger, V. Almstrum, A. Korhonen, J. A. Velazquez-Iturbide, W. Dann, and L. Malmi. Exploring the role of visualization and engagement in computer science education. In *Report of the Working Group on "Improving the Educational Impact of Algorithm Visualization"*, 2002.
25. S. Palmiter and J. Elkerton. An evaluation of animated demonstrations for learning computer-based tasks. In *Proc. of the ACM SIGCHI'91 Conference on Human Factors in Computing Systems*, pages 257–263, 1991.
26. W.C. Pierson and S.H. Rodger. Web-based Animations of Data Structures Using JAWAA. In *Proc. 29th SIGCSE Technical Symposium on Computer Science Education*, pages 267–271, 1998.
27. L.P. Rieber, M.J. Boyce, and C. Assad. The effects of computer animation on adult learning and retrieval tasks. *J. Computer Based Instruction*, 17:46–52, 1990.
28. G. Rößling. Collection of animations. URL: http://www.animal.ahrgr.de/.
29. J.T. Stasko. Algorithm Animation Research at GVU. http://www.cc.gatech.edu/gvu/softviz/algoanim/.
30. J.T. Stasko. Using Student-Built Algorithm Animation as Learning Aids. In *Proceedings of the 1997 ACM SIGCSE Conference*, pages 25–29, 1997.
31. J.T. Stasko, J. Domingue, M.H. Brown, and B.A. Price. *Software Visualization: Programming as a Multimedia Experience*. MIT Press, Cambridge, MA, 1997.
32. M. Syrjakow, J. Berdux, and H. Szczerbicka. Interactive Web-based Animations for Teaching and Learning. In *Proceedings of the 32nd Winter Simulation Conference*, pages 1651–1659. Society for Computer Simulation International, 2000.
33. A. Tal and D. Dobkin. Visualization of Geometric Algorithms. *IEEE Transactions on Visualization and Computer Graphics*, 1(2):194–204, 1995.

Multilingual Sentence Hunter*

Julie Yu-Chih Liu and Jun-Lin Lin

Yuan Ze University, Chung-Li 320 Taiwan, Republic of China
{imyuchih, jun}@saturn.yzu.edu.tw

Abstract. Learning by example is an effective language learning technique. However, most language learning tools only provide a rather limited collection of example sentences and a simple searching-by-keyword interface, making example sentences that meet user demand difficult to find. To resolve this problem, this work introduces a Query By Sentence Pattern technique to provide a flexible query interface, and then proposes several algorithms to extract example sentences from the Web. Results of this study demonstrate that the proposed framework effectively searches for example sentences.

1 Introduction

With advances in computer technology, many tools have been developed to assist writing. For example, most word processing programs provide spelling and grammar checking, so each sentence written should contain no typographical errors and be grammatically correct. However, due to the complexity of natural language, incorrect or awkward sentences can still pass spelling and grammar checkers.

Learners occasionally wonder whether they are using a language correctly when learning. When doubts occur, example sentences can be quite useful to dispel the doubts. This learning-by-example technique is highly effective in many areas. A dictionary can be very useful when looking for example sentences. Highly effective Internet dictionary search services like OneLook [1] can search for a word or a wildcard pattern from hundreds of dictionary providers on the Web.

Although dictionaries are useful for learning the correct usage of words or idioms, dictionaries cannot always find an example sentence that is similar to one already written for two reasons. First, most digital (including web-based) dictionaries only allow searching for single words or common phrases. Dictionaries are very hard to use to find example sentences that match a specific sentence pattern (e.g., sentence patterns like "has taught ... differently" or "extensively studied ... poorly understood"). Second, even if a sophisticated query interface were provided, searching sentences that match a specified sentence pattern could still return nothing due to the limited collection of example sentences in any dictionary.

---

* This research is based on work supported by the National Science Council under Grants NSC 94-2623-7-155-006 and NSC 93-2213-E-155-053.

M. Dean et al. (Eds.): WISE 2005 Workshops, LNCS 3807, pp. 84–93, 2005.

Resolving the above problems requires both a flexible query interface and a huge corpus of sentences. A flexible query interface should allow users to query by entering a sentence pattern, instead of single words or phrases. The corpus of sentences should provide adequate access performance, but should not incur much cost to build or to use. This study presents a novel framework that meets these two goals.

2 Query by Sentence Pattern

The query interfaces of most language learning tools allow searching by words or phrases. Such query interfaces can only search for example sentences that contain the specified words or phrases and, thus, are quite inflexible. For example, these query interfaces can be used to specify a query to look for sentences containing terms t_1 and t_2, but cannot constrain the order of appearance of t_1 and t_2 within a sentence.

To more accurately describe the constraints of example sentences, this study introduces the Query by Sentence Pattern (QSP) technique, which expresses a *sentence pattern* as a sequence of term sets, where each *term set* is a set of query terms. A *query term* is a string consisting of a single word or phrase, plus punctuation if desired. A sentence S matches a sentence pattern P if and only if S contains a query term from each term set in P, and the order of appearance of these query terms is the same in both S and P. A prefix (or suffix) constraint can also be added to a sentence pattern to require a query term from the first (or last) term set of the sentence pattern to appear at the beginning (or end) of a sentence. An example and a formal definition are given below.

Example 1. Given a sentence pattern $P = <\{$ "denote"$\}$, $\{$ "as", "by"$\}$, $\{$ ".", "!"$\}>$ with the suffix constraint enabled, any sentence matching P must end with a period or an exclamation mark, and has a form like "...denote ...as ..." or "...denote ...by ...".

Definition 1. *Given a sentence pattern $P =< ts_1, ts_2, \cdots, ts_n >$ and a sentence S, S matches P if and only if there exists some sequence $T =< t_1, t_2, \cdots, t_n >$, $t_i \in ts_i$ for $i=1$ to n, such that "$t_1 * t_2 * \cdots * t_n$" is a substring of S, where $*$ denotes any string of characters. If P is prefix (or suffix) constraint enabled, then t_1 (or t_n) must also appear at the beginning (or end) of S.*

How can the QSP technique be used in practice? A possible scenario is when a learner is uncertain whether a term used with another one is common. The learner can construct a sentence pattern with these terms, and search for example sentences that match the sentence pattern. Another scenario is writing a sentence which might not be syntactically correct. The writer can omit the part of the sentence that he is certain of, convert the remaining part into a sentence pattern, and search for example sentences that match the sentence pattern. For example, a writer could write a sentence "...even people like ( ) ( ) ...", but wondered whether the word in the first pair of parentheses should be "he" or "him", and whether the word in the second pair of parentheses should be "think" or "thinks". Then, he can construct a sentence pattern <{"even people like"}, {"he", "him"}, {"think", "thinks"}> to search for example sentences. The writer discovers from the example sentences returned that "him" and "think" should be used in this sentence.

In the scenarios above, if example sentences are found, then the sentence pattern is probably a commonly used pattern, and can be used to construct new sentences. If, however, no example sentences are found, then the user still has to determine whether the sentence pattern should be used to construct new sentences. Three possible reasons exist for why no example sentences are found. First, the sentence pattern might be incorrect or not commonly used, in which case this sentence pattern should be avoided when constructing sentences. Second, the sentence pattern in question might be too specific. This problem can be resolved by simplifying the sentence pattern to make it more general. Third, the corpus of sentences might be not large enough to cover a wide variety of sentence patterns. To resolve this problem, a huge corpus should be used.

3   Web as a Corpus of Sentences

A huge corpus of sentences is required for the QSP technique to work. However, such a corpus is quite expensive to build from scratch. The World Wide Web, or Web for short, is probably the largest and fastest-growing modern source of information, and thus certainly qualifies as a huge corpus of sentences. Using the Web as a corpus of sentences has many advantages . First, it is enormous. Second, it is multilingual. Third, it reflects the real use of languages and is up to date. And finally, the Web is virtually free, with no construction, storage or maintenance cost for using it.

However, some obstacles must be overcome in order to use the Web as a corpus of sentences. First, the Web is document-based, not sentence-based. Each web page is a document, and must be parsed into sentences before it can be matched against a sentence pattern. Parsing a document into sentences is not a trivial problem, but many techniques have been proposed [2][3][4] to handle this problem accurately.

Second, because the Web is enormous, searching the Internet to retrieve documents can be quite time-consuming even with a powerful computer. This problem can be resolved using powerful search engines like Google, Yahoo, and AltaVista. A query to the search engines is constructed by putting together the query terms of a sentence pattern. The responses to this query are the web pages that contain these query terms. Notably, these query terms might not appear in the same sentence in these web pages. The web pages are then parsed into individual sentences. Finally, the regular expression, converted from the sentence pattern, is used to filter sentences that match the sentence pattern.

Third, the quality of sentences is hard to control. The Web contains documents written at different times and with different written styles. Many sentences retrieved from web-based forums or newsgroups are written in spoken language, and frequently with overly use of abbreviations (e.g., "u" for "you", "r" for "are", "plz" for "please"). The quality of sentences retrieved from the Web can be controlled by adding constraints to the search. Intuitively, PDF and DOC files are less likely to contain grammatically incorrect sentences than other files. Therefore, the quality of sentences can be improved by simply limiting the search to only PDF and/or DOC files on the Web (see Example 2). Limiting the search to certain sites or domains (e.g., "www.newsweek.com", ".org", and ".gov") can also help control the quality of sentences.

Example 2. Five key phrase queries (see column 1 in Table 1) were individually sent to Google. Without file type restriction, all five queries found some matched web pages. However, only three phrases found some matched web pages when file type was restricted to PDF, revealing that they are more commonly used than the other two.

Table 1. Number of web pages returned by Google with or without file type restriction

Key phrase	No file type restriction	Restrict file type to PDF
"the correct *usage* of words"	381	17
"the correct *usages* of words"	4	0
"can also help *control*"	3400	177
"can also help *controlling*"	2	0
"can also help *to control*"	519	72

Even with the help of search engines, retrieving multiple web pages is still time-consuming. Many previous works bypass this problem by first searching the Web to build a local corpus [5]. This local corpus approach faces similar problems to traditional corpora. If the local corpus is too small, then querying against it may return few or no results. However, if the local corpus is too large, then it needs significant resources to build and store it, contradicting the objective of building a low-cost corpus. Using the Web as a corpus, rather than just as the source of a local corpus, eliminates cost of building and storing a corpus.

4 Extracting Example Sentences from the Web

4.1 Search Results from Search Engines

Many search engines regularly crawl the Web to build a database of all visited web pages. Some search engines, such as Google and Yahoo, also cache each visited web page locally. When a user issues a query to a search engine, the query is searched against the database to find a list of matching entries, where each entry generally contains 1) a *snippet* description, 2) a hyperlink to the *cache* and 3) a hyperlink to the *source* of a matching web page.

The *snippet* description of a matching web page is mainly determined by the keywords in the query. For example, both Google and Yahoo appear to pull the snippet description from areas of a matching web page surrounding the use of any keyword in the query. A snippet is usually only a few lines long; may also contain incomplete sentences, and may use ellipses "..." to indicate omission of words from the original web page. Each search request can usually return the snippets of tens of matching web pages. More snippets can be retrieved at subsequent requests if more matching web pages are available.

However, retrieving a cached web page requires a separate request to the search engine. As the cache of a web page is a snapshot of the web page taken when the search engine crawled the Web, its size is much larger than its corresponding snippet. The most up-to-date document does not need to be retrieved from the source of each matching web page to extract example sentences from the search results returned by search engines. Either snippet or cache is sufficient to fulfill this job, as described next.

4.2 Extracting Example Sentences from Search Results

Given a sentence pattern, as described in Section 2, a query to a search engine is first constructed by putting together all query terms of the sentence pattern. Then, each matching entry returned by the search engine corresponds to a web page containing all query terms of the sentence pattern. Finally, example sentences can be either extracted directly from the *snippet* of each matching entry or from the *cache*. The resulting algorithms are called, respectively, *SnippetOnly* and *CacheOnly*.

Figure 1 shows the SnippetOnly algorithm. The advantage of the SnippetOnly algorithm is its speed. Because the SnippetOnly algorithm does not request cached web pages, and a snippet is only a few lines long, it takes very little time to process a matching entry returned from the search engine. However, since snippets often contain ellipses "..." to indicate omission of words, it may contain incomplete sentences. To handle this problem, the SnippetOnly algorithm simply removes any matching sentences containing "...", as described in Step 9 of the algorithm.

Because the snippets omit words from the original web pages and contain incomplete sentences, the quality of the sentences retrieved from snippets may be poor, even after eliminating sentences containing "...". This phenomenon is inevitable since the algorithms used by search engines to generate snippets of web pages are not intended for extracting complete sentences but for highlighting the corresponding web pages in relation to a query. However, the quality of sentences parsed from snippets could directly impact the performance of the SnippetOnly algorithm.

The CacheOnly algorithm retrieves sentences from cached web pages to enhance the quality of sentences. The CacheOnly algorithm simply replaces lines 7-9 of the SnippetOnly algorithm with the algorithm fragment in Fig. 2. However, the CacheOnly algorithm makes too many requests for cached web pages, significantly slowing it down. Notably, a search request to Google usually takes less than one second, but requesting a cached web page from Google may sometimes take more than four seconds.

Input: a sentence pattern P, and the number of example sentences n
Output: a set E of example sentences that match P
 1. **let** $E = \phi$;
 2. Convert the sentence pattern P into a regular expression R;
 3. Build a query Q to a search engine by putting together all query terms of P;
 4. Submit Q to the search engine, and retrieve a list of matching entries;
 5. **while** ($|E| < n$ and there are more matching entries) {
 6.   **for each** matching entry {
 7.   Parse the *snippet* of the entry into sentences;
 8.   Use R to find matching sentences from the *snippet*;
 9.   Add the matching sentences without "..." to E;
10.   }
11.   **if** ($|E| < n$)
12.   Request the search engine for more matching entries;
13. }
14. **return** E;

Fig. 1. Algorithm SnippetOnly

 1.   Request the cached web page of the entry from the search engine;
 2.   Parse the cached web page into sentences;
 3.   Use R to find matching sentences from the cached web page;
 4.   Add the matching sentences to E;

Fig. 2. Fragment of the CacheOnly Algorithm

 1.   Parse the snippet of the entry into sentences;
 2.   Use R to check whether the snippet contains any matching sentence;
 3.   **if** (the snippet contains a matching sentence without "...")
 4.   add the matching sentence to E;
 5.   **else if** (the snippet contains a matching sentence with "..."){
 6.   Request the cached web page of the entry;
 7.   Parse the cached web page into sentences;
 8.   Use R to find matching sentences from the cached web page;
 9.   Add the matching sentences to E;
10.   }

Fig. 3. Fragment of the S&C Algorithm

This work introduces a hybrid of SnippetOnly and CacheOnly, called S&C, to compromise between speed and sentence quality. The S&C algorithm, like SnippetOnly, first checks the snippet to look for matching sentences. If the snippet contains no matching sentence, it is simply disregarded. If the snippet contains a matching sentence *without* "...", then it is an example sentence, and the corresponding cached web page does not have to be retrieved. However, if the snippet contains a matching sentence *with* "...", then it is probably not a complete sentence, but the corresponding cached web page is likely to contain a matching sentence. Hence, as in the CacheOnly algorithm, the cached web paged is retrieved to look for matching sentences. The S&C algorithm simply replaces lines 7-9 of the SnippetOnly algorithm with the algorithm fragment in Fig. 3. It makes fewer requests for cached web pages than the CacheOnly algorithm, but it can provide better sentence quality than the SnippetOnly algorithm.

Since retrieving and processing cached web pages consumes much time, parallel processing can improve both the CacheOnly and the S&C algorithms by letting them process more than one matching entry in parallel. Consequently, the retrieval and processing of each cached web page overlapped significantly, thus reducing the total response time.

5   Implementation and Evaluation

5.1   Implementation

The Multilingual Sentence Hunter (MSH) was built to verify the feasibility of the proposed methodology. MSH is written in Java, and is hosted on an Apache Tomcat server. MSH uses Google API [6] to submit search queries and request cached web pages. Once the search results (either snippets or cached web pages) are returned from Google, some preprocessing is required before they can be parsed into sentences. Both snippets and cached web pages are in HTML format in Google. Therefore, the first step in processing snippets or cached web pages should be to remove HTML tags.

After removing HTML tags from snippets and cached web pages, the result is ready to be parsed into sentences. Parsing a document into sentences may require different algorithms for various languages. For instance, sentences often end with a "." in English, but with a "o" in both Chinese and Japanese. Additionally, in Chinese and Japanese, question marks and exclamation points can be either half-width (as in English) or full-width. In order to parse documents written in various languages, MSH uses the BreakIterator class in Sun Java SDK, which determines sentence boundaries in many languages with acceptable accuracy. More accurate parsers for various languages can be developed to override the default parser, if needed. Finally, each sentence is checked against the input sentence pattern (see Definition 1), and matching sentences are then returned to the user.

MSH implements five different algorithms, SnippetOnly, CacheOnly (both Single-threaded and Multiple-threaded versions), and S&C (both Single-threaded and Multiple-threaded versions). For brevity, these five algorithms are respectively denoted as SO, CO_S, CO_M, S&C_S, and S&C_M. The multiple-threaded algorithms (CO_M and S&C_M) use multiple threads to achieve parallel processing of each cached web page. Each thread retrieves a cached web page, removing its HTML tags, parsing it into sentences, and filtering out matching sentences. Since Google API returns at most 10 matching entries per search request, MSH uses up to 10 threads, one for each Google matching entry.

5.2   Experimental Results

The experiments used two datasets. Dataset 1 contained 60 English sentence patterns, and Dataset 2 contained 20 Chinese sentence patterns. Two experiments were conducted, as described below.

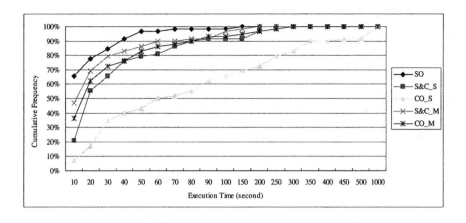

Fig. 4. Cumulative frequency histogram of execution time

Experiment 1 compares the performance of five different algorithms, SO, CO_S, CO_M, S&C_S, and S&C_M, using Dataset 1. This experiment measured the time required for each algorithm to extract 10 example sentences. Figure 4 shows the cumulative frequency of execution time of these five algorithms. The experimental results clearly indicate that SO outperforms the other four algorithms because it does not read cached web pages. Conversely, CO_S suffers from reading cached web pages sequentially, and thus has the worst performance. By either reading the cached web pages in parallel or checking snippets first to avoid reading the cache, CO_M, S&C_S, and S&C_M significantly improve the performance of CO_S.

Experiment 2 evaluated the number of example sentences that MSH could find within 30 seconds. Table 2 shows the results of Experiment 2. This test mimics the case of a user who is willing to wait for 30 seconds for his query results. Since multiple-threaded algorithms S&C_M and CO_M are more effective than their single-threaded counterparts S&C_S and CO_S, this experiment did not consider either S&C_S or CO_S. Both Datasets 1 and 2 were used to see the impact of different languages.

As shown in Table 2, the order of the average number of sentences returned by these algorithms was S&C_M > CO_M > SO for Dataset 1, but SO > S&C_M > CO_M for Dataset 2. The different results for Datasets 1 and 2 could be caused by the following reasons. First, the snippets generated by Google are less fragmented for Chinese than for English. Restated, the snippets for Dataset 2 contain more complete sentences than those for Dataset 1. As shown in Table 2, S&C_M makes fewer cached web page requests than CO_M for Dataset 2, indicating that S&C_M is more effective at reducing cache requests using the snippets for Dataset 2 than using the snippets for Dataset 1, which also explains why SO performs best with Dataset 2. Second, Google search request is faster for Chinese than for English. Table 2 shows that, with SO, the average number of Google search requests is 10 for Dataset 1, but is 13 for Dataset 2, probably

Table 2. Results of Experiment 2 using either Dataset 1 or Dataset 2

algorithm		num. of sentences returned			num. of Google search requests			num. of Google cached web page requests		
		SO	S&C_M	CO_M	SO	S&C_M	CO_M	SO	S&C_M	CO_M
Dataset 1	avg.	32	**41**	37	10	5	3	0	12	33
	max.	80	122	117	13	9	5	0	25	50
	min.	1	1	1	6	2	1	0	3	10
Dataset 2	avg.	**32**	20	16	13	7	3.75	0	5	37.5
	max.	99	71	72	18	13	4	0	16	40
	min.	1	1	1	10	4	3	0	0	30

because the number of Chinese web pages is smaller than that of English web pages. Third, the sentence patterns in both datasets may have quite different characteristics. Some sentence patterns contain terms that are frequently used together, but others do not. Different mixtures of these sentence patterns may produce quite different results. However, S&C_M outperforms CO_M with both datasets.

6   Related Work

The Web plays an important role in linguistic research. Many works use the Web to build a corpus. Hutchinson [7] proposed a technique to build a corpus of sentences containing discourse markers from the Web. This corpus can then be used for empirical linguistic study of discourse markers. Resnik and Smith [8] developed a system for building a parallel corpus by extracting parallel text from the Web. Parallel corpora are important for studying machine translation.

Linguist's Search Engine (LSE for short), developed by Resnik and Elkiss [5], provides interfaces to build a searchable collection of sentences from the Web and to search for sentences from the collection. To build a collection of sentences, the user specifies which phrases must or must not appear in a sentence. LSE uses the Altavista search engine to find web pages that are likely to contain sentences of interest; extracts those sentences of interest from these web pages, and finally stores the sentences in a searchable LSE collection. Since Altavista does not provide access to cached web pages like Google and Yahoo, LSE needs to read each web page from its source, which usually takes more time than reading from the cache. Furthermore, each LSE collection is stored locally in the LSE system. Therefore, building a large LSE collection can consume much time and space. The LSE search interface allows the user to input an example sentence, modify the syntactic structure of the sentence, and finally search for sentences with the same syntactic structure and lexical content from a user-specified LSE collection. Although powerful, such an interface is more suitable for linguists than for ordinary language learners.

7   Conclusion

Unlike previous work, this work uses the Web (or more precisely, a view of the Web provided by search engines) directly as a corpus, instead of building a local corpus from the Web. Since no corpus is built or stored locally, searching for example sentences effectively becomes very important. This work shows that example sentences can be extracted from the Web in a timely manner by using snippets, cached web pages, or both. Moreover, the performance can be further improved with an intelligent scheme to read cached web pages in parallel. Besides using the Web as a corpus, MSH provides a Query by Sentence Patterns interface. Overall, MSH helps language learners easily find example sentences from the Web.

References

1. OneLook Dictionary Search. http://www.onelook.com/
2. Palmer, D.D., Hearst, M.A.: Adaptive multilingual sentence boundary disambiguation. Computational Linguistics, **23(2)**. (1997) 241–269
3. Reynar, J. C., Ratnaparkhi, A.: A Maximum Entropy Approach to Identifying Sentence Boundaries. In: Proc. of the 5th Conf. on Applied Natural Language Processing (1997) 16–19
4. Stamatatos, E., Fakotakis, N., Kokkinakis, G.: Automatic Extraction of Rules for Sentence Boundary Disambiguation. In: Proc. of the Workshop in Machine Learning in Human Language Technology, Advance Course on Artificial Intelligence (1999) 88–92
5. Resnik, P., Elkiss, A.: The Linguist's Search Engine: Getting Started Guide. Technical Report: LAMP-TR-108/CS-TR-4541/UMIACS-TR-2003-109, University of Maryland, College Park, November 2003. Update of 20 January 2004.
6. Google Web APIs. http://www.google.com/apis/
7. Hutchinson, Ben: Mining the web for discourse markers. In: Proc. of the 4th Int'l Conf. on Language Resources and Evaluation. (2004) 407-410
8. Resnik, P., Smith, N.A.: The Web as a Parallel Corpus. Computational Linguistics, **29(3)**. (2003) 349-380

Design and Implementation of a Web-Board System for the Adaptive School Web Site Construction

Jeonghun Lee[1] and Woochun Jun[2]

[1] Seoul Donam Elementary School, Seoul, Korea
cman27@dreamwiz.com
[2] Dept. of Computer Education, Seoul National University of Education, Seoul, Korea
wocjun@snue.ac.kr

Abstract. Due to advances in Web technologies, many schools have now their own Web sites as a center of the communication for diverse groups such as students, their parents, teachers, and others. However, among diverse Web-based communications tools, their bulletin board systems are usually based on the commercially developed boards that do not usually reflect educational environments and adaptive features. The purpose of this research is to develop the Web-board system for the adaptive school Web site construction. Using concept of customization and optimization, our Web-board system is designed to reflect the educational environments as well as the user characteristics. The proposed Web-board system has the following characteristics. First, our system promotes communication among users through their personalized Web pages generated by our proposed algorithm. Second, our system provides Web-boards that reflect necessary Web-board elements in school environments. Third, our system allows easy access to the system through user-friendly interface.

1 Introduction

With the development of information communication technology, especially Web technologies, many schools now have their own Web sites. The main purpose of the sites was to provide site visitors with brief information on schools. However, the simple Web sites have evolved in terms of their contents as well as the functions of the Web sites, and became a communication space among relevant parties such as students, their parents, teachers and others [5,13,14]. Communication can be conducted via diverse tools such as bulletin boards, e-mail, chatting, and other electrical media. Among diverse communication tools, bulletin boards have become a major role of sharing materials and communication in school Web sites. However, Web maters (also called administrators) usually generate bulletin boards through ordinary Web-board systems, and system developers tend to provide bulletin boards without reflecting educational environments. Moreover, with rapidly growing contents and pages, users have more difficulties in accessing right information at the right time.

The purpose of this research is to develop the Web-board systems for the adaptive Web site that can reflect educational environments and users' characteristics on system usages. This paper is organized as follows. In Section 2, theoretical

M. Dean et al. (Eds.): WISE 2005 Workshops, LNCS 3807, pp. 94–103, 2005.

backgrounds are introduced. In Section 2, adaptive Web site and the types of bulletin boards are also explained. Section 3 is related to the design of the Web-board system for the adaptive school Web site. It includes an algorithm of the adaptive school Web site. The implementation of the Web-board system is explained in Section 4. Finally, conclusions and future work are presented in Section 5.

2   Theoretical Backgrounds

2.1   Definition of Adaptive Web Sites

Although Web sites are now major communication tool for diverse users, major problem in current Web sites is that the initial sites are seldom updated timely and in the right forms. Because user's access to the sites is dynamic and time dependent, static Web sites cannot meet user's information needs, and eventually lose user's interest. In order to overcome this problem, the concept of adaptive Web sites based on artificial intelligence techniques is introduced [1,10,12]. According to Etzioni, an adaptive Web site can be defined as follows: A Web-based system is designed to improve its own structures and/or forms through learning visitors' accesses [3,11]. The main advantage of the adaptive Web site is that it helps user save time and efforts in navigation, and also allows Web masters to spend less time for site management.

2.2   Implementation of Adaptive Web Sites

Two major approaches for adaptive Web site construction are *customization* and *optimization* [2,10,15].

-Customization
Customization means that information is provided in timely manner according to user's (visitor's) requirements and interests. As the interface is designed individually for users, users can be more satisfied. Using customization, the adaptive Web sites allow users to choose their necessary information. It also automatically predicts users' navigation paths through internal processes.

-Optimization
While *customization* is relevant to the effective navigation of individual user, *optimization* is for every user. The adaptive Web sites can learn the past and potential visitors' characteristics, and change their structures and/or forms adaptively.

-Implementation procedure
The implementation of the adaptive Web sites consists of two procedures, monitoring and transformation. The former is related to information on access frequency, navigation, visitor profile, and unexpected operation problems, etc. The latter is concerned with the actual transformation of structures and/or forms by using monitoring results.

2.3   Web-Board and Bulletin Board System

A Web-board is the program that enables users to generate and manage bulletin board systems in a Web server through databases. Bulletin board system (BBS) is the two-way media that have searching, posting, and replying functions. Since it is usually open to every user, its purpose is to share information rather than exchanging private messages.

According to the usage of bulletin boards, bulletin board systems can be classified into 6 categories such as free bulletin board, Q&A bulletin board, FAQ bulletin board, announcement bulletin board, resource center, and visitors' book, respectively. On the other hand, bulletin board systems can be classified into three types by their forms, date-type board, reply-type board, and comment-type board, respectively.

2.4 Related Works

Related works on adaptive Web site construction are as follows.

In [6], an implementation methodology of adaptive Web site is presented. The methodology is designed to improve structures and appearances of Web sites by analyzing sequential access patterns of visitors. In their work, index pages can be generated by analyzing Web server log data.

In [9], an algorithm for implementing adaptive Web sites is introduced. The algorithm needs to find frequent item sets first and apply Markov chain to those sets in order to construct adaptive Web sites.

In [8], characteristics of existing Web boards are analyzed. Based on the analysis results, a new type of Web board is designed and implemented. They also suggest a standard for Bulletin board structures.

In [7], a bulletin board supporting Web-based discussion study is designed and implemented. In order to design their bulletin board, they first find promoting and impeding factors for bulletin board users. Based on the results, their bulletin board is designed to reflect factors promoting interaction among students and feedback from teachers.

In [16], an interactive bulletin board installation program is designed and implemented. The purpose of the program is to support easy installation of appropriate bulletin board types for users' Web site. The program also allows Web masters to install various types of bulletin board and generate bulletin boards with the same functions as many as they want.

In [4], existing school Web sites are classified into 4 types, public relations, teaching-learning, information sharing, and communication, according to functions of school Web sites. They also classify those functions further into particular elements and examine percentage of particular elements adopted by schools. Table 1 shows the summarization of their results.

Prior research on adaptive Web sites and Web-board shows that they were independently treated. Moreover, the application domains and educational environments are not reflected in developing Web-board for the adaptive Web site. The purpose of this research is to develop the Web-board systems for the adaptive Web site that can reflect educational domains and users' characteristics on system usages.

Table 1. Survey results of school Web sites according to its functions[4]

Functions	Elements	Perc(%)	Functions	Elements	Perc(%)
Public Relations	Announcement	100	Info. Sharing	Class Web site	75
	Greetings from principal	92		Data room for students	64
	Introduction to teachers	91		Internet library	47
	School history	89		Internet newspaper	31
	School facilities	86		Data room for parents	20
	Education plan	81	Communication	Free bulletin board	95
	Special ability & aptitude	35		Visitors' boards	83
	School album	30		Alumni & parents boards	78
	Merits of school	20		Counseling	68
Teaching-Learning	Materials	83		Applause	62
	Web sites	81		Suggestion	60
	Web study room	32		Q & A	59
	S/W list	5		Discussion	34
Info. Sharing	Data room for teachers	95		Chatting	20
	General data room	82		Board for teacher only	11

3   Design of Web-Board System for Adaptive School Web Sites

3.1   Design Principles of the Proposed Web-Board System

Design principles of the proposed Web-board system are as follows.

First, individual Web utilization for customization and optimization is classified by the proposed algorithm generating index pages. Individual index page is generated for close user groups, while index pages through analyzing utilization of total visitors are presented for guests.

Second, most popular bulletin board type is identified through in-depth analyses of school bulletin board systems, and it is generated by the proposed Web-board system.

Third, Web master has a separate page for overall management such as generation, modification & deletion of bulletin board as well as membership management.

Fourth, members are classified into Web master, teachers, students, and their parents. Teachers, after subscription, need to go through authorization process. Students' parents can subscribe only if their children have already subscribed.

Finally, for the consistent design, the environments for SSI (Server Side Include) application are presented.

3.2 Algorithm for Adaptive Page Construction

Individual index pages of this Web-board depend on the utilization of the sites by users. That is, users' activities such as reading and posting contents on the bulletin board are reflected for generating individual index pages. Although a simple way of analysis is to count the number of clicks, it is not widely accepted as a measure of the bulletin board utilization.

Logistic function and step function have dummy variables whose values are changed from 0 to 1. In logistic function, as x is increased, y is changed smoothly. Figure 1 shows the logistic function.

On the other hand, y value of step function is always 1 for some value of x. Figure 2 shows step function.

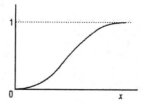

Fig. 1. Logistic function

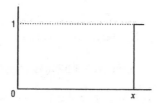

Fig. 2. Step function

The main advantage of the logistic function can control convergence speed. However, the number of clicks is a major factor for its slope. On the other hand, for step function, user's activities can be reflected as a value easily. Therefore, in this work, index pages are generated using step function.

In the Web-board system of this research, individual index pages are generated by the step function below. It is to reflect degree of meaningful activities rather than number of clicks by assigning weighting factors to reading and writing activities, respectively.

$$ka = \left[\left. \sum_{i=0}^{n} Rai \middle/ Rt \right. \right] + \left[\left. \sum_{i=0}^{n} Wai \middle/ Wt \right. \right]$$

$$(* \ 0 < Rt < 1, \ 0 < Wt < 1)$$

Where,

ka: Degree of reflection for creating individual index page

a: Bulletin board

i: Contents posted in bulletin board

Rai: Score of reading contents i in bulletin board a

Wai: Score of writing contents i in bulletin board a

Values of this function are determined by constant Rt and Wt. Web master can assign adjusting scores for different activities, that is, reading, frequent but less active participation, and writing, less frequent but active participation. It may assume that the higher is the value of reflection, the more the bulletin board is utilized. Individual pages are presented according to the order of values. By clicking hyperlinks users can move to the desired pages.

3.3   Flowchart for Web-Board Administration

Web masters can install and manage Web-board systems in a flow as shown in Figure 3.

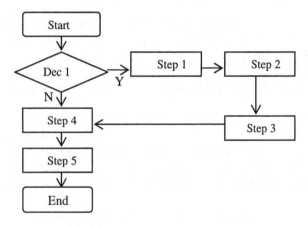

Fig. 3. Flowchart for Web-board administration

Where

Dec 1: Initial installation?

Step 1: Database information input

Step 2: Database generation

Step 3: Web master's information generation

Step 4: Web master login

Step 5: BBS and member management

Information on databases is installed in the process of initialization, and databases required for bulletin board generation are automatically created. After that, Web master can input his or her information. After logging in, Web master have the authorization for membership management such as level adjustment and deletion of members, and also bulletin board administration such as generation, modification, and deletion of bulletin board.

4 Implementation of Web-Board System for Adaptive School Web Sites

Implementation environments for this Web-board system are shown in Table 2.

Table 2. Implementation environments

Item	Option
Web Server	IIS 5.0
DBMS	SQL server 2000
Language	ASP 3.0, Html, VBscript, Javascript
Authoring tool	Namo editor 5.0, Edit plus

4.1 Web-Board System Installation

Web maters can generate the screen for accessing databases by decompressing and execution of ./setup/setup.asp. Inputting IP address, name, administrator name, passwords to the database created as ODBC (Open Database Connectivity) automatically generates tables for creating bulletin boards. By applying OLE-DB type to linking databases, a Web server and a database server can be used in a distributed manner.

After completing database linkage and table generation, a screen for Web master's logging in is generated. Using session concept, the Web master has the right to authorize every screen. Making move to an important page without Web master's right automatically moves back to Web master's screen. Figure 4 and Figure 5 show the database environment input screen and Web master login screen, respectively.

Fig. 4. DB Environment input screen   **Fig. 5.** Web master login screen

4.2 Web Master Screen

In Web master screen, overall membership management and bulletin board management is managed. Especially, bulletin board can be generated, and the preview of generated bulletin board provides its styles and IP address. Modification of bulletin board types and other options is possible, and also entire bulletin board can be deleted.

Clicking 'creating bulletin board' icon generates a screen for generating a bulletin board. Bulletin board types, title, name, color, and other options can be created in this screen. Screen width adjustment, file and text inputs for consistent design through SSI, and the number of posting materials are also created. Finally, the number of messages per screen can be established.

The menu for membership management has functions such as retrieving member information, modifying member level and its status. Membership is categorized into four, teachers, students, students' parents, and alumni, respectively. Especially, students' parents can become members only when their children are already members. Figure 6 and Figure 7 show the Web master screen and bulletin board generation screen, respectively.

   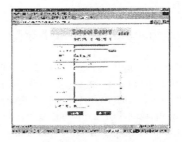

Fig. 6. Web master screen   **Fig. 7.** Bulletin board generation screen

A bulletin board can be generated as one of 8 categories, that is, generic, materials, announcement, visitors, privacy, link, image and discussion, respectively. While announcement, visitors, and image bulletin boards are date-type boards, generic, materials, image, privacy and discussion bulletin boards are comment-type boards. Figure 8 and 9 show generic and image bulletin boards, respectively.

Fig. 8. Generic board   **Fig. 9.** Image board

4.3 Customization Pages

Customization pages are presented based on users' utilization after member's logging in the system. Bulletin boards are presented in the order of users' utilization right after login, and visiting hyperlinks allow users to move to the relevant items. Automatic and periodic refresh provides the latest information. Figure 10 and Figure 11 show membership management screen and pilot adaptive Web site, respectively.

Fig. 10. Membership management screen   **Fig. 11.** Pilot adaptive web site

5 Conclusions and Further Work

School sites have usually confronted growing number of users, diverse users' requirements and contents, which result in the complex accessibility to relevant information in the right time. Moreover, in spite of the importance of interactions in the bulletin board of school sites, it is frequently treated the same as ordinary ones. In this paper, based on the in-depth analyses of current school bulletin boards, a Web-board system is developed for adaptive school Web sites. Especially, customization is achieved through the algorithm using step function. The following desirable results are expected from this research.

First, friendliness and customization of bulletin board systems will promote students to use school sites more than before. Second, the bulletin board developed for education environments will promote interactions among relevant users such as students, teachers, and parents. Finally, Web-board is designed to install and manage with ease, which will save Web master's time and efforts.

The study can be expanded further to encompass more diverse educational environments in the future. For example, customization on the other pages of the sites in addition to bulletin boards can be an immediate research issue.

References

1. Anderson, T. and McKell, M: A Component Model for Standardized Web-based Education, Journal of Engineering Resources in Computing, Vol. 1 No. 2, (2001)
2. Bauer, J. F.: Assessing Student Work from Chatrooms and Bulletin Boards, New Directions for Teaching & Learning, No. 91, (2002) 36-46

3. Brusilovsky, P. and Rizzo, R.: Map-based Horizontal Navigation in Educational Hypertext, Conference on Hypertext and Hypermedia, Proceedings of the 13th ACM Conference on Hypertext and Hypermedia, (2002) 1-10
4. Chun, H.: A Study on Contents Construction of Elementary School Web Site through Contents Analysis, Master's Thesis, Graduate School of Education, Keimyung University, (2003)
5. Curran, K.: A Web-based Collaboration Teaching Environment, IEEE MultiMedia, Vol. 9, Iss. 3, (2002) 72-76
6. Ko, K.: A Study on Adaptive Web Site Construction using Web Mining, Master's Thesis, Graduate School, Kyunggi University, (2001)
7. Lee, J.: Design and Implementation of Electric Bulletin Boards supporting Web-based Discussion Study, Master's Thesis, Graduate School, Korea National University of Education, (2003)
8. Lee, S.: Design and Implementation of Bulletin Board for Educational Web Sites, Master's Thesis, Graduate School, Korea National University of Education, (2003)
9. Lee, S.: A Study on Adaptive Web Site Construction using Web Mining, Master's Thesis, Graduate School, Hanyang University, (2001)
10. Papanikolaou, K. A., et. al.: Personalizing the Interactions in a Web-based Educational Hypermedia System: the case of ISPIRE, User Modeling and User Adapted Interaction, Vol. 13, Iss. 3, (2003) 213-267
11. Perkowitz, M. and Etzioni, O.: Adaptive Sites: an AI Challenge, Proceedings of the 15th International Joint Conference on AI, (1997)
12. Ray, U.: Prepare Engineers for a Future with Collaborative Technology, Computer Applications in Engineering Education, Vol. 6, No.2, (1999) 99-104.
13. Spence, L. J. and Wadsworth, D.: Using an Electronic Bulletin Board in Teaching Business Ethics: En Route to a Virtual Agora, Teaching Business Ethics, Vol. 6 No. 3, (2002) 335-354
14. Slator, B. M., et. al.: Virtual Environments for Education, Journal of Network and Computer Applications, Vol. 22, Iss. 3, (1999) 161-174
15. Tetiwat, O. and Lgbaria, M.:   Web-based Learning and Teaching Technologies: Opportunities and Challenges, Journal of Engineering Resources in Computing, Vol. 1 No. 2, (2000) 17-32
16. Yoon, S: A Study on Interactive Bulletin Board Installation Program, Master's Thesis, Graduate School of Industry, Pukyung National University, (2003)

Developing Web-Based Learning Scenarios Using the IMS Learning Design: The ASK-LDT Environment

Demetrios Sampson[*], Pythagoras Karampiperis, and Panayiotis Zervas

Department of Technology Education and Digital Systems,
University of Piraeus, Greece
Advanced eServices for the Knowledge Society Research Unit,
Informatics and Telematics Institute, Centre for Research and Technology Hellas, Greece
{sampson, pythk, pzervas}@iti.gr

Abstract. The need for e-learning systems that support a diverse set of pedagogical requirements has been identified as an important issue in web-based education. Until now, significant R&D effort has been devoted aiming towards web-based educational systems tailored to specific pedagogical approaches. As a response to pedagogical concerns towards standardization and interoperability needs, Educational Modeling Languages (EMLs) were introduced. These languages attempt to provide a formal way of representing the educational process in a commonly agreed manner. Nevertheless, still there exist very few web-based educational systems that support EMLs. One of the key issues to be considered when designing web-based educational systems to support EML is the adoption of easy-to-use tools for the definition of learning scenarios. In this paper we present the ASK Learning Designer Toolkit (ASK-LDT), a learning scenarios graphical authoring system that utilizes the IMS Learning Design specification.

1 Introduction

During the last years, several web-based educational systems have been proposed aiming to address specific pedagogical approaches. The main drawback of those systems is that they are closed, self-contained systems that cannot inter-exchange either educational content or activities. Additionally, the supported content and learning scenarios are a-priori designed to serve and support a specific pedagogical approach. As a result they are non-flexible in supporting different pedagogical approaches and they require extensive redesign effort in order to be used in different domains.

On the other hand, several Learning Management Systems already exist (e.g. Blackboard, WebCT, Lotus Learning Space, learn eXact etc.) delivering web-based courses with limited pedagogical flexibility, but are able to share/exchange learning content in the form of learning objects.

As a response to pedagogical concerns towards standardization and interoperability needs, Educational Modeling Languages were introduced, offering a standardized

---

[*] Corresponding author.

M. Dean et al. (Eds.): WISE 2005 Workshops, LNCS 3807, pp. 104–113, 2005.

way to associate educational content, activities and actors in a learning scenario [1], enabling the inter-exchange of not only content, but also pedagogical scenarios. Nevertheless, there exist only few web-based educational systems that support EMLs [2], due to the lack of EML-based graphical tools that provide easy-to-use authoring systems.

In this paper we present the ASK Learning Designer Toolkit (ASK-LDT), an authoring system that provides a graphical user interface for the definition of learning scenarios based on the use of IMS Learning Design specification, the specification emerged from the OUNL/EML. The paper is structured as follows: In section 2, we discuss the evolution of Educational Modeling Languages focusing on the principles of the IMS Learning Design specification. Section 3 presents the current developments in web-based educational authoring systems that support the IMS Learning Design specification. In Section 4, we present the ASK-LDT, an authoring system developed to overcome the limitations of the current IMS LD-based authoring tools.

2 Modeling Educational Processes

The term "Educational Modeling Language (EML)" was first introduced in 1998 by researchers of the Open University of the Netherlands, as a pedagogical meta-model, that is, a model for describing pedagogical models, intending to express the learning process beyond content navigation and structuring [1]. The CEN/ISSS Learning Technologies Workshop defines an EML as "a semantic information model and binding, describing the content and process within a 'unit of learning' from a pedagogical perspective in order to support reuse and interoperability" [3].

Educational Modeling Languages are intended for describing, reproducing and reusing not only educational resources, but also events and roles associated with teaching and learning processes. This objective has been based on the fact that learning occurs not only through interaction with knowledge resources, but also through interactions within learners' social and working environment [4]. In literature, a number of EMLs have been proposed including:

- PALO: an Educational Modeling Language developed at the Department of Languages and Computer Systems of UNED (Universidad Nacional de Educación a Distancia), Spain. PALO is structured using a five level information model that describes content, activities, structure, scheduling and management processes [5].
- LMML: A Learning Material Markup Language developed at the University of Passau, Germany, based on a meta modeling architecture for knowledge management [6].

Despite the variety of EML languages and approaches, the EML that has attracted by far the most attention is the "Educational Modeling Language" developed by the Open University of the Netherlands (OUN-EML) [1].

Recently, the OUN-EML converged to an international specification for modeling educational processes, namely, the IMS Learning Design (IMS LD) [7] adopted by the IMS Global Consortium. The rational and the principles of the IMS Learning Design specification are presented in the next section.

The key assumption of the IMS Learning Design specification is that regardless of the adopted pedagogical strategy, learners attain learning objectives by performing a series of activities in the context of an educational environment.

Within this context, an activity can be formally defined as a triple containing the content that is delivered by an educational system, the actors participating in the learning activity (such as the learner or a group of learners, the tutor etc.) and their corresponding interactions. These interactions include three types, namely, interactions with the learning content, interactions with the educational environment and interactions between the participating actors.

Following the notation of the IMS LD, the different participating actors are called roles and they are divided in two main classes, namely the Learner Role and the Support Role. These roles can be sub-typed allowing the definition of refined learner and support roles. For example a learner can be a task leader or a group participant and the support roles can be a tutor or a task reviewer in a collaborative problem-solving activity.

Furthermore, the IMS LD formulation provides a notation schema for the description of activities taken place in a specific Environment. These activities can be Learning or Support Activities. A Learning Activity is attaining a learning objective per individual actor and a Support Activity is meant to facilitate a role performing one or more learning activities.

The IMS LD specification is implemented at three Levels. Learning Design Level A includes the following elements: a series of activities (for example assessment, discussion, simulation), performed by one or more actors (learners, teachers etc.) - roles, in an environment consisting of learning objects or services. Level B introduces properties about participating roles and conditions upon flow of activities. Level C introduces notifications to participating roles (triggered events - e.g., if a student asks a question, the teacher needs to be notified that a response is needed).

3   Authoring Tools Based on the IMS-LD

Despite the development of different Educational Modeling Languages and the agreement on a common specification, that is, IMS Learning Design specification there are still only a few web-based educational systems that support EMLs and even less of them provide a graphical user interface for the design of pedagogical scenarios [2].

Until recently, research effort has been focused in defining information models to express the dynamics of the learning process and development of tools intending to prove the capacity of these models to express several pedagogical approaches. As a result, these tools did not focus on the provision of an easy-to-use interface for the end-users (pedagogical designers, subject experts etc), but were limited in the implementation of the underline EML model.

In this section, we present the main initiatives related to the development of web-based education authoring tools inspired by EML and/or following the IMS LD specification. In order to compare these authoring tools, we have classified them in two main classes, namely, the form-based tools and the graphical-based tools. Additionally, we have classified these tools based on the level of IMS Learning Design that they support.

3.1 Form-Based Tools

Form-based Learning Design authoring tools are tools that provide form-based interfaces for the definition of the learning scenarios. The main advantage of these tools is that they provide direct control of the Learning Design information model elements. However, they are rather difficult to be used by less experienced designers and they require pre-processing of the structure of the desired scenario in order for the designer to be able to express it directly in XML notation. Examples of such tools include:

- The Reload project (www.reload.ac.uk/) is building on the current developments of the Valkenburg Group (www.valkenburggroup.org) concerning Educational Modeling Language (EML) and the associated IMS Learning Design Specification. The Reload Editor, supports authoring of Learning Designs level A through form-based user interfaces [2]. Additionally, it integrates a content packaging mechanism that allows exporting of a learning design in the form of a content package.
- The Alfanet project (alfanet.ia.uned.es) that aims to develop adaptive services for web-based learning. Within the context of the Alfanet project an authoring tool supporting IMS LD level A and B has been developed, allowing the designer to create and edit web-based courses. The Alfanet LD Editor is designed reflecting the structure of the IMS LD information model. As a result it provides flexibility in defining activity properties and conditions, in balance of user-friendliness [8]. Additionally,Alfanet project has developed a runtime LD engine, called CopperCore that supports IMS Learning Design Level A, level B and C.
- CopperAuthor   is   an   open-source   form-based   editor (sourceforge.net/projects/copperauthor) developed by the Open University of Netherlands. CopperAuthor supports IMS Learning Design Level A and calls CopperCore through web-services to support validation and play of the designed Units of Learning.

3.2 Graphical Tools

Graphical-based Learning Design authoring tools are tools that provide drag-and-drop interfaces for the definition of the learning scenarios. Their main advantage is that they support the definition of a pedagogical scenario without requiring pre-existing knowledge on the details of the IMS Learning Design information model. Examples of such tools include:

- The LearningSequence developed by Eduplone (eduplone.net), is an activity based exportable workflow tool for tutor - learner interaction in e-learning environments. The tool is based on IMS Learning Design Level A and provides simple pedagogic templates which can be applied to learning resources.
- The MOT+ editor developed by the University of Quebec, provides a graphical user interface for describing instructional scenarios. The MOT+ editor can be configured to create learning designs conforming to IMS LD level A [9].
- elive Learning Design (www.elive-ld.com) in co-operation with cogito GmbH, is currently developing an integrated toolset for design, documentation and

optimization of didactic scenarios, called "elive LD-Suite". The application will support e-Learning and Blended Learning Designs as well as scenarios focusing exclusively on conventional face to face settings.

– The LAMS developed by WebMCQ is a learning management system inspired by EML and IMS Learning Design that provides an authoring tool based on the use of user-friendly drag-and-drop user interfaces [10]. The limitation of this environment is that it supports only linear sequence of pre-defined activities, thus cannot implement complex scenarios.

Due to the complexity of the structure of the IMS Learning Design information model, it is recognized in the literature that the implementation of graphical authoring tools are essential for providing an easy-to-use IMS LD-based authoring system [2, 10].

On the other hand, in order to design complex learning scenarios the implementation of IMS LD Level B is required. IMS LD Level B provides the information model for defining conditions upon the flow of activities allowing the design of complex activity structures that extend the linear activity sequence defined in level A. For example in IMS LD Level A, even a simple branch based on the results of a quiz question cannot be modeled, since in the IMS LD schema the result of the quiz be captured only as property and the branching can be defined only as condition.

To this end, in this paper we present ASK-LDT, an authoring system that provides a graphical user interface for the definition of learning and support activities based on the use of IMS LD Level B. The main advantage of this tool is the automatic generation of the XML coding of IMS LD Level B, enabling pedagogical designers to focus on the design of a pedagogical scenario, rather than on the details of how the desired scenario is implemented in the XML schema of the IMS Learning Design specification.

4   The ASK Learning Designer Toolkit

The ASK Learning Designer Toolkit (ASK-LDT) [11] is an authoring tool based on the use of IMS LD Level B specification that provides the environment for a pedagogical designer to define complex learning scenarios. Earlier versions of ASK-LDT have been presented elsewhere [12].

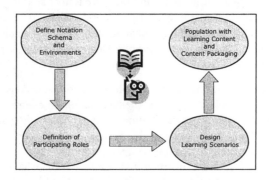

Fig. 1. ASK-LDT authoring process

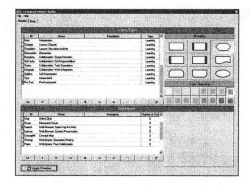

Fig. 2. Defining Notation Schema and Environments

ID	Name	Description	Type
Intro	Introduction		Learning
Chapter	Lesson: Chapter		Learning
Simulation	Lesson: Simulation Activity		Learning
Discussion	Discussion		Learning
Grouping	Collaboration: Group Formation		Learning
SetTasks	Collaboration: Set Responsibilities		Learning
Tasks	Collaboration: Task Completion		Learning
Integrate	Collaboration: Work Integration		Learning
SelfAss	Self Assessment		Learning
Test	Assessment		Learning
Pre-Test	Pre-Assessment		Learning

Fig. 3. Defining Activity Types

The core design concept of the ASK-LDT is to provide a graphical user interface for the design and sequencing of learning activities, which, on one hand uses a standard xml-based low-level notation language for the description of learning scenarios (so as, to be able to inter-exchange learning activities between different systems), and on the other hand enables pedagogical designers to use their own design notation (high-level notation) for the definition of learning scenarios. Furthermore, ASK-LDT supports metadata for learning resources that conform to the IEEE Learning Object Metadata 1484.12.1-2002 standard [13], as well as, the use of content objects that conform to Sharable Content Object Reference Model v1.2 [14] and IMS Content Packaging v1.1.3 [15].

The authoring process supported by ASK-LDT consists of the following steps (Fig. 1):

– *Definition of Notation Schema and Environments.* At this step (Fig. 2) the ASK-LDT supports the pedagogical designer in defining the activity types he/she wants to support in a learning scenario, as well as, in defining a notation schema for each activity type specified. During this step the designer has the ability to characterize each activity type as "learning" or "support" activity, following the IMS LD Notation (Fig. 3).

ID	Name	Description	Number of LOs
Chat	Online Chat		0
Forum	Discussion Forum		0
Search	Web-Browser: Searching the Web		0
Lecture	Web-Browser: Content Presentation		0
ConceptM	Concept Map		0
Sharing	WorkSpace: Document Sharing		0
Peers	WorkSpace: Peer Collaboration		0

Fig. 4. Defining Environments

For each activity type defined the designer specifies the preferred design notation (schema and color) that will be used for the graphical representation of the pedagogical scenario.

Additionally, during this step the designer defines the environments in which the activities are taking place. An environment can be a web-based environment such as an on-line chat, a discussion forum etc., or a stand alone software tool such as an annotation tool, a search engine etc.

For each environment specified the designer can provide a set of learning objects required from an end user to interact with the corresponding environment (Fig. 4).

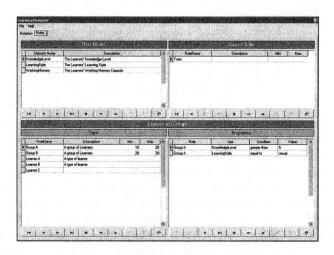

Fig. 5. Defining Participating Roles and Groups

– *Definition of Participating Roles.* At this step (Fig. 5) the designer defines the participating roles in the desired learning scenario.

Each role can be defined based on specific attributes of a user model, enabling the definition of refined roles and groups. For example, the designer can specify that Group A consists of learners with good knowledge of the subject and another group, Group B, consisting of learners with medium knowledge.

– *Learning Scenario Design.* During this step (Fig.6) the designer specifies the activity sequence of a scenario using a graphical user interface.

For each activity the designer defines the participating roles, the environment in which the specific activity is taken place, as well as, the method by which this activity will be completed and/or terminated (for example user choice or time limit). The time limit is often used in testing activities where a learner is required to finish a test in a specific time frame. Alternatively, this functionality can be used for associating a sequence of activities within a time schedule.

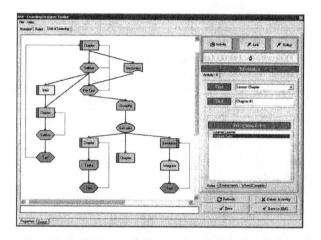

Fig. 6. Designing a Pedagogical Scenario

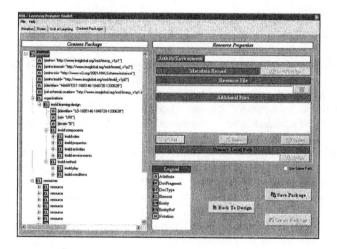

Fig. 7. Content Packaging

Content Packaging. This is the final step (Fig.7) in the authoring process, in which the content components required to support the designed activities are specified. The intended user of this step is the subject expert, who is responsible for populating the pedagogical design with the required content objects. After the design of the pedagogical scenario (previous step), the ASK-LDT automatically generates the XML coding of IMS LD Level B that corresponds to the designed scenario. Once the XML coding generation, the subject expert is requested to associate for each resource defined, the required content objects that support the designed scenario. For each resource, additional required components (e.g. images that are used within an html page) can be specified, as well as, metadata records that conform to the IEEE LOM standard.

5   Conclusions

In this paper we discussed the evolution of Educational Modeling Languages and presented the current developments in authoring systems that support the IMS Learning Design specification, the standardized extension of the OUNL/EML. Then, we presented the ASK Learning Designer Toolkit (ASK-LDT), an authoring tool based on the use of IMS LD Level B specification that provides the environment for a pedagogical designer to define complex learning scenarios.

Acknowledgements

The work presented in this paper is partially supported by European Community under the Information Society Technologies (IST) programme of the 6th FP for RTD - project ICLASS contract IST-507922 and the Leonardo da Vinci programme - project eAccess contract EL/2003/B/F/148233.

References

1. E. J. R. Koper, Modelling units of study from a pedagogical perspective: the pedagogical metamodel behind EML, 2001. Available online at: http://eml.ou.nl/introduction/docs/ped-metamodel. pdf, last visited 10 April 2005.
2. Bill Olivier, Learning Design Update, 2004, [Online] Available at: http://www.jisc.ac.uk/uploaded_ documents/Learning_Design_State_of_Play.pdf, last visited 10 April 2005.
3. A. Rawlings, P. Van Rosmalen, R. Koper, M. Rodriguez-Artacho, P. Lefrere, Survey of Educational Modeling Languages (EMLs) Version 1.0, CEN/ISSS Learning Technologies Workshop, 2002 [Online]. Available at:
http://www.cenorm.be/cenorm/businessdomains/businessdomains/isss/activity/emlsurveyv 1.pdf, last visited 10 April 2005.
4. R. Koper, B. Olivier, Representing the Learning Design of Units of Learning, *Educational Technology and Society*, 7(3), 2004, 97-111.
5. M. Rodriguez-Artacho, M.F. Verdejo Maillo, Modeling Educational Content: The Cognitive Approach of the PALO Language, *Educational Technology and Society*, 7(3), 2004, 124-137.

6. C. Süß, B. Freitag, P. Brössler, Metamodeling for Web-Based Teachware Management. *Proc. of the International Workshop on the World-Wide Web and Conceptual Modeling (WWWCM`99)*, Paris, France, 1999, 360-373.
7. IMS Learning Design Specification Version 1.0. [Online]. Available at: http://www.imsglobal.org/learningdesign/index.cfm, last visited 10 April 2005.
8. P. Van Rosmalen, J. Boticario, Using Learning Design to Support Design and Runtime Adaptation. In R. Koper and C. Tattersall (Eds.), *Learning Design: A Handbook on Modelling and Delivering Networked Education and Training*, Springer-Verlag, 2005, 291-301.
9. G. Paquette, I. de la Teja, Mi. Leonard, K. Lundgren-Cayrol, O. Marino, An Instructional Engineering Method and Design Tool. In R. Koper and C. Tattersall (Eds.), *Learning Design: A Handbook on Modelling and Delivering Networked Education and Training*, Springer-Verlag, 2005, 161-184.
10. J.R. Dalziel, Implementing Learning Design: The Learning Activity Management System (LAMS). *Proc. of the 20th Annual Conference of the Australian Society for Computers in Learning in Tertiary Education*, Adelaide, Australia, 2003.
11. Sampson D., Karampiperis P., and Zervas P., ASK-LDT: a Web-based Learning Scenarios Authroing Environment based on IMS Learning Design. International Journal on *Advanced Technology for Learning (ATL)*, ISSN 1710-2251, Special issue on *Designing Learning Activities: From Content-based to Context-based Learning Services*, vol. 2(3), October 2005
12. Karampiperis P., Sampson D., Designing Learning Services for Open Learning Systems utilizing IMS Learning Design. *Proc. of the 4th IASTED International Conference on web-based Education (WBE 2005)*, Grindelwald, Switzerland, 2005, 279-283.
13. IEEE Draft Standard for Learning Object Metadata, IEEE P1484.12.1/d6.4, 2002. [Online]. Available at: http:// ltsc.ieee.org/wg12/files/ LOM_1484_12_1_v1_Final_Draft.pdf, last visited 10 April 2005.
14. ADL Sharable Content Object Reference Model (SCORM), Advanced Distributed Learning Initiative. [Online]. Available at: http://www.adlnet.org, last visited 10 April 2005.
15. IMS Content Packaging (CP) Specification, IMS Global Learning Consortium Inc. [Online]. Available at: http://www.imsglobal.org/, last visited 10 April 2005.

Towards the Use of Web Services to Support the Provision of Learning Environments in Educational Modeling Languages

Manuel Caeiro-Rodríguez, Martín Llamas-Nistal, and Luis Anido-Rifón

University of Vigo, Department of Telematic Engineering,
C/ Maxwell S/N E-36310, Spain
{Manuel.Caeiro, Martin.Llamas, Luis.Anido}@det.uvigo.es

Abstract. This paper is focused on the use of Web services for the modeling and provision of learning environments in Educational Modeling Languages (EMLs). EMLs have been proposed to support the modeling of 'Units of Learning' (e.g. a course, a lesson, a lab practice). Such modeling involves the specification of the actors (e.g. learners, tutors), the data used, the required applications and services, the tasks to be performed and the process in which all these entities are arranged. An important part of this modeling comprises learning environments where existing services and applications are intended to be integrated. This paper is concerned with the application of Web services ideas and specifications to satisfy the requirements involved in such modeling. In addition, several management issues related with Web services are considered that enable to separate the applications and services used from the control and coordination required to interact with them.

1 Introduction

The use of tools, services and applications during instruction is a common practice. Both in conventional face-to-face educational scenarios and in e-learning systems, learners and academic staff (e.g. tutors, teachers, etc.) are intended to use different tools, services and applications during their daily activities: pens and paper, blackboards, loudspeaker systems, lab instruments, text editors, calculators, etc. In this paper we are interested on enabling the provision of such tools, services and applications in a kind of e-learning environments.

The provision of e-learning environments is a main component in Educational Modeling Languages (EMLs) [1]. EMLs are proposed to support the modeling of 'Units of Learning' (UoLs), as for example a course or a lab practice, to enable the provision of computational support that supports the enactment of such UoLs. The modeling involves the specification of the actors (e.g. learners, tutors), the data managed, the environments available, the tasks to be performed, etc. Part of the core involves the learning environments where existing services and applications have to be integrated, controlled and managed. This integration requires the consideration of two separated stages:

M. Dean et al. (Eds.): WISE 2005 Workshops, LNCS 3807, pp. 114–123, 2005.

- *The modeling of the UoL.* This stage involves the description of the instructional process, including the learning environments where participants (e.g. learners, tutors) are intended to carry out certain learning activities. Such description involves the services and applications that must be available in each environment, together with the mechanisms required to control their management and use. Eventually, it should be possible to carry out a UoL in different learning scenarios that satisfy the descriptions.
- *The execution of the UoL.* This stage is concerned with the execution of the UoL, including the provision of the intended learning environments as they were modeled in the previous stage. This requires that the UoL contains appropriate information to enable the location and integration of appropriate services and applications, and their management and use.

This paper is concerned with the application of Web services ideas and specifications to facilitate the provision of EML learning environments. The idea is to treat the services and applications to be integrated in these environments as Web services. The use of ontologies describing Web services will enable to separate the specification of the capabilities required in a certain UoL learning environment from the eventual tools used in a particular instantiation scenario. In this way, it will be possible to use different systems to solve the same requirement.

The paper is organized as follows. Next section introduces EMLs. Section three considers requirements on EMLs learning environments. In section four, a solution based in Web services for the provision of EMLs learning environments is discussed. This solution is extended identifying a set of common management services required in collaborative scenarios in section five. The paper finishes with some conclusions.

2   Educational Modeling Languages

EMLs have been proposed to support the modeling and execution of UoLs. They consider a set of entities and relationships, arranged in well defined meta-models, that enable to capture in a kind of computational model (i.e. the UoL) the resources and the instruction intended to be used to achieve a certain learning. Furthermore, UoLs may be packaged as reusable building blocks in the form of Learning Objects (LOs) [2] to enable their reuse and transfer between different learning systems. Eventually, UoLs are devoted to support the enactment of the models by appropriate computational systems, supporting the provision and management of the resources and the instruction in the intended form.

The main EML ideas were considered by several projects in the first years of the current century [1]. Rob Koper from the Open University of the Netherlands was the first to name his proposal as EML [3]. Then, he actively contributed to a new IMS standard proposal, the IMS Learning Design (LD) specification [4], which is based on his initial EML. Currently, LD is considered the reference EML by an increasing community of e-learning researchers, system developers and instructional designers that base their works on this specification.

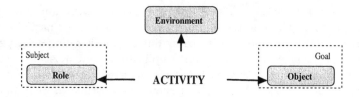

Fig. 1. Main elements of a basic EML meta-model

To support the modeling and execution of UoLs an EML is focused not on pedagogical approaches or instruction mechanisms, but on the coordination of the entities (e.g. persons, documents, tools, etc.) involved in instruction (e.g. the documents that can be accessed by a learner, the kind of communication that can be maintained between a learner and a tutor, the tools that can be used by a learner in a certain moment, etc.) together with the establishment of particular goals that drive and control the way in which such entities are intended to interact. To allow this kind of modeling, EMLs' meta-models use to be arranged in accordance with an Activity scheme involving three main entities (cf. figure 1): (i) the Goals that have to be achieved in each Activity, which are usually related with an Object to be produced; (ii) the Subject(s) that have to carry out each Activity (e.g. learners and staff); and (iii) the Environment where each Activity has to be carried out (composed by resources, services, etc.). These three elements made up the base of a typical EML meta-model. In addition, most of the UoLs (those including more than one activity) involve another key element: the order or sequence in which Activities are intended to be attempted.

In this way, EMLs support the modeling of the variety of pedagogical approaches. It is possible to describe UoLs based on the conventional idea of resource transmission (they comprise a particular kind of coordination issues between resources and a learner establishing which resources can be accessed by the learner at each moment), but also UoLs that involve new pedagogical approaches using more complex coordination issues and entities (interactions between several learners, between learners and teachers, resources to be used by teachers, intelligent agents that provide some kind of functionality, etc.)

3   Environments in Educational Modeling Languages

The basic structure of EMLs involves learning activities that have to be carried by certain users (e.g. learners, tutors) in particular environments. These environments are made up by artifacts (e.g. properties, documents, etc.), applications and services, that can be used by learners and academic staff to achieve the established learning goals. This section is focused on capturing the requirements that should be satisfied to support the modeling and provision of such environments in EMLs. The final idea is that an instructional designer is able to model the environment (including applications and services) where users should work, and a computational system is able to provide it.

3.1   Applications and Services in EMLs

The applications and services intended to be used by learners and academic staff during instruction involve many different forms [5]. Depending on the subject topic (e.g. mathematics, chemistry, language) and the pedagogical approach (e.g. behaviorist, constructivist, socio-cultural) it is possible to consider many different artifacts, applications and services. A great amount of these functionalities are already supported by computational systems that are not related with EMLs. The recently proposed IMS Abstract Framework [6] and E-Learning Framework [7] initiatives include the identification of functionalities in existing learning systems. The idea behind EMLs is not to provide these functionalities as an internal part of the languages, but to enable the composition of environments that include access to existing systems. The following list gathers a representative set of services and applications that should be considered for inclusion in EML learning environments:

- *Stand-alone applications*: simulators, word processors, calculators, games, assessment applications, data bases, etc.
- *Communication applications and services*: e-mail, bulleting boards, chat, instant messaging, file transfer, document synchronizing, awareness, etc.
- *Shared applications*: whiteboards, shared editors, shared files, group decision tools, group calendars, etc.
- *Collaborative applications and services*: audio-video conferences, virtual worlds, virtual reality environments, games, etc.

These applications and services involve functionalities that should be considered in the final UoL execution, but they are not contained in the UoL package [8]. They are provided by the system that executes the UoL. In this way, the instructional design modeling is separated from the services and applications used in practice. In this situation, it is necessary to consider the integration, control and management of these services and applications.

3.2   Requirements to Support EMLs' Environments

The EML approach to support the variety of required learning environments is to enable the integration and use of existing applications and services. This approach involves the separation of the instructional design (concerned with the coordination of activities, users, information, functionalities, etc.) from the final systems that provide such functionalities. For this purpose, we identify the following high-level EML requirements:

- *Automatic discovery*. It should be possible to specify in the UoL the service or application functionality that is required in the learning environments. The engine devoted to execute the UoL should be able to locate a system that provides the required functionality in a dynamic way. Obviously, it is possible to consider several alternatives satisfying it or to fail in the search. In the current IMS LD services are pre-defined and it is not possible to set new services directly.

- *Automatic Invocation of operations.* The applications and services considered are mainly devoted to be used by learners and tutors. Anyway, it should be possible to specify the invocation of certain operations in accordance with conditions modeled in a UoL (e.g. to start-up a chat session when a learner fails a test, to modify the execution mode of a simulator from novice to expert). Such operations should be invoked on the service or application by the EML execution engine autonomously. Furthermore, these operations should enable the transfer of data from the engine to the service and vice versa. The following types of operations should be supported: one-way, request-response, solicit-response and fault.
- *Composition and Interoperation.* Some times it is desired to combine several applications and services in order to provide a comprehensible functionality (e.g. a collaboration environment including a chat, a whiteboard, file transfer, etc.) or an application that requires other applications or services to work properly (e.g. a shared editor requires a file manager). Therefore, it should be possible to specify the combination and interoperation of several systems in a UoL. Moreover, in certain scenarios, it should be required to specify the way in which different systems should interoperate (e.g. to consider permissions concerned with the available operations in the file manager).
- *Monitoring.* It should be possible to transfer information about the status of execution of an application or service to the UoL execution engine. Many times, the interactions of learners with the tools are of interest from an instructional point of view (e.g. the activity of a learner in a simulator). Then, the instructional designer can consider the processing of this information (e.g. filtering, summarizing, pattern matching) to decide the instruction.

4   A Web Services Proposal for Educational Modeling Languages

This section proposes Web services as a solution to EML environments enabling the integration of existing applications and services.

4.1   About Web Services

A Web service is an abstract notion that must be implemented by a concrete software or hardware entity [9]. The conventional purpose of Web services is not to describe applications accessed by human users, but by other Web services and computational systems [10]. By the contrary, the applications and services to be integrated in EML learning environments are mainly intended to interact with learners and teachers. Anyway, the Web service capabilities are very useful, since it enables the satisfaction of the requirements considered in the previous section concerned with functionality discovery, management and control. Otherwise, our main focus is not on taking advantage of the issues about Web service orchestration or choreography, which are oriented towards the structured execution of several Web services.

Several specifications are being proposed to support Web services ideas. We consider the use of Web Services Description Language (WSDL) [11] and Web Ontology Language for Web Services (OWL-S) [12]. These specifications are not concerned on how Web services are implemented. Their main focus is on supporting the semantics of Web services, as the shared expectation about its behavior. OWL-S relies on WSDL for service interaction [13].

4.2   Modeling of Units of Learning

The idea is to enable the instructional designer to model the applications and services that should be included in the environments of the UoLs. The labor of the instructional designer involves the following points:

- *Service Description.* The instructional designer should be able to specify the desired functionalities and capabilities of the applications and services to be used in EMLs environments. This can be done through the Service Profile and Process Model of OWL-S. During runtime, the discovery is concerned with the location of applications and services with the specified capabilities. The comparision should be based on ontologies where the capabilities requested and offered are annotated in accordance with well established taxonomies. Inference logic on these ontologies may reveal various degrees of similarities which should be used to select between different offerings.
- *Invoking Operations.* Once a particular Web service is selected it has to be incorporated in a certain UoL environment and operations may be invoked on it. Messages are then created using the agreed format and sent to services that reply with messages back to the client. This description of what operations to invoke is performed in the UoL in accordance with the agreed WSDL interface and OWL-S Grounding, and considering the OWL-S Process Model. For example, in a conference room to assign a UoL user to certain conference privileges, or to finish a conference session when certain condition is satisfied. The operations on the service intended to be used only by users are not required to be described in a semantic notation.
- *Composition and interoperation.* The composition and interoperation between several Web services requires in a first stage to locate the appropriate Web services. Then, it is necessary to invoke operations in each one of them [14]. Both the Web service description information for location and operation invocation will be described in the UoL using OWL-S and WSDL.
- *Monitoring.* The Web-service can generate events that need to be captured. These events should be described indicating the output operations and parameters produced by the service. The instructional designer should be able to specify how to process the events produced by Web services.

4.3   Execution of Units of Learning

The execution of UoLs involves the control and organization of the entities as they were modeled by the instructional designer. Activities have to be offered to learners and academic staff, and environments have to be composed integrating data and the Web services specified. The system devoted to perform these tasks is named as Learning Management System (LMS). In relation with Web services, the first LMS task involves the search and location of Web services satisfying the required capabilities. The second task is concerned with the interaction with the Web service invoking operations when appropriate and receiving information.

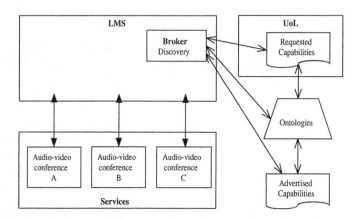

Fig. 2. Illustration of how Web services are used in the provision of EML learning environments

- *Service location.* Usually a kind of broker is required that enables to search in different locations, c.f. figure 2. Capability matching means to compare the requested service description with the advertised services descriptions. This process is based on the use of appropriate ontologies and taxonomies. The matching of the interface is very important to enable the instructional designer in the modeling of service operations. In other way, the operations would not be executed in the service.
- *Service Interaction.* Service interaction is concerned with the invocation of operations in the Web service, their composition and monitoring. Operation invocations are performed in accordance with the operations modeled in the UoL, produced in correspondence with the WSDL interface of the selected Web service. Different Web services can have different ways of invoking the same operations (e.g. the operation to close a chat session may return different parameters). Therefore, the ontology used to locate Web services should have to include information about the WSDL interface.

5   Educational Modeling Languages Extensions for Collaborative Web Services Support

Collaborative applications used in UoL share a set of functionality that may be applicable to several final communicative and collaborative services. For example, the way in which communication sessions are initiated and finished may be shared by a chat service, a whiteboard service or a conference service. The proposal presented in this section involves the identification of these kinds of common behaviors and their modeling in the UoLs, independently of the final communication or collaboration Web services. The concrete idea is to extend IMS LD. In this way, the instructional designer is enabled to specify the way in which the collaboration has to be carried out, coordinating the behavior of participants and other entities and without constraining the final applications to be used. Next, we propose some common services that may be used by several communication or collaboration scenarios:

- *Session management.* It is concerned with the initiation and finish of a collaborative service instances. In certain scenario a chat session is initiated when the learning environment is created and it is finished when it is destroyed. In other scenario, learners are enabled to initiate a new task session whenever they want.
- *Membership management.* It is concerned with the participants that can use a certain collaborative service. It is possible to define lists of required participants, allowed participants, etc. For example, the instructional designer can specify that some tools require the presence of a participant to enable their operation (e.g. a teacher in a conference tool).
- *Authorization management.* It is concerned with the permissions assigned to participants to use, access or manipulate the artifacts available in a learning environment. The more simple form is concerned with the visibility of a certain data or service. More complex behaviors may involve the use of particular service operations. In this case, the specification of the authorizations is performed in the UoL, but the control has to be performed in the Web service. Therefore, it is required to invoke a particular operation in the Web service indicating that a certain participant has the intended permissions.
- *Floor control management.* It is concerned with the dynamic control of certain rights in the services. For example, the right to talk in a conference service can be transferred between the participants. It is possible to consider different policies related to control the way in which rights are transferred. For example: free, moderated, discourse, etc.
- *Version control management.* It is devoted to control a decide when a new version has to be issued on some artifact. For example, the modification of a document for a certain participant has to produce a new version.
- *Time stamp management.* It is devoted to control when some time stamp has to be issued on some artifact (e.g. when some participant performs a particular operation on an artifact, when some task is concluded, etc.). The typical use of time stamps is to signal special events in files or other variables.
- *Presence management.* It is devoted to control the presence and state of the different participants that may be involved in a certain activity. The considered states may vary from available in the current task, to busy in other task, to not connected. This service provides information and events that may be used by other services. It is possible to consider conditions to invoke other services when appropriate.

The identification of these common services enables to separate the particular functionality intended in the UoL from the collaboration or communication services used. The different services are intended to be modeled through the definition of policies that determines the way of operation. For example, floor control policies determine how some rights are dynamically transferred between participants. In this way, different tools with different capabilities could be modified or interchanged in the same learning environment without requiring the modification of the policies for session management, membership management, etc. Eventually, these functionalities may be supported by specialized parts of the LMS or directly by the particular Web services (e.g. the conference system can provide membership management functionality). This approach based on the separation of concerns and policies enables to provide a modular approach for the modeling of UoL and development of LMSs.

6   Conclusions

EMLs have been proposed to enable the modeling of UoLs, but there are many issues that remain to be solved. The modeling of learning environments including applications and services is one of the more critical points because it involves the interaction with external systems. In this paper we propose a solution based on Web services that provides a flexible and dynamical approach. The proposal involves the extension of current IMS LD specification to support a more adaptable way of interoperation with services, enabling the integration of existing resources. It is focused both on enhancing reusability and interoperability, supporting the execution of the same UoLs in different LMSs and using different final applications and services. The advantage of this proposal is mainly related with the benefits of web services: possibility to use different services with the same course, different users can use applications developed by different vendors, etc.

The most noticeable motivation for the use of web services is that the number of services used in e-learning increases rapidly. Teachers should be enabled to use the applications and services they want freely. In this way, the proposal separates the decision of the final application and services intended to be used from the policies and mechanisms that control the way in which such artifacts are going to be used and related with learners and tutors. This is a main contribution to the EML development.

Acknowledgements

This work has been partially supported by the *Xunta de Galicia* under grant PGIDIT02PXIC32202PN.

References

1. Rawlings, A., Rosmalen van, P., Koper, R., Rodrguez-Artacho, M., Lefrere, P.: CEN/ISSS WS/LT Learning Technologies Workshop: Survey of Educational Modelling Languages (EMLs) (2002) [On-line] Available at http://sensei.lsi.uned.es/palo/eml-version1.pdf
2. IEEE LTSC: IEEE 1484.12.1-2002 Learning Object Metadata standard, IEEE official standard. E. Duval (ed.) (2002) [On-line] Available at http://ltsc.ieee.org/wg12/files/LOM_1484_12_1_v1_Final_Draft.pdf
3. Koper, R.: Modeling units of study from a pedagogical perspective - The pedagogical metamodel behind EML, Open University of the Netherlands (2001)
4. IMS Global Consortium: IMS Learning Design Information Model, Final Specification, R. Koper, B. Olivier, T. Anderson (Eds.) (2003) [On-line] Available at http://www.imsglobal.org/learningdesign
5. Dalziel, J. R.: From Re-usable E-learning Content to Re-usable Learning Designs: Lessons from LAMS (2005) [On-line] Available at http://www.lamsinternational.com/CD/html/resources/whitepapers/Dalziel.LAMS.doc
6. Smythe, C.: The IMS Abstract Framework: Applications, Services, and Components. Version 1.0 (2003) [On-line] Available at http://www.imsglobal.org/af/index.cfm
7. Wilson, S., Blinco, K., Rehak, D.: An E-learning Framework. A Summary (2004) [On-line] Available at http://www.jisc.ac.uk/uploaded_documents/Altilab04-ELF.pdf
8. IMS Global Consortium: IMS Content Packaging, Final Specification, C. Smythe, A. Jackl (eds.) (2004) [On-line] Available at http://www.imsglobal.orgs/packaging
9. W3C: Web Services Architecture. W3C Working Group Note (2004). [On-line] Available at http://www.w3.org/TR/2004/NOTE-ws-arch-20040211/
10. W3C: Web Service Description Usage Scenarios, W. Sadiq, S. Kumar (eds.) W3C Working Draft (2002) [On-line] Available at http://www.w3.org/TR/ws-desc-usecases/
11. W3C: Web Services Description Language (WSDL) Version 2.0 Part 1: Core Language. R. Chinnici, J.-J. Moreau, A. Ryman, S. Weerawarana (ed.) W3C Working Draft.
12. Sycara, K.: Dynamic Discovery, Invocation and Composition of Semantic Web Services, Springer-Verlag, Berlin (2004)
13. Martin, D., Burstein, M., Lassila, O., Paolucci, M., Payne, T., McIlraith, S.: Describing Web Services Using OWL-S and WSDL. DAML-S Coalition working document, (2003)
14. Rajasekaran, P., Miller, J. A., Verma, K., Sheth, A. P.: Enhancing Web Services Description and Discovery to Facilitate Composition. 1st International Workshop on Semantic Web Services and Web Process Composition, San Diego, California (2004)

A Framework for Monitoring the Unsupervised Educational Process and Adapting the Content and Activities to Students' Needs

Iraklis Varlamis[1], Ioannis Apostolakis[2], and Marianthi Karatza[3]

[1] Department of Informatics, Athens University of Economics and Business,
Patision 76, Athens, Greece
varlamis@aueb.gr
[2] National School of Local Government, Technical University of Crete, Greece
apost@ced.tuc.gr
[3] Bank of Cyprus, Athens, Greece
mkaratza@bankofcyprus.gr

Abstract. The growth of internet and the evolution of supporting infrastructures motivated universities and other educational institutions to adopt new teaching methods. These unsupervised methods are focused on the dissemination of the educational material and the evaluation of the users through tests and activities. The user behavior is not monitored and the performance of users cannot be reasoned in most cases. We strongly believe that the monitoring and analysis of the users' behavior in a distance course may help on improving the course plan and the quality of the reading material. In this direction we define the framework for an unsupervised educational process that combines reading material and examinations and monitors the user performance throughout the educational process. We detail on how this framework can be implemented using web technologies, thus creating a web-based educational application. We additionally define the methodology and tools that can be employed for monitoring and processing users' data.

1 Introduction

The progress of network technologies and infrastructures helped the evolution of distant training and education. A feature of e-learning and e-education programs is the diversity of the educatees' learning abilities and needs. While in e-education, the tutor provides the content and the general directions and sporadically gives clarifications and advices to the class, in e-learning programs, usually, the educational process is unsupervised. The students deal with a predefined content and search for answers on precompiled answer sets, tutorials and the web. The problems that both programs confront are: a) Lack of direct contact between the student and the tutor, b) Difficulty in content personalization, c) Confusion of students due to the abundance of information.

This work presents a web-based educational system that monitors and analyses the students' behavior while they browse the *educational material* and answer the *tests* and *problems* of the worksheet. Usually tests are used for evaluating if students have

M. Dean et al. (Eds.): WISE 2005 Workshops, LNCS 3807, pp. 124–133, 2005.
© Springer-Verlag Berlin Heidelberg 2005

acquired the offered knowledge. However, the successfulness of a worksheet in achieving the educational goals is strongly related to the quality of the offered knowledge.

The innovative aspect of our work is that questions and reading material are used in combination to achieve the educational aims. The learning activities (LAs or student evaluation activities) reflect the educational aims and the educational material is the supportive means for achieving these aims. Low performance or participation in the test activities, from the users' perspective, is indicative of deficient material and inefficient educational and evaluation process. In this paper, we provide a methodology for detecting these deficiencies and correcting them in order to improve users' performance and facilitate knowledge acquisition. According to the methodology, which is applicable in both behaviorist and constructivist learning theories, students are free to selectively browse the learning material, to search the web or other sources, to discuss about the questions and to ignore certain activities. Students' behavior is being monitored and analyzed and the course is being rearranged, in order to increase the usability of content and activities and improve the impact on students.

In the rest of the paper, we refer to related systems, present our methodology and provide the framework for a self-adaptive educational process based on students' performance in learning activities. Finally, we conclude with the functional and architectural design of a web based system (WISE - Web based Intelligent System for Education) that supports the adaptive training process. The modularity of material and activities in WISE enforces reusability, offers flexibility in course set-up and encourages students' interactivity.

2 Related Work

In the proposed work, the effectiveness of the educational material is examined under the prism of students' participation and performance in the tests. Intelligent tutoring systems, such as ActiveMath [12], ELM-ART [16] provide advanced support in problem solving and do not use the problems to increase comprehension. Adaptive hypermedia systems such as KBS-Hyperbook [8] and MetaLinks [15] capitalize on the presentation of content while neglecting the learning activities. [2] presents an adaptive web educational system, in which assessment activities are not related to the educational process.

As far as it concerns the evaluation of web based educational systems, several works limit their statistical analysis to the users' evaluation of the system's capabilities [10] or the interestingness of a module [3]. The same holds for approaches that use data-mining techniques for analyzing data [13, 4].

Test activities are powerful educational tools. They can be used for students' evaluation, they motivate students in structuring their efforts, they facilitate evaluation of teaching material and they reinforce learning by guiding students on the skills they should concentrate on. When activities are properly matched to the teaching material [9], it is necessary to be in a variety of forms that accommodate the various students' preferences. In the rest of the paper, there is no distinction between constructivist (experimenting, practicing, summarizing and reading) and behavioral activities. Worksheets may contain activities such as multiple choice or short answer questions, matching questions, true-false, problem solving etc, which are widely used in web courses. The advantage of such activities is that they offer fast and automatic evaluation of students' answers.

3   Methodology

The proposed methodology divides the educational process into three phases: *pre-assessment, reading* and *post-assessment*. In each phase users undergo the same evaluation procedure and their actions are recorded. Users access the educational material, during the second phase, in the order of their preference.

Data collected in all phases is processed using statistical and data mining techniques. The undeniable evidence that the goals have been achieved is that the average scores of users in the evaluation activities increase. Analysis of users' performance in the tests may reveal deceptive and confusing questions that hinder users from acquiring knowledge and achieving the goals of the course. The methodology can be enhanced with constructivist approaches, i.e. by allowing students to submit test questions, or modify the test layout and the timings for each question set.

3.1   Definition of the Course Structure and the Educational Aims

The first step in an educational process is the *definition of aims*: what is expected from e-learners to know before the educational procedure (pre-requisites i.e. baseline knowledge and skills) and what will be their gain in knowledge and skills after the procedure has finished. A course outline, syllabus or concept map [6] should be the output of this process and will be used as roadmap for the web course.

Another issue is to define what *kind of assignments* and other activities will be made available for the students. In an unsupervised environment, long answer questions cannot be automatically evaluated and should be avoided. Multiple-choice or "point and click" questions can be monitored and evaluated more easily. Finally the proper *reading material* should be found and combined with activities in order to achieve the educational aims.

3.2   Preparation of Teaching Material and Learning Activities

The next step towards an adaptive educational process is to prepare the informative material, collect and organize sources in a meaningful and readable way. The material should be brief, clear and up to the point, so that it does not confuse novice users. Additional material can be offered to expert users upon request (and not by simply following hyperlinks). The material should be modular so that it can be easily composed and restructured by adding or removing hyperlinks [6].

Similarly, test activities should be created for the educational aims. Different type of tests, serving the same purpose (*synonym* activities), must be made available. Both educational and evaluation material is accumulated into a database (Content Database), thus creating a knowledge base of teaching modules which can support the educational process.

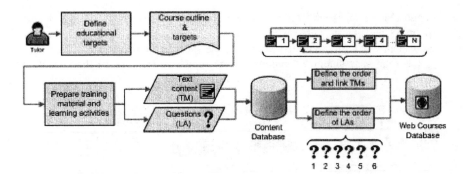

Fig. 1. Preparation of educational material, learning activities and courses

3.3   Organize the Course

Once the content database is populated, the next step is to organize the course structure. The two basic types of modules used for the course are the teaching material (TM) and the learning or test activities (LA). For simplicity we assume that the TM modules are composed by a few paragraphs of text whereas the LA modules are multiple-choice and matching questions. The tutor initially selects, arranges and links the LAs and TMs, thus converting plain texts into web courses. The structure of every web course is stored in the Web Courses Database. The initial course structure gradually evolves as more students take the same course and more input is acquired.

3.4   Run the Course

In every course the students pass through the following phases:

♦ *Pre-assessment*: They preview all the questions in a predefined order and for a limited period of time. They are encouraged to answer only the questions they know and ignore those that are confusing or unfamiliar to them. Their answers, and the questions they omitted, are recorded in this phase. Since students have not accessed the TM yet, we get an indication on the initial knowledge level of each student.

♦ *Reading*: Students start from an introductory page and browse the TMs by following the links created by the tutor. They go back and forward to the teaching modules (texts and multimedia), while in the same time they review and answer the questions without order or time limit.

♦ *Post-assessment*: In this phase, students are able to revise their answers, without accessing the TM. In an alternate version, students may answer all the questions from start (without revision). This allows the teacher to know the knowledge incorporated by the students.

The students' actions and answers are recorded in each phase and are stored in a database, in the form of access logs (web-access database). Specifically:

♦ In the pre-assessment phase we record: a) the LAs that the student failed and succeeded, b) the LAs ignored, c) the time spent in each specific LA.

♦   In the reading phase we record: a) the order of visit of the TMs and the time
    spent, b) the LAs answered whilst reading a TM and the success or failure, c) the
    time spent in a LA (subtracted from the time spent in the respective TM).
♦   In the final assessment we record: a) the revised questions, b) the correct and
    wrong answers.

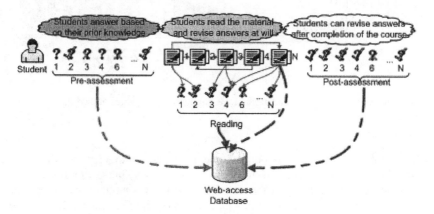

Fig. 2. Evaluation of students in the three phases of the educational process

Data analysis helps in locating bad or misleading content and questions and
reorganizing the course in a more meaningful manner. Reorganization comprises of
replacing confusing activities (with high failure degree) with synonym activities from
the database, merging more than one LAs into a single unit and splitting a LA into
smaller units. In an offline process, the tutor rephrases the unclear questions, creates
new teaching material adds or removes links, changes the order in the LAs and TMs
of a course etc.

The framework for analyzing the collected data and drawing useful results on the
usability and clarity of the provided content follows. We define an indicative but not
exhaustive set of measures. We emphasize on their semantics and on their
combination in order to produce interesting results.

4   A Framework for the Analysis of the Results

The analysis of the collected data can be performed using commercial -SPSS
Clementine, Palisade StatTools, and other freeware tools. However, custom
algorithms for statistical and web usage analysis can be implemented. The analysis
can be of three types: 1) Statistical analysis of the teaching material's and the
evaluation activities' accessibility, 2) Navigation pattern analysis, of the order in
which users access the TMs and LAs, 3) Combined analysis on how the TMs affect
success or failure in TMs.

The aim of the analysis process is to measure the validity and reliability of content
and tests as stated by [7]. As far as it concerns the usability of a course we distinguish
between *activities usability* (section 4.1) and *content usability* (section 4.2) and
attempt to quantify them. Then we combine those measures to get an indication on the

course impact (section 4.3) in users' performance [1]. Finally, we discuss on more complex factors (section 4.4) of the learning process such as time and sequence and give insights on how to improve course effectiveness.

4.1 Usability of Activities

For each LA, during the three phases, we count the following: a) *TotalAnswers*: the number of users that answered the LA (question), b) *CorrectAnswers*: the number of users that correctly answered the LA, c) *WrongAnswers*: the number of users that failed in the LA, d) *TotalUsers*: the number of users that took the course.

Thus we have three indicators on the usability of an activity:

$$LA\_Interest: \frac{TotalAnswers}{TotalUsers}, LA\_Success: \frac{Success}{TotalAnswers}, LA\_Failure: \frac{Failure}{TotalAnswers}$$

A question answered by many users (regardless of the result) is easy to comprehend and more possible to achieve its aim. A question of interest and high success rate in the pre-assessment phase is simplistic with limited value for the educational process and can be omitted or replaced by another question (not a synonym one). A question with high interestingness, but high failure during the pre-assessment phase is a challenge for the educational process. The aim is to maintain the interestingness in a high level, while decreasing the number of wrong answers by assisting users with the reading material.

4.2 Usability of Content

For the usability of training material (TMs) we count the following: a) *UserAccesses:* The number of distinct users that access a node, b) *AccessesPerSession:* The mean number of times a page is accessed by the same user inside a session (a course). We then define the interesting and centrality of a TM, which indicate the usability of a content node.

$$TM\_Interest: \frac{UserAccesses}{TotalUsers}, TM\_Centrality: \frac{AccessesPerSession}{Accessibility}$$

Nodes with low accessibility are either difficult to reach (low connectivity) or are not properly described (i.e. wrong hyperlink titles are used). Nodes that are accessed many times inside the same session (by the same user) are either very important for the user (high centrality) or are very difficult to comprehend. The tutor should consider splitting the content into more nodes.

4.3 Impact on Users' Performance

We strongly believe when teaching material is properly combined with the learning activities the efficacy of the educational process is increased. The analysis on the accessibility of content should be done under the prism of the supported activities. We use the following measures:

TM_Impact: The mean number of questions answered while reading a TM.

TM_PositiveImpact: The number of questions, which were initially answered wrong and corrected after reading a TM node.

TM_NegativeImpact: How many questions were changed from correct to wrong after reading a certain TM node.

These TM nodes that exceed a threshold of negative influence should be rewritten and this must be done in accordance to the questions influenced.

4.4 Advanced Analysis

By adding a time dimension into our analysis (i.e. the time each user spends in a question or web page) we get very interesting results. Complex and demanding questions should be reconsidered for their usability in the educational process. Content nodes which are neglected by the users should be omitted from the course. Additionally, if a specific TM does not help in answering a question, this is a fact that the node is of low importance.

The web-access data collected through the educational process has an inherent sequence dimension (sequence of accessing TM nodes, answering LAs, revising answers in the post-assessment phase). Analysis of these sequences (web-usage mining), leads to interesting access patterns [5].

The first step towards this direction is to define the *"path"* – the sequence of TMs – accessed by each user for answering a question. For simplicity, based on Miller's work [14] on the limits of human capacity in acquiring knowledge, we assume that a path contains the last 7 (at most) nodes that the user visited before answering the LA. We also define *"same paths"*, those that contain the same nodes with the same order and *"similar paths"*, those that contain the same nodes but with a different order.

We consider the *participation* of a node in the set (number of distinct paths it belongs to). For the paths that correspond to the learning activities, we define two measures: a) *Path_Support:* The percentage of users that used similar paths, b) *Path_Confidence:* The percentage of users that used the same path.

Finally, we define *"frequent paths"*, with Path_Support over a predefined threshold and apply web usage mining algorithms on them.

A joint analysis of the above factors indices gives valuable hints on how content and activities should be organized. For example:

+ A *frequent path* with 3 TM nodes that leads to a correct answer gives the following rule: Visitors of the first 2 nodes *must* visit the third node in order to successfully accomplish the learning activity. As a result, a hyperlink pointing to the third node can be added in both TM nodes.
+ Paths with high support and low confidence indicate that the content of TM nodes should be read in total and thus the nodes should be merged in a single node. This is feasible only for nodes with low participation.
+ TM Nodes with low influence and low participation can be either merged with others, deleted or converted to external references.
+ A high LA_StayTime in an activity may due to the complexity of the activity but also to an ambiguous question definition. Such questions should be revised, rephrased or replaced by "synonyms".

5 Architecture and Technologies Employed

The proposed methodology is to be implemented into *WISE*, a *W*eb based *I*ntelligent *S*ystem for *E*ducation. The general architecture of the WISE system is a typical client-server one with a web server in the front and a database in the back-end. In the following, we provide suggestions on the technologies that can be used for the efficient delivery of web courses to remote students and give a simple sketch of the user interface. Finally we present our thoughts for transforming an e-learning tool into a learning community platform [11].

5.1 Educational Material

The tutor creates the teaching material and the questions using a web page development tool or a custom application that generates simple HTML or XML documents (snippets). The use of XML for describing educational material and activities offers high adaptability and reusability. XML nodes can be easily transformed, split or merged in a new document. In the course design phase, tutors combine the snippets into a complete course by defining order of TAs and LAs, their alternatives etc, without special knowledge of web development tools. Material in other formats (pdf files, presentations, documents etc) can be provided through links.

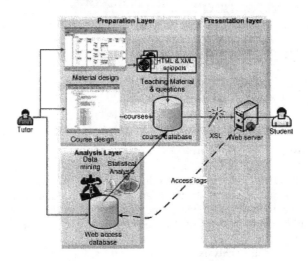

Fig. 3. The proposed architecture

5.2 Publishing Web Courses

Once the material and the questions have been stored in the database and the course and evaluation outline have been set up, the publishing phase follows.

Languages that transform XML to HTML (i.e. XSL) can be used to create presentation templates for a course. The templates are created once by expert web designers and reused through the educational process.

5.3 The Student's Interface

A simple user interface (web page) facilitates students' work while keeping their focus on the evaluation activities. A *top frame* that contains the reading material (text, flash animation, images, audio and video), a *navigational frame* (with navigation buttons for the course) in the middle for choosing the questions to answer and a *bottom frame* where the question will be presented are sufficient for the whole procedure. The bottom frame contains the evaluation activity, which may range from a simple multiple-choice question to a complex web component (activeX component or java applet) that simulates a point-and-click activity. The small frame on the bottom of the window contains the list of activities and a pair of navigation buttons for selecting activities. A sketch of the user interface is presented in Fig 4.

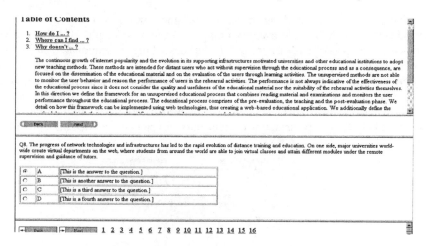

Fig. 4. The user interface

6 Conclusions - Future Work

This work presents a methodology for adapting the reading material and test activities to the user needs and interests, as these are detected throughout the educational process. Intelligent monitoring of the users' actions inside the web-based teaching environment and in depth analysis of the collected data may expose the deficiencies of the material and activities and lead to reformulations.

The framework for the analysis of collected data along with some measures and indications that can be drawn were presented. The next step is to define a concrete set of measures for course evaluation based on the literature.

The generic architecture of the WISE system (*W*eb based *I*ntelligent *S*ystem for *E*ducation) was presented. The system is currently in the design phase, so we presented the technologies that we plan to use for the development. The development of the WISE system and its evaluation on a real educational process will allow us to define which measures are of importance for the evaluation and amelioration of the process. The next step for the WISE system is to support interactive design of courses, based on students' feedback and comments. This will provide a platform for building learning communities instead of simply supporting e-learning process.

References

1. Avouris, N., Dimitracopoulou, A., Daskalaki, S., & Tselios, N. (2001). Evaluation of Distance-Learning Environments: Impact of Usability on Student Performance. International Journal of Educational Telecommunications 7(4), 355-378
2. Brusilovsky, P., Karagiannidis, C., and Sampson, D. (2004) Layered evaluation of adaptive learning systems. International Journal of Continuing Engineering Education and Lifelong Learning 14 (4/5), 402 - 421
3. Chu, K., Chang, M., & Hsia, Y. (2003). Designing a Course Recommendation System on Web based on the Students' Course Selection Records. World Conference on Educational Multimedia, Hypermedia and Telecommunications 2003(1), 14-21.
4. Donnellan, D., & Pahl, C. (2002). Data Mining Technology for the Evaluation of Web-based Teaching and Learning Systems. World Conference on E-Learning in Corp., Govt., Health., & Higher Ed. 2002(1), 747-752.
5. Eirinaki, M., Vazirgiannis, M., Varlamis, I., (2003) "SEWeP: Using Site Semantics and a Taxonomy to Enhance the Web Personalization Process", 9th ACM SIGKDD.
6. Gaines, B.R., Shaw, M. L. G. (1995), Concept maps as hypermedia components. Int. J. Human Computer Studies 43(3): 323-361
7. Gronlund, N. E., and Linn, R. (1990) Measurement and Evaluation in Teaching. (6th ed.) New York: Macmillan.
8. Henze, N., & Nejdl, W. (2001). Adaptation in open corpus hypermedia. International Journal of Artificial Intelligence in Education, 12(4), 325-350.
9. Jacobs, L. C., and Chase, C. I. (1992) Developing and Using Tests Effectively: A Guide for Faculty. San Francisco: Jossey-Bass.
10. Kim, M., & Orrill, C. (2003). Evaluating a Web-based Professional Development System: Learning to Teach in Technology Studio (LTTS). World Conference on Educational Multimedia, Hypermedia and Telecommunications 2003(1), 1301-1308.
11. Lambropoulos, N. & Zaphiris, P. (2005). User-Centred Design of Online Learning. Hershey, PA, USA: Idea Publishing.
12. Melis, E., Andrès, E., Büdenbender, J., Frishauf, A., Goguadse, G., Libbrecht, P., Pollet, M., & Ullrich, C. (2001). ActiveMath: A web-based learning environment. International Journal of Artificial Intelligence in Education, 12(4), 385-407.
13. Merceron, A., Yacef, K. (2004). Mining Student Data Captured from a Web-Based Tutoring Tool: Initial Exploration and Results. Journal of Interactive Learning Research 15(4).
14. Miller, G. A. (1956). The Magical Number Seven, Plus or Minus Two: Some Limits on Our Capacity for Processing Information, The Psychological Review, 1956, vol. 63, pp. 81-97.
15. Murray, T. (2003). MetaLinks: Authoring and affordances for conceptual and narrative flow in adaptive hyperbooks. International Journal of Artificial Intelligence in Education, 13(2-4), 197-231.
16. Weber, G., Brusilovsky, P. (2001). ELM-ART: An adaptive versatile system for Web-based instruction. International Journal of Artificial Intelligence in Education. 12(4), 351-384.

Web-Based Assessment Tests
Supporting Learning

Sylvia Encheva[1] and Sharil Tumin[2]

[1] Stord/Haugesund University College, Bjørnsonsg. 45, 5528 Haugesund, Norway
sbe@hsh.no
[2] University of Bergen, IT-Dept., P. O. Box 7800, 5020 Bergen, Norway
edpst@it.uib.no

Abstract. Students perform better academically when they are thought using a curriculum infused with Web-enabled computer technology. They become more motivated and interested in schoolwork as a result of being thought using such a curriculum.

The aim is to deliver content to an individual learner, i.e., corresponding to his/her level of knowledge and understanding. The presented system supports the educational use of Web-enhancing courses and computer-aided formative and summative assessments. Subjects' contents are arranged in a structure that allows them to be used in classroom teaching and as effective self-study materials.

The obtained results guarantee the usefulness of a full-scale implementation of Web-based tutorial model in the following years. Both lecturers and students expressed a desire to expand their usage of computer technology.

Keywords: Web-based assessment, e-learning.

1 Introduction

In the usual academic education students are viewed as passive recipients of information. The new information age demands an educational concept developing students' abilities to deal with problems that are not obvious today [2].

Assessment of learning is a critical part of the learning and instruction process [29]. The need for tests assessing students' ability to use knowledge in an interrelated way is discussed in [4]. The importance of delivering high-quality assessment tests is discussed in [8]. Teachers have found that the use of Web-enabled computer technology in a classroom enables them to effectively deliver course content, assess student comprehension, and foster the development of learning communities. Being provided with interactive examples, animations, java applets and different tests with immediate feedback, students became engages of the work instead of receivers of information.

This article focuses on a system containing interactive tests that assessing critical thinking. Students are asked to interpret data, identify conclusions, draw conclusions, and hypothesize explanations. Research [20] implies that interactive-engagement classes can achieve at higher levels than more didactic classes.

M. Dean et al. (Eds.): WISE 2005 Workshops, LNCS 3807, pp. 134–143, 2005.
© Springer-Verlag Berlin Heidelberg 2005

The paper is organized as follows. Related work is presented in Section 2. Presentation of contents is discussed in Section 3, some learner issues are considered in Section 4. Assessment tests are considered in Section 5 and directing students in the system is described in Section 6. The system architecture is described in Section 7. Our experience using the system is described in Section 8. The paper ends with a conclusion in Section 9.

2   Related Work

Pedagogical, operational, technological, and strategic issues faced by those adopting computer-assisted assessment is described in citeBull , [30], [13] and [12]. How to integrate assessment and instruction is discussed in [9].

Adaptive testing is presented in [7] and a level-based instruction model is proposed in [31]. Interactive dialogs in a mathematics teaching are generated by the system in [28]. Generate comparable scores even though different test takers receive different test questions is explained in [15].

The importance of being able to properly judge the confidence of one's answers is discussed in [6]. A critical source of information for learning is emotion [22]. They engage meaning and predict future learning because they involve our goals, beliefs, biases, and expectancies [5]. The learning orientations and their effect on individual learning is considered in [27].

Projects such as CANDLE [14], Edutella [16], SeLeNe[18], and ORL [17] investigate the use of various standarts for the exchange of educational metadata. LMSs such as WebCT and Blackboard, provide integrated assessment tools, while others like Question Mark's Perception and Hot Potatoes specialize in assessment engines. These general purpose assessment tools offer instructors test creation and test management interfaces based on Web-forms for producing different type of quizzes such as true-false, multiple choice, calculated, short answer, matching, and paragraph. These interfaces range from simple to complex, depending on the functionalities provided.

3   Presenting Contents to Students

Initially students are presented with theory and supporting examples, where it is explicitly stated which part is recommended for additional reading as being more difficult and/or less relevant to the current curriculum. The system provides different levels of presentation with respect to problem solving. Each level has tutorial material generated for it; since it is important to target tutorial tasks at the student's ability, this is seen as being of more educational benefit than offering the same tutorials to all students and then assigning a student to a level based upon the grade the student achieves [1]. It is incorporated by including different help functions. Different students are provided with different pages according to their needs. Additional explanations and examples helping to clear current difficulties and misconceptions are provided without use of human tutors.

4   Learning Issues

It is commanly accepted that how students think or prefer to process information has the strongest effect on how they learn. Such view underestimates the role of emotions and intentions. The learning orientations represent an individual's complex, intrinsic manipulation of key psychological variables (affective, and cognitive influences) as they approach and experience learning [26].

The following learning orientations are presented in [27].

Transforming learners are holistic thinkers. They commit great amounts of learning effort and use short-term goals as steps to accomplish important, long-term, transformational goals. They prefer to rely on themselves to learn.

Performing learners are usually self-motivated in learning environments that interest them. They are somewhat responsible for their learning but often rely on others for motivation, coaching, scheduling, and direction.

Comforming learners strongly prefer routine, structure, and support. They learn best in well-structured and directive environments.

Resistant learners do not usually believe that academic learning is helpful for achieving personal goals.

4.1   High-Level Thinking

Bloom's taxonomy [3] was created for categorizing level of abstraction of questions that occur in educations. The levels in the taxonomy are very useful to develop both the critical and creative thinking. Critical thinking involves logical thinking and reasoning including skills while the aim of creative thinking is to stimulate curiosity and promote divergence.

Presenting students with tests where all the correct answers should be chosen and/or answers require integration of several components or approaches is used for assessing their conceptual thinking.

Theoretically grounded and empirically supported strategies that can be used to improve the development and assessment of students' critical thinking skills are presented in [24].

5   Assessment Tests

Assessment tests are based on tailored testing. The first item is of average difficulty. A correct answer is followed by a more difficult item. The level of difficulties is increasing until an item is followed by a wrong answer.

If first item gets wrong answer, an easier item is presented afterwords. The items get easier until an item gets a correct answer. If at least one item is correct and at least one item is incorrect, a maximum likelihood estimation of the student's standing is obtained. When a point estimate is obtained, a local standard error of measurement for the student is computed. The system then chooses an item for that particular student that is expected to provide the maximum information for that student.

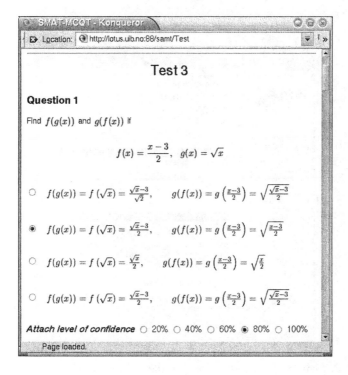

Fig. 1. Attach a level of confidence

The student is asked to mark all the correct answers to every question and to attach a level of confidence (20%, 40%, 60%, 80%, 100%) (Fig. 1).

After each submission, the system gives the student immediate result of her current performance compared with her previous results (competition against oneself) and her best performance compared with the results of the whole class (competition against other learners). A student receives an immediate feedback (Fig. 5) from the system after each submission in the form of a bar graph of her score showing the distribution on correct, wrong and not-answered questions together with the current standing score, status and the results of her submission history. On her request the system shows also her score in relation to the current minimum, average and maximum of the whole class. This will provide him/her with information of his/her current standing on a particular assessment.

6   Directing Users

Directing Users in a system supporting Web-enhanced courses should prevent users from becoming overwhelmed with information and losing track of where they are going, while permitting users to make the most of the facilities the system offers.

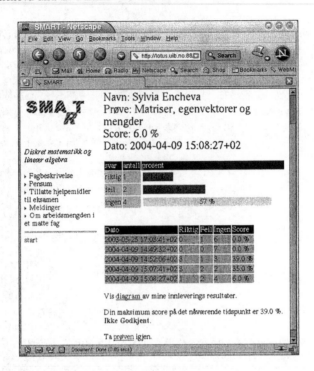

Fig. 2. A feedback page with current status and results of submission history

In this system a new topic is recommended to a student after assessing her knowledge:

i) The system first suggests a test for the student and based on her response recommends one of the levels α, β, γ, or δ (in the current version) as a start. However, users have an opportunity to place themselves in any of the levels α, β, γ, or δ, according to their opinion.

ii) The system gives information about the amount of theory and problems to be considered as the content of a 2×45 min lecture and recommends related problems to be solved for further reading. Based on student's responses while solving the recommended problems, the system either gives suggestions for solving problems from the database that will clear a misconception (if necessary) or advises students to proceed with another topic.

iii) The system gives information about the level of knowledge of each user, compares the results of every user with the results of the class, compares the results of different classes, and provides information on the amount of students going back to a particular problem and/or a statement. This helps content developers to improve on certain parts by including further explanations and better examples.

The system guides the student downwards according to her mistakes and brings her upwards using the same path without a human tutor. Suppose γ is the current level where the first mistake occurs. The system then brings the student to level β for reading suitable theory and solving new examples, evaluating her understanding of the material on level β. If the student is making another mistake at level β she will be sent to level α for reading another suitable theory and solving new examples, evaluating her understanding of the material on level α, i.e.

$$\gamma \xrightarrow{\ 0\ } \beta \xrightarrow{\ 1\ } \alpha.$$

Suppose the problem is cleared up on level α, i.e., α is the lowest level in this case. The system goes back to level β where the student is presented with a new test. If the test results on level β are satisfactory the system brings the student to the same point in γ where the first mistake occurred. If the student fails the test at level β automatic help is offered and then a new test is suggested. On any level the system distinguish wrong answers caused by miscalculation, lack of knowledge, and misconception. Here the student is guided through a path

$$\alpha \xrightarrow{\ 2\ } \beta \xrightarrow{\ 3\ } \gamma.$$

By automatically tracking the student's path in response to his/her answers, the system helps him/her to learn from her mistakes. Thus the student will not spend time and effort keeping track of his/her path.

7   System Architecture

The framework is composed of three main components: base system, content, and runtime support.

Base System
Apache is used as a Web server with a Python interpreter extention using a PyApache module. PostgreSQL is used as a relational database that supports SQL.

Python is an object-oriented scripting language. Having a Python interpreter compiled into an Apache Web server increases performance and reduces response time significantly. A standard Apache implementation with Common Gateway Interface (CGI) scripts can also be used. However, this will lead to a performance penalty in that a Web server needs to start a new external Python interpreter each time a CGI script is called.

A relational database management system (DBMS) is used to store tests and users' data. PostgreSQL provides us with database support for flexible implementation. All data is stored in a relational database and can be queried programmatically by Python scripts using Simple Query Language (SQL). Other relational databases such as MySQL and Oracle can be used instead.

Contents
Presenting mathematical concepts on the Web is a major problem for many educators who wish to publish their tutorials and assignments using extensive

mathematical notations. In our case all mathematical equations and formulas are converted to PNG images files by *latex2html*. We have developed contents on a Linux workstation. We also make some modifications to the original *latex2html* to conform to our style.

Runtime support
Dynamic HTML pages are created by server-side scripts written in Python. Python programs are also used for database integration, diagnostics, and communication modules.

8   Experience

For the experiment we consider a course thought by one lecturer to three groups of students without any use of Web-enabled computer technology and three groups of students with use of Web-enabled computer technology. In a group of about 90 undergraduate engineering students in linear algebra the percentage of failure has decreased by 36% and their average grade is improved by 24%.

Another experiment is following a group of students taking a course in linear algebra and a course in calculus. The two subjects take place in two consecutive semesters, thought by the same lecturer using the system. Our statistics shows a stable tendency of about 25% increased number of students attending lectures and about 40% increased number of students interacting with Web-based tutorials and tests in the second semester. To our surprise we notice nearly 50% increased number of students taking personal contacts with the lecturer seeking deeper understanding of topics compulsory for the subject and topics under link 'for those who have special interest'.

Teachers have found that the use of Web-enabled computer technology in a classroom enables them to effectively deliver course content, assess student comprehension, and foster the development of learning communities. Being provided with interactive examples, animations, java applets and different tests with immediate feedback, students became engages of the work instead of receivers of information.

Web-based tests indicate that students tend to work more slowly under negative marking directions and complete fewer items than in the same test taken with right scoring. Students under right scoring instructions guess more than under negative marking directions, and higher ability students guess more than lower ability ones. This might be because the higher ability students either are more confident or follow directions better. Under negative marking, low ability students omit fewer items than high ability. Students should be told explicitly about the scoring that is being used. If negative marking is used, it is important to indicate that answering based on partial knowledge (ie. being able to eliminate some options) is generally advisable, but random guessing is not.

The scoring distribution graphs are shown (Fig. 3). The date for the type and topic of feedback were not remarkably different for the three different assessments. The control group was taking the same subject and had no access to Web-based tutorials and Web-based assessments. Applying Web-based as-

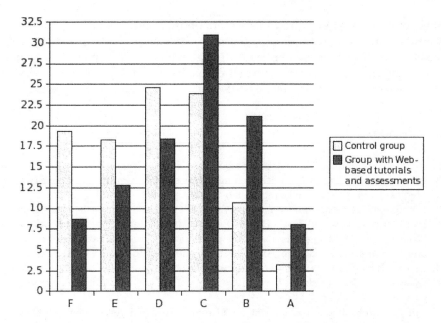

Fig. 3. Percentage of students falling into each grade category

sessments resulted in a much wider distribution of scores, indicating that such grading helped the rates in the group make more discriminating judgments about the quality of the presentations.

9   Conclusion

To prepare students for a job situation where they have to deal with problems that are not yet recognized, they should experience solving complex problems with a requirement for making a decision in a limited amount of time.

This study explored the potential of a Web-based blended learning to improve engineering students achievements in studying mathematics on undergraduate level. Students perform better academically when they are thought using a curriculum infused with Web-enabled computer technology. They become more motivated and interested in schoolwork as a result of being thought using such a curriculum.

Developing an item pool of questions tailored for individuals with different learning orientations is both difficult and time consuming. A cooperation among educational organizations is a possible solution but it needs serious consideration of security issues.

Web-based tests indicate that students tend to work more slowly under negative marking directions and complete fewer items than in the same test taken with right scoring. Students under right scoring instructions guess more than under negative marking directions, and higher ability students guess more than lower ability ones. This might be because the higher ability students either are more confident or follow directions better. Under negative marking, low ability students omit fewer items than high ability. Students should be told explicitly about the scoring that is being used. If negative marking is used, it is important to indicate that answering based on partial knowledge (ie. being able to eliminate some options) is generally advisable, but random guessing is not.

References

1. Bergeron, B., Morse, A. and Greenes, R. : A Generic Neural Network Based Tutorial Supervisor for C.A.I. 14th Annual Symposium on Computer Applications in Medical Care, IEEE Publishing (1989)
2. Birenbaum, M.: Assessment 2000: towards a pluralistic approach to assessment. In M. Birenbaum and F. J. R. C. Dochy (Eds.), Alternatives in assessment of achievements, learning processes and prior knowledge. Evaluation in education and human services. Boston, MA Kluwer Academic Publishers (1996) 3–29
3. Bloom, B.S. (Ed.): Taxonomy of educational objectives: The classification of educational goals: Handbook I, cognitive domain. New York ; Toronto: Longmans, Green (1956)
4. Bull, J., McKenna, C.: Blueprint for Computer-assisted Assessment, Routledge-Falmer (2003)
5. Cytowic, R.: The man who tasted shapes. New York: Time Warner (1993)
6. Gardner-Medwin, A.R.: Confidence assessment in the teaching of basic science. Association for Learning Technology Journal **3** (1995) 80–85
7. Guzmàn, E., Conejo, R.: A model for student knowledge diagnosis through adaptive testing. Lecture Notes in Computer Science, Vol. 3220. Springer-Verlag, Berlin Heidelberg New Jork (2004) 12–21
8. Janvier, W.A., Ghaoui, C: Using Communication Preference and mapping Learning Styles to Teaching Styles in the Distance Learning Intelligent Tutoring System-WISDeM. Lecture Notes in Artificial Intelligence, Vol. 3190. Springer-Verlag, Berlin Heidelberg New Jork (2003) 185–192
9. Jensen, M.R., Feuerstein, R.: The learning potential assessment device: From philosophy to practice. In C.S. Lidz (Ed.), Dynamic assessment: An interactional approach to evaluating learning potential. NY, Guilford Publications, Inc. (1987) 379–402
10. de Jong, T., Ferguson-Hessler, M.G.M.: Types and qualities of knowledge. Educational Psychologist **31** (1996) 105–113
11. Hartley, J.R.: Interacting with multimedia. University computing **15** (1993) 129–136
12. Harper, R.: Correcting computer-based assessments for guessing. Journal of Computer Assisted Learning **19** (2003) 2–8
13. Hirsh, L., Saeedi, M., Cornillon, J., Litosseliti, L.: A structured dialogue tool for argumentative learning. Journal of Computer Assisted Learning **20**(1) (2004) 72–80
14. http://www.candle.eu.org
15. http://www.calicocat.com/irt.html
16. http://edutella.jxta.org/
17. http://www.dpi.vic.gov.au/dpi/nrenfa.nsf/
18. http://www.dcs.bbk.ac.uk/selene/

19. Hron, A., Friedrich, H.F.: A review of web-based collaborative learning: factors beyond technology. Journal of Computer assisted Learning **19** (2003) 70–79

20. Huffman, D, Goldberg, F., Michlin, M.: Using computers to create constructivist environments: impact on pedagogy and achievement. Journal of Computers in mathematics and science teaching **22**(2) (2003) 151–168

21. Lepper M.R., Woolverton M., Mumme D., Gurther G.: Motivational techniques of expert human tutors: Lessons for the design of computer-based tutors. In S.P. Lajoie, S.J. Derry (Eds.): Computers as cognitive tools. LEA, Hillsdale, NJ (1993) 75–105

22. LeDoux, J.: The emotional brain. New York: Simon and Schuster (1996)

23. http://www.livemath.com

24. Lynch C. and Wolcott, S. K.: Helping your students develop critical thinking skills. The Idea Center (2001)

25. Maio, Y., Holst S., Holmer, T., Zentel, P.: An actively-oriented approach to visually structured knowledge representation for problem-based learning virtual environments. Designing Cooperative Systems. IOS Press, Amsterdam (2000)

26. Martinez, M.: Chapter 7: Know Thyself: Taking Charge of Your Online Learning. In White, K. & Baker, J. (eds.), The Student Guide to Successful Online Learning: A Handbook of Tips, Strategies, and Techniques, Allyn & Bacon (2003)

27. Martinez, M.: Adaptive Learning: Research Foundations and Practical Applications. In Stein, S., and Farmer, S., S. (eds.), Connotative Learning. Washington D.C.: IACET (2004)

28. Mora, M.A., Moriyòn, R., Saiz, F.: Role-based specification of the behavior of an agent for the interactive resolution of mathematical problems. Lecture Notes in Computer Science, Vol. 3220. (2004)

29. Nitko, A.: Curriculum-based continuous assessment: a framework for concepts, procedures and policy. Assessment in education **2** (1995) 321–337

30. Oliver, M., MacBean, J., Conole, G., Harvey, J.: Using a Toolkit to Support the Evaluation of Learning. J. of Computer Assisted Learning **18**(2) (2002) 199–208

31. Park, C., Kim, M.: Development of a Level-Based Instruction Model in Web-Based Education. Lecture Notes in Artificial Intelligence, Vol. 3190. (2003) 215-221

A Personalized Mobile Learning System Using Multi-agent

Jin-hee Ko, Chihoon Hur, and Hanil Kim

Department of Computer Education, Cheju National University,
Jeju, 690-756, Korea
littletomato7942@hotmail.com, pareahab@msn.com,
hikim@cheju.ac.kr

Abstract. Due to the recent development of the wireless communication industry, the learning system using the mobile technology, which is not restricted by time and space, has been researched. However, a learning system based on the level of users and a personalized service in accordance with the individual characteristics has been insufficient. Therefore, this paper proposes a system to offer a personalized service by adding the multi-agent system to the mobile English words learning system.

1 Introduction

Due to the recent development of wireless communication and popularization of mobile devices, the learning system using mobile devices has been developed. Using mobile devices, learners can study anywhere anytime. Accordingly, the mobile learning system has been researched. However, the existing systems have been insufficient to fully offer a learning service based on levels in accordance with the characteristics of users because they don't use the feedback on the changing information of users effectively. As a result, the users got the service not suitable for their level and they couldn't use the learning system effectively. Thus, they lost interest in learning. Therefore, this paper proposes a personalized learning system based on the characteristics of each user.

Personalization means offering goods, service, or related information to each customer based on his personal characteristics. The basic goal of the personalized system is to offer service that customers may want or need even though they didn't ask or choose it [1]. The methods of personalization include Rule-based Filtering, Collaboration Filtering, Learning Agent, and Content-based Filtering. In general, the hybrid personalization method is used with weak points and strong points complementing each other. With this personalized service, users are able to reduce search time and the cost of using the service, get personalized service, and raise loyalty to the personalized system. However, in the process to collect information of users for personalization, if the users are required to give excessive personal information, they may be reluctant or give wrong information. Therefore, excessive personal information should not be asked.

In the systems researched before, the agent system was used as one way to offer a personalized service. The agent system automatically handles the work wanted by

M. Dean et al. (Eds.): WISE 2005 Workshops, LNCS 3807, pp. 144–151, 2005.

users. Moreover, the multi-agent system is a conglomerate of agent systems. It solves complicated problems, which cannot be solved by one agent, with the cooperation of multi-agent [2].

This paper uses agents with different roles to offer a personalized service. Also it aims to offer an automated personalized service through the multi-agent system.

2 Related Research

2.1 The Existing English Learning System

In the case of the English Learning System researched before, it attempted to offer a learning service based on the user's level using the user's information. However, it was insufficient. Moreover, it was insufficient to offer an adaptive service based on the characteristics of the user with the feedback on the changing learning evaluation information while the user was using the learning system. Otherwise, the utilization of the feedback information was low.

[3] used a strong point of Instant Messenger in that it is popularized and has broad usage. However, Instant Messenger has a weak point in that communication is impossible without a conversation partner. In order to overcome this, the Messenger Agent was adopted. However, since it is the system using messenger, users have difficulty in English learning using animated pictures or pictures. In this system, voice service cannot be offered and only textual English learning is possible.

[4] made up the system for English learning based on classes or chapters. The function in which the users directly control the system was added. As a result, self-directed learning, in which the users can learn based on their level and they can learn repetitively, is possible. However, since learning is done by the choice of users, users may choose the wrong learning service which is not for their level. Moreover, it is a system in which users passively use the system rather than an automated English learning service based on the system. In addition, it was insufficient to offer an English learning service based on the characteristics of users since the utilization of the feedback information on learning results of users is low.

[5] used the Item response theory and the Intelligent Tutoring System for suitable learning based on the user's level. Moreover, it analyzed the feedback on the learning information of users and applied it to the system. As a result, English learning suitable for each user is possible. However, the classification or evaluation of English learning contents is classified as general contents. Therefore, it is insufficient to offer a suitable learning method for each user by detecting their hidden characteristics.

Therefore, this paper attempts to offer a personalized service to each user using the agent system of a server and a client. The agent system of the client collects characteristic information of users and sends the feedback to the server. As a result, the system can work adaptively to changes in learning characteristics of users.

2.2 The Mobile English Learning System Based on the WIPI

The system structure. Our research tem developed an English Words Learning System in which anyone can use without restriction on space by using popularized cellular phones. However, this English Words Learning System can't offer a personalized service to users since it has nothing whereby it can measure the characteristics of users. Therefore, this paper attempts to offer a personalized service to users by developing the Multi-agent System. The existing system has 7 basic functions shown in Fig. 1.

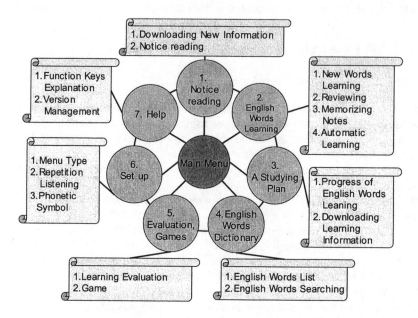

Fig. 1. Function Configuration Diagram of the English Words Learning System

Fig. 2 shows segments of the English Learning System to run each function. When you click on the 'Introduction screen' and 'Learning start' first, the 'DoointroEx class', main screen moving function, is initiated. It consists of seven modules with the above basic functions.

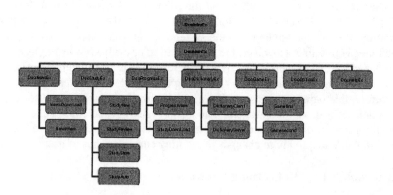

Fig. 2. Class Configuration Diagram of the English Words Learning System

Fig. 3. Main Screen   **Fig. 4.** Notice Reading   **Fig. 5.** English Words Learning

Materialized screen. The client of the English Learning System consists of 20 screens. The main screen consists of 2 level stages. The main functions include 'notice reading', 'English Words Learning', 'English Words Searching', and English words learning through 'games' [6].

3 The Mobile English Learning System

Our research team developed the English Learning System in which anyone can use it without restriction on space by using popularized cellular phones. Moreover, we are developing the Multi-agent System for the personalized service.

3.1 The Multi-agent System Structure

As shown in fig. 6, this system consists of three agents for a server and a client, and three databases for personalization.

The first agent is the Interface Agent to offer interface to users. The Interface Agent classifies clients who access the server and offers a personalized service to them. The second agent is the English Words Recommending Agent. It enables learning based on levels using the information of users. It consists of a Collaboration Filtering Agent, Character Analysis Agent, and English Words Management Agent. The Collaboration Filtering Agent compares and analyzes the user with the user group with similar characteristics to the user based on his profile and learning pattern. Then, it recommends an English words pattern suitable for him. The Character Analysis Agent analyzes the English words learning tracking and recommended history of the user and recommends a suitable English words learning pattern for the user. The English Words Management Agent is in charge of the management of the English Words Database including the classification of English words suitable for the user. The third agent is the Adaptation Agent. It updates the User Database through the learning results of the user. It changes the User Database using the feedback on learning evaluation results or clickstream through learning or evaluation of the user on the client. Then, it stores the adaptive user information in the User Database.

As for a database, on the server side, there is a User Database and an English Words Database. On the client side, there is a Client Database. The Client Database stores the English Words Learning System setup information and downloaded English words form the server.

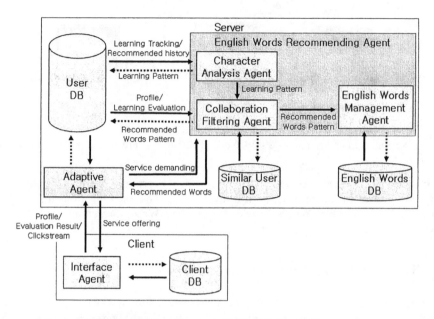

Fig. 6. Multi-Agent System Structure for English Words Learning System

3.2 The Interface Agent

When the user accesses the server through a mobile device, the Interface Agent sends the ESN (Electronic Serial Number) to the server. Then, the server searches the User Database to figure out whether it's the first access or not. If the ESN is not contained in the User Database, it represents the first access. If it's the first access, on the mobile device of the user, the screen to input the setup information and the screen to evaluate the level of him are shown. If it's not the first access, the user can learn English words based on his level.

While the user uses this system, the Interface Agent collects the English Words Learning System's clickstream. It includes the time taken to learn English words, tracking of English words learning, and English words learning system usage methods of the user. Then, the Interface Agent sends the learning clickstream and the results of evaluation of the user from among the many functions of the English Words Learning System to the Adaptation Agent of the server through the wireless Internet.

3.3 The English Words Recommending Agent

The English Words Recommending Agent consists of the Collaboration Filtering Agent, Character Analysis Agent, and English Words Management Agent. The Collaboration Filtering Agent and the Character Analysis Agent analyze the user database and send the recommended English words pattern to the English Words Management Agent.

The Collaboration Filtering Agent analyzes the user based on the profile of him in the user database, and learning pattern from the Character Analysis Agent. Then, it detects the user group similar to the user using the analyzed information of him. Finally, it detects an English words pattern to offer the user by comparing and analyzing the similar user database and the user database.

The Character Analysis Agent analyzes the English words learning pattern of the user based on the user learning tracking and the recommended history in the User Database. Then, it confirms the English Words Learning System usage and the English words learning methods which the user has difficulty in learning using the analyzed user learning information. It sends analyzed results to the Collaboration Filtering Agent.

The English words pattern confirmed by the Collaboration Filtering Agent and the Character Analysis Agent are sent to the English Words Management Agent. The English Words Management Agent classifies suitable English words for the user in the English Words Database in the server using the user information analysis results from the Collaboration Filtering Agent and the Character Analysis Agent. Then, it sends them to the Interface Agent through the Adaptive Agent. Moreover, it is in charge of the management of the English Words Database including classifying new English words and storing them in the English Words Database.

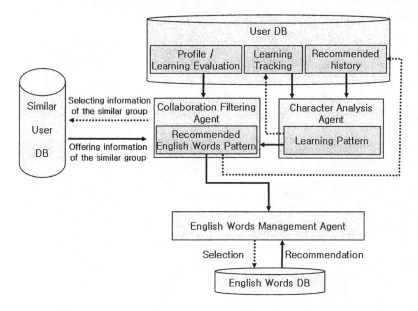

Fig. 7. English Words Recommending System Structure

3.4 The Adaptation Agent

The Adaptation Agent collects real-time the English Words Learning System usage clickstream or learning evaluation of the user on the client through the Interface Agent of the client. It analyzes learning tracking of the user based on the collected information. Then, it updates the User Database using the analyzed results. Moreover, when the user uses the English Words Learning System again, the server offers a personalized service to him using updated contents.

3.5 Database

As for the database, on the server side, it consists of a User Database and an English Words Database. The User Database stores the user profile, learning tracking and recommended history for the user. The English Words Database stores English words in the English Words Learning System. On the client side, it stores setup information of the client and English words information downloaded from the server.

The initial database in the User Database includes the user profile, input by the user in the first access to the server, and the user level evaluation information. When the user uses the English Words Learning System, the analyzed results of the system learning information of the user from the Adaptation Agent are stored in the User Database. With this analyzed user learning information, the user can learn suitable English words in accordance with his changing learning levels or patterns.

The English words database stores English words used in the English Words Learning System. English words in the English Words Database are managed by the English Words Management Agent. Suitable English words for the user are offered by the English Words Management Agent.

The Client Database stores the English Words Learning System setup information of the user, English words downloaded by the user from the access to the server, and the progress of English Words Learning.

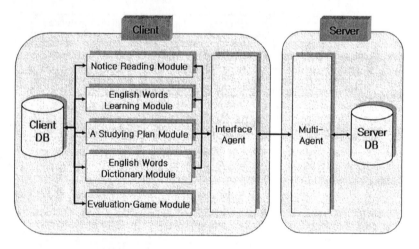

Fig. 8. The Database Relation of the Server and the Client

4 Conclusion

Due to the development of wireless Internet technology, the environment to use educational contents anywhere anytime is established. Also, this system uses cellular phones, accessible anywhere anytime, with a high popularization rate. Therefore, it is expected that the user can use the English Words Learning System with interest without restriction on time and space. Moreover, this system offers English words learning service based on the level of the user using the multi-agent to offer a personalized service to the user. Therefore, it is expected that effective English words learning is possible.

Acknowledgement

This research was supported by the MIC (Ministry of Information and communication), Korea, under the ITRC(Information Technology research Center) support program supervised by the IITA(Institute of Information Technology Assessment).

References

1. Y.J. Na, I.S. Ko, K.H. Han: A Design of a Recommendation System for one to one Web Marketing: Korea Information Processing Society VOL. 11-D NO. 07pp, Korea (2004) 1537-1542
2. http://blog.naver.com/poopu6/100003905135
3. B.J. Kim, J.H Han: The Design and Implementation of Messenger Agent for Elementary English Education: Korea Information Processing Society VOL. 11 NO. 02pp. Korea (2004) 0171-0174
4. J.Y. Ku, H.O. Lee: Web Courseware Design and Implementation of Elementary English 6 Grade for self-directed Learning Ability Extension: Korea Information Processing Society VOL. 11 NO. 02pp. Korea (2004) 1093-1096
5. Y.S. Lee, J.W. Cho, B.U. Choi: Design and implementation of an Intelligent Tutoring System for Mobile English Learning: Korea Information Processing Society VOL. 10. NO. 05pp. Korea (2003) 0539-0550
6. E.Y. Kang, J.H. Ko, H.I. Kim: Design and Implementation of a Mobile English Words Learning System based on WIPI: Korea Information Processing Society VOL. 12. NO. 01pp. Korea (2005) 1005-1008

Collaborative Web-Based Nursing Practice Learning System

Woojin Paik[1], Nam Mi Kang[2], Heejung Choi[3], and Eunmi Ham[4,*]

[1] Dept. of Computer Science, Konkuk University,
322 Danwol-Dong, Chungju-Si, Chungcheongbuk-Do, 380-701, Korea
wjpaik@kku.ac.kr
[2, 3, 4] Dept of Nursing Science, Konkuk University,
322 Danwol-dong, Chungju-si, Chungcheongbuk-do, 380-701, Korea
{nmkang03, hchoi98, hem2003}@kku.ac.kr

Abstract. Nurses collaborate with other medical professionals including doctors, lab technicians, and other nurses to provide patient care. Especially, the nurses often work as a team to take care of multiple patients. However, it is fairly often for the team members to work at different time in different location as they are assigned to work in different shifts. Traditionally, the nurses keep the written patient records for the others to review and also have brief face-to-face meetings as one shift ends and the next shift starts. This process tends to be one-way communication from the nurses, who collected and/or analyzed the patient information, to other nurses in the same team without much opportunity to feedback or clarification. Although, this approach works well for the experienced nurses, the novice nurses or the nursing students in the internship settings require fairly long time to get used to it. To remedy this problem, we are developing a web-based nursing practice collaborative system, which can also act as an in-practice learning system to enable better communication and also group decision making. We designed the system to facilitate collaborative learning by a team of nurses through helping each other to work toward to achieve the goal of best nursing care.

1 Motivation: Collaboratively Developing Nursing Care Plan

According to North American Nursing Diagnosis Association (NANDA), a nursing diagnosis is defined as a critical judgment about individual, family, or community responses to actual or potential health problems or life processes. The goal of a nursing diagnosis is to identify health problems of the patient and his/her family. A diagnosis provides a direction for the forthcoming nursing care [1].

In addition to the actual skills of caring for the patients, the nursing education put heavy emphasis on developing nursing diagnosis capabilities. Thus, nursing students and novice nurses spend a lot of time learning to come up with a correct diagnosis given particular patient data. A traditional method for teaching the nursing diagnosis subject is for the nursing students to work in the actual hospital setting as student

---

* Corresponding author.

M. Dean et al. (Eds.): WISE 2005 Workshops, LNCS 3807, pp. 152–161, 2005.

interns. During the internship, the students assist medical staff in various situations. However, the most important task to be completed by the student interns is to generate a nursing care plan for a particular patient.

The nursing care plan includes the systematic explanation of the facts gathered during the patient assessment stage and also the analysis of the facts. In addition, the plan describes the nursing diagnosis based on the facts and the analyses. The nurses develop a plan of care that prescribes interventions to attain outcomes then include them in the planning documentation. The care plan is prepared to provide continuity of care from nurse to nurse, to enhance communication, to document the nursing process, to serve as a teaching tool, and to coordinate provisions of care among disciplines [2].

Typical nursing care plan includes the background information about the patients such as the general biographical information, the medical history, various health related information, physical and mental state assessment results, nursing diagnoses, suggested interventions, and expected outcomes. Often certain information such as the medication records is also included. However, much of the information is conveyed as narratives of the nurses and the direct quotes from the patients. In the nursing process literature, patient data are regarded as either subjective or objective data. Subjective data are what the client reported, believed, or felt. Objective data are what can be observed such as vital signs, behaviors, or diagnostic studies [2]. This distinction is important as the reliability and validity of the data as well as the data collection methods differ. Nurses try to find additional supporting evidences when making judgments mainly based on the subjective data.

The nurses compile patients' conditions in the form of the facts that the nurses observed, monologue by the patient, patient's answers to the nurse' questions, and the patient's condition conveyed by others such as family members. Then, the nurses often summarize the factual information. The nurses form their evaluation of the patient's condition based on the summarized factual information.

Usually, each student intern is assigned to one patient during his/her internship and thus expected to produce one nursing care plan for the assigned patient. Each student works alone. However, this process does not simulate the actual clinical setting of many nurses collaboratively taking care of many patients. The nurses often work as a team to take care of multiple patients. But, it is fairly often for the team members to work at different shift. Therefore, we decided to group students into three-person teams to make the students' internship experience closer to the actual practice. The internship requirement was changed so that each team collaboratively generates the nursing care plans for three patients.

In a typical clinical setting, there tends to be one-way communication amongst the nurses without much opportunity for feedback or clarification mainly due to the time constraints imposed on the working schedule of the nurses. Instead, the nurses keep the written patient records for the others to review and also have brief face-to-face meetings as one shift ends and the next shift starts. However, we considered this practice to be less accommodating for the students and the novice nurses. Thus, we decided to introduce the collaborative learning concept where small independent groups of students work together as a team to help each other learn [3]. We developed a collaborative web-based nursing practice learning system and required the students to use the system to generate the nursing care plans during their internship.

Our collaborative web-based nursing practice learning system includes the patients and/or their guardians as the active participants by allowing them to enter subjective information about the patients by themselves. Any nursing team member, who is available and has access to the patients, can review the patient-entered information then fill-in the missing information and/or clarify any doubtful information entered into the system. Any nurse, who happens to observe any noticeable patient behavior or symptom, can enter the objective information to the system. Other team members can review the stored information then provide additional information or ask clarification questions to the other member, who collected and entered the information. Decisions such as the nursing diagnoses or the treatment plan can be proposed and entered into the system by a team member. Other team members can question or modify what others proposed via online discussions until everyone in the team agrees with the decisions.

2 Collaborative Web-Based Nursing Practice Learning System

We designed the collaborative learning system as a web-based system to maximize the accessibility by the nurses, the patients, and the instructors, who are overseeing the internship students. The system consists of three subcomponents. Figure 1 is a flow chart showing how three components interact to generate a nursing care plan, which is the final product of the collaborative web-based nursing practice learning system.

The first component is referred as the Patient Information Survey System. This system is used to collect the subjective data about the patients. The system is implemented as a web-based survey, which is accessible via a Tablet PC. The Tablet PC is wirelessly linked to the network. The web survey pages displayed on the Tablet PC are directly fetched from a remote web server. The data entered on the web-based survey is directely fed into a remote database server. The Tablet PC can be given to a patient or the patient's guardian if the patient cannot fill out the survey physically. Our goal of using the wireless Tablet PC is to maximize the mobility of the data collection tool by bringing the data entry system to the patients instead of bringing the patients to a fixed station PC. The web-based survey was designed and implemented mainly as a point-and-click interface with the minimum typing requirements. The main goal of this design decision was to reduce any difficulties that the patients and/or the guardians might encounter when using a computerized survey form especially when they are not used to computers.

The types of subjective data gathered by Patient Information Survey System include the biographical information such as name, gender, age, occupation, religion, education level, marital status, admission date, and the main symptoms. In addition, the patient's medical history, medical diagnosis and the prescription information are also collected. The patient's developmental history starting from when the patient was an infant to his/her current age was also collected. Finally, the patient's general health related information such as drinking & smoking pattern, dietary & defecation habit, personal hygiene, sleeping pattern, existing health conditions or risks, interpersonal relations, factors affecting the stress increase, stress management methods, financial condition, familial loading, and family tree are collected.

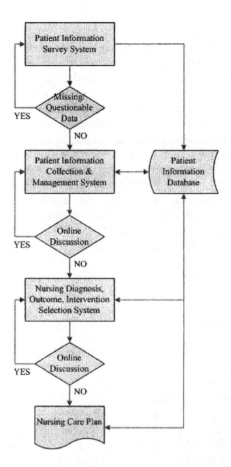

Fig. 1. Collaborative web-based nursing practice learning system components

After the patients and/or the guardians complete the web-survey, the nurses go over the collected data to check whether there is any missing or questionable data. If there are data, which need to be entered or verified, the nurses meet the patients and/or the guardians in person to collect the data. Through this process, we wanted to simulate the typical procedure of the outpatient clinic settings where the patients fill out the paper forms regarding their general health issues during their first visit and the interview with the nurses before the patients' see the doctors.

The second component is the Patient Information Collection and Management System. The main use of this system is for the nurses to collect the objective information about the patients and also to enter the analyses based on the observations. Another important use of this system is for the nurses to communicate with other nurses about the observations and the analyses. We regard the analysis based on the observations as the same cognitive activity as the nurses' evaluation of a particular patient condition. After the nurses analyze the factual information about a patient, the nurses determine the conditions to be of a certain type then select an appropriate course of action. Finally, the instructors can use the system to monitor the internship progress when the system is used by the internship students.

The system is implemented as a web-based collaborative information management and communication system, which is accessible via a wirelessly connected Personal Digital Assistant (PDA). All accessible information from the PDA is managed by the web-based interface, which is linked to the web server and the database server.

To collect the objective data, the nurses mainly use the voice recording function in the PDA to store what they observed as the digital audio. The nurses can also enter the information by using the on-screen keyboard or the hand recognition function of the PDA. The types of objective data collected with the Patient Information Collection and Management System include mental state assessment outcome such as general appearance of the patient, attitudes & behavior, mood or affect, thoughts, perception, cognition, intellectual function, insight, expectation about the admission outcome by the patient and/or family, patient's future plan, patient's defense mechanism, and the psychodynamics. These types of data were specifically collected as the system is developed and tested for the Psychiatric Nursing internship.

The nurses can review both the subjective data collected with the Patient Information Survey System and the objective data on the PDA. Although, the same information can be viewed on both the Tablet PC and the PDA, the PDA is only used by the nurses as it takes some training to use the system.

As the nurses review the collected information and their associated analyses, they can reach different analyses or form questions. Then, the nurses can post their alternative analyses and the questions on the Patient Information Collection and Management System. The nurses in a team will discuss the posted alternative analyses and questions until certain agreements are reached by the majority of the team members.

In the internship settings, the instructors can also participate in the discussions to guide the students to the right direction. The students definitely learn when the instructors' intervene and lead the discussion. However, we believe that the significant web-based learning occurs when the team members collaboratively work toward to solve the problem online.

The third component of the Collaborative web-based nursing practice learning system is the Nursing Diagnosis, Outcome, and Intervention Selection System. This system is used as an online collaboration tool for the nurses to synthesize every piece of patient information that has been collected and analyzed. There is no information collection function in this system. The nurses will initially propose one or more nursing goals to achieve given the patient's conditions. Once the goal is determined collaboratively, the nurses will select one or more nursing diagnoses. There are 167 NANDA approved nursing diagnoses [1]. The nurses examine the defining characteristics of each diagnosis against the patient information then select the most appropriate diagnoses. There is a mapping table from each diagnosis to a set of potential nursing outcomes. There are 330 nursing outcomes [4]. Not all outcomes in the matching set will be applicable to the patient in consideration. Thus, the nurses need to go through each outcome in the matching set then select the best possible outcomes based on the pre-selected goals, diagnoses, and the patient conditions. Finally, there are 514 nursing interventions [5]. Each nursing outcome is also linked to a set of interventions although, not all interventions in the matching set will be applicable to the patient in care. Therefore, the nurses will be required to review each intervention in the matching set to select the most potentially effective interventions to be applied.

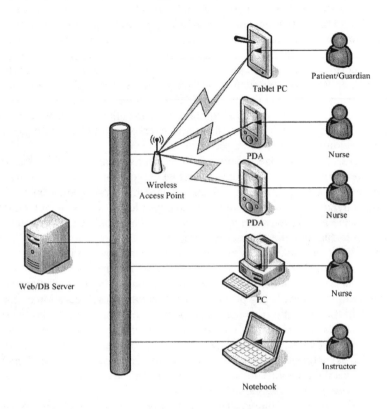

Fig. 2. Collaborative Nursing Practice Learning System Use Diagram

The Nursing Diagnosis, Outcome, and Intervention Selection System include both synchronous communication tools such as an Internet messenger and asynchronous communication tool such as a threaded discussion board. The nurses can carry out online discussions as a group decision process by using the web-based interface of the Nursing Diagnosis, Outcome, and Intervention Selection System. Since, all information is transferred back and forth from the web server and the Patient Information Database in the database server, the nurses can participate in the online discussion from any Internet connected devices such as PDAs, notebooks, or PCs. The instructors can also access the system to monitor and evaluate the student activities if the system is used as a part of an internship. The Figure 2 shows the schematic view on how the nurses, patients/guardians, and the instructors access the overall Collaborative Web-based Nursing Practice Learning System.

3 Web-Based Collaborative Learning

We designed the Collaborative Web-based Nursing Practice Learning System to provide an optimal learning environment, which is capable of supporting high learning performance with maximum satisfaction and utilization as well as minimum effort and time [6]. Our system supports the maximum utilization, minimum effort, and minimum time as the nurses can access the system at anytime and at any place by using a web-based interface available on any Internet connected devices. The nurses are able to develop the patient care plans collaboratively without being restricted by time and space. With the ubiquitous mode system access, the students can continue to learn the nursing process and the instructors can continue to monitor and evaluate the student progress. We consider the ubiquitous and the collaborative nature of the system use also provide maximum satisfaction to everyone participating in the nursing care plan development and learning process.

The process of knowledge building in collaborative learning is characterized by six cognitive activities [7]. They are: 1) mutual exploration of issues; 2) mutual examination of arguments; 3) agreements and disagreements; 4) mutual questioning of positions; 5) dynamic interaction; and 6) weaving of ideas. Our system facilitates all six activities and also allows them to occur in a web-based online environment.

Our system supports the 'mutual exploration of issues' by enabling the nurses to collaboratively review and clarify the patient/guardian provided subjective information as well as collaboratively collect the objective information. Our system also allows the nurses to 'examine the arguments mutually', 'agree and disagree', and 'question positions mutually' by providing the functionalities to question or comment in response to the evaluations or the analyses of the objective information posted by other nurses. These exploration, examination, agreement, disagreement, and questioning form the 'dynamic interactions' amongst the nurses due to the built-in synchronous and asynchronous communication functionalities of the system. Finally, our system provides the capability to 'weave ideas' during the collaborative generation of nursing diagnoses, outcomes, and interventions.

Mason [8] noticed that online dialogue often never reaches synthesis or closure. However, we had not noticed this problem during the preliminary field testing of our system. It is probably due to the fact that the student interns had a clearly defined goal as well as a firm deadline to reach the goal. In addition, we believe that the students were motivated to cooperate with each other and come to the conclusions without side tracking due to the fact that the instructor was capable of monitoring and evaluating the work progress by accessing the system at anytime without the knowledge of the students. However, we also believe that our system functionalities enabled the students to fully exercise six learning quality criteria [9] such as brainstorming, articulating, reacting, organizing, analysis, and generalization.

There were two major objectives for the students to achieve during their internship. One object was for the students to be able to correctly select the most appropriate nursing diagnoses and their associated outcomes and interventions based on the vast amount of subjective and objective data about a real patient. Before the students took the internship course, they took a regular lecture-based class on the subject of nursing diagnosis, outcome, and intervention. Thus, the internship experience for this subject was an exercise to apply the theories into practice.

However, the second object of observing and concisely recording the patient conditions as well as evaluating the objective data was a new learning task for the students. We hypothesize that a nurse utilizes causal knowledge specific to the nursing process if he/she can analyze the factual information about a patient then determines the conditions to be of a certain type and also selects a course of action.

The following show three actual examples from the nursing care plan prepared by the student interns where the evaluative statements are followed by factual information. The nursing care plan was originally written in Korean and the texts were translated manually. 'HS' and 'JK' refer to a pseudo name of the patients. Each sentence is marked with two sets of tags to show the beginning and end of the factual information and the evaluative statements. These tags are inserted manually just to show the demarcation of the factual information and the evaluative statements.

1) <Factual Information> HS said "I hope my nervousness goes away soon". </Factual Information>, <Evaluation> Based on the statement, HS seems to understand about his condition well. </Evaluation>

2) < Factual Information> Since HS was voluntarily admitted to the hospital last time, </ Factual Information>, <Evaluation> it is believed that HS is positively thinking about the treatments that HS is receiving. </Evaluation>

3) < Factual Information> As the patient stated that he never had a relationship with a female and also did not have many male friends, </ Factual Information >, <Evaluation> it is likely that JK have been having a difficult interpersonal relationship since he was a teenager. </Evaluation>

The primary learning objective for the students was to write sensible and consistent evaluative statements given factual information. To do that, the students reviewed what others have recorded and discussed online the differences from their own evaluation if there were any. Since all team members were responsible for a nursing care plan for one patient, they had to reach an agreement. This exercise promoted the collaboration learning by the students as they all had to learn to assess the patients' conditions correctly.

4   Implementation and Preliminary Evaluation

We developed a prototype Collaborative Web-based Nursing Practice Learning System as a database-backed website. The MySQL database was used to store the patient information database. There are two versions of the same websites. One was for the PDA and the other was for the rest of the devices such as Tablet PC, notebook, and ordinary PC. The Apache web server and the database server are running on a HP ProLiant ML150 Xeon server with 2 CPUs and 1 GB of main memory, and 72GB of hard disk. The operating system of the server is RedHat Linux. For the preliminary evaluation of the system, we used one Tablet PC (HP Compaq Tablet PC TC 1100) running Windows XP Table Edition and three PDAs (HP iPAQ TM Pocket PC h5550) running Windows CE. We also used a wireless router (Linksys Wireless-G Broadband Router) to enable the wireless connection for the Tablet PC and the PDAs.

The preliminary evaluation was conducted with six senior nursing students from the Department of Nursing Science, Konkuk University in Chungju, Korea in June 2005. Three students acted as the nurses and the other three acted as hypothetical patients. The goal of the evaluation was mainly to test the functionalities of the Collaborative Web-based Nursing Practice Learning System. The students, who were involved in the evaluation, completed an internship course in the previous year. In the previous year, the format of the internship was a traditional one where each student developed a nursing care plan for one patient. The students mainly used paper and pencil to record what they have observed then prepared the nursing care plan at the end of the internship. The test subjects thought the prototype Collaborative Web-based Nursing Practice Learning System was easy to use and required less time to complete. However, we were not able to obtained a reliable evaluation of the web-based collaborative learning aspect of the system..

We are currently conducting a full scale evaluation of the system as a part of the 'Psychiatric Nursing' course, which is being offered in the Fall 2005 semester. The course is offered at the Department of Nursing Science, Konkuk University in Chungju, Korea. The course is for the Juniors, who are majoring in the nursing science. Thus, we plan to have an in-depth report of this evaluation at the workshop in November 2005.

5 Summary and Future Work

Although we are clearly in the early stages of developing a prototype Collaborative Web-based Nursing Practice Learning System, we find preliminary evaluation of the system to be quite promising and eager to share our experiences in developing an a web-based collaborative learning system with other researchers.

We expect system to aid both nursing students and practitioners learn various aspects of the nursing process. They can review what others have done and conduct online discussions to learn from each other.

We have developed a prototype Collaborative Web-based Nursing Practice Learning System, which enables the nurses to work as a team to solve nursing problems collaboratively. In addition, we expect the system to be an effective teaching platform for the nursing students. We have not yet finished the formal evaluation of the system. However, we expect to report the evaluation results at the workshop.

We have implemented a simple authentication method to protect the data. To use the system, the users need to get a user identification and password from the system administrator. For the system evaluation, the supervising instructor acted as the system administrator. We have implemented a simple security measure as we are evaluating the system as a part of an internship, which requires sharing of the collected data and the corresponding analysis outcomes for the collaborative learning and the course evaluation purposes. However, we plan to introduce more stringent security and data protection system in place to protect the patients' privacy when we release a production system.

References

1. Sparks. S.M. and Taylor, C.M., Nursing Diagnosis Reference Manual 5th Edition, Springhouse, Springhouse, Pennsylvania. (2000).
2. Doenges, M. and Moorehead, M.F., Application of Nursing Process and Nursing Diagnosis: An Interactive Text for Diagnostic Reasoning 4th Edition, F.A. Davis Co., Philadelphia, Pennsylvania. (2003)
3. Damon W., Peer education: the untapped potential. Applied Development Psychology 5, 331-343. (1984)
4. Moorhead, S., Johnson, M., and Maas, M., Nursing Outcomes Classification (NOC) 3rd Edition, Mosby, St. Louis. (2003).
5. Dochterman, J.M. and Bulechek, G.M., Nursing Interventions Classification (NIC) 4th Edition, Mosby, St. Louis. (2004)
6. Lee, Y. and Geller, J., A Collaborative and Sharable Web-based Learning System. Association for the Advancement of Computing in Education (AACE), 2(2). 35-45. (2003).
7. Harasim, L., Collaborating in Cyberspace: Using computer conference as a group learning environments. Interactive Learning Environments, 3(2). 119-130. (1993)
8. Mason, R.D. (ed.), Computer Conferencing. The last Word. Victoria. Beach Holme Publishers. (1993)
9. Stahl, G., Reflections on WebGuide: Seven Issues for the Next Generaton of Collaborative Knowledge-Building Environment. Proceedings of the Computer Support for Collaborative Learning (CSCL) Conference. Palo Alto, CA, Lawrence Erlbaum Associates: 575-581. (1999)

Learning Object and Dynamic E-Learning Service Technologies for Simulation-Based Medical Instruction

Stanley Y.W. Su[1], Gilliean Lee[2], and Sem Lampotang[3]

[1] Database Systems R&D Center, CISE department, University of Florida
[2] Department of Math and Computing, Lander University
[3] Department of Anesthesiology, University of Florida
su@cise.ufl.edu, glee@lander.edu, SLampotang@anest.ufl.edu

Abstract. Simulations are increasingly used for instruction and training purposes in many application areas such as commercial and military aviation, battlefield management, building construction, product manufacturing, medical education and others. However, most simulation systems are monolithic, ad hoc and non-reusable. In this work, we apply learning object and e-learning service technologies to modularize an existing Web-based simulation system called the Virtual Anesthesia Machine (VAM). Instructional materials associated with the components of the simulation system are encapsulated as reusable Atomic Learning Objects, each of which consists of content items, practice items, assessment items, meta-information and constraints. Instructional materials associated with the entire simulation system is modeled as a Composite Learning Object having a structure of activities, which is used by a Learning Process Execution Engine to enact the process of delivering contents, instructing learners to use the simulation system for practice on what they learn, and performing assessment to evaluate the performances of learners in learning the functions and operations of the simulation system and its components. An event-trigger-rule server is used in an event-driven, rule-based execution of a learning process to make the learning process active, adaptive, customizable and flexible.

1 Introduction

Complex medical equipment are regularly used in hospitals and clinics where patient safety depends on the proper interactions between skilled practitioners and equipment [1, 2]. Even though anesthesia is increasingly safe, critical accidents in which patients are seriously injured still occur [1, 3]. Misuse of equipment is far more common than pure equipment errors/failures in the medical environment. Human error is a dominating factor in up to 90% of the problems caused by equipment [3, 4].

VAM is a Web-based simulation system developed at the University of Florida. It, together with an on-line workbook, can be accessed by registered users free of charge through Web-enabled personal computers. It is international in scope and features legends in 22 languages and is used in over 336 institutions and programs worldwide. The VAM web site at http://vam.anest.ufl.edu receives more than 2,000,000 hits per year.

M. Dean et al. (Eds.): WISE 2005 Workshops, LNCS 3807, pp. 162–171, 2005.

A major advantage of VAM is that users can focus on learning about anesthesia without being distracted by the concern of placing an actual patient at risk [6]. Also, it is a cost-efficient way to learn because it is free to use and does not require any actual anesthesia equipment or patient. In addition, practitioners and medical students can learn the inner workings of the anesthesia machine because the VAM is a transparent reality simulator; i.e., it is a model-driven, display-based simulation that represents internal, abstract and invisible functions with explicitly visible and manipulatable symbols to assist learners in exploring, developing and confirming mental models. The focus of the simulation is on high fidelity behavior rather than life-like appearance [5].

In spite of VAM's success and advantages, there are a number of limitations in the existing system. First, it is a monolithic system in that the components and their accompanying instructional materials, questions and answers for practice and questions for assessment are not modularized to make them reusable for constructing other simulation systems. Second, users of VAM and its workbook can freely operate on any part of the system and access any content of the workbook. Although, the workbook provides some guide for structured exercises, the learners can choose not to follow the guide. Lastly, the ability of the existing VAM system to adapt and customize its instruction delivery to suit the learners' profiles and needs is currently limited to language and medical gas color code. The aim of this work is therefore to apply the learning object and e-learning service technologies developed at the Database Systems R&D Center to address these limitations.

The organization of this paper is as follows. Related works are discussed in Section 2. The definition models for defining atomic learning objects and composite learning objects are introduced in Section 3. Section 4 explains how we use learning object models and an e-learning service system to model the components of VAM, deliver contents to learners, direct them to VAM for practice, and perform assessments. A summary is given in the last section.

2   Related Work

There are several Web contents that provide learning materials on anesthesia machines. The resource by Dosch [8] provides extensive Web contents about a variety of anesthesia machines. The material by College of Veterinary Medicine, Washington State University [9] is a comprehensive resource that covers circuits, vaporizers, gas cylinders, pressure regulators, flow meters, scavenging, ventilators, and endotracheal tubes. However, they do not provide simulation software for practice, or a way of assessment to measure learners' understanding. Gas Man [10] is a commercial product for teaching, simulating and experimenting with anesthesia uptake and distribution. It provides a tutorial and simulation software. The text tutorial is not accessible on the Web; it is published as a book. To the authors' knowledge, no anesthesia simulation system has been developed based on learning object technology at the time of writing.

There are several research and standardization efforts in developing learning process models.   SCORM's Content Aggregation Model [11] and Cisco's Reusable Learning Object (RLO) [12] are two of the popular models that organize learning contents/objects for effective delivery. A tree structure, which is commonly used to present the 'table of contents' of a book or training manual, is generally used to model a learning process. The tree structure is employed in SCORM, and Cisco's RLO.

SCORM's Sequencing Definition Model [13] is a rule-based sequencing model, which supports adaptive execution of an activity tree using sequencing rules and the status of learning objectives. The rules are in the form of *'if condition, then [action/behavior]'*.

The SCORM's Sequencing Definition Model provides a number of desirable concepts and features such as the flexible navigation through an activity tree, the rule-based execution model that includes sequencing rules and rollup rules, and the idea of adaptive sequencing facilitated by its execution model. However, there are two limitations in our opinion. First, the definition of learning objects in SCORM does not explicitly distinguish content, practice, and assessment items as Cisco's RLO, which is adopted in our work. Distinguishing these learning items allows dynamic binding and flexible presentation of learning objects [14]. Second, non-leaf activities in an Activity Tree neither present contents nor perform assessment in SCORM [13]. We believe that it is useful to allow a non-leaf node to present an introduction, a summary, and assessment item of the contents covered by its child activities.

3   Learning Object Model

A *Learning Object (LO)* is a granule of instruction designed to meet a specific instructional objective. In our work, it is modeled in terms of content items, practice items, assessment items needed to cover a subject of learning, and the sequence of their delivery. The bundling of content, practice and assessment items to form an LO is important because practice provides a learner an opportunity to perform what he/she has learned, and assessments provide a way to evaluate how much he/she has learned. This modeling approach is different from the existing Web infrastructure, which provides only contents without the means to determine what users have learned from the contents. Additional to the three types of items, meta-data, which characterizes the LO itself, is added in an LO specification [12, 15]. The meta-data is expressed in terms of a set of attributes such as title, keywords, author, cost, material type, language, difficulty level, target age, etc. and their value constraints. The meta-data of LOs are stored in a registry, which provides a search facility for finding LOs.

We distinguish three types of learning resources. They form a hierarchy based on the order of their construction. Figure 1 illustrates the hierarchy of the learning resources, and their relationships. The lowest type of resources in the hierarchy is called *learning asset*, which represents multimedia resources (text, graphs, video and audio tracks, web-pages, etc.) available on the Web. The next level of resource is called Atomic Learning Object (ALO), which consists of multiple content, practice and assessment items, each of which can be specified and presented to learners in the form of any type of multimedia learning asset. In this work, we use ALOs to encapsulate the instructional materials associated with the components and sub-components of a simulation system.

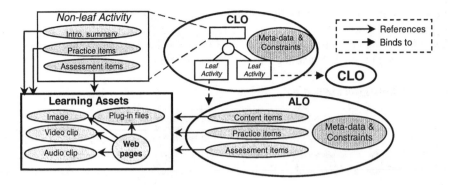

Fig. 1. Three Types of Learning Resources and Their Relationships

By encapsulating instructional materials of each component of an anesthesia machine as an ALO, the ALO can be reused to teach the functions and operations of other anesthesia machine designs or other medical equipment such as intensive care unit ventilators, medical gas blenders and cardiopulmonary bypass machines that share some components with an anesthesia machine. An ALO that covers a smaller granule of instruction will be more easily reused since it includes less contextual information [12]. The top level LO is called Composite Learning Object (CLO), which is modeled as a tree-structured learning process that contains activities, connectors, and links as modeling constructs. A CLO allows a non-leaf activity to include learning items. In contrast, a leaf activity specifies the binding information used to search for and bind to an ALO or a CLO either statically or dynamically [16]. Connectors located between a parent and its child activities specify the sequencing control modes for selecting child activities.

In addition to learning object models, we maintain learner profiles that include learners' identification, demographics, accessibility, background and preference information such as date of birth, name, languages, preferred learning styles, disability, interests, learning history, learning goals, etc. The information is used for the adaptation of the sequencing of learning contents and the dynamic selection of LOs.

3.1 Event-Driven, Rule-Based Execution of Learning Process

Learners have diverse backgrounds, competencies, needs and interests. We believe that LOs and the e-learning services provided by an e-learning service system should have the following four dynamic properties: active, flexible, adaptive and customizable. They should be *"active"* in that operations on them can automatically trigger rules to enforce policies and constraints, coordinate learning activities, and notify peers and content producers to achieve collaborative e-learning. They should be *"customizable"* in that the structures, enabled/disabled status of activities and sequencing control modes can be customized to suit individual learners before the processing of a CLO by using the information provided in *learners' profiles*. They should be *"adaptive"* in that activities can be retried, skipped, exited, enabled or disabled, and sequencing control modes can be updated at runtime to adapt to the *learner's performance* (i.e. assessment results). They should be *"flexible"* in that small granules of LOs and multimedia assets can be used to flexibly compose larger objects, and a request for an object can be flexibly bound to a suitable LO dynamically. In our work, active, flexible, adaptive and customizable e-learning services are achieved by event-driven, rule-based execution of CLOs and the ALOs referenced by them.

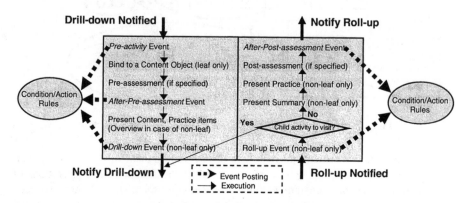

Fig. 2. Tasks in an Activity Node at Runtime

The execution of an activity in an activity tree consists of a sequence of event postings, activity code executions and rule invocations as illustrated by Figure 2. The condition-action rules specified in a non-leaf activity may contain 1) pre-activity rules, 2) after-pre-assessment rules, 3) drill-down rules, 4) roll-up rules, and 5) after-post-assessment rules. At each of the above five stages of processing a non-leaf activity, an event is posted to trigger the processing of the corresponding condition-action rules.

During the processing of a leaf-activity, events are also posted at the points of pre-activity, after-pre-assessment and after-post-assessment to trigger relevant rules. Since the condition parts of these rules may check a learner's profile, progress status and assessment result at each stage of processing a leaf or non-leaf activity, appropriate actions can be taken to suit the specific learner in a specific learning context. The action part of a rule may specify "Skip Activity", "Retry Activity", "Exit Activity", "Incomplete Activity", "Satisfy Activity", "Enable/Disable Activity", "Hide Activity from Choice", "Assess", "Update the sequencing control mode of a Connector", etc., so that the delivery sequence of activities can become adaptive, flexible and customizable. Customization of a learning process instance is performed by the pre-activity rules attached to the root activity of the learning process instance. Adaptation based on a learner's performance can be accomplished by event-triggered rules during other stages of processing a learning process instance.

A leaf activity can bind to an LO dynamically that suits a learner's profile and competency at the time of execution. The binding information specified in a leaf activity can describe or refer to data values, learner profile information, and assessment results and be used to generate a query to the LO Broker. A list of LOs that satisfy the query conditions together with their descriptions is returned. The learner can select an LO from the list for learning.

There are four learning approaches (or architectures) proposed by Clark [7]: Receptive, Directive, Guided Discovery, and Explorative. Due to learners' different learning styles and performance needs, it is desirable to support these different learning approaches [17]. Sequencing control modes [11] that define the sequencing behavior among the child nodes of a non-leaf node in an activity tree can be modified to limit learner's control over the learning path. For example, the 'Choice' mode gives learner the freedom to choose any child activities as the next activity, while 'Forward Only' mode does not allow learners to choose the next activity. In our work, multiple learning approaches are supported by using rules to adapt the sequencing control modes to suite a learner's profile, competency and progress. Rules invoked during the enactment of a learning process model by the Learning Process Execution Engine can also disable or replace activities, thus altering the activity tree dynamically.

4 Application in Medical Instruction

VAM is composed of a transparent reality simulator developed using Macromedia Director, and a workbook delivered in Macromedia FlashPaper format. The simulator currently supports 22 languages, and the workbook is in 11 different languages. The languages of the user interface as well as the color code for medical gases are changed according to a learner's selection or user profile.

The workbook consists of three parts. Part 1 covers the basic concepts of the anesthesia machine. Part 2 teaches input/output controls of VAM. Users can adjust gas pipelines, valves, gas flow meter knobs, buttons, etc, and visually observe the effects of the adjustment on the flow of molecules of gases, the readings of pressure gauges, valves, etc. Part 3 covers safety exercises and is composed of six sections, each of which covers the high pressure system, the low pressure system, the breathing circuit, the manual ventilation, the mechanical ventilation, and the scavenging system, respectively. Each section is comprised of a set of learning objectives written in questions, a set of questions and answers (Q&As), and a set of post-assessment questions. Each Q&A has a question, an answer, a VAM demonstration, an explanation, and learning objectives. The post-assessment questions (quiz) can be answered on-line at a Website specified in the workbook.

The workbook, the simulator and the quiz Web site need to be used together for effective delivery of learning experience. However, the current VAM system is not structured in order to provide a smooth transition between those learning resources. Even though directions are provided in the workbook, it is the responsibility of a learner to open the workbook online, to start the simulator, to go to the quiz Website at appropriate times.

4.1 Encapsulating VAM as Learning Objects

There are two main advantages to create LOs that encapsulate the workbook contents, the VAM simulator, and the quiz problems. First, each LO can be reused for instruction of other types of anesthesia machines, which may use the same or similar component(s). Second, it is possible to deliver learning experiences provided by the workbook's contents, the use of the simulator for practice, and the use of quiz problems for assessment in a seamless fashion and under the control of the e-learning service system.

In this work, we created an ALO for Part 1 and another ALO for Part 2 of the workbook. Part 3 is composed of several ALOs each of which contains instructional materials to cover a component of the anesthesia machine. For these ALOs, the workbook contents are extracted and regenerated as separate HTML pages. The quiz problems available at the quiz Website are extracted and used as post-assessment items. We constructed a CLO for modeling the entire VAM instruction as an activity tree, in which each of the leaf activities is bound to an ALO. Figure 3 shows the activity tree of the CLO, and the relationship among the ALOs and VAM resources.

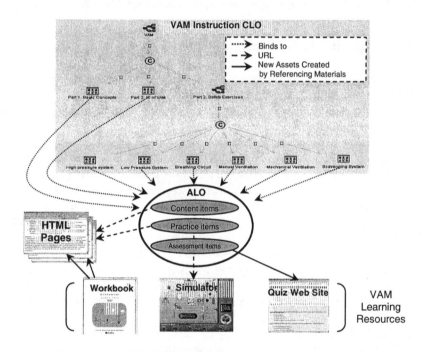

Fig. 3. Construction of Learning Objects using VAM Learning Resources

An ALO bound to a leaf activity of Part 3 begins its presentation with a set of learning objectives of the ALO. Then a sequence of several content and practice items of the workbook is delivered. A content item is presented to the learner in the form of Q&A. A practice item, presented as a Web page, includes a demonstration scenario related to the Q&A, and provides a Web link for invoking the VAM simulator. The delivery sequence of the items follows the order in the workbook. After finishing the content and practice items, post-assessment items in the multiple-choice format are provided and the result is graded. All these content, practice and assessment items are delivered in sequence through a Web user interface of our e-learning service system. Figure 4 shows the Web user interface that presents a practice item as a URL. By clicking the link to the practice item, a new Web browser that presents the practice item will popup. The user can then invoke VAM by clicking the link in the Web browser, and follow the demonstration scenario of the practice.

Fig. 4. Web User Interface (left) and a Practice Item (right)

4.2 Dynamic Execution of VAM Instruction

A number of dynamic techniques, including sequencing rules and dynamic binding, are incorporated in the design of the VAM CLO to achieve adaptive, customizable, and flexible delivery of instruction. They are described below:

(1) A learner is *required* to *take the content, practice,* and *assessment items* to satisfy an activity. In the activities 'Part 1 Basic Concepts' and 'Part 2 IO of VAM', all the learning items have to be delivered to a learner in order to make each of the activities 'Satisfied'. This is specified by an after-post-assessment rule *"if [true], then [set the activity 'Satisfied']"* in each activity.

(2) Dissimilar contents are delivered to different learners depending on the *learning goals* specified in their *learner profiles*. The pre-activity rule of the root activity 'VAM' checks if a learner's goal is related to anesthesia. If it is, then a non-leaf activity 'Part 3 – Safety Exercises', which contains the details of system components and exercises, will be delivered to the learner. Otherwise, the non-leaf activity is *disabled* so that the contents in the activity and its child activities are not presented to the learner. In the CLO, we consider that the activity 'Part 3 – Safety Exercises' covers too much details for a person without a learning goal in anesthesia.

(3) ALOs written in the *language* of a learner's preference will be chosen and delivered. The language requirement is specified as a binding constraint of a leaf activity. For example, in the CLO, activities 'Part 1-Basic Concepts' and 'Part 2-IO of VAM' can be bound to ALOs that are written in either English or Korean, depending on the language specified in the learner's profile model.

(4) Various *learning approaches* that suit different learners' backgrounds and preferences are supported. A learner with the background knowledge of anesthesia or a preference to the learning approach, *guided discovery,* is given the freedom to choose the next activity when the non-leaf activity 'Part 3 – Safety Exercises' is delivered. That is, the *Choice* sequencing control mode is set in the connector of the activity 'Part 3 – Safety Exercises'. On the other hand, a learner who prefers the *receptive* or *directive* learning approach will be restricted to choose the next activity; i.e., the Flow sequencing control mode will be set in the connector. A *customized* LO is delivered by a pre-activity rule of the root activity.

(5) *Depending on the performance* of a learner, a *post-assessment* can be conducted in the 'Part 3 – Safety Exercises' activity. There is an after-post-assessment rule in the activity stating *"If [4 or less children are satisfied], then [conduct Post-assessment], else [set the activity 'Satisfied']"*, and each child activity of 'Part 3 – Safety Exercises' is designed to conduct a post assessment. If the assessment results are satisfactory in four or less child activities, a post-assessment is presented to the learner. Otherwise, the parent activity will be set to 'Satisfied'.

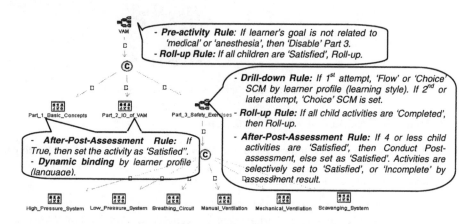

Fig. 5. Condition/Action Rules and Dynamic Binding Defined in 'VAM' Instruction CLO

(6) A learner is required to *re-take* the instruction of components (activities) that he/she has *failed*. If a learner takes the optional assessment in 'Part 3 – Safety Exercises' activity discussed in (5), the assessment result is analyzed to identify the parts (components) of VAM that the learner should focus on. By referring to the status of learning objectives that are set by the assessment result, the system can figure out the components where the learner has difficulties. An after-post-assessment rule in 'Part 3 – Safety Exercises' sets the status of its child activities as 'Incomplete' for the unsatisfactory parts, and as 'Satisfied' otherwise. When the learner re-takes the 'Part 3 – Safety Exercises', the status of the activities (Attempted or Satisfied) are shown to the learner so that he/she would know which activities to take in order to complete and satisfy the CLO. The rules that facilitate the dynamic execution of 'VAM' CLO are shown in Figure 5.

5 Summary

In this work, we have applied the developed technologies (i.e., learning object models, authoring tools, Web-service infrastructure, e-learning service system, and event-driven, rule-based execution of learning processes) to modularize the Web-based Virtual Anesthesia Machine and make the instructional materials of its components reusable for instructing other simulation systems that made use of these components. We have also demonstrated that the event-driven, rule-based execution of a learning process, which models the VAM instruction as a composite learning object, can make the instruction delivery and assessment active, customizable, flexible and adaptive.

References

1. Dalley, P., Robinson, B., Weller, J., and Caldwell, C., The Use of High-Fidelity Human Patient Simulation and the Introduction of New Anesthesia Delivery Systems, *Anesthesia and analgesia*, 99:1737–1741 (2004).
2. Reason, J., Human error: models and management. *BMJ*, 320:768–770 (2000).
3. Weinger, M., Anesthesia equipment and human error. *Journal of clinical monitoring*, 15:319–323 (1999).
4. Williamson, J., Webb, R., Sellen A, et al., Human failure: an analysis of 2000 incident reports, Anaesthesia and intensive care, 21:678–683 (1993).
5. Lampotang S, Lizdas D. E., Gravenstein N, and Liem E. B.: Transparent reality, a simulation based on interactive dynamic graphical models emphasizing visualization. Educational Technology. In press.
6. Virtual Anesthesia Machine: Teaching without Risk, *UniSci* (January 28, 2002); http://unisci.com/stories/20021/0128025.htm
7. Clark, R., Four Architectures of Instruction, *Performance Improvement*, 39(10), 31-37 (2000).
8. Dosch, M., The Anesthesia Gas machine (2004); http://www.udmercy.edu/crna/agm/index.htm
9. Anesthesia Information from the College of Veterinary Medicine, Washington State University (2004); http://www.vetmed.wsu.edu/depts-anesthesia/equipment/equipment.html
10. Gas Man (2004); http://www.gasmanweb.com.
11. Advanced Distributed Learning, Sharable Content Object Reference Model (SCORM) 1.3: Sequencing and Navigation (2004); http://ADLNet.org
12. 12 Termaat, B., Crowley, R., Agua, B., Tabor, M., McGough, B., Darling, S., et.al, Reusable Learning Object Strategy: Designing and Developing Learning Objects for Multiple Learning Approaches (2004); http://business.cisco.com/servletwl3/FileDownloader/iqprd/104108/104108_kbns.pdf
13. Advanced Distributed Learning, Sharable Content Object Reference Model (SCORM): The SCORM Content Aggregation Model (2004); http://ADLNet.org
14. Lee, G., Zhang, X., and Su, S.Y.W, Learning Object Models, Authoring Tools, and Learning Object Registry Service for Achieving Dynamic and Collaborative E-Learning, *Proceedings of the 7th IASTED International Conference on Computers and Advanced Technology in Education*, 321-327 (2004).
15. Johnson, L. F., Elusive Vision: Challenges Impending the Learning Object Economy, New Media Consortium, Macromedia® white paper (2003).
16. Lee, G., and Su, S.Y.W, Learning Object Models and E-learning Service Infrastructure for Virtual e-Learning Communities, *Lecture Notes in Computer Science 3143: Advances in Web-based Learning – ICWL 2004 – Third International Conference*, 371-378 (2004).
17. Barritt, C., Using Learning Objects in Four Instructional Architectures, *ISPI Networker*, 18(7), (2002); http://www.svispi.org/networker/2002/0702a1.htm.

Time – Space Trade-Offs in Scaling up RDF Schema Reasoning

Heiner Stuckenschmidt[1] and Jeen Broekstra[2]

[1] Vrije Universiteit Amsterdam
[2] Aduna, Amerfoort

Abstract. A common way of reducing run time complexity of RDF Schema reasoning is to compute (parts of) the deductive closure of a model offline. This reduces the complexity at run time, but increases the space requirements and model maintenance because derivable facts have to be stored explicitly and checked for validity when the model is updated. In this paper we experimentally identify certain kinds of statements as the major sources for the increase. Based on this observation, we develop a new approach for RDF reasoning that only computes a small part of the implied statements offline thereby reducing space requirements, upload time and maintenance overhead. The computed fragment is chosen in such a way that the problem of inferring implied statements at run time can be reduced to a simple form of query re-writing. This new methods has two benefits: it reduces the amount of storage space needed and it allows to perform online reasoning without using a dedicated inference engine.

A common way of reducing run time complexity of RDF Schema reasoning is to compute (parts of) the deductive closure of a model offline using the deduction rules specified in the RDF Semantics Specification [6] and work on the expanded model at query time. Most implementations of RDF reasoning use existing approaches like the RETE algorithm [3] that have originally been invented for Deductive Databases and Rule-based Expert systems. Obviously there is a trade-off between run-time complexity and the amount of space needed to store the deductive closure. In the first part of this paper we analyze these space requirements of computing the deductive closure using a number of large real-life RDF models and compare it to the minimal space needed for storing the model. We argue that the fact that existing algorithms for offline closure computation work quite well is mainly a consequence of the fact that the scenarios in which they were applied are still far away from the vision of Semantic Web reasoning as they work on a relatively small amount of centrally stored data. In a recent study Guo et al. revealed the limitations of current systems with respect to handling large amounts of data both in terms of upload and query time [4]. Another serious problem of closure computation is the need to recheck the validity of derived statements when the model is changed. This revision process is known to be very expensive in theory and in practice [2]. In the paper, we propose a novel strategy for RDF reasoning that combines offline computation based on an extensional semantics for RDF schema with a simple

M. Dean et al. (Eds.): WISE 2005 Workshops, LNCS 3807, pp. 172–181, 2005.

form of online reasoning. We evaluate our method with respect to space requirements and run-time behavior. The paper is organized as follows. In section 1 we briefly recall the foundations of RDF reasoning based on [5] focussing on a proof system for RDF schema as well as the notion of closure and reduction. In section 1.1 we compare the space complexity of closure and reduction for some real-life models and discuss the closure computation approach. In section 2 we introduce a new reasoning strategy for RDF schema and show its completeness and correctness. In section 3, we report the result of experiments with applying the approach to the data used in section 1.1. We close with a discussion of general space-time trade-offs and the specific characteristics of the proposed method.

1   Analysis of Space Requirements

RDF models can be seen as a set of statements or as the graph induced by these statements. RDF schema models are RDF models where a subset of the triples use a designated vocabulary with a special meaning defined in the RDF Semantics Specification. The special meaning allows us to derive new statements. In the following, we briefly describe a proof system for RDF schema that has been proposed by [5].

The RDF semantics specification [6] does not only provide a model theoretic semantics for RDF and RDF schema, but also provides and alternative specification of the semantic in terms of a deduction system. The deduction system consists of the set of axioms about the nature of RDF and RDF schema statements and a set of inference rules that can be used to derive new statements from existing ones. We list these deduction rules below[1], because we extensively refer to individual rules throughout the paper. For the set of axioms, we refer to the specification.

$$\frac{(X \ A \ Y)}{(A \ \text{type Property})} \tag{1}$$

$$\frac{(A \ \text{domain} \ X), (U \ A \ Y)}{(U \ \text{type} \ X)} \tag{2}$$

$$\frac{(A \ \text{range} X), (Y \ A \ V)}{(V \ \text{type} \ X)} \tag{3}$$

$$\frac{(U \ A \ B)}{(U \ \text{type Resource})}$$

$$\frac{(B \ A \ U)}{(U \ \text{type Resource})} \tag{4}$$

$$\frac{(U \ \text{subPropertyOf} \ V), (V \ \text{subPropertyOf} \ X)}{(U \ \text{subPropertyOf} \ X)} \tag{5}$$

$$\frac{(U \ \text{type Property})}{(U \ \text{subPropertyOf} \ U)} \tag{6}$$

$$\frac{(A \ \text{subPropertyOf} \ B), (U \ A \ Y)}{(U \ B \ Y)} \tag{7}$$

$$\frac{(U \ \text{type Class})}{(U \text{subClassOf Resource})} \tag{8}$$

---

[1] We deliberately omit rules concerned with the treatment of literals. All results in this paper are also valid if we include them.

$$\frac{(U \texttt{ subClassOf } X), (V \texttt{ type } U)}{(V \texttt{ type } X)} \tag{9}$$

$$\frac{(U \texttt{ type Class})}{(U \texttt{ subClassOf } U)} \tag{10}$$

$$\frac{(U \texttt{ subClassOf } V), (V \texttt{ subClassOf } X)}{(U \texttt{ subClassOf } X)} \tag{11}$$

$$\frac{(U \texttt{ type ContainermembershipPoperty})}{(U \texttt{ subPropertyOf member})} \tag{12}$$

$$\frac{(U \texttt{ type Datatype})}{(U \texttt{ subClassOf Literal})} \tag{13}$$

The semantics specification also provides a proof that the proof system corresponds to the model-theoretic semantics in the sense that the set of all statements that can be derived by iteratively applying the deduction rules are exactly those statements that follow from the model-theoretic semantics. Given an RDF model, we can compute the closure using the proof system by recursively applying rules 1 to 13 until no rule can be applied.

1.1   Experiments

In order to be able to better judge the impact of closure computation in terms space requirements compared to the minimal and the actual representation of a model, we performed a number of experiments with real life data. We used the Sesame system [1] for performing a number of reasoning experiments on realistic data sets. The system uses a forward chaining strategy that is applied when RDF data is uploaded [2]. Besides using the standard rule set mentioned above, the system can also perform reasoning using different sets of inference rules specified in a specific format. We use this feature later to implement an alternative reasoning approach.

Table 1. Increase of statements (factor)

	type	subClassOf	overall
CIA Fact Book	11.03	6.67	1.15
TAP KB	5.19	5.27	2.24
Teknowlegde	2.71	4.86	2.47
Wordnet	2.78	7.73	2.66
Average	6.13	6.6	2.18

Not surprisingly the differences in the extent of the available schema has a major impact on the distribution of types of statements in the closure. We see that for the first two models that do not contain extensive schema information, the kind of statements that increase are the type statements. For the models with a richer schema, the main increase can be observed in the amount of subclass relations. Table 1 summarizes the degree of increase for these types of statements. We see that while the average increase of the model is by a factor of 2.18, the average increase of type statements is 6.13, the one for subclass statements is 6.6.

Looking at the use of the different inference rules, we see that the extent of the schema information has a significant impact on the kinds of rules that are used to derive new statements. For the first two data sets, we see that almost only rules that derive type statements are applied. In particular, these are rules 2, 3, 4 and 9. In the presence of richer schema information like in the case of the latter two models, much more rules become relevant in closure computation. We can see that rules 2,3 and 9 still play a role. In addition, rules that derive subclass statements become important. In particular rules 7,8,10 and 11 play a significant role in computing the closure.

Coming back to our questions of how we can reduce the space requirements while still allowing for efficient schema-aware querying at runtime, we can draw a number of conclusions from the results of the experiments. The main conclusion is that type and subclass relations offer the greatest potential for reducing the size of the model to be stored if they are not computed offline, but are derived at runtime. This can be done by excluding the corresponding rules that we identified in the second part of the experiment from the offline computation step.

Considering the nature of the different relations, we argue that only excluding type statements from the closure is the best approach for achieving our goals. The reason for this is the following:

1. The type relation shows a significant increase in all models, regardless of whether the model has an extensive schema or not.
2. Computing the transitive closure of the subclass hierarchy is a major part of closure computation as the derivation of other statements, in particular type statements relies on it. We can assume that deriving type statements can be done with almost no overhead if the closure of the subclass relation has already been computed.
3. As updating the closure in the face of changing information is a major bottleneck of the approach, it is preferable to exclude information from the stored closure that is likely to change. In the case of RDF, it is clear that the schema part of a model is more stable than the instance information. Therefore the set of type statements will change more often than the set of subclass statements when instances are added or deleted.

In summary, we conclude that excluding redundant type statements - type statements that can be inferred from the original model using the deduction system in section 1 and to compute them at query time. This goal can be achieved by delaying the application of the corresponding inference (in particular rules 2,3, 4 and 9) and performing reasoning at run time instead.

2   Schema Closure: A Novel Approach

In this section, we provide details of the approach sketched at the end of the previous section. In particular, we define a set of deduction rules for inferring only schema statements off-line. Further, we present an algorithm for schema aware query answering that is based on query rewriting techniques for answering queries about facts that are not contained in the explicit statements.

2.1   A Proof System for Schema Closure

The goal of the proof system is to infer all derivable statements from an RDF model except for implicit type statements. For this purpose we include all rules that do not

create new type statements. These are rules 5,6,8,10,11,12 and 13. Just using this reduced set of rules is problematic, because some rules of this set have type statements in
the rule body (rules 6, 8, 10, 12 and 13). This means that we will also lose inferences
at the schema level if we just omit the other rules. Instead we take an approach, where
we restrict the application of general type inference rules to cases where they compute
certain type statements that are potentially input to other rules.

We have to pay special attention to rule 7, because it potentially derives any kind of
statement. There are different options of dealing with this situation:

- We can include rule 7 into the set of rules for off-line computation. This guarantees
  that we do not miss any schema statements, but also means that we might compute
  some undesired type relations.

- We can restrict the use of rule 7 to cases where the derived statements is a potential input for one of the other rules. This guarantees that we do not generate any
  unwanted statements in the off-line phase, but it also means that we might miss
  statements about non-schema elements.

In our approach we decided to chose the first option. This leads to slightly larger models,
but reduces the complexity of online reasoning. The reason for choosing to include rule
7 is that in many cases, it does not play a significant role in the closure computation and
will therefore not lead to a major increase in the model size.

Rule Instantiation. We restrict the general type inference rules by replacing them with
a set of instantiated rules. In these rules, some of the variables have been replaced by
the names of schema elements.

Rule 1: For the case of rule 1 this is not necessary, because it only compute type
statements with respect to the class 'Property'. As these statements are input to rule 6,
we leave rule 1 unchanged.

Rule 2: This rule compute general type statements based on a combination of domain definitions. We instantiate the variable X by schema elements that occur in the
bodies of other inference rules, in particular `Class`, `Property`, `Datatype` and
`ContainerMembershipProperty`. This leads to a set of four rules that replace
rule 2 in the proof system:

$$\frac{(A \text{ domain Class}),(U\ A\ Y)}{(U \text{ type Class})}$$

$$\frac{(A \text{ domain Property}),(U\ A\ Y)}{(U \text{ type Property})}$$

$$\frac{(A \text{ domain Datatype}),(U\ A\ Y)}{(U \text{ type Datatype})}$$

$$\frac{(A \text{ domain ContainerMembershipProperty}),(U\ A\ Y)}{(U \text{ type ContainerMembershipProperty})} \tag{14}$$

Rule 3: This rule is equivalent to rule 2 except that it uses range definitions for
inferring general type statements. Consequently, we instantiate rule 3 in the same way
as rule 2. This leads to a set of four rules that replace rule 3 in our proof system:

$$\frac{(A \text{ range Class}),(Y \ A \ V)}{(V \text{ type Class})}$$

$$\frac{(A \text{ range Property}),(Y \ A \ V)}{(V \text{ type Property})}$$

$$\frac{(A \text{ range Datatype}),(Y \ A \ V)}{(V \text{ type Datatype})}$$

$$\frac{(A \text{ range ContainerMembershipProperty}),(Y \ A \ V)}{(V \text{ type ContainerMembershipProperty})} \tag{15}$$

Rule(s) 4: These rule is somewhat trivial as it only creates statements indicating that the subject and the object of a statement are of type resource. As these statements are not further used in any rule we omit these rules.

Rule 9: This rule computes new type relations based on existing ones and information about subclasses. We can restrict it to schema elements by instantiating it in the same way as rule 2 and 3. We replace rule 9 by the following set of instantiated deduction rules:

$$\frac{(U \text{ subClassOf Class}),(V \text{ type } U)}{(V \text{ type Class})}$$

$$\frac{(U \text{ subClassOf Property}),(V \text{ type } U)}{(V \text{ type Property})}$$

$$\frac{(U \text{ subClassOf Datatype}),(V \text{ type } U)}{(V \text{ type Datatype})}$$

$$\frac{(U \text{ subClassOf ContainerMembershipProperty}),(V \text{ type } U)}{(V \text{ type ContainerMembershipProperty})} \tag{16}$$

Schema Closure. The modifications to the original set of inference rules described above provides us with a proof system that defines a subset of the closure of a model that that contains the complete schema information but only a subset of the instance data. We denote this subset as 'schema closure' and formally define it in the following way:

Definition 1. *Let S be a deduction system consisting of rules 1, 5-8, 10-13, 14-16. The schema closure of a model G is the maximal model G' such that $G \vdash_S G'$. We denote the schema closure of an RDF graph as sc(G).*

As the schema closure is created by applying a rule set that contains a subset of the original inference rules or refinements of original rules the resulting set of statements is a subset of the complete closure and a superset of the statements explicitly contained in the model. Our previous experiments suggested that computing the schema closure offline and storing it instead of the original model and using online reasoning to bridge the gap between schema closure and closure of a model constitutes a near-optimal trade-off between space requirements for storing the model and time complexity of computing the closure. Before we test this claim in a second set of experiments, we draw our attention to the online-reasoning part.

2.2   Online Reasoning by Query Rewriting

The price of reducing the size of the model to store is that we still have to perform parts of the reasoning online. It turns out however, that the way we determined the statements

to be pre-computed allows us to simply expand queries posed against the schema closure by replacing those parts of the query that ask for instance level statements by a
more complex query expression (of a fixed size !) that involves some schema elements.
This means that we do not need an inference engine to provide schema-aware querying
support as the same functionality can be achieved by a query-preprocessor expanding
the query and sending it on to any RDF query engine. In the following, we describe the
query expansion strategy and show that it is correct and complete.

Query Rewriting. We assume a query language that uses sets of triple patterns to define the subset of the RDF model to be selected. This assumption does not limit our
approach as many widely used RDF query languages such as RDQL and SeRQL are
based on this paradigm. In order to completely answer queries in such a language, we
have to provide special mechanisms for triple patterns that contain a type relation. These
patterns potentially match statements that were not included in the schema closure but
can be derived using the RDF semantics. The fact that the schema closure contains all
schema related statements, we can use special view definitions to replace these patterns
by extended ones that used compiled schema information to also capture implicit statements. We use special kinds of view definitions where the head is a single triple pattern
and the body is a set of triple patterns. When rewriting a query, we use these view definitions to replace triple patterns that correspond to the head of a view by the set of
patterns in its body.

Let us first consider view definition for substituting type statements. The first view
definitions we use is a direct counterpart of rules 4a and 4b.

$$(S \text{ type Resource}) \leftarrow \{(S \ X \ Y)\} \qquad (17)$$

$$(S \text{ type Resource}) \leftarrow \{(X \ Y \ S)\} \qquad (18)$$

The second view definition is a counterpart of rule 9. The difference to the direct use
of the rule is the fact that the model we are querying is known to explicitly contain all
subclass statements. This means that no further reasoning about the subclass hierarchy is
required. The query will directly return all statements that can be inferred using rule 9.

$$(S \text{ type } O) \leftarrow \{(O \text{ subClassOf } X),$$
$$(S \text{ type } X)\} \qquad (19)$$

The most complex way of inferring type statements is in terms of a combination of
subclass, subproperty and domain restrictions. Before being able to use rule 2 to infer
that r1 is of type E, we first have to derive $(P \text{ subPropertyOf } R)$ in order to be able
to apply rule 7. Afterwards, we have to derive $(C \text{ subClassOf } E)$ in order to establish
the goal using rule 9. These intermediate facts, however, are already contained in the
schema closure. We can use this fact to define the following view that explicitly contains
the three statements necessary to establish the type relation.

$$(S \text{ type } E) \leftarrow \{(C \text{ subClassOf } E),$$
$$(P \text{ subPropertyOf } R),$$
$$(R \text{ domain } C),$$
$$(S \ P \ X)\} \qquad (20)$$

Note that this view definition is general enough to also capture the cases where the subclass and/or the subproperty relation does not have to be inferred but are contained in the model. This case is covered, because the schema closure also contains the statements defining each class to be a subclass of itself and every property to be a subproperty of itself (compare rules 5 and 10).

We can use the same idea to define a view definition that covers the derivation of type statements using a combination of subclass, subproperty and range statements.

$$(S \ \texttt{type} \ E) \leftarrow \{(C \ \texttt{subClassOf} \ E),$$
$$(P \ \texttt{subPropertyOf} \ R),$$
$$(R \ \texttt{range} \ C),$$
$$(X \ P \ S)\} \qquad\qquad (21)$$

The online reasoning part now consists of replacing triple pattern that contain a type statement by the union of all possible re-writings of the respective pattern shown in equations 17 to 21 and evaluating it over the schema closure of the model.

3 Experiments

The primary aim of our approach is to reduce the amount of data that has to be stored explicitly. By doing this we do not only hope to reduce the memory consumption but also to reduce upload and revision time for RDF schema models. A secondary goal is to allow online query processing without a dedicated rule engine. In order to test the first goal, we carried out a second set of experiments using the Lehigh university benchmark [4]. This benchmark consists of a fixed schema about universities including aspects like departments, employees and courses. Further, the benchmark has a statement generator that can be used to randomly produce instance data of arbitrary size. For our experiments, we created data for eight universities with an overall size of about one million statements. In the experiments we uploaded this data to two versions of the Sesame system. The first version used the build-in inference engine that computes the complete closure of the model using the rule set shown at the beginning of the paper. In the second version, we implemented the rule set for computing the schema closure using Sesames custom inferencer. Both experiments were carried out on a PC with an AMD Athlon 64 3000+ processor with a 2 Ghz CPU and 1 GB ram 512 MB of which were reserved as a heap for java process. We used Java 2 version 1.4.2 and Sesame 1.1-RC2 with MySQL 4.0.21nt as a physical storage. The results from the experiments are discussed in the following.

The first aspect we looked at is the size of the model in terms of number of statements. In particular, we were interested in the relation between the number of additional statements in the closure and in the schema closure as well as the relation to the overall size of the model. Figure 1a shows the number of statements added. The experiment shows that the use of the schema closure instead of the full closure leads to significant reduction of the number of statements added. In the case of the full closure the number of statements added is more than 40% of the number of explicit statements. In this case it means that we have to deal with almost half a million additional statements. For the schema closure, the number of statements added is less than 5% of the number

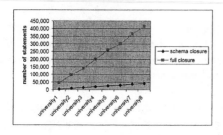 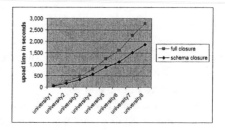

(a) Growth of inferred statements   (b) Upload time for the models

Fig. 1. Use of Inference Rules

of original statements. This difference is quite significant as it amounts to a ration of
1:10 when comparing the size of the different closures. We also analyzed the impact of
the reduced number of statements on the upload time for the model. The question was,
whether the computation of the schema closure instead of the full closure significantly
reduces upload time. Figure 1b shows the results of this experiment. We can see that
the reduction in the size of the model also leads to a reduced upload time. In the case
of larger models like the one used in the experiment, the difference is significant. In the
experiment shown, an upload of the model with full closure computation took about 45
minutes whereas the upload of the model with a schema closure computation only took
about 30 minutes. This is a reduction of the upload time of more than 30%.

We can expect that the reduction of the size of the closure has a similar effect on
other management task. In particular, this will hold for the update of an RDF model
which currently is a very expensive task, because for each inferred statement we have
to check whether it is still supported by the ground facts. We also compared the results
of querying the closure and using the method proposed here. We were able to show that
the method actually delivers the same results.

4 Discussion

We presented an approach for RDF schema reasoning to support schema aware query
answering that combines partial offline closure computation with view based query
rewriting. The approach has the same advantage as a complete offline schema computation in the sense that an RDF query engine can be used to compute answers without
further reasoning. On the other hand, the reduction of the closure to a subset of the
complete closure reduces space requirements and upload time which is particularly significant when working with very large models. We expect similar improvements for
other time consuming tasks such as the update of a model. For smaller models of computing the complete closure is still a valid approach. We implemented and tested our
method on a benchmark dataset using the Sesame system.

In contrast to other rewriting-based approaches like [8], we cover the complete RDF
semantics by pre-computing the transitive closure of hierarchical relations. This pre-
compilation is also provided for example by the SWI semantic web library [9], but they
do not provide methods for completing the closure in the online reasoning step. Both
methods have problems in dealing with domain and range restrictions.

References

1. J. Broekstra, A. Kampman, and F. van Harmelen. Sesame: A generic architecture for storing and querying rdf and rdf schema. In *The Semantic Web – ISWC 2002* [7], pages 54–68.
2. Jeen Broekstra and Arjohn Kampman. Inferencing and truth maintenance in rdf schema: exploring a naive practical approach. In *Workshop on Practical and Scalable Semantic Systems (PSSS) at the Second International Semantic Web Conference (ISWC)*, Sanibel Island, Florida,, October 2003.
3. C.L. Forgy. A fast algorithm for the many pattern / many object pattern match problem. *Artificial Intelligence*, 19:17–37, 1982.
4. Yuanbo Guo, Zhengxiang Pan, and Jeff Heflin. An evaluation of knowledge base systems for large owl datasets. In D. Plexousakis, S. McIlraith, and F. van Harmelen, editors, *Proceedings of the 3rd International Semantic Web Conference (ISWC)*, Lecture Notes in Computer Science. Springer, 2004.
5. C. Gutierrez, C. Hurtado, and A. O. Mendelzon. Foundations of semantic web databases. In *ACM Symposium on Principles of Database Systems (PODS)*, Paris, France, June 2004.
6. Patrick Hayes. Rdf semantics. Recommendation, W3C, 10 February 2004 2004.
7. I. Horrocks and J. Hendler. *The Semantic Web - ISWC 2002*, volume 2342 of *Lecture Notes in Computer Science*. Springer, 2002.
8. Ora Lassila. Taking the rdf model theory out for a spin. In *The Semantic Web - ISWC 2002* [7], pages 307–317.
9. Jan Wielemaker, Guus Schreiber, and Bob Wielinga. Prolog-based infrastructure for rdf: Scalability and performance. In Dieter Fensel, Katia Sycara, and John Mylopoulos, editors, *The SemanticWeb - ISWC 2003, Second International SemanticWeb Conference*, volume 2870 of *Lecture Notes in Computer Science*, pages 644 – 658, 2003.

OWLIM – A Pragmatic Semantic Repository for OWL

Atanas Kiryakov, Damyan Ognyanov, and Dimitar Manov

Ontotext Lab, Sirma Group Corp.,
135 Tsarigradsko Chaussee, Sofia 1784, Bulgaria
{naso, damyan, mitac}@sirma.bg
http://www.ontotext.com

Abstract. OWLIM is a high-performance Storage and Inference Layer (SAIL) for Sesame, which performs OWL DLP reasoning, based on forward-chaining of entilement rules. The reasoning and query evaluation are performed in-memory, while in the same time OWLIM provides a reliable persistence, based on N-Triples files. This paper presents OWLIM, together with an evaluation of its scalability over synthetic, but realistic, dataset encoded with respect to PROTON ontology. The experiment demonstrates that OWLIM can scale to millions of statements even on commodity desktop hardware. On an almost-entry-level server, OWLIM can manage a knowledge base of 10 million explicit statements, which are extended to about 19 millions after forward chaining. The upload and storage speed is about 3,000 statement/sec. at the maximal size of the repository, but it starts at more than 18,000 (for a small repository) and slows down smoothly. As it can be expected for such an inference strategy, delete operations are expensive, taking as much as few minutes. In the same time, a variety of queries can be evaluated within milliseconds. The experiment shows that such reasoners can be efficient for very big knowledge bases, in scenarios when delete operations should not be handled in real-time.

1 Introduction

The Semantic Web requires scalable high-performance storage and reasoning infra-structure in order to mach the expectations for a hype of ontologies and structured metadata. The major challenge towards building such infrastructure is the expressivity of the underlying standards: RDF(S), [6], and OWL, [2]. Although RDF(S) is a simple Knowledge Representation (KR) language, it is already a challenging task to implement a repository for it, which provides performance and scalability comparable even to entry-level relational database management systems (RDBMS). Going up the stairs of the Semantic Web stack, the challenges for the repository engineers are getting more and more serious. Even the simplest dialect of OWL (Lite) is a description logic (DL) with no obvious algorithms allowing for efficient inference and query answering over reasonably scaled knowledge bases (KB).

Logical programming (LP) is a common name used for rule-based logical dialects and systems, such as PROLOG, Datalog, and Flora. OWL DLP is emerging as a new dialect, offering a promising compromise between expressive power, efficient reasoning, and compatibility. It is defined in [3] as the intersection of the expressivity of OWL DL and LP, which is more clearly layered on top of RDFS.

M. Dean et al. (Eds.): WISE 2005 Workshops, LNCS 3807, pp. 182–192, 2005.

The two principle strategies for rule-based inference are, as follows:

- **Forward-chaining**: to start from the known facts and to perform inference in an inductive fashion. The goals could be different: to answer a particular query; to infer a particular sort of knowledge (e.g. the class taxonomy).
- **Backward-chaining:** to start from a particular fact or a query and to verify it or get all possible results, using deductive reasoning. In essence, the reasoner decomposes the query or the fact into alternative or simpler facts, which are available in the KB or can be further, recursively, transformed.

Let us imagine a repository, which performs total forward-chaining; after each update to the KB, the *inferred closure*[1] is computed and made available for query evaluation or retrieval. This strategy is known as *materialization*. The advantages and disadvantages of this approach are discussed at length in [1].

This paper presents the implementation of OWLIM – a semantic repository, based on full materialization, providing support for a fraction of OWL, close to OWL DLP. We present a benchmark for examining the performance of the repository, report the results, and discuss the advantages and disadvantages of the approach taken.

Section 2 presents OWLIM with its specifics, optimizations, and limitations. Section 3 presents the ontology and the dataset that we use as a basis for the benchmark, described in section 4. The fifth section presents the results from the experiment; section 6 comments on related work and section 7 concludes the paper.

2   OWLIM

OWLIM is the short name of the `OWLMemSchemaRepository` SAIL (Storage and Inference Layer) for Sesame[2], which supports partial reasoning over OWL DLP. It is an in-memory reasoning implementation; the latter means that the full content of the repository is loaded and maintained in the main memory, which allows for efficient retrieval and query answering. Although the reasoning is handled in-memory, this SAIL offers a relatively comprehensive persistency and backup strategy.

Technically, OWLIM v.2.0 is an extension of the `RdfSchemaRepository` SAIL of Sesame v.1.2.1. Thus, the results reported represent an evaluation of a tuning of Sesame and can be considered indicative for its robustness. More information related to various aspects of its specification, architecture, and implementations can be found in [1]. The modifications in OWLIM can be summarized as follows:

- The set of entilement rules supports some OWL primitives (see section 0);
- Concurrent multi-thread inference: it delivers serious improvements of the inference speed for machines with multiple processors or Hyper-Threading;
- The persistence implementation is derived from `RdfSchemaRepositoryV2` (underlying OWLIM v.1.0). It was further optimized, as a serious performance bottleneck in the file operations was removed.

---

[1] "Inferred closure" is the extension of a KB with all the facts which could be inferred from it.
[2] One of the most popular Semantic Web repositories, http://www.openrdf.org, [1].

- Optimizations speeding-up the delete operation – a number of improvements were made to the implementation of `RdfSchemaRepository`.

Along with the SAIL, the distribution of OWLIM also contains a custom RMI factory, which allows the remote access to the SAIL layer. OWLIM, together with its documentation can be downloaded from http://www.ontotext.com/owlim.

2.1 Reasoning and Language Support

OWLIM uses for reasoning the in-memory rule entilement engine of `RdfSchemaRepository`. The engine can be configured with a set of inference rules, which determines the supported semantic. Each rule has a set of premises, which conjunctively define the body of the rule. The premises are RDF statements, which can contain free variables. The rule head contains one or more consequences, each of which is an RDF statement, without free variables, not already introduced in the body.

As a basis, `RdfSchemaRepository` is configured with a set of rules which cover the model-theoretic semantics of RDFS, as defined in [5]. More details about the implementation and motivation can be found in [1]. OWLIM extends these rules with a set, which support the following OWL constructs: `SymmetricProperty`, `TransitiveProperty`, `inverseOf`, `equivalentProperty`, `sameAs`, `FunctionalProperty`, `InverseFunctionalProperty`. The full list of the axioms can be found in the OWLIM documentation.

We are currently investigating the extension of the set of rules to make possible full support of OWL DLP. Extensions towards more expressive LP fragments are straightforward, taking the rule-based inference engine used.

2.2 Persistence

The persistency of OWLIM is implemented through N-Triples files. The repository can be spread into several files. All but one of these files are considered read-only; there is a single file (let us name it `persist`) that is considered both an input for loading and a target, where new statements are stored.

The backup strategy implemented, ensures that no loss of newly asserted triples can occur in cases of power failure or abnormal termination – the detailed description is presented in OWLIM's documentation. Although relatively simple, this strategy had proven to be very efficient and reliable, through the couple of years for which `RdfSchemaRepositoryV2` and OWLIM has been used as a semantic repository for different applications of the KIM platform, http://www.ontotext.com/kim.

2.3 Limitations

The limitations of OWLIM are related to its reasoning strategy. In general, the expressivity of the language supported cannot be extended in the direction of DL. The rule-engine behind OWLIM is limited in expressivity by the Horn logic.

The "total materialization" strategy has its obvious drawbacks, as discussed in [1] (section 6). For specific ontologies and KBs, the count of the implicit statements can appear to grow rapidly[3]. What is even more important, the delete operation is really slow, which means that OWLIM is not suitable for applications where removal of data is a typical transaction.

The most obvious disadvantage of the in-memory reasoning is that the size of the KB, which can be handled, is limited by the size of the available RAM. Considering the currently available commodity hardware, OWLIM can handle millions of statements on desktop machines and above ten millions on an almost-entry-level server.

3 Ontology and Dataset

We took the PROTON light-weight upper-level ontology as a basis for our experiment. It contains about 300 classes and 100 properties, providing coverage of the general concepts necessary for a wide range of tasks, with special focus on named entities and concrete domains (i.e. people, organizations, locations, numbers, dates, addresses). The ontology is encoded in a fragment of OWL DLP. It is split into four modules: System, Top, Upper, and KM. The PROTON ontology itself and related documents can be found at http://proton.semanticweb.org.

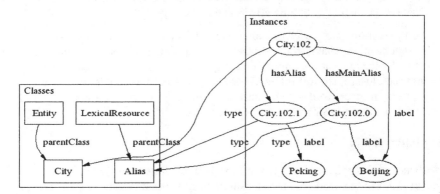

Fig. 1. Sample Representation of an Entity Description

PROTON is also heavily used within the KIM platform. As a start, part of KIM is the so-called World Knowledge Base (WKB), which consist of thousands of entity (instance) descriptions. Each entity is described by its most specific type, aliases, attributes (e.g. the latitude of a Location), and relations (e.g. subRegionOf of another Location). A simplified schema of the entity representation is demonstrated in Fig. 1. WKB is populated with entities of general importance, which serve as a seed for KIM to perform automatic semantic annotation of text and ontology population. The full variant of WKB consists of more than 200,000 entities, which have been gathered semi-automatically out of a big number of publicly available datasources. The small variant of WKB, which is used here, contains about 40,000

---

[3] Still, for many real-live scenarios the amount of implicit statements is comparable to this of the explicit ones – for instance KIM and the examples available in section 6 of [1].

entities, of which about 8,000 organizations (mostly big companies, with their industry codes, associated through the `activeInSector` property); 6,000 persons;
12,000 locations, including continents, global regions, and countries with their provinces, 4,400 cities, oceans, seas, etc. Each location has geographic coordinates and
several aliases (including different language variants), as well as co-positioning relations (e.g. `subRegionOf`). More information about the compilation of WKB and its
usage in KIM can be found at http://www.ontotext.com/kim/docs.html.

4   Benchmark Organization

The experiment loads initially non-synthetic ontology and instance data. Then it starts
uploading more quasi-real knowledge in transactions of about 10,000 statements each.
Upload transactions are performed until either the target upload transactions count or
the memory limit is reached. After each ten uploads we measure, as follows:

- The upload speed, in terms of explicit statements per second;
- The speed for evaluation of two queries. Each of these queries is evaluated
  10 times, for the sake of accuracy. As long as OWLIM evaluates all the queries in-memory, caching effects cannot be expected.

Delete transactions are performed after each 100 upload transactions. We remove a
single statement, the one stating the label of last created city. The important point here
is that under the current implementation, any delete transaction causes invalidation of
the inferred closure, so, full inference on top of the current content of the repository
takes place. In other words, such transactions indicate the time for calculation of the
full inferred closure, over repository of the corresponding size.

4.1   Initialization

The benchmark application starts OWLIM with all following files, given as "background" knowledge, loaded in the repository during initialization:

- `owl.rdfs` – the standard OWL schema;
- `protons.owl`, `protont.owl`, `protonu.owl`, `protonkm.owl` – the
  four modules of PROTON ontology. The namespace prefixes used below
  are respectively: `psys`, `ptop`, `pupp`, `protonkm`.;
- `kimso.owl` and `kimlo.owl` – a couple of small KIM specific ontologies, defining auxiliary primitives such as `hasAlias`;
- `wkb.nt` – the small version of KIM's WKB in N-Triples format, which ac-
  counts for most of the volume of the initial repository.

After loading the above files, OWLIM is in the state in which it is used in the KIM
platform; this is to say we start with ontology and KB used in a real application. The
explicit statements in the repository are about 0.5 millions – this figure can be seen as
a starting point at the charts in section 0. The inferred closure adds about 0.5 million
statements – which means, that due to the total materialization strategy of OWLIM, it
holds at this stage about 1 million statements in memory.

4.2   Upload Transactions

Each upload transaction adds one new city and a number of other entities related to it. We created a new instance of pupp:City, which is linked as sub-region of an arbitrarily chosen province from the WKB. Due to the fact that WKB covers all the provinces (or states) for most of the countries in the world, this strategy guarantees: (i) connectivity between the real KB and the synthetically generated one; (ii) some inference takes place, at least for the closure of the transitive sub-region relation, considering that provinces are "nested" in countries, which are nested in regions and continents; and (iii) good spread of the synthetically generated cities all over the globe.

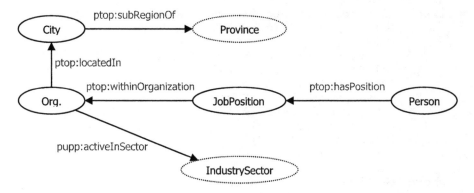

Fig. 2. Synthetic Description of City and Related Entities

Ten new organizations are created, and related to the synthetic city. The organizations are related to an arbitrarily selected industry sector from the WKB, in order to extend the connectivity of the synthetic data with the real KB. 38 new instances of ptop:Person are created and related for each organization (i.e. 380 per city) and related to it through positions. The pattern of entities created within a transaction can be seen at Fig. 2. Notice that the province and the industry sector are dashed to indicate that those are not newly created, but just randomly chosen from WKB. For each of the new entities, we generate their aliases (one of which is the main alias) and a label, in the manner depictured at Fig. 1.

The number of persons per organization is tuned so that the description of the city and its related entities consists of 10,033 statements. It turns out that the upload of a city description causes extension of the inference closure with about 9,000 implicit statements. Measuring the speed after each 10 upload transactions, means measuring the upload and storage of about 100,000 explicit statements and the inference of roughly the same amount of implicit ones.

4.3   Queries

We made two test queries, a simple and a more complex one. Both queries are encoded in SeRQL, which is a language developed for Sesame, as an improvement of RQL. A description of SeRQL can be found in section 3.5 of [1].

Query 1:

```
select   OL,CL
from    {C} rdf:type {pupp:City},
        {C} ptop:subRegionOf {wkb:Continent_T.4},
        {O} ptop:locatedIn {C},
        {O} rdf:type {ptop:Organization},
        {C} rdfs:label {CL},
        {O} rdfs:label {OL}
```

Query 2:

```
select distinct PL,OL,SL,CL
from    {S} pupp:subSectorOf {wkb:SIC_H},
        {O} pupp:activeInSector {S},
        {O} ptop:locatedIn {C},
        {C} ptop:subRegionOf {wkb:Continent_T.4},
        {O} rdf:type {pupp:City},
        {Pos} ptop:withinOrganization {O},
        {Pos} ptop:holder {Pos},
        {Per} kimso:hasAlias {A} rdfs:label {AL},
        {C} rdfs:label {CL},
        {S} rdfs:label {SL},
        {Per} rdfs:label {PL},
        {O} rdfs:label {OL}
where  AL like "*son*" ignore case
```

The first query lists all the names of organizations in Europe (identified through its URI in WKB – wkb:Continent_T.4). It involves joining of a pattern of 6 statements. The results, indicate that the transitive closure of ptop:subRegionOf has been calculated, as there were not cities declared explicitly to be part of Europe.

The second query returns the list of all people having "son" as part of one of their aliases and working for organization in Europe, which are active in sub-sector of "Finance, Insurance, And Real Estate" (identified in WKB with wkb:SIC_H). This query involves a pattern of 12 statements and a literal constraint, which does not allow for easy indexing and optimization (without a full-text search system built in). In addition to what is already checked with Query 1, the results of the second query indicate that pupp:subSectorOf is closed properly (usually, the organizations are active in a more specific sector below wkb:SIC_H). It also checks the inference of ptop:holder on the basis of its inverse property ptop:hasPosition.

The number of results returned by both queries grows proportionally to the size the repository. For instance, the number of results returned after adding 200 cities (i.e. for a repository of size 2.5 million statements) is respectively 1042 for Query 1 and 3714 for Query 2. Considering that the benchmark application fetches all the results from the repository and the cardinality of the results, this test provides also an indication for the speed of fetching results.

4.4 Test Hardware

We had measured the performance of the benchmark application on equipment of different scale and specificity, as presented in Table 1. Here follow some comments on the configurations:

- 2Opt5GB and 2Opt3GB are servers in the price range 2000-6000 EURO;
- 2Xeon1GB is a high-end workstation, PM512MB is a notebook;
- The amount of RAM indicated in the tables is the RAM given as maximum heap constraint to the Java virtual machine (JVM); all the machines have more physical memory than this.

Table 1. Hardware and software configurations for the different runs

Name	Configuration	RAM	JDK
2Opt5GB	2xOpteron 2.4GHz, DDR400, Red Hat Linux v.3	5GB	JDK 1.5 64-bit
2Opt3GB	2xOpteron 1.4GHz, DDR333, Win 2003 64-bit	3GB	JDK 1.5 64-bit
2Xeon1GB	2xXeon 2.4GHz, DDR333, Win XP	1GB	JDK 1.5 32-bit
PM512MB	Pentium M 1.6GHz, DDR266, Win XP	0.5GB	JDK 1.5 32-bit

5 Results

We present the results below in three charts, demonstrating: upload speed, query evaluation time for Query 2, and delete time. The chart of the diagram for Query 1, shows that the dependency is the same as for Query 2, but less steep, i.e. that the evaluation time grows in a similar but "slower" relation to the size of the repository.

Some of the data has been manually "polished" in order to clear distortions caused by garbage collection or known defects of the benchmark application. In all of these cases fixes were made so that (i) less than 10% of the data in each of the series were affected and (ii) the trends were respected as much as possible.

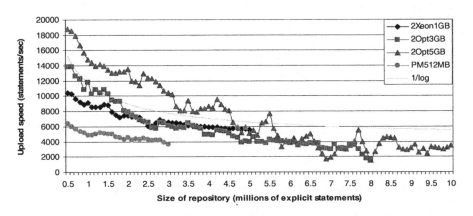

The upload speed of the fastest server starts at almost 19,000 statements/second (st/sec) and slows down to about 3,000 st/sec. Within 5GB of RAM this machine was

able to manage 10 million statements. The slowest machine starts at bit more than 6,000 st/sec and slows down to about 3,500 st/sec at 3 million statements.

The upload speed measurements needed to be smoothened, to provide clear tendencies. The chart presents the average of three consequent values in the actual series. The diagram demonstrates that the speed is falling down in reciprocal logarithmic dependency with respect to the size of the repository.

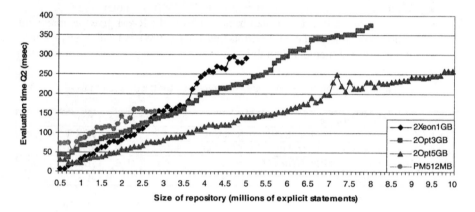

Both queries are evaluated within milliseconds. Two of the machines evaluated Query 2 for less than 30 ms with the initial size of the repository; 2Opt5GB needed ten times more (258 ms) time when the repository grew up to 10 million statements. Even the slowest machine, evaluates the complex query respectively in the range between 77 and 155 msec.

The dependency between the evaluation time and the size of the repository seems linear, which can be explained with the fact that the repository does not use any indices, which can let it behave in a more logarithmical fashion.

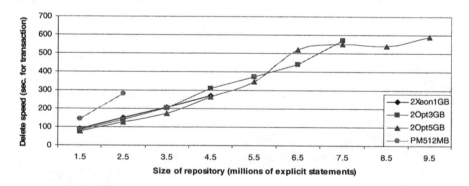

The delete operations are slow, as they perform full inference over the repository. The chart with the time necessary for completion of delete transaction demonstrates this. It takes between 77 and 144 seconds for the machines in this experiment to acomplish a delete opeation on top of a repository of size 1.5 millions statements. The time grows in an almost linear dependency to reach 10 minutes for a repository with 10 million statements.

The same performance experiments has been also conducted with a "pure", un-optimized, version of RdfSchemaRepository SAIL of Sesame v.1.2.1, which we name below Sesame-Memory. For the sake of fair comparison, the later has been extended with the persistence mechanisms of OWLIM. OWLIM v.2.0 uses the in-memory representation of Sesame, so, there were no deviations in the scalability (mostly determined by the amount of RAM available). Sesame-Memory was running on a smaller set of rules – only those for RDFS, without the OWL supporting ones in OWLIM; the inference, and the query results, of Sesame-Memory were incomplete in this test. What was compared was the speed of the inference engines. Sesame-Memory appeared 30-50% faster than OWLIM, which can be explained with the simpler set of rules. Apart from the benefit from checking fewer rules, the size of the repository was actually smaller for Sesame-Memory, because fewer implicit state-ments are generated and later on involved in further reasoning. With the growth of the repository, however, OWLIM is slow reducing the speed difference, which is an evi-dence, that the multi-threaded inference engine delivers growing improvement to the performance with the growth of the repository.

6   Related Work

For the purposes of this evaluation, we inspected two related studies. They both pro-vide interesting approaches with respect to a more comprehensive benchmarking.

SWETO, [7], is a large scale dataset for testing algorithms for discovery of seman-tic associations, developed in the LSDIS Lab, University of Georgia. The schema component of the ontology reflects the types of entities and relationships available explicitly (and implicitly) in Web sources. It is populated through knowledge extrac-tors. SWETO is intended for ontology tools benchmarking purposes; its version (1.3) is populated with well over 800,000 entities and over 1.5 million relationships. It is available as OWL files of total size about 250 MB. Overall, the SWETO dataset is similar in nature and origin to the ontologies and datasets used in this evaluation.

The Lehigh University evaluation, [4], is one of the most comprehensive bench-mark experiments published recently. It evaluates the upload and query perform-ance of 4 systems: memory-based Sesame, database-based Sesame, DLDB-OWL, and OWLJessKB. The benchmark was made with a relatively simple ontology about the organizational structure of a university and with synthetically generated datasets – for each university, a number of departments and employees with de-scriptions and relations among them were generated. The performance of the sys-tems was measured in the course of incrementally increasing the number of the universities (from 1 to 50). The smallest set is 8MB and the largest one (for 50 universities) is 583MB, described in 1000 owl files, with a total of about 6 million statements. The main conclusions are: DLDB is the best system for very large data sets where an equal emphasis is placed on query response time and completeness. Sesame-Memory is the best when the size is relatively small (e.g., 1 million triples) and only RDFS inference is required.

The evaluation reported here is very similar to the on in [4], but simpler – we evaluate a single repository with a much smaller set of queries. Note that OWLIM extends a later version what is called in [4] Sesame-Memory. Further, the evaluation there was made on a desktop machine with 512MB of RAM. Here we demonstrated that Sesame can scale much further, given server hardware. Our short-term plans include evaluation of OWLIM with respect to the Lehigh University dataset and queries, to allow for easy comparison with the results of the other systems.

7 Conclusion

This paper reported on the scalability and performance of a particular reasoning schema and implementation. We had presented OWLIM – a Sesame-based repository, which offers N-Triples persistence and supports a dialect close to OWL DLP through forward-chaining in-memory reasoning and full total materialization.

The evaluation can be summarized as follows: OWLIM can handle millions of statements on commodity hardware. The scale varies from a couple of millions on desktop machines to ten million statements on a server with few GB of RAM. The upload speed is in the range of thousands of statements/second and decreases in a sort of logarithmic dependency to the size of the repository. The delete operation is slow, but the query evaluation is very fast – even complicated queries pass in milliseconds.

We develop OWLIM in a number of directions. The applicability of the total materialization strategy should be evaluated to support more expressive languages. The rule engine can be optimized to allow for faster operation in less memory – ongoing experiments provide evidence that a ten-fold increase of the inference speed is achievable. Beyond these "gradual" improvements, we are working on a next generation repository, which should allow for efficient integration with databases and full-text search engines. We investigate strategies combining forward- and backward-chaining, without loosing the essential advantage of the inductive approaches, namely, that they allow for more straightforward RDBMS-like query optimizations.

References

1. Broekstra, J. (2005). *Storage, Querying and Inferencing for Semantic Web Languages.* Ph.D. Thesis, VU Amsterdam, ISBN 90 9019 2360. http://www.cs.vu.nl/~jbroeks/#pub
2. Dean, M; Schreiber, G. – editors; (2004). *OWL Web Ontology Language Reference.* W3C Recommendation, 10 Feb. 2004. http://www.w3.org/TR/owl-ref/
3. Grosof, B; Horrocks, I; Volz, R; Decker, St. (2003). *Description Logic Programs: Combining Logic Programs with Description Logic.* In Proc. of WWW2003, May 2003.
4. Guo, Y; Pan, Z; and Heflin, J. (2004). *An Evaluation of Knowledge Base Systems for Large OWL Datasets.* CS and Engineering Department, Lehigh University, Bethlehem, PA18015, USA, http://www.lehigh.edu/~yug2/iswc2004-benchmark.PDF
5. Hayes, P. (2004). *RDF Semantics.* W3C Recommendation, 10 February 2004. http://www.w3.org/TR/2004/REC-rdf-mt-20040210/
6. Klyne, G; Carroll, J. J. (2004). *Resource Description Framework (RDF): Concepts and Abstract Syntax.* W3C Recom. 10 Feb, 2004. http://www.w3.org/TR/rdf-concepts/
7. LSDIS and the University of Georgia. (2004). *Semantic Web Technology Evaluation Ontology (SWETO).* http://lsdis.cs.uga.edu/Projects/SemDis/sweto/

Scaling the Kowari Metastore

David Wood

MIND Laboratory,University of Maryland,
College Park, MD 20742
dwood@mindswap.org

Abstract. The Kowari Metastore is an Open Source RDF database, built with
the goal of providing large-scale storage of Resource Description Framework
(RDF) information and a means to analyze that information in near real time.
Kowari is currently the most scalable RDF database available. This paper presents a survey of options to further scale the Kowari Metastore. Options to further increase the upper bound of RDF statements which may be stored, decrease
write times, distribute computational and storage resource requirements and
improve analysis capabilities on large data sets are presented.

1 Introduction

The Kowari Metastore [12] provides a storage and analysis platform for RDF, RDFS
and OWL information.

Several systems currently exist for the storage of RDF data. These databases – often referred to as RDF stores – exist as both Open Source projects and commercial
product offerings. Since Guha's first RDF store, rdfDB [3], several other Open Source
stores have been developed. These include: Sesame [11], developed by Administrator
Nederland b.v. as part of the European IST project On-To-Knowledge; 3store [10],
developed by the University of Southampton; and Redland [2], developed by the University of Bristol. The Jena Semantic Web Framework [5], developed by Hewlett
Packard's Bristol Laboratory also provides the capability for persistent storage (thus
making it an RDF store) by utilizing a persistent backend.

Kowari is currently the most scalable of the RDF stores. The RDF stores listed
above allow for the storage of between hundreds of thousands and tens of millions of
RDF statements, whereas Kowari is currently able to store hundreds of millions of
RDF statements and query them rapidly. Figure 2 shows load times for 250 million
statements on commodity hardware, although 500 million statements is currently considered a practical limit.

Kowari was developed by Tucana Technologies, Inc from 2001-2004. A commercial product, the Tucana Knowledge Server (TKS), is based upon Kowari and has recently been purchased by Northrop Grumman Corporation. Active development of
Kowari continues as an independent Open Source project. [7]

Figure 1 shows Kowari's high-level architecture. The topmost layer provides access APIs, below which is a query engine, backed by a storage layer. The upper API

M. Dean et al. (Eds.): WISE 2005 Workshops, LNCS 3807, pp. 193–198, 2005.

layer supports many of the common Semantic Web and industry standard access APIs. The Query Engine is separated from the access API layer by a transport layer, allowing the APIs to be used across a network connection. The Session and Resolver APIs are responsible for taking access requests and directing them to the storage layer.

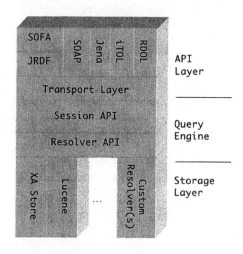

Fig. 1. Simplified Kowari architecture

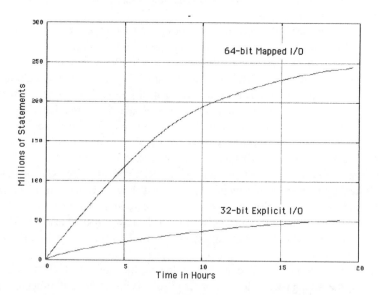

Fig. 2. Loading times for RDF statements in N3 format using manual commits on 64-bit and 32-bit machine architectures, noting the performance gains when mapped I/O is used.

Kowari clients, such as provided Java Bean, typically accept queries in the interactive Tucana Query Language (iTQL). Kowari does not yet support the upcoming SPARQL RDF query language, although work is in progress to do so.

Kowari's native data store (the XA Store) is a native Java version 1.4 transactional data store that stores RDF statements persistently on disk without the use of an external database. At its base is a series of files conceptually addressed as Adelson-Velskii and Landis (AVL) trees. Components of RDF statements consist of strings or other XSD data types. These data are mapped to numbers in a String Pool and the numbers are then stored in six indexes, also conceptually addressed as AVL trees. A Node Pool keeps track of AVL tree nodes which may be reused as they are freed.

Kowari currently scales to roughly 500 million RDF statements when run on a 64-bit operating system with a 64-bit Java Virtual Machine. Scaling is significantly reduced on 32-bit platforms due (primarily) to limitations with memory mapped file sizes.

Figure 2 shows the time required to bulk load Kowari with RDF data. Note that the curves enter a logarithmic region as the number of statements increases.

The remainder of this paper surveys ways to increase Kowari's actual or effective RDF storage and analysis capabilities.

2 Survey of Scaling Options

Kowari may be scaled in a number of ways. One obvious way is to increase the amount of data storable in a single Kowari instance. That would require a new quad store in place of the existing XA Store. Other options include enabling distributed queries and investigating specialty hardware.

The ability to simply store large amounts of RDF data is not sufficient. One wishes to be able to query that data in near real time and to perform inferencing activities against it using RDF Schema and OWL. An option to allow for improved performance of RDFS and OWL operations is also considered.

2.1 Upgrading Kowari's Native Quad Store

David Makepeace, currently of Agile TV in Brisbane, Australia, has proposed replacing the current transactional quad store in Kowari (labeled as "XA Store" in Figure 1) with a new quad store based on skip lists [9]. The goals are to (a) increase Kowari's write speeds, (b) consider the feasibility of allowing Kowari to have multiple write phases.

A skip list is a "randomized variant of an ordered linked list with additional, parallel lists. Parallel lists at higher levels skip geometrically more items. Searching begins at the highest level, to quickly get to the right part of the list, then uses progressively lower level lists." [8]

Search time in skip lists, like Kowari's current AVL Tree implementation is $O\log(n)$ where n is the number of nodes in the graph.

Insertion into Kowari's indexes based on AVL Trees occasionally require rebalancing of the tree. This rebalancing consists of rotating the appropriate subtree and may, rarely, require rotation all the way up to the tree's root. Rebalancing occurs after every insert which requires a new node be created in the AVL Tree. This can have major consequences when loading bulk data into Kowari and thus helps to practically limit the size of Kowari's store. Insertion into an index based on skip lists requires *randomly* selecting a level and inserting into that and all lower levels. The cost of rebalancing is avoided.

Mr. Makepeace has completed the initial design of the new skip list-based store and implementation is in progress.

2.2 (Re-)Implementing Distributed Query Capability

Kowari's commercial big brother, the Tucana Knowledge Server, extends the interactive Tucana Query Language to allow for distributed queries. That is, a single query may be issued which allows for multiple databases to take part in finding the answer. Instances of either Kowari or TKS databases may take part in TKS distributed queries.

The iTQL FROM clause allows multiple RDF models to be listed. WHERE clause constraints are executed against all listed models, unless they are explicitly tied to a given model via the IN specifier. In TKS, the RDF models may reside on more than one database.

An Open Source re-implementation of distributed query capability in Kowari would allow for RDF data to be distributed across multiple machines.

Re-implementation of distributed query capability in Kowari is not considered difficult, but has not yet been scheduled.

2.3 Lookup Service for Distributed Queries

Distributed query capability in TKS requires that a Unix network socket be opened to each database server in the list of models in order to determine if each server can contribute to the answer. That is, some servers may return null answers when queried. It would be useful, especially in a network of many TKS/Kowari servers, to limit the opening of sockets to those servers which can contribute to an answer.

The author proposes a lookup service, not unlike DNS in concept, which may report RDFS schemas or OWL ontologies stored in models. TKS/Kowari clients may cache that information and make use of it to determine which TKS/Kowari servers to involve in a particular query. Only those models which store a given schema or ontology may satisfy constraints involving terms from them.

It is possible that a truly scalable solution for distributed queries will require additional metadata about what is stored where. Fortunately, this information may itself be stored in and queried from Kowari.

2.4 Multiple Databases Per Machine

Multiple instances of Kowari may be run on a single machine. Unfortunately, this would only assist scalability if distributed queries were (re-)implemented and the machine in question had multiple processors, preferably 64-bit. Kowari processes run on separate processors would reduce contention between them and allow both to be utilized. Naturally, use of separate storage media on different hardware channels would be recommended.

Due to the requirements for specialty hardware, this is not considered to be a general solution.

2.5 Scalable RDF Schema and OWL Operations

Storing large quantities of RDF is one thing, but being able to make use of that information is another. Although Kowari users may perform queries to recover stored information, scalable RDF Schema (RDFS) and OWL operations have not been possible due to a combination of the use of undecidable logic in the OWL specification and untractable algorithms for OWL operations. Kowari developers have implemented Kowari as a Jena [5] storage back end and integrated the Simple Ontology Framework API (SOFA) [1] in efforts to address this problem, but the results are less than satisfactory to date.

Fortunately, Boris Motik and his colleques at the Research Center for Information technologies (FZI) and the University of Karlsruhe developed algorithms [4] to implement the SHIQ(D) subset of OWL-DL using rules. Their implementation of these ideas is KAON2, an infrastructure for managing ontologies [6].

Paul Gearon of the University of Queensland in Brisbane, Australia, is researching scalable RDF Schema and OWL operations using Kowari as an implementation platform. His approach to date, following Motik, et al, has been to implement a rules engine particular to Kowari which makes use of the fact that counts are an inexpensive operation. This rules engine is known as Krule (pronounced "cruel") for Kowari rules.

Krule rules are described in RDF. Rules may be defined in any RDF format parsable by Kowari (currently RDF/XML, N3 and NT). The structure of the rules RDF is provided in an OWL file. Krule applies a set of entailment rules to a base set of RDF statements, producing new data. The new data may be stored in the same RDF model (graph) as the original data or in a new model.

The Krule rules engine has been checked into Kowari, inclusive of rules implementations capable of passing W3C compliance tests for RDF Schema, except XSD datatype tests. Completion of full RDFS compliance and the addition of rules to implement OWL operations (probably to the level of OWL Lite plus the full cardinality restrictions from OWL Full) are expected by late 2005.

3   Conclusions

The Kowari Metastore is the most scalable RDF database currently available. Five options for further increasing the upper bound of RDF statements which may be stored, decreasing write times, distributing computational and storage resource requirements and improving analysis capabilities on large data sets were presented. Ongoing implementation of the ideas collected in this paper seem likely to allow Kowari to retain the mantle of "most scalable RDF database".

Acknowledgments

The author would like to thank Tucana Technologies, Inc. and contributors from the Open Source community for creating Kowari and Northrop Grumman Corporation for its continued support. David Makepeace designed and is implementing the skiplist-based quad store for Kowari. Paul Gearon of the University of Queensland designed and implemented the rules engine for Kowari. Professor James Hendler and UMD MIND Lab funded the preparation and presentation of this paper. The author also thanks Fujitsu Laboratory of America College Park, NTT Corp., and Lockheed Martin for funding of the University of Maryland MIND Laboratory.

References

1. Alishevskikh, A., Subbiah, G. Simple Ontology Framework API,
   http://sofa.projects.semwebcentral.org/
2. Beckett, D., Redland RDF Application Framework, http://librdf.org/
3. Guha, R., rdfDB: An RDF Database, http://www.guha.com/rdfdb/
4. Hustadt, U., Motik, B., Sattler, U.. Reducing SHIQ Descrption Logic to Disjunctive Datalog Programs. Proc. of the 9th International Conference on Knowledge Representation and Reasoning (KR2004), June 2004, Whistler, Canada, pp. 152-162
5. Jena Semantic Web Framework, http://jena.sourceforge.net/
6. KAON2, http://kaon2.semanticweb.org/
7. Kowari Metastore, http://kowari.org/
8. NIST, Definition of Skip Lists, http://www.nist.gov/dads/HTML/skiplist.html
9. Pugh, W. Skip Lists: A Probabilistic Alternative to Balanced Trees, CACM, 33(6):668-676, June 1990.
10. Threestore, http://inanna.ecs.soton.ac.uk/3store/
11. Sesame, http://www.openrdf.org/
12. Wood, D., Gearon, P., Adams, T. Kowari: A Platform for Semantic Web Storage and Analysis, Proc. of XTech 2005,
    http://www.idealliance.org/proceedings/xtech05/papers/04-02-04/

A Method for Performing an Exhaustive Evaluation of RDF(S) Importers

Raúl García-Castro and Asunción Gómez-Pérez

Ontology Engineering Group, Departamento de Inteligencia Artificial,
Facultad de Informática, Universidad Politécnica de Madrid, Spain
{rgarcia, asun}@fi.upm.es

Abstract. Interoperability is one of the main quality criteria required for Semantic Web technology. In this paper we propose a method for defining benchmark suites for evaluating the RDF(S) importers of Semantic Web technology. We also show how this method was used for developing a benchmark suite that is being used for benchmarking the interoperability of ontology development tools.

1   Introduction

Interoperability is one of the main quality criteria required for Semantic Web technology. Users need to know which tools allow them to interchange their ontologies (or part of them) with other users or with other tools, contributing to the scalability of the Semantic Web. Therefore, the need of an objective evaluation of these tools according to their interoperability, that can be adapted to each case, is of high relevance.

As most of the Semantic Web information is available as RDF(S) ontologies in the web, in this paper we propose a method for defining benchmark suites for evaluating the RDF(S) import capabilities of Semantic Web technology. This method allows to create tailored benchmark suites, focusing on the components of interest of the RDF(S) knowledge model.

We also show how this method was used to develop a benchmark suite that is being used for benchmarking the interoperability of ontology development tools, in the context of the Knowledge Web Network of Excellence.

This paper starts presenting in Section 2 an overview of the benchmarking methodology for ontology tools and showing in Section 3 how this methodology is being applied for benchmarking the interoperability of ontology development tools. Section 4 describes the method used for defining the benchmark suites in the benchmarking and Section 5 presents the resulting benchmark suite for RDF(S) importers. Finally, Section 6 discusses our results and points out ongoing and future work.

2   Benchmarking Methodology for Ontology Tools

In the last decades, benchmarking has become relevant within the business management community as a continuous process for comparing the products,

M. Dean et al. (Eds.): WISE 2005 Workshops, LNCS 3807, pp. 199–206, 2005.

services, and work processes of an organisation with those of the organisations that are recognised as representing best practices [1].

The Software Engineering community does not have a common benchmarking definition. Some authors consider benchmarking as a software evaluation method [2] while others adopt the business benchmarking definition, defining benchmarking as a continuous improvement process that strives to be the best of the best through the comparison of similar processes in different contexts [3].

A benchmark, in contrast, is a test that measures the performance of a system or subsystem on a well-defined task or set of tasks [4]. However, Sim et al. [5] propose to also measure tools and techniques to compare their performance.

This section summarises the benchmarking methodology developed by the authors in the Knowledge Web Network of Excellence [6]. The benchmarking methodology provides a set of guidelines to follow in benchmarking activities over ontology tools. This methodology adopts and extends methodologies of different areas such as business community benchmarking, experimental software engineering and software measurement as described in [6].

The benchmarking methodology for ontology tools is composed of a benchmarking iteration that is repeated forever. Each iteration is composed of three phases (*Plan, Experiment* and *Improve*) and ends with a *Recalibration* task:

- **Plan phase.** Its main goals are: to produce a document with a detailed proposal for benchmarking, including all the relevant information about it; to search for other organisations that want to participate in the benchmarking; and to agree on the benchmarking proposal and on the benchmarking planning with all the participants.
- **Experiment phase.** In this phase, the organisations must define and execute the evaluation experiments for each of the tools that participate on the benchmarking. The evaluation results must be compiled and analysed, determining the practices that lead to these results and identifying which of them can be considered as best practices.
- **Improve phase.** This phase comprises the writing of the benchmarking report, the communication of the benchmarking results to the participant organisations and finally, in several improvement cycles, the improvement of the tools and the monitorisation of this improvement.

The goal of the *Recalibration* task is not to improve the tools, but to improve the benchmarking process itself using the lessons learnt while performing it.

At the time of writing this paper, this methodology is being used in Knowledge Web for benchmarking the interoperability of ontology development tools[1]. A proposal for using this methodology for benchmarking the performance and the scalability of ontology development tools can be found in [7].

---

[1] http://knowledgeweb.semanticweb.org/benchmarking_interoperability/

3   Interoperability Benchmarking

In the benchmarking activity that is taking place in Knowledge Web, the interoperability between two ontology development tools is assessed using RDF(S) files to exchange ontologies. To exchange ontologies from one ontology development tool into another, they must first be exported from the origin tool to a RDF(S) file and then this file must be imported into the destination tool.

This scenario requires that the importers and exporters from/to RDF(S) of the ontology development tools work accurately to be able to exchange ontologies correctly. Therefore, the benchmarking is composed of the following phases:

Agreement phase. The quality of the benchmark suites is essential for the results of the benchmarking. Therefore, the first step is that a group of experts reach an agreement on the definition of these benchmark suites.

Evaluation phase 1. In this phase, the RDF(S) importers and exporters of the ontology development tools are evaluated.

Evaluation phase 2. In this phase, the ontology exchange between ontology development tools is evaluated.

The method described in the next section was used for defining the benchmark suites that are being used for benchmarking the interoperability of ontology development tools. Section 5 shows how this method was applied for defining a benchmark suite for RDF(S) importers, taking as an input the knowledge model of RDF(S).

Similarly, for defining a benchmark suite for RDF(S) exporters, a common core of the knowledge model of the ontology development tools was taken as an input. This second benchmark suite is not described in this paper because of space constraints.

4   Definition of the Benchmark Suite

The benchmark suite for evaluating RDF(S) importers is composed of benchmarks that import an ontology with a simple combination of components of the RDF(S) knowledge model (classes, properties, etc.) [8]. Assessing the import of real, large or complex ontologies can be useless if we don't know if the importer can deal correctly with simple ones. Besides, it is easier to find problems in simple cases than in complex ones.

We have considered the import of all the possible combinations of the components of the RDF(S) knowledge model to make the benchmark suite exhaustive. There are four different types of benchmarks:

- **Benchmarks that import single components.** For each component of the knowledge model of RDF(S), we defined: a benchmark to import a single component and another to import several components. For example, for *rdfs:Class*, we defined two benchmarks to import:
  - One class.
  - Several classes.

– **Benchmarks that import all the possible combinations of two components with a property.** We defined all the combinations of two components related by a property, assigning cardinalities to the relations. These cardinalities define the different number of benchmarks that will be performed. For example, for *rdfs:Class* and the property *rdfs:subClassOf*, we defined five benchmarks to import:

  - One class that is subclass of another class, being this last class subclass of a third one.
  - One class that is subclass of several classes.
  - Several classes that are subclass of the same class.
  - One class that is subclass of another class and viceversa, forming a cycle.
  - One class that is subclass of himself, forming a cycle.

– **Benchmarks that import combinations of more than two components that usually appear together in RDF(S) graphs**, such as properties that have both domain and range (*rdf:Property* with *rdfs:domain* and *rdfs:range*); statements that have subject, predicate and object (*rdf:Statement* with *rdf:subject*, *rdf:predicate* and *rdf:object*); and definitions of lists (*rdf:List* with *rdf:first*, *rdf:rest* and *rdf:nil*). For example, for a property with a domain and a range, we defined five benchmarks to import:

  - One property that has as domain a class and as range another class.
  - One property that has as domain a class and as range several classes.
  - One property that has as domain several classes and as range another class.
  - One property that has as domain several classes and as range another several classes.
  - One property that has as domain and range the same class.

– **Benchmarks that import RDF(S) graphs with the different variants of the RDF/XML syntax[2]:**

  - Different syntax of URI references: absolute URI references, URI references relative to a base URI, URI references transformed from *rdf:ID* attribute values, and URI references relative to an ENTITY declaration.
  - Language identification attributes (*xml:lang*) in tags.
  - Abbreviations of: empty nodes, multiple properties, typed nodes, string literals, blank nodes, containers, collections, and statements.

5   Resulting Benchmark Suite

The resulting benchmark suite obtained using the previous method is composed of a huge number of benchmarks, because of the large number of combinations that can exist between RDF(S) components. To make the benchmark suite more usable, we propose to prune it according to its intended use and to the kind of tools that it is expected to evaluate.

---

[2] http://www.w3.org/TR/rdf-syntax-grammar/

For example, for evaluating the RDF(S) importers of ontology development tools, we only considered the components of the knowledge model of RDF(S) that are most frequently used for modelling ontologies in these tools: *rdfs:Class*, *rdf:Property*, *rdfs:Literal*, *rdf:type*, *rdfs:subClassOf*, *rdfs:subPropertyOf*, *rdfs:range*, and *rdfs:domain*; not dealing with the rest of the RDF(S) components.

The definition of each benchmark in the benchmark suite, as Table 1 shows, includes the following fields:

- An identifier, for tracking the different benchmarks.
- A description of the benchmark in natural language.
- A graphical representation of the ontology to be imported in the benchmark.
- A file containing the ontology in the RDF/XML syntax.

Table 1. An example of a benchmark definition

Identifier	I14
Description	Import one class that has the same property with several other classes
Graphical representation	
RDF/XML file	```<rdf:RDF xmlns="http://www.w3.org/2000/01/rdf-schema#"
xmlns:g1="http://www.test.org/graph14#"
xmlns:rdf="http://www.w3.org/1999/02/22-rdf-syntax-ns#"
xmlns:rdfs="http://www.w3.org/2000/01/rdf-schema#">
<Class rdf:about="http://www.test.org/graph14#class1">
<g1:prop1 rdf:resource="http://www.test.org/graph14#class2"/>
<g1:prop1 rdf:resource="http://www.test.org/graph14#class3"/>
</Class>
<Class rdf:about="http://www.test.org/graph14#class2"/>
<Class rdf:about="http://www.test.org/graph14#class3"/>
</rdf:RDF>```

The resulting benchmark suite[3] contains 72 benchmarks grouped in the following categories: class benchmarks, metaclass benchmarks, subclass benchmarks, class and property benchmarks, property benchmarks, subproperty benchmarks, property with domain and range benchmarks, instance benchmarks, instance and property benchmarks, and syntax and abbreviation benchmarks. Table 2 shows the benchmarks corresponding to the first three categories and Table 3 shows the graphical representations of these benchmarks.

---

[3] http://knowledgeweb.semanticweb.org/benchmarking_interoperability/
rdfs_import_benchmark_suite.html

Table 2. Benchmarks that import classes, metaclasses, and subclasses

Id.	Description
Class benchmarks	I01 Import just one class
	I02 Import several classes with no properties between them
Metaclass benchmarks	I03 Import one class that is instance of another class, being this last class instance of a third one
	I04 Import one class that is instance of several classes
	I05 Import several classes that are instance of the same class
	I06 Import one class that is instance of another class and viceversa
	I07 Import just one class that is instance of himself
Subclass benchmarks	I08 Import one class that is subclass of another class, being this last class subclass of a third one
	I09 Import one class that is subclass of several classes
	I10 Import several classes that are subclass of the same class
	I11 Import one class that is subclass of another class and viceversa, forming a cycle
	I12 Import just one class that is subclass of himself, forming a cycle

Table 3. Graphical representation of the benchmarks shown in Table 2

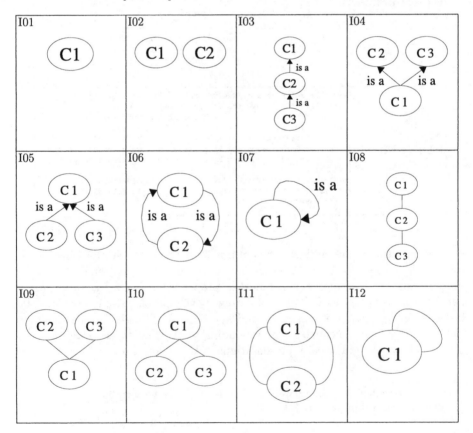

The execution of each benchmark in the benchmark suite comprises the following steps:

1. To define in the ontology development tool the expected result of importing the RDF(S) ontology.
2. To import the file with the RDF(S) ontology into the tool.
3. To compare the imported ontology with the expected ontology to check whether they are the same.

Although these steps can be performed manually, some automatic mean of performing them (or part of them) is highly advised when dealing with many benchmarks, specially for comparing the expected ontology with the imported one.

The expected results of a benchmark execution are:

- If the tool passes the benchmark or does not.
- If not, the reasons for not passing the benchmark. It could be because of a wrong implementation of the importer or because the tool cannot represent the RDF(S) component in its own knowledge model.
- If the tool does not pass the benchmark and is corrected to pass it, the changes performed.

The last two results have the goal of obtaining from the tool developers the practices used when developing the RDF(S) importers. This can allow to extract, if possible, the best practices performed by these developers.

6   Conclusions and Future Work

In this paper we present a method for defining benchmark suites for evaluating the RDF(S) import capabilities of Semantic Web technology. There are other benchmark suites for RDF like the RDF Test Cases [9], but they are not exhaustive enough and they are not flexible enough to be used for different evaluations. The RDF Test Cases are quite concrete, as they just deal with certain issues addressed by the RDFCore Working Group.

We also show how the method was applied for defining a benchmark suite for evaluating the RDF(S) importers of ontology development tools, and how this benchmark suite is being used for benchmarking the interoperability of ontology development tools in Knowledge Web.

This method was also used to define a benchmark suite for evaluating the RDF(S) exporters of ontology development tools[4]. Instead of taking as an input the RDF(S) knowledge model, a common core of the knowledge models of the ontology development tools was used to define the benchmark suite. The method can also be used to define benchmark suites specific to other languages such as OWL[5] or specific to the knowledge model of a certain tool.

---

[4] http://knowledgeweb.semanticweb.org/benchmarking_interoperability/
rdfs_export_benchmark_suite.html

[5] http://www.w3.org/TR/owl-features/

One important issue when defining benchmark suites with this method is to prune the resulting benchmark suite to make it more usable, as considering all the relations between RDF(S) components can result in thousands of benchmarks.

Combining the definitions of the benchmarks, the benchmark suites can be improved to include new benchmarks with more complex structures or with a higher number of components.

One future line of work would be to define different RDF(S) benchmark suites for different kinds of tools (ontology editors, ontology repositories, etc.) and for different kind of ontologies (ontologies with linear taxonomies, with graphs with cycles, with metaclasses, etc.).

Acknowledgments

This work is partially supported by a FPI grant from the Spanish Ministry of Education (BES-2005-8024), by the IST project Knowledge Web (IST-2004-507482) and by the CICYT project Infraestructura tecnológica de servicios semánticos para la web semántica (TIN2004-02660).

References

1. Spendolini, M.: The Benchmarking Book. AMACOM, New York, NY (1992)
2. Kitchenham, B.: DESMET: A method for evaluating software engineering methods and tools. Technical Report TR96-09, Department of Computer Science, University of Keele, Staffordshire, UK (1996)
3. Wohlin, C., Aurum, A., Petersson, H., Shull, F., Ciolkowski, M.: Software inspection benchmarking - a qualitative and quantitative comparative opportunity. In: Proceedings of 8th International Software Metrics Symposium. (2002) 118–130
4. Sill, D.: comp.benchmarks frequently asked questions version 1.0 (1996)
5. Sim, S., Easterbrook, S., Holt, R.: Using benchmarking to advance research: A challenge to software engineering. In: Proceedings of the 25th International Conference on Software Engineering (ICSE'03), Portland, OR (2003) 74–83
6. García-Castro, R., Maynard, D., Wache, H., Foxvog, D., González-Cabero, R.: D2.1.4 specification of a methodology, general criteria and benchmark suites for benchmarking ontology tools. Technical report, Knowledge Web (2004)
7. García-Castro, R., Gómez-Pérez, A.: Guidelines for Benchmarking the Performance of Ontology Management APIs. In: To appear in Proceedings of the 4th International Semantic Web Conference (ISWC2005), Galway, Ireland (2005)
8. Brickley, D., Guha, R.: RDF Vocabulary Description Language 1.0: RDF Schema. W3C Recommendation 10 February 2004 (2004)
9. Grant, J., Beckett, D.: RDF Test Cases. W3C Recommendation 10 February 2004 (2004)

Towards Automatic Generation of Semantic Types in Scientific Workflows[*]

Shawn Bowers[1] and Bertram Ludäscher[2]

[1] UC Davis Genome Center
[2] Department of Computer Science,
University of California, Davis
{sbowers, ludaesch}@ucdavis.edu

Abstract. Scientific workflow systems are problem-solving environments that allow scientists to automate and reproduce data management and analysis tasks. Workflow components include *actors* (*e.g.*, queries, transformations, analyses, simulations, visualizations), and *datasets* which are produced and consumed by actors. The increasing number of such components creates the problem of discovering suitable components and of composing them to form the desired scientific workflow. In previous work we proposed the use of *semantic types* (annotations relative to an ontology) to solve these problems. Since creating semantic types can be complex and time-consuming, scalability of the approach becomes an issue. In this paper we propose a framework to automatically derive semantic types from a (possibly small) number of initial types. Our approach propagates the given semantic types through workflow steps whose input and output data structures are related via query expressions. By propagating semantic types, we can significantly reduce the effort required to annotate datasets and components and even derive new "candidate axioms" for inclusion in annotation ontologies.

1 Introduction

Scientific analyses are often performed as a series of computation steps, grouped together to form the logical stages of an analysis. For example, pre-processing input data, applying one or more statistical or data-mining techniques, and post-processing and visualizing analysis results or discovered patterns may each be constructed from a number of smaller computation steps. Scientific-workflow systems (*e.g.*, TAVERNA, TRIANA,[1] and KEPLER [13]) have emerged as more versatile, extensible environments, compared with shell scripts and spreadsheets, to model and execute such analytical processes. Scientific workflows are useful to design [6] and execute end-to-end processes, and to enable the composition and sharing of computation steps, allowing scientists to more quickly experiment with and run complex analyses. Scientific workflows systems also provide scientists with a single point of access to heterogeneous data and computation services from multiple scientific disciplines and research groups. Providing such access

---

[*] This work supported in part by NSF/ITR SEEK (DBI-0533368), NSF/ITR GEON (EAR-0225673), and DOE SDM (DE-FC02-01ER25486).
[1] See taverna.sourceforge.net and www.trianacode.org, respectively.

M. Dean et al. (Eds.): WISE 2005 Workshops, LNCS 3807, pp. 207–216, 2005.

enables "cross-cutting" science, *e.g.*, allowing ecological and genomic data to be mixed or complex statistical models to be combined across disciplines. A major challenge in providing this capability are semantic and terminological differences across scientific domains. Even within a discipline such as ecology, these problems exist, making data integration and service composition difficult both automatically and for a scientist. Our work focuses on providing rich metadata and ontologies to help bridge this gap and to enable wide-scale data and workflow interoperability. We have developed a framework for registering the semantics of data and services based on *semantic types*, which are mappings from datasets or services to concept expressions of an ontology. Our framework has been used to (semi-)automate data integration [2,14] and service composition [5], and is currently being developed and used within the KEPLER scientific workflow system [2]. Providing semantic types, however, can be time-consuming for data and service providers, thereby limiting the applicability of metadata-intensive approaches to scientific data management.

In this paper, we describe an approach to make the management of semantic types more scalable by automating the generation of intermediate types within workflows. Our approach propagates the given semantic types through actors whose input and output data structures are related by a query expression, possibly approximating an actor's function. In Section 2 we introduce the propagation problem and describe the benefits of our approach. In Section 3 we present our semantic-type framework. In Section 4 we develop our approach for propagating semantic types; related and future work is discussed in Section 5.

2   The Propagation Problem

For our purposes, a *scientific workflow* consists of a number of *actors*, which are connected via directed edges called *channels* (Figure 1). An actor is a component (*e.g.*, a web service, shell command, local function, remote job) that can consume and produce data tokens. An actor has zero or more uniquely named *ports* designated as either input or output. With each port we can associate a *structural type* (or *schema*) S describing the structure of data (tokens) flowing through that port. KEPLER's structural type system, inherited from Ptolemy II [7], includes atomic types, *e.g.*, `string` and `double`, and complex types such as `list` and `record`. In a workflow, actors exchange information using channels that link an output port (token producer) to one or more input ports (token consumers). Workflows are executed according to a *model of computation* (implemented by a so-called *director* [7]), which specifies the overall workflow orchestration and scheduling. Here we assume a model of computation that corresponds to a dataflow process network [11]. Figure 1 shows a simple workflow in KEPLER for computing species richness and productivity. The workflow performs a number of distinct computations over two input datasets shown on the left of the workflow, which results in the richness and productivity derived data products shown on the right.

Semantic Type Propagation. Figure 2 depicts the problem of propagating an input semantic type α through an actor, yielding the output semantic type α'. A *semantic type* α associates elements of a schema S with concepts from an ontology O. The goal of

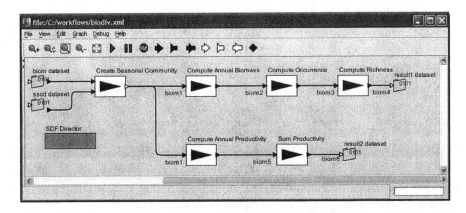

Fig. 1. Simple scientific workflow for computing species richness and productivity [9]

propagation is to automatically generate α', given α. This is only possible if something is known about the relation between elements of S and those in S'. A query expression q provides this relation. The query q can approximate[2] the actual function $f : S \rightarrow S'$ computed by the actor, *e.g.*, q might "overestimate" f such that $q(D) \supseteq f(D)$ for any input data D. The propagation problem is to determine $\alpha' : S' \rightarrow O$, the semantic type of the output, given the input type α and the query q. We denote this problem as computing $\alpha' = \alpha \circ q^{-1}$ in Figure 2, *i.e.*, the composition of α and (the inverse of) q. Based on our semantic-type framework (Section 3), we describe an initial approach towards solving this problem (Section 4). Our approach places few restrictions on where initial semantic types are given. Semantic types may be provided for input data or for inputs of some actor(s) only, significantly reducing the amount of semantic description required to reuse workflows and actors. A user may also provide additional semantic types at specific points within a workflow, *e.g.*, when the result of a computation creates new data values or adds semantic information. These semantic types are also propagated through actors. The advantages of our approach directly benefit scientific workflow engineers at various stages of workflow construction, including:

• Semantic types can be derived at **workflow design-time** (even before all actors or data are available), and thus can be used as a tool to help workflow engineers build new analyses. For example, propagated types can be presented to the user after two actors are connected, showing the resulting semantic types of combining the steps and the impact on the rest of the workflow.

• Scientific workflows can often be executed over different input datasets. The workflow's global inputs are typically quite generic, while a given dataset may have very specific semantic types. Our approach can propagate these specific semantic types of datasets, resulting in more accurate (specialized) semantic types at **data binding-time**.

• When a workflow is executed, derived data products are automatically given the propagated semantic type, minimizing the effort required to semantically type datasets at **workflow runtime**.

---

[2] Consider a filter function f that removes outliers and returns only "good" tokens. This function can be modeled as a selection σ_θ where θ is the filter condition. Obviously, $S = S'$ in this case, which means that α can be propagated as is (in fact, $\alpha' = \alpha \wedge \theta$ can be derived).

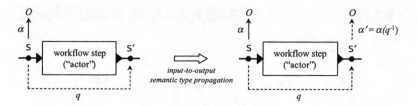

Fig. 2. Actor with semantic type α, propagated via query q, yielding semantic type α'

Another advantage of propagation is *ontology augmentation*. Consider an actor A_2 having as input species richness data. The developer of A_2 may provide a semantic type α_2 for A_2's input, stating that it was designed to "consume" RICHNESS data.[3] Assume a workflow designer has connected the output of another actor A_1 to the input of A_2, and for the output of A_1 a semantic type α_1 has been derived via propagation, indicating that A'_1s output is of type sum(OCCURRENCE), *i.e.*, the arithmetic sum (resulting from an aggregation) of OCCURRENCE data. For the link:

$$\boxed{A_1} \xrightarrow{\alpha_1 \quad \alpha_2} \boxed{A_2}$$

to be semantically type correct, we must have that α_1 is "compatible" with α_2, *i.e.*, sum(OCCURRENCE) $\sqsubseteq$ RICHNESS. If we choose to run our propagation system in "automatic mode", it will augment the given ontology O with this additional axiom. Conversely, the system can be run in "interactive mode", asking the user to determine whether the inferred axiom is correct and can be included in O, or whether there is something wrong with the connection. This example also illustrates that semantic type constraints between connected actors are "soft" in the sense that one can still execute the corresponding workflow steps, even though doing so may not be semantically meaningful. In contrast, the structural type constraint when connecting A_1 and A_2 is "hard", *i.e.*, the schema types S_1 and S_2 must satisfy a subtyping constraint $S_1 \leq S_2$ for the connection to be executable.

3   The Semantic-Type Framework

Query Expressions. Actors may have an associated *query expression* q, which may be derived from the component implementation (*e.g.*, from a script or generated data transformation) or explicitly given by a service provider (*e.g.*, for "black-box" actors whose inner workings are unknown). The most general form of a query expression is a logic constraint $\varphi_{SUS'}$, associating schema elements of the input port(s) S of an actor with those of its output port(s) S'. In analogy to data integration terminology, we can call q an *Output-as-View* (OAV) mapping if it has the form $q = P_{S'} :- \varphi_S$, and an *Input-as-View* (IAV) mapping if it has the form $q = P_S :- \varphi_{S'}$. Here, q is a logic atom defining data elements of the output schema S' (or the input schema S) in terms of the query φ_S (or $\varphi_{S'}$) over S (or S', respectively). In this paper we focus on query expressions

---

[3] We use SMALLCAPS to denote concepts from an ontology O.

given in the OAV form. Query expresssions can contain the standard relational operators select, project, join, union, and group-by with aggregation (*i.e.*, sum, count, avg, min, and max). Note that a query expression q does not need to exactly capture the function f being computed by an actor. It is sufficient if q approximates f such that all structural associations between S and S' are preserved. These structural associations will then be used to propagate the semantic types from S to S'.

We use Datalog notation [1], extended with aggregrate functions and grouping, to denote query expressions. Relations are denoted using capitals (Biom, Sscd, etc.) and variables are in lower-case $(x, y, \dots)$. For example, query q_1 approximates the *Create Seasonal Community* component of Figure 1:

$$\text{Biom1}(o, y, s, t, p, b) \; :\text{-} \; \text{Biom}(o, y, s, t, p, b), \; \text{Sscd}(p) \qquad (q_1)$$

This query selects Biom tuples (returned as Biom1 tuples) whose p-values are present in the Sscd data set. Biom represents a relational table consisting of measurements (with measurment-id o) of biomass b for a particular species p, year y, season s, and plot t. The Sscd relation contains species found within a particular community.

Query expressions can contain group-by with aggregate operators syntactically written $agg(x|\bar{y})$, where agg is the name of the aggregate operation, x is the aggregation variable, and $\bar{y}$ is a comma-separated list of grouping variables. We introduce a new variable in the head of an aggregate query and assign it (using the "$\leftarrow$" symbol) to the aggregate expression. For example, query q_2 gives the annual biomass for each plot and species (the *Compute Annual Biomass* actor):

$$\text{Biom2}(y, t, p, z \leftarrow \text{sum}(b | y, t, p)) :\text{-} \text{Biom1}(o, y, s, t, p, b) \qquad (q_2)$$

Union operations are expressed in the normal way using multiple rules. For example, query q_3 returns annual occurrence measurements (the *Compute Occurrence* actor):

$$\text{Biom3}(y, t, p, 1) :\text{-} \text{Biom2}(y, t, p, b), \; b > 0 \qquad (q_3)$$
$$\text{Biom3}(y, t, p, 0) :\text{-} \text{Biom2}(y, t, p, b), \; b \leq 0$$

Ontologies. We use description logic to express ontologies, which are used to formally define the terms (*concepts*) in a given domain and their relationships (*roles*). The OWL-DL standard is also used in KEPLER for storing and exchanging ontologies. A simple ontology is shown in Figure 3, representing definitions for ecological measurements (concept OBSERVATION) and ecological concepts such as ABUNDANCE, RICHNESS, etc. According to the underlying description-logic definitions (not shown in the figure), every observation has exactly one observed property (*e.g.*, abundance) and item (*e.g.*, species), and one or more spatial and temporal contexts. We assume a reasoning system is available to compute subsumption hierarchies from concept and role definitions. We use subsumption in particular to determine whether channels defined between actors are semantically compatible.

Semantic Types. Each structural type of a dataset, input, or output port, may be given a semantic type, which in its most general form is a logic constraint α_{SUO} associating schema elements S with concept expressions from an ontology O. We consider a syntactic form that we call *Terminology-as-View* (TAV) in which the ontology structure O is "virtually populated" with elements from the data schema S, thereby establishing the desired semantic type $\alpha = \alpha_S \to \alpha_O$. More precisely, we consider semantic types having the form $\alpha = \forall \bar{x} \exists \bar{y} \, \alpha_S(\bar{x}) \to \alpha_O(\bar{x}, \bar{y})$, where $\alpha_S(\bar{x})$ is a query over a data structure S, linking selected elements (captured via bindings of the variables $\bar{x}$) to concept expressions $\alpha_O(\bar{x}, \bar{y})$ over the ontology O.

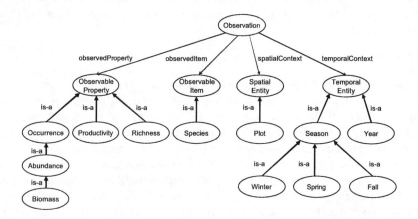

Fig. 3. Simplified ecological measurement ontology shown graphically

$$\text{Biom}(o, y, s, t, p, b) \qquad\qquad \to \text{OBSERVATION}(o) \qquad\qquad\qquad\qquad (1)$$
$$\text{Biom}(o, y, s, t, p, b) \qquad\qquad \to \text{TEMPORALCONTEXT}(o, y) \wedge \text{YEAR}(y) \qquad (2)$$
$$\text{Biom}(o, y, s, t, q, b) \wedge s = \text{`W'} \to \text{TEMPORALCONTEXT}(o, s) \wedge \text{WINTER}(s) \qquad (3)$$
$$\text{Biom}(o, y, s, t, q, b) \wedge s = \text{`S'} \to \text{TEMPORALCONTEXT}(o, s) \wedge \text{SPRING}(s) \qquad (4)$$
$$\text{Biom}(o, y, s, t, q, b) \wedge s = \text{`F'} \to \text{TEMPORALCONTEXT}(o, s) \wedge \text{FALL}(s) \qquad (5)$$
$$\text{Biom}(o, y, s, t, p, b) \qquad\qquad \to \text{SPATIALCONTEXT}(o, t) \wedge \text{PLOT}(t) \qquad\quad (6)$$
$$\text{Biom}(o, y, s, t, p, b) \qquad\qquad \to \text{OBSERVEDITEM}(o, p) \wedge \text{SPECIES}(p) \qquad (7)$$
$$\text{Biom}(o, y, s, t, p, b) \qquad\qquad \to \text{OBSERVEDPROPERTY}(o, b) \wedge \text{BIOMASS}(b) \quad (8)$$

Fig. 4. An example semantic type linking `biom` elements to ONTOLOGY elements

Figure 4 gives example semantic-type constraints linking schema elements of the `Biom` data structure S used above to concepts and roles from the ontology O given in Figure 3. Line (1) states that every measurement in `Biom` represents an OBSERVATION. Line (2) states (i) that all year values in `biom` are instances of the YEAR concept, and (ii) that the year instance is a temporal context of the corresponding observation instance. Lines (3–5) are similar, but contain an additional condition on the value of the season, and lines (7–8) annotate species and biomass values.

4   Propagating Semantic Types

We divide our approach for propagating semantic types through actors into three classes of increasing expressibility for query expressions: conjunctive queries (*i.e.*, containing only select, project, and join operations); conjunctive queries with aggregation; and conjunctive queries with aggregation and union.

The Conjunctive Case. Let query q and semantic type α be of the form:

- $q = \forall \bar{u} \exists \bar{v} \, P_{S'}(\bar{u}) :\text{-} \varphi_S(\bar{u}, \bar{v})$
- $\alpha = \forall \bar{x} \exists \bar{y} \, \alpha_S(\bar{x}) \rightarrow \alpha_O(\bar{x}, \bar{y})$

Here, $P_{S'}$ is a logic atom over the output schema S' and φ_S is a query over the input schema(s) S. Similarly, for semantic types α, we relate instances of a schema S with those of an ontology O via subformulas α_S and α_O, respectively.

The basic idea of computing $\alpha' = \alpha \circ q^{-1}$ is as follows. We would like to relate instances of the output schema S' with instances of O. Assume a substitution that satisfies φ_S (in q) implies α_S (in α). For this substitution we can establish the desired relation between S' and O, denoted abstractly as S' $\overset{q^{-1}}{\leadsto}$ S $\overset{\alpha}{\leadsto}$ O. More precisely, we consider q as a logical constraint of the form:

$$q(\bar{u}) = P_{S'} \rightarrow \underbrace{Q_1 \wedge \cdots \wedge Q_n \wedge \psi}_{\varphi_S}$$

and α of the form

$$\alpha(\bar{x}) = \underbrace{A_1 \wedge \cdots \wedge A_k}_{\alpha_S} \rightarrow \alpha_O$$

where $P_{S'}$ is a logic atom over the output schema S', Q_i and A_j are logic atoms over the input schema(s) S, and ψ and α_O are quantifier-free formulas. We assume that all $\exists$-quantified variables ($\bar{v}$ and $\bar{y}$ above) have been eliminated through Skolemization so that q and α can be seen as (implicitly) $\forall$-quantified formulas with variables $\bar{u}$ and $\bar{x}$.[4]

For propagating α "through" q we use the inverse of q, *i.e.*, the left-to-right ('head $\rightarrow$ body') direction of the query ('head :- body'). This direction is the one used in LAV-style query rewritings (*e.g.*, for sound views) and also corresponds to the usually implicit direction in Datalog-style rules (aka Clark's completion [10]). More precisely, q is defined by the equivalence $\forall \bar{u} \exists \bar{v} \, P_{S'}(\bar{u}) \leftrightarrow \varphi_S(\bar{u}, \bar{v})$ where intuitively, if $\varphi_S(\bar{u}, \bar{v})$ is a result of the query q (in a model M), then $P_{S'}(\bar{u})$ must also be true (in M) [10,12].

Observe that q can be written as a conjunction $q_1 \wedge \cdots \wedge q_n \wedge q_\psi$ with $q_i = P_{S'} \rightarrow Q_i$, and $q_\psi = P_{S'} \rightarrow \psi$. If we assume there is a substitution σ that unifies some atom Q_{i_0} and some A_{j_0}, *i.e.*, $Q_{i_0}^\sigma = A_{j_0}^\sigma$ [5], we can infer from $q_{i_0} = P_{S'} \rightarrow Q_{i_0}$ and α a new semantic type α'_{i_0} of the form:

$$\alpha'_{i_0} = P_{S'}^\sigma \wedge (\alpha_S \setminus A_{j_0})^\sigma \rightarrow \alpha_O^\sigma$$

---

[4] We assume that the variables $\bar{u}$ in $q(\bar{u})$ are disjoint from the variables $\bar{x}$ in $\alpha(\bar{x})$.

[5] T^σ denotes the result of applying σ to a term T.

where $(\alpha_S \setminus A_{j_0})$ is the conjunction $A_1 \wedge \cdots \wedge A_k$ with A_{j_0} removed. It is easy to show that the semantic type α'_{i_0} is implied by q_i and α. In this way, by successively "resolving away" atoms A_j from α_S with matching atoms Q_i from φ_S, we can obtain new semantic types α' that relate elements of the output schema S' to those in the ontology O.

Example 1 (Propagation for Conjunctive Queries). Consider query q_1 expressed as a first-order formula:

$$\text{Biom1}(o,y,s,t,q,p,b) \rightarrow \text{Biom}(o,y,s,t,q,p,b) \wedge \text{Sscd}(p) \tag{1}$$

This formula can be resolved with semantic-type expression (8) in Figure 4, resulting in the new formula:

$$\text{Biom1}(o,y,s,t,q,p,b) \rightarrow \text{OBSERVEDPROPERTY}(o,b) \wedge \text{BIOMASS}(b) \tag{2}$$

Observe that we now have biomass values b for the output schema Biom1 semantically typed as BIOMASS instances, linked through the OBSERVEDPROPERTY role.

Handling Aggregation. The approach for propagating conjunctive queries can also be used for aggregation, due to the particular syntactic representation used to express aggregate operators. As mentioned in Section 2, we perform an additional step for aggregate queries that connects aggregate operators to certain ontology concept defintions, which can be further used to infer new connections between components. The following simple example demonstrates how propagation is used with aggregation.

Example 2 (Propagation for Aggregate Operators). Consider the following Skolemized query q for the *Compute Richness* actor of Figure 1:

$$\text{Biom4}(y,t,r \leftarrow \text{sum}(c \mid y,t)) \rightarrow \text{Biom3}(y,t,f_p(y,t,c),c) \tag{1}$$

and the following (additional) output semantic type of the *Compute Occurrence* actor[6]:

$$\text{Biom3}(y,t,p,c) \rightarrow \text{OCCURRENCE}(c) \tag{2}$$

We can resolve (1) and (2) above, resulting in the new formula:

$$\text{Biom4}(y,t,r \leftarrow \text{sum}(c \mid y,t)) \rightarrow \text{OCCURRENCE}(c) \tag{3}$$

Observe that in this example we have "preserved" the fact that r is the sum of a variable c, and that values for c are OCCURRENCE instances. Thus, we can see that r is exactly the sum of OCCURRENCE. For propagated semantic types of this form, we also propagate a semantic-type expression where r is an instance of a new concept formed from the aggregate name and c's assigned concept. Thus, for the previous propagated semantic type we also propagate:

$$\text{Biom4}(y,t,r \leftarrow \text{sum}(c \mid y,t)) \rightarrow \text{sum}(\text{OCCURRENCE})(r) \tag{4}$$

With this additional step it becomes possible, *e.g.*, to determine that the *Compute Richness* actor can safely be connected to other actors that input RICHNESS data, leveraging definitions in the ontology such as sum(OCCURRENCE) $\sqsubseteq$ RICHNESS. Here, sum(OCCURRENCE) represents an ontology concept that is "linked" with a certain functionality in the query expression language.

---

[6] *e.g.*, given by the actor developer to account for the new data produced by *Compute Occurrence*.

Handling Union. Let the union query q be of the form:

$$q = \forall \bar{u} \exists \bar{v}\ P_{S'}(\bar{u})\ :\text{-}\ \varphi_S^1(\bar{u}, \bar{v})$$
$$\forall \bar{u} \exists \bar{v}\ P_{S'}(\bar{u})\ :\text{-}\ \varphi_S^2(\bar{u}, \bar{v})$$

which can also be written as the constraint $q(\bar{u}) = P_{S'} \rightarrow \varphi_S^1 \vee \varphi_S^2$ for $\varphi_S^1 = Q_1^1 \wedge \cdots \wedge Q_n^1 \wedge \psi^1$ and $\varphi_S^2 = Q_1^2 \wedge \cdots \wedge Q_n^2 \wedge \psi^2$. To resolve q and α, we rewrite q into clausal form, generating the two formulas $q'(\bar{u}) = P_{S'} \wedge \neg\varphi_S^2 \rightarrow \varphi_S^1$ and $q''(\bar{u}) = P_{S'} \wedge \neg\varphi_S^1 \rightarrow \varphi_S^2$.

Observe that q' (and similarly q'') can be rewritten as a conjunction $q_1' \wedge \cdots \wedge q_n' \wedge q_\psi'$ with $q_i' = P_{S'} \wedge \neg\varphi_S^2 \rightarrow Q_i'$ and $q_\psi' = P_{S'} \wedge \neg\varphi_S^2 \rightarrow \psi^1$. Assume there is a substitution σ that unifies some atom Q_{i_0} and some A_{j_0} for a semantic type $\alpha(\bar{x}) = A_1 \wedge \cdots \wedge A_k \rightarrow \alpha_O$. From q' and α we can infer α' of the form:

$$\alpha' = P_{S'}^\sigma \wedge \neg\varphi_S^{2\,\sigma} \wedge (\alpha_S \setminus A_{j_0})^\sigma \rightarrow \alpha_O^\sigma$$

where $(\alpha_S \setminus A_{j_0})$ is the conjunction $A_1 \wedge \cdots \wedge A_k$ with A_{j_0} removed, similar to the regular conjunctive case. As before, we successively "resolve away" atoms A_j from α_S with matching atoms Q_i^1 from φ_S^1.

We note that α' may not be in the desired form for semantic types (it may not be in clausal form) because, e.g., $\neg\varphi_S^2$ may result in a disjunctive formula. For such cases, we can apply the following simple conversion. Assuming query expressions $q = P \rightarrow (Q \wedge R) \vee (Q' \wedge R')$ and semantic types $\alpha = Q \rightarrow \alpha_O$, using resolution we infer, e.g., $\alpha' = P \wedge \neg(Q' \wedge R') \rightarrow \alpha_O$, which becomes $\alpha_1' = P \wedge \neg Q' \rightarrow \alpha_O$ and $\alpha_2' = P \wedge \neg R' \rightarrow \alpha_O$.

Example 3 (Propagation for Union). Consider query q_3 as the first-order formula:

$$\text{Biom3}(y, t, p, c) \rightarrow (\text{Biom2}(y, t, p, f_b(y, t, p)) \wedge\ f_b(y, t, p) > 0 \ \wedge\ c = 0)\ \vee \qquad (1)$$
$$(\text{Biom2}(y, t, p, f_b(y, t, p)) \wedge\ f_b(y, t, p) \leq 0 \ \wedge\ c = 1)$$

and the Skolemized semantic-type propagated from the *Compute Annual Biomass* actor (note that we only include the result z of the original aggregate operator):

$$\text{Biom2}(y, t, p, z) \rightarrow \text{OBSERVEDITEM}(f_o(y, t, p), p) \wedge \text{SPECIES}(p) \qquad (2)$$

Rewriting (1) into clausal form gives:

$$\text{Biom3}(y, t, p, c) \wedge \neg(\text{Biom2}(y, t, p, f_b(y, t, p)) \wedge\ f_b(y, t, p) > 0 \ \wedge\ c = 0) \rightarrow \qquad (3)$$
$$\text{Biom2}(y, t, p, f_b(y, t, p)) \wedge\ f_b(y, t, p) \leq 0 \ \wedge\ c = 1$$

$$\text{Biom3}(y, t, p, c) \wedge \neg(\text{Biom2}(y, t, p, f_b(y, t, p)) \wedge\ f_b(y, t, p) \leq 0 \ \wedge\ c = 1) \rightarrow \qquad (4)$$
$$\text{Biom2}(y, t, p, f_b(y, t, p)) \wedge\ f_b(y, t, p) > 0 \ \wedge\ c = 0$$

Resolving (2) and (3), *e.g.*, results in the new annotation:

$$\text{Biom3}(y, t, p, c) \wedge \neg(\text{Biom2}(y, t, p, f_b(y, t, p)) \wedge\ f_b(y, t, p) \leq 0 \ \wedge\ c = 1) \rightarrow \qquad (4)$$
$$\text{OBSERVEDITEM}(f_o(y, t, p), p) \wedge \text{SPECIES}(p)$$

We can now rewrite (5) into our desired form for semantic types.

5   Concluding Remarks

The creation of rich semantic-type annotations can be a complex task, making the problem of automatic generation of such types important for scalable "metadata-intensive" and "semantics-intensive" scientific applications. To this end, we have developed and presented a semantic-type propagation approach and sketched how queries involving selection, projection, join, aggregation, and union could be handled. Our approach is based on an inference procedure similar to the chase [1], which itself can be seen as a form of resolution [4]. Propagating semantic types is also related to work on data provenance [3,8] where the focus (in terms of propagation) is on supporting simple text-based annotations of relational table cells (instead of formulas over schemas), and on augmenting SQL to allow users to state specific schemes for propagating these value-based annotations to query results. In contrast, our semantic types are formal logic-based descriptions linking structural types to ontologies. These semantic types can be propagated within the framework of scientific workflows. We are currently investigating the properties of a specialized inference procedure, based on algorithms in [15] for composing mappings given by logic constraints. We plan to implement semantic type propagation within KEPLER as part of future work.

References

1. S. Abiteboul, R. Hull, and V. Vianu. *Foundations of Databases*. Addison Wesley, 1995.
2. C. Berkley, S. Bowers, M. Jones, B. Ludaescher, M. Schildhauer, and J. Tao. Incorporating semantics in scientific workflow authoring. In *Proc. of SSDBM*, 2005.
3. D. Bhagwat, L. Chiticariu, W. C. Tan, and G. Vijayvargiya. An annotation management system for relational databases. In *Proc. of VLDB*, 2004.
4. J. Biskup and A. Kluck. A new approach to inferences of semantic constraints. In *In Proc. of Advances in Databases and Information Systems*, 1997.
5. S. Bowers and B. Ludäscher. An ontology-driven framework for data transformation in scientific workflows. In *Proc. of DILS*, volume 2994 of *LNCS*, 2004.
6. S. Bowers and B. Ludäscher. Actor-oriented design of scientific workflows. In *24th Intl. Conf. on Conceptual Modeling (ER)*, 2005.
7. C. Brooks, E. A. Lee, X. Liu, S. Neuendorffer, Y. Zhao, and H. Zheng. The Ptolemy II Manual (vol. 1-3). Technical report, UC Berkeley, 2004.
8. P. Buneman, S. Khanna, and W. C. Tan. Why and where: A characterization of data provenance. In *Proc. of ICDT*, volume 1973 of *LNCS*, 2001.
9. D. Chalcraft, J. Williams, M. Smith, and M. Willig. Scale dependence in the species-richness-productivity relationship: The role of species turnover. *Ecology*, 85(10), 2004.
10. K. L. Clark. Negation as failure. In *Logic and Databases*. Plenum Press, 1977.
11. E. A. Lee and T. M. Parks. Dataflow process networks. *Proc. of the IEEE*, 83(5), 1995.
12. M. Lenzerini. Data integration: A theoretical perspective. In *Proc. of PODS*, 2002.
13. B. Ludäscher, I. Altintas, C. Berkley, D. Higgins, E. Jaeger, M. Jones, E. A. Lee, J. Tao, and Y. Zhao. Scientific workflow management and the kepler system. *Concurrency and Computation: Practice & Experience*, 2005. to appear.
14. B. Ludäscher, A. Gupta, and M. E. Martone. Model-based mediation with domain maps. In *Proc. of ICDE*, 2001.
15. A. Nash, P. A. Bernstein, and S. Melnik. Composition of mappings given by embedded dependencies. In *Proc. of PODS*, 2005.

A Semantic Distance Measure for Matching Web Services

Arif Bramantoro, Shonali Krishnaswamy, and Maria Indrawan

School of Computer Science and Software Engineering,
Monash University, Victoria, Australia
Bramantoro@gmail.com
{Shonali.Krishnaswamy, Maria.Indrawan}@infotech.monash.edu.au

Abstract. A key issue in web services is matching that involves comparing user requests with advertised services and finding the best available ones. In semantic web services, an ontology is used by the matching system to determine the semantic relationship between the requests and the registered services. In this paper, we propose that the semantic relationship can be measured quantitatively in order to provide a more precise similarity measures between the requested and advertised services and to produce a better ranking of relevant services. We proposes and develops a Semantic Distance Measure that is tailored to provide a quantitative measure that indicates similarity between advertised and requested services. We establish that such a measure is an effective means of discriminating services at a level of granularity that is able to enhance the matching process in semantic web services.

1 Introduction

Web services are loosely coupled and reusable software components that can be distributed over internet technologies and open standards [1]. A critical step in the process of web services is matching. The main task of web services matching is to compare user requests with advertised services and to find the best available ones. To bring the matching of web services to its success, there is a need for a language to describe web services content and a matching algorithm that is able to recognize when a user request matches an advertised service [3]. The existing work for web services is based on XML syntax to describe web services content and to provide keyword-based matching. This work lacks well-defined semantics and has therefore led to the on-going research based on the semantic web services [4].

In semantic web services, data have a structure and an ontology describes the semantic of the data [5]. An ontology defines a conceptualization of a domain related to concepts, attributes, and relations [6]. The concepts provide model entities of interest in the domain. They are typically structured into a taxonomy tree where each node represents a concept and each concept has its parent as general concepts [5].

In semantic web services matching, service providers can advertise their web services via a well-defined description language and ontology, such as DAML-S [7] and OWL-S [8]. The matching system then allows services requesters to upload their requests which are encoded in specific description language and ontology as well. From this point, the matching system determines the relationship between the requests and the registered services in an ontology.

M. Dean et al. (Eds.): WISE 2005 Workshops, LNCS 3807, pp. 217–226, 2005.

There have been several matching techniques developed for matching semantic web services such as Colucci et al. [9], Elgedawy [10], Wang and Stroulia [11], Paolucci et al. [3] and Pahl and Casey [13]. These techniques differ in their support for variant result sets, extent of semantic support, degrees of matching and presentation of ranked results. These matching strategies exploit the semantic relation available between advertised and requested services. However, the main limitation of these works is the lack of quantitative measures for specifying the extent of similarity. Current semantic web services matching techniques have degrees of matching which are discrete and at a coarse level of granularity. A quantitative measure provides a more precise measurement and therefore can produce a better ranking of relevant services. Another advantage of measuring the similarity between services quantitatively is a finer level of granularity in matching result. In fact, while similarity and distance between services in ontology implicitly exist, none of the observed techniques is able to provide quantitative measures of similarity between concepts in the matching process.

This paper proposes that matching in semantic web services can be enhanced through the use of measures that quantify the "semantic distance" [12] between concepts in web services ontology. We demonstrate that a matching process based on Semantic Distance Measures will overcome the issues discussed above by refining and quantifying the degrees of the matching.

2   Semantic Distance Measures in Web Services Matching

In this paper, we contend that semantic distance can represent in quantitative terms the degree of matching between a service request and a service advertisement. There are four degrees of similarity in [3] determined by minimal distance between concepts in ontology. We now illustrate how these degrees of similarity can be strengthened by precise quantitative measures of similarity.

In Paolucci's model [3], the first degree of similarity is *exact match*. It returns an advertised service that is the same as a requested service. For example, if a user is looking for the service that sells Sedan, then an advertised service that sells Sedan is considered as *exact match*. *Exact match* in [3] also returns an advertised service which is the parent of the requested service. For example in figure 1, if a user is looking for the service that sells a Sedan, then the advertised service that sells a Car is also considered as an *exact match*. Paolucci et al. in [3] argue that this case of matching can be considered as *exact match* since by advertising a Car, provider will commit to provide every service which is subclass of that service. However, this assumption is not always true as it is possible to provide only certain sub-classes (e.g. only Sedans and no SUVs).

The second degree of matching is termed *plug-in match*. It returns an advertised service that is a grandparent of a requested service. It is not specified in [3] whether the great-grandparent or great-great-grandparent services are considered also as plug-in or not. For example in figure 1, if an SUV is requested, then according to the definition of plug-in, a service which advertises its capability as Vehicle will be returned.

The third degree of matching is termed subsumes match. It returns an advertised service that is a child of a requested service. For example in figure 1, if a Car is requested, then according to the definition of subsumes match, a service which advertises its capability as Sedan will be returned. In this degree of matching, there is no difference between advertised services which are a child and a grandchild of requested service, regardless of which level the advertised services is at.

The last degree of matching is termed *fail match*, which shows no subsumption relation (parent-child relation) between an advertised service and a requested service. Even though an advertised service and a requested service have the same parent (or grand parent) in ontology, they are still considered as *fail match* in [3]. For example in figure 1, if the requested service is a Sedan and the advertised service is a Bus, then a *fail match* is returned.

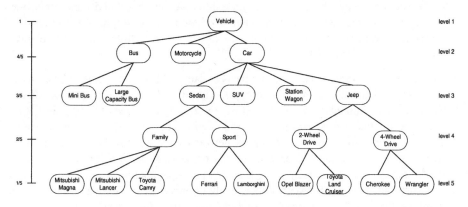

Fig. 1. The Example of Vehicle Ontology

We identify from above discussion of Paolucci's model that there are certain limitations. Firstly, a more precise measurement can produce a better ranking of relevant services. The matching result should not be only in the form of four discrete degrees, but should be at a finer level of granularity. For example, the Vehicle ontology in figure 1 shows that Sedan is semantically closer than Ferrari with respect to Vehicle. However, in [3] both services which sell Sedan and Ferrari are considered as *subsumes match* if the requested service is Vehicle.

Secondly, we identify that not all of the services without a subsumption relation should be considered as fail match. Especially, the services which have the same parents should not be considered as fail match. For example, the service which sells Lamborghini should be ranked as some degree of matching to a service which sells Ferrari. This is because there is possibility that a user who wants to buy Ferrari may also considers buying Lamborghini since they are both Sports cars.

We anticipate that a matching process based on Semantic Distance Measures will overcome these issues by refining and quantifying the degrees of the matching.

Therefore, we formulate the notions of our proposed model as follows.

1. The highest degree of matching is *exact match* where the requested service and the advertised service are exactly the same.
2. A requested service and an advertised service which has the child-parent relationship in the ontology should be higher in similarity than these services

which have the parent-child relationship. For example, if Sports car is requested, then a service which advertises Sedan should be higher in similarity than a service which advertises Ferrari. It can be seen from the Vehicle ontology in figure 1 that Sport is a child of Sedan and Sport is a parent of Ferrari.

3. The services in a lower level of the ontology should be ranked relatively closer to one another than the services in the higher level of ontology. According to Sussna's observation in [14, 15], concepts which are located deeper in the tree tend to be more closely related to one another than those higher in the tree. Therefore, we consider assigning a different weight for different level in the ontology. For example in figure 1, the services which sell Ferrari and Lamborghini (level 5 in the ontology) should be closer to one another than the services which sell Sedan and SUV (level 3 in the ontology).

4. The services which have the same parent should be considered closer than the services with the grandparent-grandchild relation. For example, the relationship between Ferrari and Lamborghini should be ranked closer than the relation between Ferrari and Sedan.

These above considerations form the basis of our SDM for matching web services. As we can see from the example ontology in figure 1, the similarity or the distance between services implicitly exists. Therefore, there is a need to exploit this similarity or distance by the use of quantitative and explicit measures. By using semantic distance, the similarity or the relatedness between concepts can be measured. The concepts refer to a particular sense of words or services in term of web services. According to Budanitsky in [12], there are three principal approaches that can be used to measure the distance between concepts dictionary-based, Thesaurus-based, and semantic networks. [12]. According to Lee et al. in [16], semantic networks are defined as "any representation interlinking nodes with arcs, where the nodes are concepts and the links are various kinds of relationships between concepts." Since this view of a semantic network has structured similarity to web services ontologies, we will focus the discussion only on this approach. In semantic networks, WordNet [17] is widely used as the encoding of lexical knowledge.

2.1 Incorporating Semantic Distance Measures in the Matching Process

As it is not always the case that an *exact match* to a requested service exists, every advertised service in the ontology should be able to be measured against requested services quantitatively. However, we need to satisfy all the requirements for matching web services as discussed previously. There are several measures of Semantic Distance that have been developed. In this research, we modify the SDM proposed by Hirst and St-Onge in [18] to facilitate application in the context of semantic web services. There are three major relations in Hirst and St-Onge's framework, i.e.: extra-strong, medium-strong, and strong. The definition of medium-strong is defined by the following formula:

$$\text{weight} = C - \text{path length} - k \times \text{number of changes of direction} \tag{1}$$

where C and k are constants, C set to 8 and k set to 1^{1}. By using the formula in equation 1, Hirst and St-Onge emphasize on the length of the path and the direction changing. It can be inferred from the formula that the longer the path the lower the weight and the more changes of direction the lower the weight.

We now explain our proposed modification of the Semantic Distance formula in equation 1 proposed by Hirst and St-Onge's in [18]. In their paper, the formula is used to measure the relations between nouns in Word-Net. However, our SDM algorithm applies the measurement for services in web service ontology. The concepts of nouns in [18] is replaced with web services inputs and outputs parameters while the taxonomy tree of WordNet in [18] is replaced with the ontology of web services.

The following formula can be used to have semantic distance measurement as well as satisfying all the requirements for matching web services.

- Let S_1 be the requested service from user and S_2 be the advertised service.
- Let lw be the level weight for each path in ontology. It depends on the depth of the ontology. To count the level weight lw, we use the following formula:
  $$lw = \frac{(n - \ln - 1)}{n}$$ where $\ln$ is the level of the node in the ontology.
  For example, the Vehicle ontology in figure 1 has five levels. Therefore, we weigh the edges in the topmost level as 1, the second level as 4/5, the third level as 3/5, the fourth level as 2/5 and the lowest level as 1/5.
- Let C be the constant. We follow Hirst and St-Onge in setting C to 8. The logical explanation for this value is for not neglecting other values in the formula
- Let $PathLength$ be the number of edges counted from service S_1 and S_2 in the ontology. For example the service Ferrari and SUV have the value of $PathLength = 4$
- Let $NumberOfDownDirection$ be the number of edges counted between service S_1 and S_2 which direction is downward. For example figure 1, Ferrari and SUV have 1 value of $NumberOfDownDirection$, while SUV and Ferrari have value of 3

Our proposed formula for measuring the semantic distance between service S_1 and S_2 is:

$$sdm(s1,s2) = C - lw*PathLength - NumberOfDownDirection \tag{2}$$

The formula in equation 2 only works for measuring the distances between services in the single inheritance ontology. While this research focuses on the matching between services in a single ontology, we present an extension to our proposed SDM to facilitate its use in multiple inheritance ontologies. The formula to count Semantic Distance Measure for matching web services which use multiple inheritance ontologies is as follow:

$$sdm(s1,s2) = C - lw*PathLength - NumberOfDownDirection + mcp(s1,s2) \tag{3}$$

---

[1] We communicated personally with Hirst to obtain these values.

The difference between the formula in equation 2 and 3 is the additional $mcp(s1,s2)$ in equation 4. The $mcp(s1,s2)$ is used to measure the number of most common parents in multiple inheritance ontologies. The formula is as follow:

$$mcp\ (s1;s2) = -\log \sum_{l=1}^{n} \frac{NumberOfMostCommonParents(s_1,s_2)_l}{l \times n} \tag{4}$$

where n is the depth of ontology which is measured in nodes and $NumberOfMostCommonParents$ is the number of parents in level l. This formula is useful to measure the distance between two services which are not only related in one ontology, but also present relations in other ontologies.

3 Evaluation

We implemented a matching engine based on our proposed SDM to conduct evaluations. The matching engine uses the following technologies in its implementation:

There are four supporting technologies used by SDM Matching Engine. The supporting technologies used in our SDM Matching Engine architecture are outlined as follows:

- **JDOM** [21]is an XML parser for Java. It provides a simple API for XML (SAX) and XML Document Object Model (DOM).
- **Jena [22]**is a Java framework for supporting semantic web applications. *Jena* is an open source software developed by HP Semantic Labs. *Jena* provides a programmatic environment for RDF, RDS and Web Ontology Language (OWL).
- **Jess** [23] s a Java expert system shell (*Jess*) and serves as a rule engine and scripting environment written in Java. *Jess* is developed by the Sandia National Laboratories. We use *Jess* to store the web service ontologies and to query the relationship between web services in the ontology.
- **OWLJessKB [24]** is a successor to *DAMLJessKB* which is a description logics reasoner for ontologies written in DAML+OIL. *OWLJessKB* provides extended reasoning for OWL by utilizing *Jena* and *Jess*. It provides a Java API that supports the reading and retrieval of web service ontologies (OWL).

To perform the evaluation, we only consider one parameter of each service for one matching process even though our SDM application can accommodate multiple parameters and combine the matching result from input and output matching. The reason for matching only one parameter is we want to focus on the matching process. By matching one parameter we hope that we can simplify comparison of the matching results between our approaches.

We use the simple example of a Vehicle Selling Service (shown in Figure 1) to show how SDM is used to match between a requested service and an advertised service. The Vehicle Selling Service is also used in Paolucci's model [3]. In our SDM, the Vehicle Ontology used by the Vehicle Selling Service is extended with several concepts. A larger ontology is needed to demonstrate the benefits of our SDM. Figure 1 shows the Vehicle ontology used by Vehicle Selling Service. The root concept of the Vehicle ontology is *Vehicle*. Each concept in this ontology has a level weight. The deeper a concept is in the ontology the level weight tends to decrease as shown in figure 1. For example, the concept *Bus*, *Motorcycle* and *Car* have level weight of $^4/_5$. On the other hand, the level weight for *Sedan*, *SUV* and *Station Wagon* is $^3/_5$. In order to focus on the matching process, we only examine the output parameters which are based on the Vehicle ontology. We assume that all cases use *Price* as the input of the services. It means that to be able to run the services, the user should input the *Price* value of the required vehicle.

3.1 Case 1

Table 2 shows the result of SDM matching between a requested and advertised service in case 1.

Table 2. Matching Result for Case 1

Requested service:	
- input:	Price
- output:	Sedan
Advertised service:	
- input:	Price
- output:	Sedan
Result from matching:	
- SDM input:	100 %
- SDM output:	$(8-(^3/_5+^3/_5)*0-0)/8 * 100\% = (8/8) * 100\% = 100\%$
- In Paolucci's model:	exact match

In this case, the user wants to buy a *Sedan* while the advertised service sells *Sedan* also. Since both requested and advertised service have the same input and output services, it returns a perfect value (100%). This result also shows that the concepts of input and output parameters are located in the same position in the ontology. According to Paolucci [3], this case returns a matching degree of *exact match*.

3.2 Case 2

Table 3 shows the result of SDM matching between a requested and advertised service in case 2. In this case, the user wants to buy *Sedan* while the advertised

Table 3. Matching Result for Case 2

Requested service:	
- input:	Price
- output:	Sedan
Advertised service:	
- input:	Price
- output:	Car
Result from matching:	
- SDM input:	100 %
- SDM output:	$(8-(^3/_5+^4/_5)*1-0)/8 * 100\% = (6.6/8)*100\% =$ 82.5%
- In Paolucci's model:	exact match

service sells *Car*. Since *Sedan* is a child of *Car* in the Vehicle ontology, it returns 82.5%. According to Paolucci [3], this case still returns a matching degree of *exact match*. It is clear that a quantitative measure based on Semantic Distance, allows explicit articulation between differences such as case 1 and this case.

3.3 Case 3

Table 3 shows the result of SDM matching between a requested and advertised service in case 4. In this case, the user wants to buy *Sedan* while the advertised service sells *Sport*.

Table 3. Matching Result for Case 3

Requested service:	
- input:	Price
- output:	Sedan
Advertised service:	
- input:	Price
- output:	Sport
Result from matching:	
- SDM input:	100 %
- SDM output:	$(8-(^3/_5+^2/_5)*1-1)/8 * 100\% = (6/8)*100\% = 75\%$
- In Paolucci's model:	subsumes match

Since *Sedan* is a parent of *Sport* in the Vehicle ontology, it returns 75%. It is noteworthy that in comparing this result with case 2, we see that through SDM, the relationship of similarity between a *Sedan* and a *Sports* car is weaker than the relationship between a *Sedan* and a *Car*. It is evident that a *Sports* car has certain specific semantics that can not be generalized to all *Sedans*, while in case 2 a *Sedan* is a *Car* and a *Sedan* is a less specific requirement than a *Sports* car.

3.4 Case 4

Table 4 shows the result of SDM matching between a requested and advertised service in case 5. In this case, the user wants to buy *Ferrari* while the advertised

Table 4. Matching Result for Case 4

Requested service:	
- input:	Price
- output:	Ferrari
Advertised service:	
- input:	Price
- output:	Sport
Result from matching:	
- SDM input:	100 %
- SDM output:	$(8-(^1/_5+^2/_5)*1-0)/8 * 100\% = (7.4/8)*100\% = 92.5\%$
- In Paolucci's model:	exact match

service sells *Sport*. Since *Ferrari* is a child of *Sport* in the Vehicle ontology, it returns 92.5%. This result has a higher degree of match than case 2 since the concepts are located in a lower part of ontology. According to Paolucci [3], this case returns a matching degree of *exact match*. Again, it can be seen that we are able to in this case establish a high degree of similarity without terming it as an *exact match*, which it is not.

We performed several other evaluation cases that we are unable to present in this paper due to space considerations. We also performed evaluation with other ontologies that illustrate similar results of the benefits of quantitative similarity measures in matching semantic web services.

4 Conclusion and Future Work

In this paper, we have proposed a formula to measure the Semantic Distance between services through concepts specified in an ontology. We established that Semantic Distance Measures are suitable for determining similarity between requested and advertised web services, thereby facilitating in performing the task of matching in the selection process. Our approach exploited service profiles that are available and provides a quantitative means of specifying the extent to which an advertised service meets the requirements of a user's request. This is significant because it allows us to return a finer level of granularity for each degree of matching. In summary, the primary contribution of our research is that we have developed a Semantic Distance Measure to provide a quantitative similarity measures to support matching in semantic web services. Currently, our model does not support multiple inheritance ontologies. Therefore, the enhancement of our model to incorporate Semantic Distance Measurement between services in multiple inheritance ontologies is a proposed extension.

References

1. Wang H, Huang JZ, Qu Y, et al. Web Services: Problems and Future Directions. In *Web Semantics: Science, Services and Agents on the World Wide Web, April 2004*. Vol1(3), pp. 309-320.
2. McIlraith SA, Son TC, Zeng H. Semantic Web Services. In *IEEE Intelligent Systems, 2001*. Vol16(2). pp 46-53.
3. Paolucci M, Kawmura T, Payne T, et al. Semantic Matching of Web Services Capabilities. In *First International Semantic Web Conference, June 2002, Sardinia, Italy*. pp. 333-347.
4. Berners-Lee T, Hendler J, Lassila O. The Semantic Web. In *Scientific American, 2001*. Vol284 (5). pp. 34–43.
5. Doan A, Madhavan J, Dhamankar R, et al. Learning to Match Ontologies on the Semantic Web. In *VLDB Journal, Special Issue on the Semantic Web, November 2003*. Vol12(4), pp. 303-319.
6. Fensel D. Ontologies: Silver Bullet for Knowledge Management and Electronic Commerce. *Springer-Verlag, 2001, Berlin*.
7. DAML Services Coalition (alphabetically A. Ankolekar MB, J. Hobbs, O. Lassila, D. Martin, S. McIlraith, S. Narayanan, M. Paolucci, T. Payne, K. Sycara, H. Zeng). DAML-S: Semantic Markup for Web Services. In *Proceedings of the International Semantic Web Working Symposium (SWWS), July 30-August 1, 2001, Stanford University, CA, USA*.

8. OWL-S Coalition. OWL-S 1.0 Release. Available at http://www.daml.org/services/owl-s/1.0/ (last accessed November 05, 2005).
9. Colucci S, Di Noia T, Di Sciascio E, et al. Description Logics Approach to Semantic Matching of Web Services. In *Proceedings of the 25th International Conference on Information Technology Interfaces 2003 (ITI 2003), June 16-19, 2003, Dubrovnik, Croatia.* pp. 545-550.
10. Elgedawy I. A Conceptual Framework for Web Services Semantic Discovery. In *Proceedings of On The Move (OTM) to meaningful internet systems, pages 1004–1016, Italy, 2003. Springer Verlag.*
11. Wang Y, Stroulia E. Flexible Interface Matching for Web-Service Discovery. In *Proceedings of the Fourth International Conference on Web Information Systems Engineering 2003 (WISE 2003), December 10-12 2003, Roma, Italy.* pp. 147-156.
12. Budanitsky A. Lexical Semantic Relatedness and Its Application in Natural Language Processing. Technical Report, *CSRG-390, August 1999.*
13. Pahl C, Casey M. Ontology support for web service processes. Proceedings of the 9th European software engineering conference held jointly with 10th ACM SIGSOFT international symposium on Foundations of software engineering. pp. 208 - 216 2003.
14. Sussna M. Word Sense Disambiguation for Free-Text Indexing Using a Massive Semantic Network. In *Proceedings of the Second International Conference on Information and Knowledge Management 1993 (CIKM-93), Arlington, Virginia.* pp. 67-74.
15. Sussna MJ. Text Retrieval Using Inference in Semantic Metanetworks. PhD thesis, University of California, San Diego, 1997.
16. Lee JH, Kim MH, Lee YJ. Information Retrieval Based on Conceptual Distance in IS-A Hierarchies. In *Journal of Documentation, June 1993.* Vol49(2). pp. 188-207.
17. Miller GA. Nouns in WordNet. In *Christiane Fellbaum, editor, WordNet: An Electronic Lexical Database*, chapter 1, pp. 23-46. The MIT Press, Cambridge, MA, 1998.
18. Hirst G, St-Onge D. Lexical Chains as Representations of Context for the Detection and Correction of Malapropisms. In *Christiane Fellbaum, editor, WordNet: An Electronic Lexical Database, chapter 13, pp. 305-332.* The MIT Press, Cambridge, MA. 1998.
19. http://www.daml.org/services/owl-s/1.1/BravoAirService.owl (last accessed April 25, 2005).
20. http://www.daml.org/services/owl-s/1.1/CongoService.owl (last accessed April 25, 2005).
21. Hunter J, McLaughlin B., JDOM API Javadoc Specification. Technical Report, 2004. Available at http://www.jdom.org/docs/apidocs/ (last accessed June 2, 2005).
22. McBride B. Jena: Implementing the RDF Model and Syntax Specification. In *Proceedings of the Semantic Web Workshop (WWW2001), May 2001, Hongkong, China.*
23. Friedman-Hill E. Jess in Action. Manning Publications Company, October 2003.
24. Kopena J, Regli W. DAMLJessKB: A Tool for Reasoning with the Semantic Web. In *IEEE Intelligent System, May/June 2003.* Vol18(3). pp. 74-77.

A Web Mining Method Based on Personal Ontology for Semi-structured RDF

Kotaro Nakayama, Takahiro Hara, and Shojiro Nishio

Dept. of Multimedia Eng., Graduate School of Information Science and Technology,
Osaka University, 1-5 Yamadaoka, Suita, Osaka 565-0871, Japan

Abstract. In order to improve Semantic Web Mining, as a precondition, there have to be enough data that are "well"-structured by linking to other web resources. However, Semantic Web data in real world, such as RSS and Dublin Core, are just semi-structured documents in most cases, because the main part of the content is still mixed with text data. In this paper, we propose a new Web Mining method based on Personal Ontology, a concept dictionary in the local machine personalized for each user which maps to web resource. Our approach accomplished Semantic Web Mining for semi-structured data such as RSS.

1 Introduction

The World Wide Web became a huge data source. Billions of pages are publicly available, and it is still growing dramatically. Thus, the internet has become an important infrastructure of information for most people. Recently, Web Mining, that can discover knowledge from huge amounts of web pages, has become an urgent research area in computer science.

The word "Web Mining" has several aspects because Web Mining is a wide research area. In fact, Web Mining is classified into several categories by the data source and the technique. The advanced essential techniques are based on various research areas such as database, natural language processing, information retrieval, data mining, and so on. Over the last few years, Web Mining become a hot topic and numerous attempts has been made to bring out the potential of WWW from these various aspects.

In addition to this, as the "Semantic Web[3]" is growing, "Semantic Web Mining[1]" has been noticed as the next step of Web Mining. In order to improve Semantic Web Mining, as a precondition, there have to be enough data based on Semantic Web data formats (RDF/OWL) which are "well"-structured by linking to other web resources. However, Semantic Web data in real world, such as "rss:title" or "rss:description" in RSS, are just semi-structured documents in most cases, because the main part of content is still mixed with text data. This form of the data connection is called "Semantic forests[8]." This means many small, disconnected, shallow resource trees. The structure of such a forest

M. Dean et al. (Eds.): WISE 2005 Workshops, LNCS 3807, pp. 227–234, 2005.

is isomorphic to that of an XML document. The connection form should be "Semantic webs", another form that consists of a large networks of resources linking to each other.

Semantic Web Mining techniques cannot be used for the data which forms Semantic forests due to the lack of links between web resources. Therefore, the way how to change the Semantic forests into Semantic webs became a hot topic on the Semantic Web Mining research. In this paper, we propose a Semantic Web Mining method for semi-structured RDF such as RSS that analyzes both text part and structured part in web resources.

Our method creates references to other web resources from RDF data by using Text Mining techniques. We designed the mechanism to make it scalable by using *Personal Ontology*, a concept dictionary personalized for each user. The mechanism does not refer the web resources on the WWW while inference. Instead of that, it refers the map of web resources on Personal Ontology.

In the next section of this paper, we give an overview of works relate to our research. Our approach and algorithm is described in section 3. We explain about our developed annotation system following this method in section 4. Finally, we make a conclusion of this research in section 5.

2   Related Works

Two fast-developing research areas, Web Mining and Semantic Web Mining, relate to our research. In this section, we give an overview of these related works to clarify our approach and contributions.

2.1   Web Mining

Web Mining is a research area of Data Mining which deals with the extraction of interesting knowledge from the World Wide Web. Web Mining researches are classified into three categories from the data source and the techniques; "Web Structure Mining," "Web Usage Mining," and "Web Content Mining[7]." The goal of Web Structure Mining is to mine hidden relations by analyzing the relations (Hyperlinks) between web pages and structure of page. Page Categorization methods and page ranking methods such as the PageRank[9] algorithm on Google are typical examples of the Web Structure Mining. In the PageRank algorithm, information about reference between pages is used to capture the relative importance of web pages in order to improve the quality of search engine. The goal of Web Usage Mining is to track the user's behavior by analyzing weblogs, log data of user access on both the server and the client machine. Web Usage Mining has a lot of applications such as the discovery of bottlenecks, usability measuring, user pattern discovery, user categorization, and so on. The goal of Web Content Mining is to analyze the contents of pages. It focuses on the text information available in web pages. The source data mainly consist of textual data in web pages. Typical applications are content-based categorization and content-based ranking of web pages.

2.2   Semantic Web Mining

The purpose of Semantic Web is that programs (Agents) search for information instead of humans by processing RDF, a machine-understandable data format. Therefore, the relations between web resources are quite important.

Semantic Web Mining aims at integrating techniques on the two fast-developing research areas, Semantic Web and Web Mining. The purpose of Semantic Web Mining is to improve the results of Web Mining by exploiting the new semantic structures in the Web. Furthermore, Web Mining can help to build the Semantic Web data[1].

As a concrete research example, Maedche et al.[10] are advancing the research which tries the construction of ontology by mining the Semantic Web data[10]. Purpose of the research is to create ontologies and concepts (semi-)automatically. That research is quite challenging and using several techniques such as machine learning, information retrieval and agent interface in order to discover semantics from web resources.

In Semantic Web Mining, no difference is made between Web Structured Mining and Web Contents Mining because the content describes the structure of Web resources[1]. However, it is just an ideal. The problem how and by whom the meta-data is created still remains even though "rdf:about," an entry which is used to link to other web resources.

3   Hybrid RDF Mining

As we mentioned before, there are no enough links to other Web resources in most cases. That is to say it is "semi"-structured data, not "well"-structured yet. "rss:title" and "rss:description" are typical examples. Of course, many entities to link other resources, including "foaf:knows", are already defined. However, lack of semantics still remains and it should be more structured and annotated well in order to improve the Semantic Web Mining.

As a solution, we propose a new Web Mining method based on Personal Ontology, a concept dictionary in the local machine personalized for each user which maps to web resource. The purpose of this method is to add annotation automatically for such not well-structured data.

3.1   Personal Ontology

Personal Ontology is the core part of our approach. In the Semantic Web, agent programs should search and explore the WWW as a front-end interface instead of users because the data will be described by machine-understandable format. However, in a distributed environment like WWW, conflicts with opinions of users and missing links are big problems. Additionally, the concept of each user depends on the culture and organization the user belongs to. To maintain a robust ontology in the distributed environment, it is natural that each user has his own personalized dictionary and agents manage it instead of the user. Furthermore, from the view of scalability, it is not a practical solution to relay

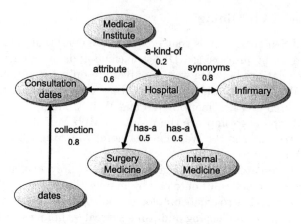

Fig. 1. Personal Ontology.

the relation between web resources. Therefore, we propose Personal Ontology, a concept dictionary that stores the map for web resources on the WWW. The characteristic feature of the Personal Ontology is that it has a Certainty Factor(CF) to keep the robustness of the dictionary instead of using the two value paradigm such as "Correct/Incorrect" or "0/1." Figure 1 shows an example of Personal Ontology.

This example shows the word "Hospital" and its relations to other words. These words are connected to other words by relation, such as "a-kind-of." We used the "WordNet[11]," a machine readable lexical dictionary of English which has a huge amount of vocabulary, as an initial data for Personal Ontology. The Personal Ontology is maintained by agent programs while the system is running.

3.2   Web Resource Mapping for RDF

We propose an automated resource mapping algorithm for RSS. In this algorithm, we analyze the text part in RSS and explore the web resources which relate to the terms in the text part. Then, links are automatically added (RDF:about) to the RSS.

Analyzing RDF: This process extracts text parts of RDF files at first. Then, as preprocessing, it performs stemming and tagging by using Brill's tagger[2]. The reason why we decided to use the tagger is that it is a simple but practical tool for real-time analyzing. Finally, it creates a word list that contains words marked as nouns or unknown words by the tagger.

Capturing the Importance by Lead-Method: There are several well-known methods based on statistics techniques to extract important words from articles. Although tfidf[12] is a typical and popular technique for this aim, it is not suitable for RSS because the text part in RSS is too short and distributed in general cases. In addition to this, its approach that counts frequencies of words cannot extract hidden topics. Thus, we decided to develop a new algorithm which explores the relation of words from Personal Ontology. This algorithm consists of the following two steps.

The first step is the extraction of important words by using the Lead method[6]. The basic idea of the Lead method is that "the lead part in article is more important than other parts." The second step is the exploration of the words. In this step, we recalculate the importance of words by exploring the relations between words which are stored in the Personal Ontology. In this clause, we explain detailed procedure of the first step. We defined W, a list of combinations of word w and the importance p, as follows:

$$W = \{(w_1, p_1), (w_2, p_2), ..., (w_i, p_i), ...\}.$$

$$p_i = \sum_{k=1}^{l} (length(doc) - position(w_{i,k})) / length(doc).$$

l denotes how many times w_i appears, $length(doc)$ denotes the total number of words in the document, and $position(w_{i,k})$ denotes the position of kth w_i. Added to this, the title entities in RSS should be more important than other entities, thus we multiply $p_i (\geq 1)$ to the importance of words which appears in the title part.

Recalculation of Importance: As we explained above, the proposed algorithm consists of two steps. In this clause, we explain detailed procedure of the second step, exploring words to recalculate the importance of words. In this process, we define $GetRelations(w)$, a function which gets all words relate to word w as w_j, the kind of relation between w and w_j as r_j, and the certainty factor as c_j. R_w, a list of combination of these elements, is defined as follows:

$$R_w = \{(w_1, r_1, c_1), (w_2, r_2, c_2), ..., (w_j, r_j, c_j, ...)\}.$$

In the second step, the function RE is recursively called for all words extracted by the Lead method. The detailed algorithm is as follows:

Algorithm. $RE(w, p)$
1   **if** $p < \delta$ **then return**;
2   $R_w = GetRelations(w)$;
3   **for each** $(w_j, r_j, c_j) \in R_w$ **do**
4       $s = p \cdot c_j \cdot cf(r_j)$;
5       $S_w = S_w + s$;
6       $RE(w_j, s)$;

---

cf is a function that returns a coefficient determined by the kind of relation r between words. Table 1 shows the coefficients returned by $cf(r)$ for the given relations between words A and B.

We designed this algorithm that the importance decreases as the trace of words is branched off. Finally, the extracted words are sorted by its total score, and the scores are used to map web resources to the entry. The web resource mapping information is not stored in original file on the WWW. Instead of this, the mapping information is stored into Personal Ontology for next time.

Table 1. Coefficients returned by cf(r)

relation	$cf(r)$	example
A same-as B	1.00	PC is same as personal computer
A is-a-kind-of B	0.75	Thinkpad(A) is a kind of PC(B)
B is-a-kind-of A	0.50	Thinkpad(B) is a kind of PC(A)
A relates-to B	0.25	Thinkpad(A) relates to PC(B)

Updating the Personal Ontology: The word list should be resorted by the total score S_w of word w, then the c_j value between top n resources should be increased. This approach is similar to the concept of *Cooccurrence-based similarity of words*[13]. If there is no relation between words ranked as top n resources, a new relation, i.e., "A relates-to B," is generated and added to both A and B.

4   Implementation

To examine the practicality of Personal Ontology, we developed an auto annotation system for RSS. Figure 2 shows the architecture of the system.

The flow of the process is as follows. At first, as a preparation, we build a web server on a local machine to construct a Personal Ontology written by RDFS/OWL from WordNet. Several researches have addressed the conversion of WordNet into Web ontology. [5] is one of the conventional works. However, only few attempts have so far been made at the mapping to natural language. Thus, machines couldn't process the semi-structured RDF because of this problem on missing link to natural

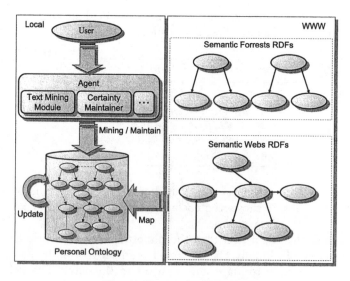

Fig. 2. System Architecture

language. We want to say the importance of mapping between web resource and natural language with special emphasis. Thus, we defined meta-data on the Personal Ontology by using the "rdfs:label" attribute on RDFS (RDF Schema), a vocabulary description language for RDF. The tagged document below is an example of a definition of word "Hospital" by using RDFS/OWL.

```
...
<wn:Noun rdf:about="&wn;106690409" />
<wn:WordObject rdf:about="&wn;hospital" />
<rdf:Description rdf:about="&wn;106690409">
  <wn:wordForm rdf:resource="&wn;hospital" />
  <rdfs:label>hospital</rdfs:label>
  <wn:glossaryEntry>
    a medical institution where sick or injured people are given medical...
  </wn:glossaryEntry>
  <wn:hyponymOf rdf:resource="&wn;106689915" />
</rdf:Description>
...
<rdf:Description rdf:about="&wn;106689915">
  <wn:wordForm rdf:resource="&wn;medical_institution" />
  <rdfs:label>medical institution</rdfs:label>
</rdf:Description>
...
```

The numbers in the document, such as 106690409 and 106689915, are just identifiers for each word in WordNet. In our implementation, we used the numbers as a part of the URI to identify each web resource.

5   Conclusion

In this paper, we proposed Hybrid Web Mining based on Personal Ontology. Additionally, we developed an auto annotation system for RSS to examine the practicality of the Personal Ontology. We plan to develop a Semantic Web search engine to conduct an experiment and evaluate the algorithm of this research. We believe that this approach can help to solve the Semantic forests problem and improve the quality of information retrieving on Semantic Web.

On the other hand, there are several issues such as quality of Text Mining and user-interface for meta-data annotation. Especially, improving the quality of Text Mining is an urgent issue in our research. We didn't process the phrase in document, but processed just individual words. we now plan to use N-Gram analyzing, extracting new words and mining technical words from Web-based encyclopedia.

Weblog is also a remarkable future work of our research because Weblog is noticed in the Semantic Web research area because of the potential as a publishing tool on the WWW[4]. We also notice this paradigm as an interface to publish the metadata because one of the issues in our project is how to add new relations between words in the Personal Ontology.

References

1. B. Berendt, A. Hotho, and G. Stumme, "Towards Semantic Web Mining," Proc. of International Semantic Web Conference, pp. 264–278, 2002.
2. E. Brill, "A Simple Rule-based Part of Speech Tagger," Proc. of Conference on Applied Computational Linguistics (ACL), pp. 112–116, 1992.
3. T. Berners-Lee, J. Hendler, and O. Lassila, "The Semantic Web," Scientific American, pp. 35–43, 2001.
4. S. Cayzer, "Semantic blogging and decentralized knowledge management", Communications of the ACM, Vol. 47, No. 12, pp. 47–52,2004.
5. C. Ciorascu, I. Ciorascu, and K. Stoffel, "knOWLer Ontological Support for Information Retrieval Systems," Proc. of SIGIR Conference, 2003.
6. H. P. Edmundson, "New Methods in Automatic Extracting," Journal of ACM, Vol. 16, No. 2, pp. 264–285, 1969.
7. F. M. Facca and P. L. Lanzi, "Mining Interesting Knowledge from Weblogs: A Survey," Data and Knowledge Engineering, Vol. 53, No. 3, pp. 225–241, 2005.
8. G. A. Grimnes, P. Edwards, and A. Preece "Learning Meta-descriptions of the FOAF Network," Proc. of International Semantic Web Conference, pp. 152–165, 2004.
9. P. Lawrence, B. Sergey, M. Rajeev, and W. Terry, "The PageRank Citation Ranking: Bringing Order to the Web," Technical Report, Stanford Digital Library Technologies Project, 1999.
10. A. Maedche and S. Staab, "Ontology Learning for the Semantic Web," IEEE Intelligent Systems, Vol. 16, No. 2, pp. 72–79, 2001.
11. G. A. Miller, "WordNet: A Lexical Database for English," Communications of the ACM, Vol. 38, No. 11, pp. 39–41, 1995.
12. G. Salton and C. Buckley, "Term-Weighting Approaches in Automatic Text Retrieval," Information Processing and Management, Vol. 24, No. 5, pp. 513–523, 1988.
13. H. Schutze and Jan O. Pedersen, "A Cooccurrence-based Thesaurus and Two Applications to Information Retrieval," International Journal of Information Processing and Management, Vol. 33, No. 3, pp. 307–318, 1997.

SPARQL Query Processing with Conventional Relational Database Systems

Stephen Harris and Nigel Shadbolt

IAM, University of Southampton, UK
{swh, nrs}@ecs.soton.ac.uk

Abstract. This paper describes an evolution of the 3store RDF storage system, extended to provide a SPARQL query interface and informed by lessons learned in the area of scalable RDF storage.

1 Introduction

The previous versions of the 3store [1] RDF triplestore were optimised to provide RDQL [2] (and to a lesser extent OKBC [3]) query services, and had no efficient internal representation of the language and datatype extensions from RDF 2004 [4].

This revision of the 3store software adds support for the SPARQL [5] query language, RDF datatype and language support. Some of the representation choices made in the implementation of the previous versions of 3store made efficient support for SPARQL queries difficult. Therefore, a new underlying representation for the RDF statements was required, as well as a new query engine capable of supporting the additional features of SPARQL over RDQL and OKBC.

2 Related Work

The SPARQL query language is still at an early stage of standardisation, but there are already other implementations.

2.1 *Federate*

Federate [6] is a relational database gateway, which maps RDF queries to existing database structures. It concentrates on compatibility with existing relational database systems, rather than as a native RDF storage and querying engine.

2.2 Jena

Jena [7] is a Java toolkit for manipulating RDF models which has been developed by Hewlett-Packard Labs. It has largely complete support for SPARQL features over the in-memory store provided by the Jena engine. There is also a SQL back-end available, sparql2sql, which provides persistent storage through a SQL database.

M. Dean et al. (Eds.): WISE 2005 Workshops, LNCS 3807, pp. 235–244, 2005.

2.3 Redland

The Redland Framework [8] also has substantial support for SPARQL queries
over its in-memory and on-disk stores, but does not have a query engine that
translates into relational expressions in the way that 3store and sparql2sql do.
3store uses the RDF parser and SPARQL query parser components from Redland, which were a great help in reducing the implementation effort.

3   The Design of the 3store RDF Knowledge Base

The overall architecture of this version of 3store (version 3) is broadly based on
the previous versions. The basic design, in which the RDF query expressions are
transformed to an SQL query expression containing a large number of simple joins
across a small number of tables has been shown to perform and scale well [9].

3.1 Platform

For scalability and portability reasons the software is developed for POSIX compliant UNIX environments in ANSI C. C is efficient and can easily be interfaced
to other languages such as PHP, Perl, Python, C++ and Java.

As in previous versions of 3store, MySQL was chosen as the sole persistent
back-end. Although the MySQL optimiser is not particularly sophisticated it has
already be shown in 3store versions 1 and 2 to be adequate for optimising RDF
graph matching queries of the form produced by the 3store query translator.

3.2 Three Layer Model

The existing RDF engines that support medium sized knowledge bases and
database back-ends (such as Jena and Redland, discussed in Sections 2.2 and 2.3
respectively) mostly evaluate queries in the RDF part of the engine, rather than
in the underlying database. We believe that this misses an opportunity to let the
database perform much of the work using its built-in query optimiser (based on
its understanding of the indexes). Our experiences from the previous versions of
3store indicated that this can quantitatively reduce query execution times. The
3-layer model of HYWIBAS[10] and SOPHIA[11] is used to perform multi-level
optimisations, and enable efficient RDBMS storage. Like SOPHIA, and unlike
HYWIBAS, 3store uses a unified storage mechanism for both classes and instances, in part due to the underlying RDF syntax of RDF Schema. 3store's
layers can be characterised as RDF Syntax, RDF Representation and Relational
Database System, which are comparable to HYWIBAS' Knowledge Base System,
Object Data Management System and Relational Database System.

4   RDF–SQL Mapping

The mapping between RDF and SQL has been changed since the previous version
of 3store. In the previous version resources (URIs) and literals were kept in

separate tables, requiring the use of outer joins to return values. Resources and literals are now kept in a single table, which allows inner joins to be used to return values, at the cost of a larger table.

4.1   Hashing Function

Resources and literals are internally identified by a 64 bit hash function. This is used so that string comparisons can be kept to a minimum and to reduce the storage requirements per statement.

Discrimination. As before a portion of the MD5 function [12] is used for it's efficiency and universality (a hash function is universal if it has the property that the probability of a collision between keys x and y when $x \neq y$ is the same for all x and y [13]). However recent concerns over MD5's security [14] suggest that it may be better to seek out a hash function that provides greater protection from the possibility of hash collisions where security is a concern.

In order to allow the URI <http://aktors.org> to be easily distinguished from the literal string "http://aktors.org" the hash space is divided into two segments. Literals occupy the lower half of the 64 bit hash space and URIs occupy the upper half, such that $hash(literal(x)) \text{ \& } 2^{63} = hash(uri(x))$.

Additionally the literal hash values are modified by applying the bitwise exclusive-or operator to bit ranges of the literal hash and the integer identifier of the datatype and language. This ensures that that hash value for an integer literal "100" is distinct from the float, string etc. literals with the same lexical form, "100". This stage is not strictly necessary, but it facilitates certain comparisons and joins we wish do do in the query language, and enables some optimisations.

Collisions. The system detects colliding hashes for differing RDF nodes at assertion time. Though there is no obvious way to recover from this state, it is possible to warn the user and reject the RDF file containing the colliding hash. This could potentially happen though a pair of URIs engineered to collide. With the current state of the art in MD5 collisions they would both have to be at least 1024 bytes long [14], and it would take an extensive search to find a colliding pair that contained only characters that were legal in URIs.

The "Birthday Paradox"[1] gives the probability of an accidental hash collision occurring anywhere in a knowledge base of 10^9 distinct nodes to be around $1 : 10^{-10}$ when using an effective 63 bit hash. The situation for literal values is complicated by the exclusive-or operator, but the probability will be of a similar order of magnitude.

4.2   SQL Tabular Representation

Triples. The central table is the `triples` table (figure 1) which holds the hashes for the subject, predicate, object and SPARQL GRAPH [5] identifier. The 64 bit

---

[1] The Birthday Paradox gives the hash collision probability as $p = 1 - (1 - 2^{-s})^n$ where s is the size of the hash (in bits) and n is the number of items. However this assumes a perfectly even hashing function.

model	subject	predicate	object
int64	int64	int64	int64

Fig. 1. Structure of the `triples` table

hash	lexical	integer	floating	datetime	datatype	language
int64	text	int64	real	datetime	int32	int32

Fig. 2. Structure of the `symbols` table

integer columns hold hashes of the RDF nodes that occupy those slots in the triple. The `model` column is used to hold the `GRAPH` identifier, or zero if the triple resides in the anonymous background graph.

Symbols. The `symbols` table (figure 2) allows reverse lookups from the hash to the hashed value, for example, to return results. Furthermore it allows SQL operations to be performed on pre-computed values in the `integer`, `floating` or `datetime` value columns without the use of casts.

hash holds the value of the hash the represents this symbol (URI or literal). URIs and literals may be discriminated by checking the value of the MSB of the integer value, see section 4.1.

lexical holds the UTF-8 representation of the textual form of the symbol as it appeared in the RDF document. This allow reconstruction of the node in output documents or query results, and is used for the storage of URIs and strings.

integer, floating and datetime are computed at assertion time according to the RDF datatype of the literal to be stored. The `floating` column has multiple uses and is used to store values in the XSD decimal, float and double datatypes [15]. NULL (ω) is stored in the value columns for which there is no value of that type.

datatype and language columns hold foreign keys to the `datatypes` and `languages` tables respectively. Where the is no known RDF datatype or language for a particular literal the appropriate columns are set to ω.

Datatypes and languages. The `datatypes` and `languages` tables are joined to the `symbols` table by the id columns. Datatype could have been stored in the symbols table and joined back onto itself to recover the URI. However, the author felt that the approach of keeping it in a separate table would be more efficient overall. No benchmarking has been done to justify this decision.

The `id` column is an auto incrementing field in this implementation, though it could equally be a hash of the value as in the `triples` table.

id	uri		id	lang
int32	text		int32	char(5)

Fig. 3. Structure of the `datatypes` and `languages` tables

5   Query Execution

As far as is possible the task of executing the query is passed down to the database engine. This allows the database optimiser to operate on the query, hopefully spot optimisations that are not clear from the external view of the tables and benefit from decades of research into relational database optimisers.

5.1   Simple Graph Expression Mapping

To illustrate how the mapping to relational database expressions is performed for simple SPARQL queries imagine a query to discover the label associated to the URI `mailto:alice@example`. In SPARQL this query could be written as shown in figure 4, where `?x` is a variable to be bound by the results of the query.

```
SELECT ?x
WHERE { <mailto:alice@example.com>
              <http://www.w3.org/2000/01/rdf-schema#label> ?x . }
```

Fig. 4. Graph showing RDF structure and equivalent SPARQL query

```
CREATE TABLE tmp (
  x bigint
)

INSERT INTO tmp
SELECT object
FROM triples
WHERE predicate=0xcf75ce12336ab89a
AND subject=0xbb37ab7444225966
AND model=0

SELECT lexical, datatype, language
FROM tmp, symbols
WHERE tmp.x=symbols.hash
```

Fig. 5. Translation of query in figure 4 into SQL

This query may simply be translated into relational algebra[2] as:

$$\text{tmp}(x) \leftarrow \pi_{\text{object}}(\sigma_{\text{predicate}=hash(p)\wedge\text{subject}=hash(s)\wedge\text{model}=0}(\text{triples}))$$

$$\pi_{\text{lexical,datatype,language}}(\text{tmp} \bowtie_{x=hash} \text{symbols})$$

---

[2] In the paper describing the translation algorithm of the previous version of this software [1] the authors used relational calculus. However, some of the expressions used in this paper are more clearly expressed in relational algebra, which regrettably makes comparisons difficult.

where $hash(s)$ and $hash(p)$ are the 64 bit hash values for the URIs `mailto:alice@example.com` and `http://www.w3.org/2000/01/rdf-schema#label` respectively. Equivalently the SPARQL query may be translated into MySQL's dialect of SQL as shown in figure 5.

Where the graph pattern is more complex and contains multiple triples, the `triples` table must be joined to itself, as in:

```
PREFIX rdfs: <http://www.w3.org/2000/01/rdf-schema#>
PREFIX ex: <http://example.com/schema#>
SELECT ?uri ?homepage
WHERE { ?uri ex:homepage ?homepage .
          ?uri rdfs:label "Alice" . }
```

which becomes

$$\text{tmp(homepage, uri)} \leftarrow \pi_{t0.\text{object},t0.\text{subject}} \sigma_{t1.\text{object}=0x64489c85dc2fe078}$$
$$\wedge t1.\text{predicate}=0xcf75ce12336ab89a \wedge t1.\text{model}=0$$
$$\wedge t0.\text{predicate}=0xd290a78cfc5c100b \wedge t0.\text{model}=0$$
$$(\rho_{t0}(\text{triples}) \bowtie_{t0.\text{subject}=t1.\text{subject}} \rho_{t1}(\text{triples}))$$

$$\pi_{v0.\text{lexical},v0.\text{datatype},v0.\text{language},v1.\text{lexical},v1.\text{datatype},v1.\text{language}}$$
$$((\text{tmp} \bowtie_{\text{uri}=\text{hash}} \rho_{v0}(\text{symbols})) \bowtie_{\text{homepage}=\text{hash}} \rho_{v1}(\text{symbols}))$$

The algorithm employed to implement the transformation of these simple expressions is straightforward. First the `triples` table is joined once for each triple in the pattern and renamed as tn ($\rho_{tn}(\text{triples})$). Then the set of triples in the graph pattern is traversed and triple slots (subject, predicate or object) with constant values are constrained to their hash values. For example t1.predicate is constrained to the hash for `rdfs:label` with $\sigma_{t1.predicate=0xcf75ce12336ab89a}$. Concurrently variables are bound; when first encountered the triple and slot in which the variable appears is recorded, and subsequent occurrences in the graph pattern are used to constrain any appropriate joins with their initial binding, as in $\bowtie_{t0.subject=t1.subject}$ in the example.

To produce the intermediate results table (tmp), the hashes of any SPARQL variables required to be returned in the results set are projected, as in $\pi_{t0.object,t0.subject}$.

Finally, the hashes from the intermediate results table are joined to the `symbols` table to provide the textual representation of the results. The datatype and language columns are also projected to allow them to be returned for RDF serialisation for example, or as data in the SPARQL XML results serialisation.

Clearly, the intermediate table could be projected within the final results expression (see section 5.4). Keeping it separate at this stage of the processing has advantages when dealing with more complex expressions. It allows a simple representation of optional match expressions and can be used to circumvent the join size optimiser restrictions on some database engines (including MySQL), by breaking down the query into multiple sub expressions.

5.2   Optional Match Implementation

SPARQL's OPTIONAL operator is used to signify a subset of the query that should not cause the result to fail if it cannot be satisfied. As such it is roughly analogous to the left outer join of relational algebra.

Again, the algorithm for the transformation from SPARQL to relational algebra is quite straightforward. The triples are grouped according to what block they appear in (the single "required" block, or one of the optional blocks). Intermediate tables are produced for each block as before, but in the case of optional blocks, columns that allow joining onto the required block must also be projected. In the example below uri is the only column which is present in both intermediate tables.

The intermediate tables are then joined to the symbols table in the results phase. The symbols tables for optional intermediate tables must be outer joined, as the bindings may be ω from failed matches in the optional blocks.

Using this approach, the SPARQL query

```
PREFIX rdfs: <http://www.w3.org/2000/01/rdf-schema#>
PREFIX ex: <http://example.com/schema#>
SELECT ?uri ?homepage
WHERE { ?uri rdfs:label "Alice" .
        OPTIONAL { ?uri ex:homepage ?homepage . }
}
```

becomes[3]

$$\text{tmp}(\text{uri}) \leftarrow \pi_{\text{subject}} \sigma_{\text{object}=0x64489c85dc2fe078 \wedge \text{predicate}=0xcf75ce12336ab89a \wedge \text{model}=0}(\text{triples})$$

$$\text{opt1}(\text{homepage}, \text{uri}) \leftarrow \pi_{\text{object},\text{uri}} \sigma_{\text{predicate}=0xd290a78cfc5c100b \wedge \text{model}=0}(\text{tmp} \bowtie_{\text{uri}=\text{subject}} \text{triples})$$

$$\pi_{\text{v0.lexical},\text{v1.lexcial}}((\text{tmp} \bowtie_{\text{uri}=\text{hash}} \rho_{\text{v0}}(\text{symbols})) \bowtie_{\text{uri}=\text{uri}} (\text{opt1} \bowtie_{\text{homepage}=\text{hash}} \rho_{\text{v1}}(\text{symbols})))$$

All simple, legal optional expressions may be transformed in this way. Though a more sophisticated algorithm is required to express nested optional graph patterns.

5.3   Value Constraints

The application of value constraints can be more complex than the transformation of graph patterns. There is a simple case, where the value constraint refers only to variables that are only bound in the current block and the constraint can

---

[3] In this example the projections of the datatype and language of the returned bindings have been omitted for brevity.

be mapped into an equivalent relational expression. In this case the constraint may be applied simply by joining the `symbols` table and selecting on the appropriate column. For example, where we have `?x ex:age ?y . FILTER(?y > 30)` we can produce $\sigma_{integer>30}(triples \bowtie_{object=hash} symbols)$. However, there are many cases where this simple transformation cannot be applied, including:

Non-relational expressions. These may either be constraints that are beyond the expressive power of the relational engine (such as certain regular expressions) or extension functions that are implemented in the application layer. These must be handled by externally processing the intermediate tables or the final results table in the application layer.

Late bound expressions. Sometimes it is desirable to place constraints in optional blocks with variables that do not appear in that block. This is problematic as the bindings for that variable are not available at the time the intermediate table is selected. In this case the constraint can be transferred to the results processing step. Alternatively, if available the bindings for the variables in question can be joined to the intermediate blocks in which they appear. Delaying the selection of the FILTER constraints is undesirable as it increases the size of the intermediate tables.

Required constraints on optionally bound variables. In SPARQL it is syntactically legal to place constraints in the required block on variables that are bound only in an optional block. This has the effect of demoting the optional block to a required block, so the blocks must either be merged or the constraint must be delayed until the results phase of the query.

Additionally, there are complexities around the type constraints and promotion rules of SPARQL. On the whole these can be expressed in relational algebra, though a description of the algorithm is beyond the scope of this paper.

5.4 Optimisation

There are a number of layer two optimisations that can be performed on the query. The purpose of these is to perform transformations on the relational expressions that the relational engine would not be aware are valid (things that are specific to RDF) or to aid the relational engine in further optimisations.

Expressions such as the one in figure 4 may be optimised by simply substituting the intermediate table into the results expression, with appropriate renaming operations where necessary.

This operation may also be performed on certain simple optional match graph patterns. The query in section 5.2 is an example. As there are no constraints or dependencies between the blocks and each optional match consists of a single triple, the intermediate tables may be substituted into the results expression to form a single expression.

The benefit of this optimisation is in allowing the relational database's optimiser to work over the whole query and to allow it to bypass the construction of intermediate tables where possible. The total number of joins will be reduced as the required intermediate table does not have to be joined a second time.

Another area to which optimisation can be applied is the projection of the datatype and language attributes of a variable. Where the variable is known to be only able to bind to URI values then there is no need for these values to be projected. Equally, where the language or datatype attributes are constrained in FILTER expressions in certain parts of the query then their values are known to be constant.

6   Future Work

6.1   Complete Implementation

Not all the SPARQL features have been implemented at the time of writing. In particular, nested UNION and optional blocks have yet to be supported. They pose considerable complexities to an efficient querytranslation. It is hoped that the intermediate table building approach will be advantageous in optimising queries using these features.

6.2   Reasoning

As yet there is no support for RDFS reasoning in this version. The current plan is to forward port the 3store version 2 reasoner. This reasoner is sound but incomplete [1], and has performed well in the past.

Acknowledgments

This work was supported by the Advanced Knowledge Technologies (AKT) Interdisciplinary Research Collaboration (IRC). The AKT IRC is sponsored by the UK Engineering and Physical Sciences Research Council under grant number GR/N15764/01 and comprises the Universities of Aberdeen, Edinburgh, Sheffield, Southampton and the Open University.

References

1. Harris, S., Gibbins, N.: 3store: Efficient bulk RDF storage. In: Proceedings of the 1st International Workshop on Practical and Scalable Semantic Systems (PSSS'03). (2003) 1–20 http://eprints.aktors.org/archive/00000273/.
2. Hewlett-Packard Labs: RDQL - RDF data query language. http://www.hpl.hp.com/semweb/rdql.htm (2003)
3. Chaudhri, V., Farquhar, A., Fikes, R., Karp, P.D., Rice, J.P.: Open knowledge base connectivity. Technical report, OKBC Working Group (1998) http://www.ai.sri.com/~okbc/spec.html.
4. Beckett, D.: RDF/XML syntax specification (revised). Technical report, World Wide Web Consortium (2004)
5. Prud'hommeaux, E., Seaborne, A.: SPARQL query language for RDF. Technical report, World Wide Web Consortium (2005) http://www.w3.org/TR/rdf-sparql-query/.

6. Prud'hommeaux, E.: Optimal RDF access to relational databases. Technical report, Wold Wide Web Consortium (2004)
   http://www.w3.org/2004/04/30-RDF-RDB-access/.
7. Hewlett-Packard Labs: The Jena Semantic Web Toolkit. Technical report, Hewlett-Packard Labs (2003) http://www.hpl.hp.com/semweb/jena.htm.
8. Beckett, D.: Redland RDF Application Framework. http://librdf.org/ (2005)
9. Lee, R.: Scalability report on triple store applications. MIT tech report (2004)
   http://simile.mit.edu/reports/stores/.
10. Norrie, M., Reimer, U., Lippuner, P., Rhys, M., Schek, H.: Frames, objects and relations: Three semantic levels for knowledge base systems. Reasoning About Structured Objects: Knowledge Representation Meets Databases. In 1st Workshop KRDB'94 (1994) 20–22
11. Abernethy, N., Altman, R.: Sophia: Providing basic knowledge services with a common DBMS. Proceedings of the 5th International Workshop on Knowledge Represenation Meets Databases (KRDB '98): Innovative Application Programming and Query Interfaces (1998)
12. Rivest, R.: The MD5 message-digest algorithm. IETF RFC 1321, MIT Laboratory for Computer Science and RSA Data Security, Inc. (1992)
   http://www.ietf.org/rfc/rfc1321.txt.
13. Cormen, T.H., Leiserson, C.E., Rivest, R.L.: Introduction to Algortihms. MIT Press, Cambridge, MA (1989)
14. Klima, V.: Finding MD5 collisions on a notebook PC using multi-message modifications. In: Proceedings of the 3rd International Conference Security and Protection of Information. (2005)
15. Biron, P.V., Malhotra, A.: XML schema part 2: Datatypes second edition. W3C recommendation, World Wide Web Consortium (2004)
   http://www.w3.org/TR/xmlschema-2/.

Scalable Instance Retrieval for the Semantic Web by Approximation

Holger Wache[1], Perry Groot[2], and Heiner Stuckenschmidt[1]

[1] Vrije Universiteit Amsterdam, de Boelelaan 1081a,
1081HV Amsterdam, The Netherlands
{holger, heiner}@cs.vu.nl
[2] Radboud University Nijmegen, Toernooiveld 1,
6500GL Nijmegen, The Netherlands
Perry.Groot@science.ru.nl

Abstract. Approximation has been identified as a potential way of reducing the complexity of logical reasoning. Here we explore approximation for speeding up instance retrieval in a Semantic Web context. For OWL ontologies, i.e., Description Logic (DL) Knowledge Bases, it is known that reasoning is a hard problem. Especially in instance retrieval when the number of instances that need to be retrieved becomes very large. We discuss two approximation methods for retrieving instances to conjunctive queries over DL T-Boxes and the results of experiments carried out with a modified version of the Instance Store System.

1 Motivation

A central issue in the Semantic Web research community is the expressivity of its underlying language and the complexity of the reasoning services it supports. There is a direct correspondence between the current Semantic Web ontology language OWL and Description Logic (DL).[1] Research in DL has lead to sophisticated DL reasoners [6, 3, 5] that can be used to reason with OWL ontologies on the Semantic Web. Considering T-Box reasoning, current state of the art techniques seem capable of dealing with real world ontologies [7, 4]. However, besides T-Box reasoning, an important application domain of ontologies is A-Box reasoning, i.e., reasoning and retrieving the individuals in an ontology. Experiments have shown that state of the art DL reasoners break down for A-Box reasoning when the number of instances becomes large [8]. Present work focusses at approximation techniques to make A-Box reasoning in DLs more scalable when retrieving instances from an ontology with a large number of instances.

In this paper, we investigate optimization techniques that are based on approximate logical reasoning. The underlying idea of these techniques is to replace certain inference problems by simpler problems such that either the soundness or the completeness, but not both, of the solutions is preserved. The solutions to the simpler problems are approximate solutions to the original problem.

---

[1] More precisely two of the three species of OWL.

M. Dean et al. (Eds.): WISE 2005 Workshops, LNCS 3807, pp. 245–254, 2005.

The contribution of this work is in comparing the performance of two approximate reasoning methods proposed in the literature applied to the real world task of answering conjunctive queries over DL Knowledge Bases. For this, we used the Instance Store [8], a state of the art system developed to scale-up instance retrieval for ontologies with a large number of instances, and extended it with two approximation techniques. The Gene Ontology is used as benchmark data set to evaluate the performance of the approximation techniques.

The paper is organized as follows. Section 2 gives a brief introduction to DLs. Section 3 defines the problem of instance retrieval in the context of Description Logics, which is restricted to conjunctive queries. Section 4 gives a brief overview of two approximation methods and describes how they can be applied to the problem of instance retrieval. Section 5 gives the results of experiments with the two approximation methods applied to instance retrieval using the Gene Ontology. Section 6 concludes our work.

2   Description Logics

DLs [1] are a special type of logic that is tailored to define terminological knowledge in terms of sets of objects with common properties. Recently, DLs have become popular as a formal foundation for the Web

DL Expr.	Semantics
A	$A^{\mathcal{I}} \subseteq \Delta$
$\neg C$	$(\neg C)^{\mathcal{I}} = \Delta - C^{\mathcal{I}}$
$C \sqcap D$	$(C \sqcap D)^{\mathcal{I}} = C^{\mathcal{I}} \cap D^{\mathcal{I}}$
$C \sqcup D$	$(C \sqcup D)^{\mathcal{I}} = C^{\mathcal{I}} \cup D^{\mathcal{I}}$
$\exists R.C$	$(\exists R.C)^{\mathcal{I}} = \{x \mid \exists y : (x,y) \in R^{\mathcal{I}}\}$
$\forall R.C$	$(\forall R.C)^{\mathcal{I}} = \{x \mid (x,y) \in R \implies y \in C^{\mathcal{I}}\}$

Ontology Language OWL. The basic modelling elements of a DL are instances, concepts, and relations. These modelling elements are provided with a formal semantics in terms of an abstract domain interpretation $\mathcal{I}$, which maps each instance onto an element of an abstract domain Δ. Instances can be connected by binary relations defined as subsets of $\Delta \times \Delta$. Concepts are interpreted as a subset of the abstract domain Δ. Intuitively, a concept is a set of instances that share certain properties. These properties are defined in terms of concept expressions. Typical operators are the Boolean operators as well as universal and existential quantification over relations to instances in other concepts. The formal definitions can be found in the first table.

DL Axiom	Semantics
$C(x)$	$x^{\mathcal{I}} \in C^{\mathcal{I}}$
$P(x,y)$	$(x^{\mathcal{I}}, y^{\mathcal{I}}) \in P^{\mathcal{I}}$
$C \sqsubseteq D$	$C^{\mathcal{I}} \subseteq D^{\mathcal{I}}$
$P \sqsubseteq R$	$P^{\mathcal{I}} \subseteq R^{\mathcal{I}}$
$P \equiv R^{-}$	$P^{\mathcal{I}} = \{(x,y) \mid (y,x) \in R^{\mathcal{I}}\}$

A DL Knowledge base consists of a set of axioms about instances, concepts (potentially defined in terms of complex concept expressions), and relations. Axioms can be used to state that an instance belongs to a concept and that two instances are in a certain relation. Other type of axioms describe relations between concepts and instances. It can be stated that one concept is a subconcept of the other (all its instances are also instances of this other concept). Further, we can define a relation to be a subrelation or the inverse of another relation. The formal definition of axioms can be found in the second table.

The formal semantics of concepts and relations as defined by the interpretation into Δ can be used to automatically infer new axioms from existing definitions. In particular, given an ontology and a number of instance related axioms, we can automatically determine whether an instance belongs to a certain concept based on the expression defining the concept.

3   Instance Retrieval Queries

In this article we focus on the following instance retrieval problem:

Definition 1 (Instance retrieval w.r.t. some query). *Given an A-Box $\mathcal{A}$ and a query Q, i.e., a concept expression, find all individuals a such that a is an instance of Q, i.e., $\{a \mid \forall a \in \mathcal{A}, a : Q\}$.*

Often, an analogy is made between databases (DBs) and DL KBs. The schema of a DB corresponds to the T-Box and the DB instances correspond to the A-Box. However, A-Boxes have a very different semantics. This makes query answering in a DL setting often much more complex than query answering in a DB. Given the expressivity of DLs, retrieving instances to a query cannot simply be reduced to model checking as in the database framework because there is no single minimal model for a query. Knowledge Bases may contain nondeterminism and/or incompleteness. Therefore, deductive reasoning is needed when answering a query in a DL setting.

Conjunctive Queries. A-Box query languages have been quite weak for earlier DL systems. Usually they supported very simple A-Box queries like instantiation (is individual i an instance of concept C, i.e., $i : C$), realisation (what are the most specific concepts i is an instance of), and retrieval (which individuals are instances of concept C).

In [9] an approach for answering conjunctive queries over arbitrary DL KBs is given based on the translation of the query into an equivalent concept expression, i.e., by *rolling up* the query.

Definition 2 (Boolean Conjunctive Query). *A Boolean conjunctive query Q is of the form $q_1 \wedge \cdots \wedge q_n$, where $q_1, \ldots, q_n$ are query terms of the form $x : C$ or $\langle x, y \rangle : R$, where C is a concept, R is a role, and x, y are either individual names or variables.*

Because binary relations in a conjunctive query can be translated into an existential restriction such that logical consequence is preserved, standard DL inference methods can then be used to classify the concept expression the query is translated into as well as retrieve the instances that belong to it. [9] enables us to use an expressive query language for arbitrary expressive DL KBs.

Instance Store. DL reasoning is hard, especially in the case of instance retrieval when the number of instances grows very large. To speed up the overall cost of instance retrieval, one can address the number and cost of checking whether a single instance belongs to a query.

Instance Store [8] is developed to speed up instance retrieval by replacing costly instantiation checks $a : Q$ with database retrieval. However, Instance Store can not replace all DL reasoning steps using database retrieval. In some situations DL instantiation checks must still be performed. An analysis of the Instance Store revealed a drastic breakdown in performance in these situations, which hampers its goal to scale-up reasoning to ontologies with a large number of instances. At the moment Instance Store only supports role-free A-Boxes, i.e., relationships between instances in the A-Box are not allowed, but this was sufficient for our purpose.

4   Approximation Techniques for Instance Retrieval

There are three components of the instance retrieval problem where approximation methods can be applied:

The Query. The query can be made weaker, i.e., more general, by omitting or replacing parts of the query. The underlying assumption is that simpler queries are easier to check.

The Ontology. We assume that the query is formulated relative to a given ontology. Concept expressions in the ontology (representing for example an instantiation check) can be approximated by weaker or stronger concept expressions.

The Instance Descriptions. In order to check whether instances belong to the query, first the descriptions of instances are translated into equivalent concept expressions. Consequently, those concept expressions can be approximated by weaker or stronger concept expressions.

This section reviews the techniques of [10] and [11] that can be used to approximate instance retrieval in DL. Figure 1 gives an overview of the various components used in instance retrieval. The method of [10] was proposed to approximate satisfiability of concept expressions (usable in step 5 of Figure 1).[2] The method of [11] can be used to approximate conjunctive queries, or its concept expression counterpart (usable in steps 1 and 2 of Figure 1).

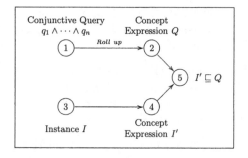

Fig. 1. Various components

---

[2] [10] should also be usable in steps 2 and 4, although not proposed originally.

Both methods propose to approximate an instantiation test using a sequence of tests $C_1, \ldots, C_n$. Assuming that less complex tests can be answered in less time, instance checking can then be speeded up. However, both methods differ in their strategy for selecting the sequence of expressions C_i to be checked successively. In general, [11] argues that the order should balance two factors:

1. The *smoothness* of the approximation. In particular, the next test C_{i+1} should lead to the next best approximation.
2. The potential contribution of the extension of C_{i+1} to the *time complexity* of the tests to be done by the system.

Approximating DL Satisfiability. In DLs, satisfiability checking can be seen as the most basic task as many reasoning services can be restated into satisfiability checks [1]. In [10] a technique has been developed to approximate satisfiability checks. Concept expressions are approximated by two sequences $C_1, \ldots, C_n$ of simpler concept expressions, obtained by syntactic manipulations, which can be used to determine the satisfiability of the original concept expression.

For every subconcept D, [10] defines the *depth* of D to be 'the number of universal quantifiers occurring in C and having D in its scope'. The scope of $\forall R.\phi$ is ϕ which can be any concept term containing D. A sequence of weaker (stronger) approximated concepts can be defined, denoted by $C_i^\top$ $(C_i^\perp)$, by replacing every *existentially quantified* subconcept, i.e., $\exists R.\phi$ where ϕ is any concept term, of depth greater or equal than i by $\top$ $(\perp)$. Concept expressions are assumed to be in negated normal form (NNF) before approximating them.

Theorem 1 ([10]). *For each i, if $C_i^\top$ is unsatisfiable then $C_j^\top$ is unsatisfiable for all $j \geq i$, hence C is unsatisfiable. For each i, if $C_i^\perp$ is satisfiable then $C_j^\perp$ is satisfiable for all $j \geq i$, hence C is satisfiable.*

The sequences $C^\top$ and $C^\perp$ can be used to gradually approximate the satisfiability of a concept expression. [10] only replaces subconcepts $D \equiv \exists R.C$ as the worst case complexity depends on the nesting of existential and universal quantifiers. Theorem 1 leads to the following for $C^\perp$-approximation:

$$(I \sqsubseteq Q)_i^\perp \text{ is not satisfiable} \Leftrightarrow (I \sqcap \neg Q)_i^\perp \text{ is satisfiable} \qquad \Rightarrow$$
$$(I \sqcap \neg Q) \text{ is satisfiable} \qquad \Leftrightarrow (I \sqsubseteq Q) \quad \text{ is not satisfiable}$$

Therefore, we are only able to reduce complexity when approximated subsumption tests are not satisfiable. When an approximated subsumption test $(I \sqsubseteq Q)_i^\perp$ is satisfiable, nothing can be concluded and the approximation continues to level $i+1$ until no more approximation is applicable, i.e., the original concept term is obtained. Analogously, from Theorem 1 one obtains that when $(I \sqsubseteq Q)_i^\top$ is satisfiable this implies that $(I \sqsubseteq Q)$ is satisfiable. When $(I \sqsubseteq Q)_i^\top$ is not satisfiable nothing can be deduced and the approximation continues to level $i+1$.

Research on this kind of DL approximation is quite limited. [10] is the only method that deals with approximation of satisfiability in DLs. Few results have only been obtained recently [2].

Approximating Conjunctive Queries. In [11] a method is introduced for approximating conjunctive queries. The method computes a sequence $Q^1, \ldots, Q^n$ of queries such that: (1) $i < j \Rightarrow Q^i \sqsupseteq Q^j$ and (2) $Q^n \equiv Q$. The first property ensures that the quality of the results of the queries doesn't decrease. The second property ensures that the last query computed returns the desired exact result.

The proposed method can easily be adapted for instantiation checks. The computed sequence $Q^1, \ldots, Q^n$ is used to generate the sequence $C_1^\Delta, \ldots, C_n^\Delta$ with $C_i^\Delta = a : Q^i$. Assuming that less complex queries can be answered in less time, instantiation checks can then be speeded up using the following implication:

$$(I \not\sqsubseteq Q') \wedge (Q \sqsubseteq Q') \Rightarrow I \not\sqsubseteq Q$$

In [11] the sequence of subsuming queries $Q^1, \ldots, Q^n$ is constructed by step-wise adding a conjunct (of the original query) starting with the universal query.

A problem that remains to be solved in this approach is a strategy for selecting the sequence of queries to be checked successively. This problem boils down to ordering the conjuncts of the query which should balance the two factors 'smoothness' and 'time complexity'.

As described in [11] the smoothness of the approximation can be guaranteed by analyzing the dependencies between variables in the query. After translating the conjunctive query to a DL expression, these dependencies are reflected in the nesting of subexpressions. As the removal of conjuncts from a concept expression is equivalent to substitution by $\top$, this nesting provides us with a selection strategy to determine a sequence of approximations S_i where all subexpressions at depth greater or equal than i are replaced by $\top$. Hence, this method is somewhat similar to $C^\top$-approximation except that it is restricted to the conjunctive query, i.e., the instance description is not approximated, and it can replace any conjunct in the query with $\top$, not only existentially quantified conjucts.

Typically, however, queries often have a very flat structure. For example, all queries used in our experiments with the Gene Ontology are of depth one. This means that S_0 is the query $\top$ whereas S_1 is already the original query. To avoid this bad approximation scheme, next we propose an improved strategy.

An Improved Approximation Strategy. To overcome the flatness of queries typically found in ontologies, we propose a strategy that also provides an order for subexpressions at the same level of depth. A possible ordering is the expected time contribution of a conjunct to the costs of the subsumption test. As measuring the actual time is practically infeasible, a heuristic is proposed.

For this purpose, we unfold the conjuncts using the definitions of the concepts from the ontology occurring in the conjunct. In order to determine a suitable measure of complexity for expressions, we consider the standard proof procedure for DLs. Most existing DL reasoners are based on tableau methods, which determine the satisfiability of a concept expression by constructing a constraint system based on the structure of the expression. As the costs of checking the satisfiability of an expression depends on the size of the constraint system, we can use this size as a measure of complexity. As determining the exact size of the constraint system requires to run the tableau method, heuristics are used for estimating the size. Based on this estimated size, we determine the order in which conjuncts at the same level of depths are considered.

In the following, we propose a method for estimating the size of the tableau for expressions in $\mathcal{ALC}$ that will be used in the experiments. The tableau rules [1] provide us with quite a good idea about an estimation of the maximal size of the tableau in the worst case. For this purpose, we define a function Φ that assigns a natural number representing the estimated size of the corresponding constraint system to an arbitrary $\mathcal{ALC}$ expression in the following way:

$$\Phi(A) = 1$$
$$\Phi(\neg A) = 0$$
$$\Phi(C \sqcap D) = 2 + \Phi(C) + \Phi(D)$$
$$\Phi(C \sqcup D) = \phi + 2 + \Phi(C) + \Phi(D) \text{ where } \phi \text{ is the current value of } \Phi(E)$$
$$\Phi(\exists R.C) = 2 + \Phi(C)$$
$$\Phi(\forall R.C) = n + n \cdot \Phi(C) \text{ where } n \text{ is the number of existential quantifiers in } E$$

A **and** $\neg A$: Atomic concepts are added as a single constraint. Negated concepts are not added as they are merely used to check the existence of a contradiction.

$C \sqcap D$: Two new constraints are added. The expressions in these constraints have to be evaluated recursively, therefore, we also have to estimate the number of constraints that will be generated by C and D.

$C \sqcup D$: Two new constraints are added and each of the constraints has to be evaluated recursively, however, we have to deal with two separate constraint systems from this point on. The number of constraints in the system at this point has to be doubled. For an estimation we add the current estimation value.

$(\exists R.C)$: Two new constraints are added, one for the relation and one restricting the object in the relation to C Object y has to be evaluated recursively.

$(\forall R.C)$: A new constraint has to be added for every existing constraint xRy in the constraint system S and each one has to be evaluated recursively. As we do not know how many of these statements are or will be in S, we use the overall number of existential quantifiers in the expression that can lead to the addition of these constraints as an upper bound.

The value Φ can now be computed for each conjunct in the query and be used as a basis for determining the order in which conjuncts at the same level of nesting are processed.

5   Experimental Evaluation

In this section experimental results are shown of the approaches described in the previous section. The main question focused on in the experiments is *if*, and if yes, in *what way* does approximation reduce the complexity of the retrieval task. We focus on the number of operations needed and the overall computation time used. The goal of our approximation approach is to replace costly reasoning operations by a (small) number of cheaper approximate reasoning operations. The approximation methods used are sound and complete. Therefore, the suitability of the approximation methods depend solely on the time gained (or lost) when classical operations are replaced by a number of approximate ones.

Our experiments were made with the Gene ontology and Instance Store [8]. The focus of our experiments are those queries where Instance Store cannot replace all DL reasoning with database retrieval, but must still check the instantiations of some instances. These instantiation checks were found to be a bottleneck in the scalability of this approach. We originally started with 17 queries (with $Q1$ to $Q6$ user formulated queries and queries $Q7$ to $Q17$ artificial), but discarded the queries that didn't require instantiation checks from further experiments.

Table 1. Performed Subsumption tests

	normal			$C^\top$			$C^\perp$			$C^\triangle$		
		true	false		true	false		true	false		true	false
Q2										L0	20	0
										L1	20	0
				L0	0	19	L0	19	0	L2	9	11
	normal	9	11	normal	9	11	normal	9	11	normal	9	0
Q8										L0	607	0
				L0	0	606	L0	606	0	L1	10	597
	normal	10	597	normal	10	597	normal	10	597	normal	10	0
Q12				L0	0	7871	L0	7871	0	L0	15	7856
	normal	15	7856	normal	15	7856	normal	15	7856	normal	15	0
Q14										L0	408	0
										L1	5	403
				L0	0	407	L0	407	0	L2	5	0
	normal	5	403	normal	5	403	normal	5	403	normal	5	0
Q15				L0	0	6693	L0	6693	0	L0	6693	0
	normal	46	6647	normal	46	6647	normal	46	6647	normal	46	6647
Q17				L0	0	7873	L0	7873	0	L0	1	7872
	normal	1	7872	normal	1	7872	normal	1	7872	normal	1	0

The results of the first experiments are shown in Table 1, which is divided into four columns with each column reporting the number of subsumption tests performed. The first column reports results for the experiment without any approximation, the second column with $C^\top$-approximation, the third column with $C^\perp$-approximation, and the fourth column with $C^\triangle$-approximation. Each column is further divided into smaller rows and columns. The rows represent the level of the approximation used, where *normal* denotes without approximation, and Li denotes the level of the approximation approach. The subcolumns show the number of subsumption tests that resulted in true or false.[3] This distinc-

---

[3] We will use the shorthand 'true subsumption test' and 'false subsumption test' to indicate these two distinct results.

tion is important, because Section 4 tells us that only when a $C^\top$-approximated subsumption succeeds, or a $C^\perp$- or $C^\triangle$-approximated subsumption test fails we obtain a reduction in complexity.

Discussion. Let us first focus on the question *if* the approximation methods can lead to any reduction in complexity. Table 1 shows that $C^\top$- and $C^\perp$-approximation cannot reduce the number of normal subsumption tests. Only $C^\triangle$ is able to reduce, except for $Q15$, all false subsumption tests to 0.

The first column in Table 1 shows that much more false subsumption tests are needed than true subsumption tests. This indicates that $C^\top$-approximation is wrong in this approach as it can only be used to lower the complexity of true subsumption tests, which is negligible when compared to false subsumption tests. This may explain its bad approximating behaviour, however, $C^\perp$ also performs badly, which does approximate false subsumption tests. Closer analysis shows that *term collapsing* [2], i.e., the substitution of terms by $\top$ or $\perp$ results in the query becoming equivalent to $\top$ or $\perp$, is the reason for this. An analysis of $C^\perp$ shows that this occurs in *all cases*.

Apart from looking at *if* an approximation method can successfully reduce the number of normal subsumption tests, we must also consider the cost for obtaining the reduction, i.e., in *what way* are the normal subsumption tests reduced. For example, approximating $Q8$ changes $607 = 10 + 597$ normal subsumption tests into 10 normal subsumption tests, $607\ C_1^\triangle$ subsumption tests, and $607\ C_0^\triangle$ subsumption tests. Thus, the number of subsumption tests may increase, but the complexity of most tests will be lower than normal. Note however, that some computations seem unnecessary as nothing can be deduced from them, e.g., the $607\ C_0^\triangle$ tests. Obviously, in this approach unnecessary subsumption tests should be minimized. Several cases can be observed in the experiments with $C^\triangle$-approximation. Either no subsumption test is unnecessary $(Q12, Q17)$, some subsumption tests are unnecessary $(Q2, Q8, Q14)$, or all subsumption tests are unnecessary $(Q15)$.

This distinction seems to influence the overall time needed when approximating a query. Table 2 reports the overall time in milliseconds needed for each query. For comparison $C^\top$ and $C^\perp$ are also reported. For queries having unnecessary subsumption tests, approximation always leads to more computation time. In those cases, reducing the complexity of subsumption tests do not weigh up to the costs of additional (unnecessary) subsumption

Table 2. Time needed for Subsumption tests (in milliseconds)

	normal	$C^\top$	$C^\perp$	$C^\triangle$
Q2	175	348	299	547
Q8	5373	8383	7753	9912
Q12	61410	93100	85764	56478
Q14	4372	6837	6017	7391
Q15	61560	90847	83714	114162
Q17	113289	158218	144689	93074

tests. For queries having no unnecessary subsumption tests, approximation does save time when compared to the normal case.

Another observation of Table 1 is that false subsumption tests for C^Δ only occur at *one level*. It seems that the conjunct that is added to the approximated conjunctive query on which the false subsumption tests occur is crucial in determining the outcome. The role of conjunct in a subsumption test is still unclear. More research is needed if this conjunct (or a group of conjuncts) can be identified in advance to speed up approximation.

6 Conclusions

Instance retrieval is one of the most important inferences in the Semantic Web. In order to make methods more scalable for ontologies with a large set of instances we investigated two approximation methods and evaluated them on a benchmark set. Both methods use a similar idea, i.e., removing parts of an expression to make it simpler to speed up retrieval. However, the method of [10] shows bad approximating behaviour because the selection and substitution of subconcepts is too restrictive. The method of [11] was extended with a heuristic for subconcept selection and shows some potential for speeding up instance retrieval. However, more research is needed to improve the heuristic and to determine if the approximation method can be used to speed up instance retrieval.

References

1. F. Baader, D. Calvanese, D. L. McGuinness, D. Nardi, and P F. Patel-Schneider. *The Description Logic Handbook - Theory, Implementation and Applications*. Cambridge University Press, 2003.
2. P. Groot, H. Stuckenschmidt, and H. Wache. Approximating Description Logic Classification for Semantice Web Reasoning. In A. Gómez-Pérez and J. Euzenat, editors, *ESWC'2005*, pages 318–332. Springer-Verlag, 2005.
3. V. Haarslev and R. Möller. RACE system description. In *Proceedings of the 1999 DL Workshop*, CEUR Electronic Workshop Proceedings, pages 130–132, 1999.
4. V. Haarslev and R. Möller. High performance reasoning with very large knowledge bases: A practical case study. In *IJCAI'2001*, pages 161–168, 2001.
5. V. Haarslev and R. Möller. RACER system description. In *IJCAR'2001*, volume 2083 of *LNAI*, pages 701–705. Springer, 2001.
6. I. Horrocks. The FaCT System. In *TABLEAUX'98*, volume 1397 of *LNAI*, pages 307–312. Springer, 1998.
7. I. Horrocks. Using an Expressive Description Logic: FaCT or Fiction? In *KR'98*, pages 636–647. Morgan Kaufmann, 1998.
8. I. Horrocks, L. Li, D. Turi, and S. Bechhofer. The Instance Store: DL Reasoning with Large Numbers of Individuals. In *Proc. of the 2004 DL Workshop*, 2004.
9. I. Horrocks and S. Tessaris. A Conjunctive Query Language for Description Logic Aboxes. In *AAAI*, pages 399–404, 2000.
10. M Schaerf and M Cadoli. Tractable reasoning via approximation. *Artificial Intelligence*, 74:249–310, 1995.
11. H. Stuckenschmidt and F. van Harmelen. Approximating terminological queries. In *FQAS'2002*, number 2522 in LNCS, pages 329–343. Springer-Verlag, 2002.

Reordering Query and Rule Patterns for Query Answering in a Rete-Based Inference Engine

Murat Osman Ünalır[1], Tuğba Özacar[2], and Övünç Öztürk[3]

Department of Computer Engineering,
Ege University, Bornova, 35100, Izmir, Turkey
{murat.osman.unalir, tugba.ozacar, ovunc.ozturk}@ege.edu.tr

Abstract. This paper describes implementation of a Rete based OWL inference engine and an optimization heuristic on this reasoner. This optimization heuristic modifies some well known optimization heuristics in needs of Semantic Web and represents a hybrid usage of them. This work measures the performance of these heuristics using Lehigh University Benchmark test data and compares the results with other common knowledge base systems. Also, some more improvements to the system is suggested as a future work.

1   Introduction

The Semantic Web is an extension of the current web in which information is given well-defined meaning, better enabling computers and people to work in cooperation[1]. For Semantic web vision to become true, there is a strong need of inference engines diverse in capability and paradigm. In this paper, we suggest a rule based reasoner (the other paradigms are DL based reasoners and theorem provers) that executes the rules using Rete algorithm.

Rete [2] is an optimized forward chaining algorithm. An inefficient forward chaining algorithm applies rules for finding new facts and whenever a new fact is added to or removed from ontology, algorithm starts again to produce facts that are mostly same as the facts produced in the previous cycle. Rete is an optimized algorithm that remembers the previously found results and does not compute them again. Rete only tests the newly added or deleted facts against rules and increases the performance dramatically. Our Rete based reasoner uses the syntax and semantics described in OWL Rules Language [3] for rules, which is a special case of axiom-based approach [4]. The reasoner modifies some well known optimization heuristics [5], related with ordering conditions in the rules and queries, in needs of the semantic web and uses these independent heuristics together.

In the next section, we describe the Rete based inference in detail. Optimization heuristics that order the conditions of the rules appropriately and hybrid usage of them are described in section three. Section four represents the performance analysis of used heuristics and hybrid usage of them. Finally chapter five concludes this paper with an outline of some potential future research.

M. Dean et al. (Eds.): WISE 2005 Workshops, LNCS 3807, pp. 255–265, 2005.

2   A Rete-Based Inference Engine

Rete is an optimized forward chaining algorithm that remembers the previously found results and does not compute them again. The inference engine uses Rete algorithm and a hybrid optimization technique on Rete in order to increase the performance. Rete algorithm is based on the reasoning process of Rete network. Following definitions give a formal representation of the concepts in a Rete network.

Let $\mathcal{O} = (\mathcal{W}, \mathcal{R})$ be an ontology where $\mathcal{W} = \{w \mid w = (s, p, o) \wedge s, p, o \in \mathcal{U}\}$ is the set of all facts in the ontology and $\mathcal{R}$ is the set of all rules related with the ontology, then every fact $w \in \mathcal{W}$ consists of a subject s, a predicate p and an object o and $\mathcal{U}$ denotes the set of constants. Given a $r \in \mathcal{R}$, $r = (lhs, rhs)$ where both lhs and rhs are lists of atoms. An atom $at = (a, i, v)$ consists of an attribute a, an identifier i and a variable v where $a, i, v \in \mathcal{T}$ and $\mathcal{T} = \mathcal{U} \cup \mathcal{V}$ where $\mathcal{V}$ denotes the set of variables. A lhs atom is called a condition. $\mathcal{C}$ is the set of all conditions of all rules $r \in \mathcal{R}$.

Given a Rete network of the ontology $\Omega(\mathcal{O}) = (\alpha, \beta)$, we denote by α the alpha network and by β the beta network. $\alpha = \{\delta(c) \mid c \in \mathcal{C}\}$ and $\delta : \mathcal{C} \to \mathcal{D}$ is a function where $\mathcal{D} = \{x \mid x \subseteq \mathcal{W}\}$. $\delta(c)$ returns the set $\{w \mid w = (s, p, o) \wedge c = (a, i, v) \wedge ((s = a) \vee (a \in \mathcal{V})) \wedge ((p = i) \vee (i \in \mathcal{V})) \wedge ((o = v) \vee (v \in \mathcal{V}))\}$ denoting all matching facts with condition c. β network consists of beta memories and join nodes where beta memories store partial instantiations of rules, which are called tokens, and join nodes perform tests for consistency of variable bindings between conditions of rules. Figure 1 explains the relationships among the formal definitions with the help of an illustration existing in [6]. In this figure rectangles show beta memory nodes, ovals show alpha memories and circles show join nodes.

The set of all beta memories is $\mathcal{PI} = \{\phi(s) \mid s \in \mathcal{S}\}$ where $\mathcal{S} = \{x \mid x = (c_1 \wedge ... \wedge c_n) \wedge r = (lhs, rhs) \wedge lhs = (c_1, ..., c_t) \wedge (1 \leq n \leq t) \wedge r \in \mathcal{R}\}$ and $\phi : \mathcal{S} \to \mathcal{I}$ is a function where $\mathcal{I} = \{x \mid x$ is a conjunctive set of $w \in \mathcal{W}\}$. $\phi(s)$ returns the conjunctive sets of facts that are matching with s. The instantiations at the end of the Rete network are handled as production nodes, abbreviated as p-nodes. $\mathcal{P} = \{\phi(s) \mid s = (c_1 \wedge ... \wedge c_t) \wedge r = (lhs, rhs) \wedge lhs = (c_1, ..., c_t) \wedge r \in \mathcal{R}\}$. Whenever a propagation reaches the end of the Rete network in other words a p-node gets activated, it indicates that a rule's conditions are completely matched and the right hand side atoms of the rule produces a new fact that will be added to the ontology.

Adding a new fact to the ontology triggers Rete network and new facts are inferred by these newly added facts without recomputing the previously found facts. The reasoner uses Rete algorithm in order to make the implicit knowledge in the OWL ontologies explicit by means of rules. The reasoner works in the following order and aims sound but not complete reasoning:

– *Parsing:* The OWL parser gets the URL of the ontology and related rules. Parser produces triples from the ontology described in OWL and the rules described in OWL Rules Language. The rules can be grouped into two:

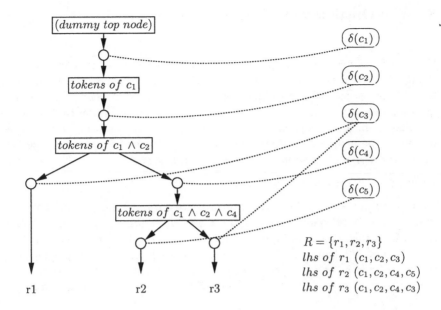

Fig. 1. An example RETE Network

- *Default rules:* These kind of rules describe the interpretation of the language in which the ontology is written. These rules are same for all ontologies written in the same language. For example, two ontologies written in OWL-Lite are interpreted with rules describing the semantics of OWL-Lite language. These rules are used to infer new facts and to check the consistency of the ontology.
- *Domain rules:* The rules in this category describe the constraints, semantics and reactions of the ontology that they are attached to.

- *Creating Rete Network:* The ontology triples are handled as facts in Rete network. The parsed rules are optimized and added to the Rete network as p-nodes and conditions. The productions of the Rete network activate the Rete network again and end in new additions or removals.
- *Editing and Querying Ontology:* Adding/removing facts/rules to/from ontology causes Rete network to activate and ends in new additions or removals. The queries, which are written in OWL-QL [7], are handled as the special cases of rules. Whenever a query is sent to the reasoner it is added to the Rete network as a new p-node without right hand side. Elements of this production node are presented as results to the user. After returning the result this node and the parent nodes, which also constitutes the query, is removed from the Rete network.

3   The Optimization Heuristics and Hybrid Usage of Them

High performance reasoning is an important issue for the Semantic Web. Although Rete is a performance optimization algorithm, there are still some optimizations to do with Rete. Some of these optimization heuristics are known for a long time, but this work represents a generic optimization that mixes and modifies them for performances close to the best. The following gives the definitions of the heuristics and explains how they increase the performance. Then the hybrid usage of these heuristics described in detail.

Heuristic 1: Place Restrictive Conditions First

This optimization reduces the intermediate data by joining restrictive conditions first. Rete tests a rule against ontology triples finding all partial instantiations of the rule. Given an ordered list $\mathcal{L}$ $((c_1), (c_1 \wedge c_2), ..., (c_1 \wedge ... \wedge c_{n-1}), (c_1 \wedge ...c_n))$ where left hand side of the rule r is a set $\{c_1, ..., c_n\}$, all partial instantiations of r is a set $\mathcal{K} = \{k_1, ..., k_n\}$ and k_x is the set of matches for the x_{th} element of $\mathcal{L}$. Let k_n be the n_{th} element of $\mathcal{K}$ and $\mathcal{E}$ (k_n) be the size of k_n then;

$\mathcal{E}$ $(k_0)=1$

$\mathcal{E}$ $(k_n) \subseteq \mathcal{E}$ (k_{n-1}) X $\delta(c_n)$

Thus ordering conditions with minimum alpha memory(restrictive) first will also decreases the size of the following instantiations. The following three methods are used in order to find the more restrictive conditions:

- *Method 1:* This method sorts the conditions ascending based on the number of edges matching with the condition. It finds the condition with minimum alpha memory m at time t, but it does not guarantee m will be the conditon with minimum alpha memory after a series of addition and deletion.
- *Method 2:* This heuristic assumes the conditions with more variables have alpha memories big in size so it sorts the conditions ascending based on the number of variables.
- *Method 3:* The usage of complex predicates is at minimum in semantic web ontologies [8]. Ontologies mainly consist of facts describing subsumption and assertion relations. Besides, the subsumption predicates in the ontologies give rise to cyclic repetitive[1] calculation and the number of facts with these predicates gets even more at the end of the inference [9]. This heuristic assumes that the number of alpha memories for conditions with complex predicates will be much smaller than the conditions with assertion or subsumption predicates. Thus the conditions with frequently used predicates are placed at the end of the conditions of the rule. This heuristic also improves the performance of additions and removals. The conditions with a frequently used

---

[1] In this work only the subsumption relationship is handled, in addition to subsumption the other transitive properties giving rise to cyclic repetitive calculation can be handled as frequently used predicates.

predicate have more possibility to change and if one of these conditions is at the end of n conditions then whenever it matches with a newly created(or deleted) fact, only one join operation would be invoked. If this condition was the first then $n-1$ join operations would be invoked subsequently [5].

Heuristic 2: Order Conditions with Common Variables Sequentially

This optimization reduces the intermediate data by ordering conditions having common variables sequentially. If the nth condition of the rule has a common variable x with $n-1^{th}$ condition then $\mathcal{E}(k_n)$ get smaller because of the restrictions have been made on x at $n-1^{th}$ instantiation.

The Hybrid Heuristic

These two heuristics can be used in a hybrid way without conflicting each other while preserving the claim that the performance of the hybrid usage will generally be better than the performance of using every heuristic separately. The heuristic works in the following order, where r is the rule to be optimized, $\mathcal{C}(r)$ is the ordered list of all conditions of r, r' is the result of the optimization and l is the last element of $\mathcal{C}(r')$:

> *Step 1:*
> - $\mathcal{C}(r') \leftarrow$ null
> - Find the most restrictive condition[2] x in $\mathcal{C}(r)$, remove x from $\mathcal{C}(r)$ and append x to $\mathcal{C}(r')$
> *Step 2:*
> - if $\mathcal{C}(r) \neq \emptyset$
>   - Find $x \in \mathcal{C}(r)$ and x is the most restrictive condition having maximum number of common variables with l, remove x from $\mathcal{C}(r)$ and append x to $\mathcal{C}(r')$
>   - *Step 2*
> - else
>   - return r'

Determination of the most restrictive condition differs for the rules and the queries. Although *Method 1* guarantees to find the facts with minimum alpha memory in the ontology while optimizing queries, it is useless for optimizing rules. Because the Rete network has not been created, the number of matching edges with a condition can not be obtained during the optimization of the rules. To determine the most restrictive condition in the rules two methods are used according to the following priorities: *Method 2, Method 3*. This means that the first condition with a complex predicate among the conditions having minimum number of variables is the most restrictive one. *Method 2* has a higher priority than *Method 3* because there are a great number of conditions in rules having three variables and returning all of the edges in the ontology. These conditions have the biggest alpha memory and method2 guarantees to place them at the end of the conditions.

---

[2] If the result contains more than one condition pick the first one.

4 Performance Analysis

We have used Lehigh University Benchmark [10] in order to evaluate the performance of the inference engine and to see the effects of the optimizations on the performance. Lehigh University Benchmark is developed to evaluate the querying performance of Semantic Web repositories over a large data set. The data set is generated according to one ontology, named univ-bench, using the synthetic data generation tool provided with the benchmark. The performance of the repositories is evaluated through a set of metrics including data loading time, repository size, query response time, and query completeness and soundness. Benchmark suite also includes 14 example queries that cover a range of types.

We compare metrics of our system with the metrics in Lehigh University Benchmark in order to evaluate the performance of the system. The table for query response times in our system is parallel to the table in [10].

Our data set is generated using the synthetic data generation tool. We have used only LUBM(1,0) data set in our benchmark. Larger data sets such as LUBM(5,0) can not be loaded because of the large memory consumption of Aegont Inference Engine. It is important to specify that we used a different test environment. We have done the tests on a desktop computer with the following specifications:

– AMD Athlon 64 3500 2200 Ghz CPU; 2 GB of RAM;320 GB of hard disk
– Windows XP Professional OS, .NET Framework 1.1

The evaluated inference engine, Aegont Inference Engine, is a part of the Aegean Ontology Environment Project[3]. The inference engine is developed to work in correspondence with the Aegont Ontology Editor. Ontology Editor is used to load and query ontologies, in other words, ontology editor can be seen as a graphical user interface to the ontology repository residing in memory. Aegont inference engine is a forward chaining reasoner like OWLJessKB [11], this means once it loads the ontology, the ontology is complete and sound according to the rules defined in the system and there is no need to make inference while answering the queries.

4.1 Results

First metric in benchmark is load time of data set. Load time of LUBM(1,0), which includes 103,074 instances, in our system is 6 minutes 41 seconds. This is fairly a good time with respect to other repositories, especially if we consider the fact that loading is the most time consuming part of the Rete algorithm.

Other metrics in the benchmark are about queries. In order to get more accurate query execution times, they are measured ten times and then their average is calculated. In our system all queries are answered with full completeness and

---

[3] It can be downloaded from http://semanticweb.ege.edu.tr/AEGONT

Table 1. Query Execution Time

Query	Metrics	Aegont	Query	Metrics	Aegont
1	Time(ms)	13	8	Time(ms)	521
	Answers	4		Answers	7790
	Completeness	100		Completeness	100
2	Time(ms)	60	9	Time(ms)	390
	Answers	0		Answers	208
	Completeness	100		Completeness	100
3	Time(ms)	23	10	Time(ms)	10
	Answers	6		Answers	4
	Completeness	100		Completeness	100
4	Time(ms)	70	11	Time(ms)	140
	Answers	34		Answers	224
	Completeness	100		Completeness	100
5	Time(ms)	532	12	Time(ms)	13
	Answers	719		Answers	15
	Completeness	100		Completeness	100
6	Time(ms)	477	13	Time(ms)	11
	Answers	7790		Answers	1
	Completeness	100		Completeness	100
7	Time(ms)	76	14	Time(ms)	546
	Answers	67		Answers	5916
	Completeness	100		Completeness	100

soundness, this results in a high F-measure value, calculated according to the formula in [10]. The system's inference level is between OWL Lite and OWL DL. This inference level is satisfied by approximately 30 rules, which are written according to the OWL entailment tests [12].

All queries are executed after optimization. We don't execute every query without optimization except some chosen queries, because they are executed extremely slower than the optimized queries. There is also one another factor on the performance of the system besides the reordering of query rule patterns. In our inference engine extra indexing mechanisms are used on the Rete network both in the Alpha and Beta part in order to make inference faster.

Query execution times of all queries can be seen on Table 1.

4.2   Evaluation of Results

The optimizations suggested and evaluated in this paper are mainly about decreasing the size of partial instantiations, i.e. count of tokens, created during the execution of the query. When we have one condition, the answering process is trivial, all constructed tokens are in the answer set. When we have two conditions, we need to check the tokens in the second condition with the tokens in the first condition in order to see whether they are in the answers set or not. The order of the conditions doesn't make a difference in a query with two conditions. So we need at least three condition to see the effects of the optimization.

Therefore, we inspect queries with number 2, 4, 7, 8, 9 and 12, since they have at least three or more conditions. During our benchmark for all of these queries query execution time is decreased. For queries 2, 7 and 9[4] the improvement is more significant as can be seen from Figure 2.

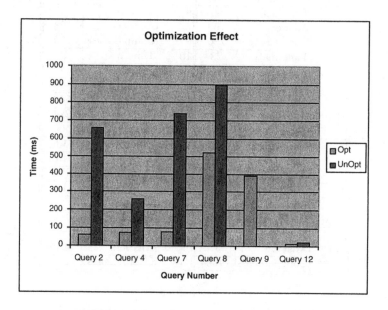

Fig. 2. Performance improvements of the queries

The reason for this improvement is the type of conditions of the query. These queries have conditions with no common variables and big alpha memories corresponding to these conditions. When these conditions are computed in a consecutive manner the possibilities to check in successive nodes will increase dramatically. To give an example lets inspect Query 2. Conditions of Query 2 can be seen in Table 2.

However, when we optimize the query we will change the order of the conditions. The optimized query order will be c, e, b, f, a, d. While optimizing the query we will start with the most restrictive condition. Most restrictive condition is the condition with the smallest alpha memory, namely c. Then we will find the conditions with common variables with c. These conditions are d and e. Condition e is more restrictive than d, therefore e will be the second condition. In third step, we will find the conditions with common variables with e which are b, d and f. Condition b is more restrictive than d and f therefore b will be the third condition. Condition f is the only condition remaining having common variables with b. f is the forth condition. a and d are remaining conditions and

---

[4] The unoptimized query execution time is much bigger than one second so it isn't shown in the figure.

Table 2. Conditions and size of their corresponding alpha memories of second query

Number	Condition		Size
a	?x rdf:type	ub:GraduateStudent	1874
b	?y rdf:type	ub:University	979
c	?z rdf:type	ub:Department	15
d	?x ub:memberOf	?z	8330
e	?z ub:subOrganizationOf	?y	463
f	?x ub:undergraduateDegreeFrom ?y		2414

Table 3. Beta memories and count of constructed tokens

Conditions	Token Count	Conditions	Token Count
a	1874	c	15
$a \wedge b$	1834646	$c \wedge e$	15
$a \wedge b \wedge c$	27519690	$c \wedge e \wedge b$	15
$a \wedge b \wedge c \wedge d$	0	$c \wedge e \wedge b \wedge f$	0
$a \wedge b \wedge c \wedge d \wedge e$	0	$c \wedge e \wedge b \wedge f \wedge a$	0
$a \wedge b \wedge c \wedge d \wedge e \wedge f$	0	$c \wedge e \wedge b \wedge f \wedge a \wedge d$	0

both of them have common variables with b, but a has a smaller alpha memory so it is the fifth condition. Finally, d is the last condition because there aren't any other remaining conditions except d. The number of tokens created during the execution of the query both in optimized and in unoptimized query pattern order is shown in Table 3.

When we compare the size of the partial instantiation of first and second execution of the same query on Table 3, we can see the reason of the difference in the execution time. The main time consuming task in adding a new query to the Rete network is constructing tokens in corresponding nodes. When the possibilities grow we will need to construct more tokens. When we execute the Query 2 in the given order we get 27519690 different possibilities to test with the alpha memory elements of fourth condition. But if we optimize it we will have only 15 different possibilities to test with the alpha memory elements of fourth condition. The cause of the difference in the execution time is the difference in the number of created tokens.

Another reason for the acceleration is the indexing mechanisms we have used in Rete network. By using these indexing mechanisms we eliminate the need for comparison tests between tokens of the previous nodes and alpha memory elements of the current node. After applying these indexing mechanisms we have decreased load time, which includes also the inference process using defined rules, of the ontology approximately from 22 minutes to 7 minutes. Since a query is a special kind of a rule, the query execution time is also affected.

The optimization overhead is negligible comparing to the speed gain. The optimization process occurs before the query execution and the optimized query is given to the inference engine. In our experiments the optimized queries have never worked slower than the unoptimized queries.

5 Conclusions and Future Work

In this paper, we suggest a query pattern reordering algorithm to improve the query performance of Rete based inference engines and evaluated the performance improvements of these optimizations on our ontology repository, namely Aegont. The optimization heuristic works well and improves the query performance as expected.

Our Rete based approach have several advantages over other ontology repositories. First of all the repository is highly dynamic and immune to changes. Whenever a rule or a query is added to the repository, there is no need to make the inference process from the beginning. Only the change to the ontology will be computed, because Rete saves the inference process in the memory. The other advantage of Rete is saving queries. By this way, we can save the highly used queries and improve the response time of the queries. And because of the dynamic nature of Rete we don't have to manage the saving process and handling the changes in the results of the query. All results of the queries will be automatically updated whenever a fact is added or removed from the ontology.

Aegont has also some more advantages over other Rete based repositories. It is optimized for speed and works almost as fast as other DL based reasoners and faster than other Rete based Reasoners evaluated in [10]. Although the load time is supposed to be the weakest aspect of the Rete based systems, the performance of loading in our system is close to the DL based systems. The performance will be decreased as more rules are added to the system, but we have already tried and saw that the system is scalable according to the rules during the rule writing process. Therefore, we don't expect a significant decrease in performance.

The main disadvantage of the system is the big memory need for ontologies. This is actually an expected result because the inference engine and the memory representation of the ontologies are designed to use for an ontology editor. They are designed for being responsive and they are immune to changes to the ontology. This means they are adapting easily to the changes in the ontology. To satisfy these needs which are necessary for an ontology editor, inference engine and memory representation of the ontology needs a large amount of memory. The solution to this problem can be seen from two different perspective:

- Decrease memory usage of the components which are absolutely necessary to be reside in memory.
- Migrate other components to a database management system using a special database schema.

Making these changes in the system will dramatically decrease the memory usage of the system, but also the speed of the system will be decreased. We will try to find a balance between speed or memory need, but ultimately there will be different versions of the inference engine for different needs.

The system will be also improved to gain more inference capabilities by adding new rules using owl test cases. The inference level will be increased to the DL level as close as possible. By improving the inference capabilities, the inference engine will give more sound and complete answers to the queries.

There are also other query optimization possibilities. Generally, query writers will include also type declarations for variables in queries. But, domain and range relations in other conditions of the query can be definitive for types of variables in conditions. For instance, in Query 2 there are three type declarations for variables, but one of them is obsolete. The second condition is obsolete because the range property of the *undergraduateDegreeFrom* object property has value "University". And from RDF Entailment Rule 3 [13] we can infer that the type of the variable y is University. So we can eliminate condition 2 and answer the query with only five conditions. This example is only one of the possibilities to improve the query performance of the inference engine.

As a result, we can say that the performance gain of the heuristics is significant and the optimizations works well as we expected. However, the system is open to improvements both in optimization heuristics, which can be diversified, and in performance of the Rete algorithm.

References

1. Berners-Lee, T., Hendler, J., Lassila, O.: The semantic web. Scientific American **284** (2001)
2. Forgy, C.: Rete: A fast algorithm for the many patterns/many objects match problem. Artif. Intell. **19** (1982) 17–37
3. Feldman, S.I., Uretsky, M., Najork, M., Wills, C.E., eds.: Proceedings of the 13th international conference on World Wide Web, WWW 2004, New York, NY, USA, May 17-20, 2004. In Feldman, S.I., Uretsky, M., Najork, M., Wills, C.E., eds.: WWW, ACM (2004)
4. Franconi, E., Tessaris, S.: Rules and queries with ontologies: A unified logical framework. In: PPSWR. (2004) 50–60
5. Ishida, T.: Optimizing rules in production system programs. In: National Conference on Artificial Intelligence. (1988) 699–704
6. Doorenbos, R.B.: Production matching for large learning systems. Technical report, Pittsburgh, PA, USA (2001)
7. Fikes, R., Hayes, P., Horrocks, I.: Owl-ql: A language for deductive query answering on the semantic web. Technical Report KSL 03-14, Stanford University, Stanford, CA (2003)
8. Staab, S.: Ontologies' kisses in standardization. IEEE Intelligent Systems **17** (2002) 70–79
9. Zhang, L., Yu, Y., Lu, J., Lin, C., Tu, K., Guo, M., Zhang, Z., Xie, G., Su, Z., Pan, Y.: Orient: Integrate ontology engineering into industry tooling environment. In: International Semantic Web Conference. (2004) 823–838
10. Guo, Y., Pan, Z., Heflin, J.: An evaluation of knowledge base systems for large owl datasets. In: International Semantic Web Conference. (2004) 274–288
11. Kopena, J., Regli, W.C.: Damljesskb: A tool for reasoning with the semantic web. In: International Semantic Web Conference. (2003) 628–643
12. Carroll, J.J., Roo, J.D.: Owl web ontology language test cases (2004)
13. Beckett, D., McBride, B.: Rdf test cases (2004)

Scalable Peer-to-Peer RDF Query Algorithm

Denis Ranger and Jean-François Cloutier

Mind-Alliance Systems LLC, New Jersey, USA
{denis, jf}@mind-alliance.com

Abstract. The execution of complex queries across peers in a timely and resource efficient manner is a difficult problem in peer-to-peer networking. A novel approach to distributed RDF queries uses a two-phased process: establish a contributor pipeline to get the raw data, then form a reader pipeline to read the results. Pipelines are created efficiently using a publish/subscribe mechanism (Pastry's Scribe framework [1]).

1 Context

Mind-Alliance is developing an information sharing platform with a fully decentralized design that supports "bottom-up", community-driven information sharing activities. The platform uses a P2P infrastructure to create RDF-based "knowledge addressable networks". A key difficulty of such networks is the ability to execute possibly complex queries in a time-efficient manner. Current solutions were deemed inadequate because:

1. Relying o n "query flooding" over unstructured P2P networks (Gnutella [2]) does not scale well, or
2. Relying on "super-peers" to handle the brunt of the work (Edutella, JXTA [3]) is overly constraining, or
3. Rely on indexing the entire knowledge base and assigning particular indexes to specific peers (RDFPeers [4]) leads to crippling "hot spots" (when a peer is responsible for holding the index, which can be be gigabytes in size, for a very popular element of the knowledge base).
4. Assuming that peers know all about the subjects they publish is inadequate for a collaboration environment where peers may contribute about similar subjects. This leaves out the entire family of query routing algorithms such as SQPeer [5].

In the target environment of this algorithm, each peer in a networked group share some of its content with the group. Peers are assumed to be of equal standing (no peer is "more equal" than the others). Content may be duplicated across peers, to the discretion of the users. It is assumed that each peer can efficiently access its own content as a semantic web graph. An algorithm was developed to support:

1. *Potentially very large P2P networks.* Centralized solutions do not scale and run into data ownership issues. Very large communities should be able to share information without a central dissemination point.
2. *Distributed RDF knowledge bases.* Each peer is a potential source of information/knowledge. RDF [6] is the W3C standard for knowledge encoding and provides a uniform format. Also, different peers may hold different pieces of information about the same subject.

M. Dean et al. (Eds.): WISE 2005 Workshops, LNCS 3807, pp. 266–274, 2005.

3. *Structured querying*(of RDF knowledge bases distributed over large P2P networks). Querying semantic web information is more involved than just locating files given one or more of their attributes. Knowledge needs to be extracted out of (or combined from) information spread over a P2P network. Complex queries need to be processed reliably (if there is an answer, it will almost certainly be found) and efficiently (the time taken is acceptable and increases only slightly with the number of peers).

The proposed algorithm has the following characteristics:

1. *No a-priori indexes*. There are no "special" peer indexing the content of the group. The ability to perform generic ad-hoc queries without knowing or limiting what the specific queries are implies that any a priori indexing would be mostly guesswork. A scheme that finds results from scratch, coupled to efficient, redundant caching and cache lookup seems more appropriate. Frequent queries are cached effectively as they occur.
2. *Read driven.*Queries remain active as long as clients are reading from it, and stop when no one cares... Query results are forwarded to clients when they actually ask for them. This avoids the drinking-from-a-fire-hose effect.
3. *The more, the merrier*. Common query results will be cached by more peers in the group, making retrieval of results quicker.

1.1 Pastry

The Pastry P2P substrate [7] provides a scalable, decentralized and self-organizing framework for routing messages from one peer to another (*routing*). Each peer in the network is aware of a small number of neighbors. Messages to another peer are efficiently routed to either a neighbor closer to the destination, or the target itself, if a neighbor.

Pastry's message routing is massively scalable.The maximum number of hops is given by formula 1 where N is the number of peers and 2^{c+1} is the number of connections per peer.

$$hops = \lceil \log_{2^c}(N) - 1 \rceil \qquad (1)$$

Fig. 1 illustrates the network connections between peers. Pastry will ensure that the connections will be adjusted appropriately as peers come and go.

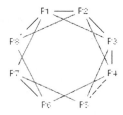

Fig. 1. Idealized node connections between 8 peers using c=1. A typical implementation would use c=4. If the 6.6 billion people on earth were peers and each peer are connected to 32 neighbors, reaching any peer from any peer would take at most 9 hops.

1.2 Scribe

In essence, this document presents how to implement a RDF search using specific message exchange using the Pastry infrastructure, and in particular, the Scribe functionality [1]. Scribe offers basic topic publish, subscribe, broadcast and *anycast* [8] mechanisms (sending a message to the first subscriber that accepts it). Scribe's framework doesn't impose limits as to what kinds of messages can be sent.

When receiving an *anycast* message, a peer may ignore the message and pass it along to the next peer, or take it out of the loop and process it. When receiving a broadcast message, the peer will process it *and* pass it along. Scribe minimizes the number of network hops and maximizes the proximity of communicating peers when performing publish and subscribe operations.

For the purpose of this algorithm, each unique query will be associated with a topic. In addition, all peers are required to subscribe to the generic "broadcast" topic.

2 Queries

Queries are translated in trees of either *atomic* or *complex* sub-queries. An atomic query is a simple, stand-alone query that all peers can execute on their local contents, without resorting to results from other peers (effectively, a leaf in the tree). A complex query uses results from other queries to produce its results, either by aggregation, filtering or calculation.

Although queries are expressed in a SPARQL [9] dialect, this algorithm only assumes that queries can be decomposed as trees of smaller queries. Fig. 2 shows a query that finds names and phone numbers of all 2005 contributors to scenarios containing the "airport" keyword, using the Dublin Core [10] and vCard [11] vocabularies.

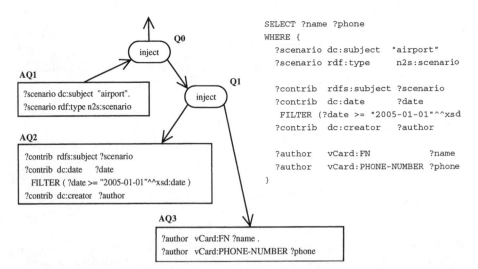

Fig. 2. Example of a possible decomposition of a query into atomic and complex sub-queries. the inject query Q_1 takes the scenarios found by atomic query AQ_1 and for each of them, runs a separate Q_2 query (and similarly for Q_2 and AQ_2).

Since all peers can execute arbitrary complex queries, the exact distinction between atomic and complex queries is somewhat fuzzy. It is not usually feasible to determine just by looking at a query, if it should be run locally on each peer. This depends on whether objects are stored as a whole on each peer, or if pieces of objects are spread out on different peers and is dependent on the application being built on top of this framework.

The algorithm addresses this ambiguity by co-locating predicates from designated namespaces (here *dc*, *vCard*, *rdf* and *rdfs*). For the same subject, all predicates from a co-located namespace will be available on the same peer. If a peer knows of author X, it will also know all other *vCard* predicates. A peer copying an author's information will also copy all the predicates.

3 Algorithm

The algorithm can be summarized as follow. When a peer needs to perform a query:

1. It first looks for another peer that is either looking for or already has the result of the query. If one is found, the peer joins the *consumer* pipeline tree rooted at a producer of the query results. Fig. 3 shows the result pipelines established when a peer (P_1) performs a query.

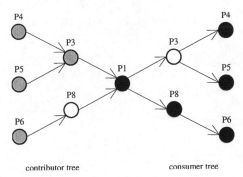

contributor tree   consumer tree

Fig. 3. Producer and consumer pipelines resulting from P1 performing a query. Gray nodes are contributors to query Q; white nodes are forwarders; black nodes are consumer of the results integrated by P1.

2. When processing a non-atomic query, the peer breaks it into smaller queries and repeat the algorithm with the smaller queries, joining consumer trees of the sub-queries.
3. When processing an atomic query, the peer establishes a *producer* pipeline tree with the current peer as a root.
4. When consumers ask for results, the producing peer will read/combine results from the produce pipeline and forward the results to the consumers (*aggregation*).

3.1 Lookup

The first phase of the algorithm involves looking around in the group for a peer that already knows (or is about to know) the results of the query of interest. This step is necessary in order to avoid redundant queries as much as possible. Some redundancy might still happen due to network outages or delays but should be kept to a minimum.

At the end of the lookup stage, peer P_1 will have a result set RS(Q) ready for processing. Results will be either coming from another peer or added by a background thread performing the query.

Pseudo-code for query lookups

```
state(Q) = looking

Subscribe to Scribe topic T(Q):
   Nodes either looking for or already
   having the answer to Q.

RS(Q) = new empty result set
Setup a wake-up timer for RS(Q)

Anycast to T(Q) the message:
   looking(Q,P₁,0):
     P₁ wants RS(Q) starting at index 0

Return RS(Q)
```

Table 1. Messages involved during the lookup phase

Origin	Target	Message	Pseudo-code

P_1	P_x	*looking*(Q,P₁,i)	`if (state(Q) == looking`
			`    && Pₓ more-powerful P₁)`
			`|| state(Q) == producing`
			`|| state(Q) == forwarding`
			
			`if i >= start of buffer`
			`Route to P₁:`
			`  consume(Q,P₁,Pₓ):`
			`  P₁ may get RS(Q) from Pₓ`
			`if state(Q) == looking,`

P_x	P_1	*consume*(Q,P₁,Pₓ)	`RS(Q) += RS(Q) from Pₓ`
			`state(Q) = forwarding`
			`disable timer for RS(Q)`
			
			`else`
			`  ignore message`

P_x	P_y	*consume*(Q,P₁,Pₓ)	`if state(Q) == looking`
			`|| state(Q) == initial,`
			
			`RS(Q) += RS(Q) from Pₓ`
			`state(Q) = forwarding`
			
			`disable timer for RS(Q)`
			`route consume(Q,P₁,Pᵧ)`
			`  to P₁`

Nodes should stay subscribed to the topic as long as they are interested in Q. Subscribers to the topic may be "volunteered" to help in producing results. This way, a peer will only perform queries that it originates, directly or indirectly. This avoids "free-loading": a rogue member of the group cannot flood the group with queries without involving the resources of its own peer.

Aggregators are the nodes in the pipelines. Reading data from the output of an aggregator will either get data from one of its input or wait until new data is available (or a new input connector is added). New connectors are added when *consume* messages are received. The method of aggregation is implementation-dependent and may be for example, *breadth-first, depth-first, local-first* (nearest results treated first), etc.

The timer will wake up P_1 after a certain wait period of inactivity. Upon waking up, if no new connectors have been added to RS(Q), P_1 will perform the query itself (either *atomic* or *complex* described in following sections).

Scribe's anycast mechanism[4] ensures that messages get delivered to the closest peer that accepts them (in this case, the closest peer that is either a forwarder or a producer). When considering an anycast message, a peer may either decide to process it or to route it to another peer. The messages in Table 1 ensure (as much as possible) that at most one node will do any query. The *more-powerful* operator designates a volunteer if many peers are querying at the same time. Note that another heuristic (such as *younger, older, less-busy*, etc) could be used.

3.2 Atomic Queries

The peer originating the atomic query (P_1) will broadcast the fact to other peers in the group. When receiving the broadcast, peers (including P_1 itself) will contribute if they have original content to contribute or if the query is *live* (the originator wants to be able to wait for new results as they happen).

Pseudo-code for atomic(AQ) performed by peer P_1

```
Broadcast on T(*):
  producing(AQ,P₁):
    P₁ needs RS(AQ)
```

Forcing new peers to contribute to known live atomic queries ensures that no potential source of results will be ignored. When a new peer joins the group, it should ask for and contribute to the live atomic queries known by its new neighbors.

If a contributing or forwarding peer intentionally or accidentally leaves the group, lower level peers will become aware of the fact (using Pastry's built-in mechanisms) and re-send the *contributing* message, thereby repairing the tree with minimal losses (the unprocessed data in the buffer of the peer that left). The "polite departure" protocol should send the remains of a peer's buffer has been sent upstream before leaving.

Table 2. Messages involved in processing an atomic query AQ

Origin	Target	Message	Pseudo-code
P_1	P_x	*producing*(AQ,P_1)	```if P_x can contribute to AQ``` `|| AQ is live,` `RS(AQ) += RS(AQ) from P_x` `state(AQ) = contributing` `if P_x != P_1,` `route to P_1:` `contributing(AQ,P_1,P_x):` `P_x contributes to AQ,` `tell P1`
P_x	P_1	*contributing*(AQ,P_1,P_x)	`RS(AQ) += RS(AQ) from P_x`
P_x	P_y	*contributing*(AQ,P_1,P_x)	`RS(AQ) += RS(AQ) from P_x` `if P_x != P_y,` `route to P_1` `contributing(AQ,P_1,P_y)`

3.3 Complex Queries

A complex query is a non-leaf node in the query tree. Typically, it will combine the results of sub-queries in some way.

Pseudo-code for complex(Q)

```
state(Q) = "producing".
QC = new Q-dependent sub-stream aggregator
RS(Q) += QC.
For each complex sub-query SQᵢ,
   QC += complex(SQᵢ)
For each atomic sub-query AQᵢ
   QC += atomic(AQᵢ)
```

The sub-stream aggregator is a query-specific consumer of the result sets of the sub-queries. In Fig. 2 , the *inject* query would take each result of another query and use it as a parameter to another query, combining all of those results as output.

3.4 Reading Results

Once the tree pipelines have been established, the peers will read results from neighboring peers. Results are read in a similar fashion whether a consumer is reading from a producer/forwarder, or a producer reading from a contributor/forwarder. Participating peers are responsible for removing duplicate results within the limit of their buffer.

Pseudo-code for P_1 reading a row of results from a result set

```
If not at end of buffer,
   return an entry from buffer
```

Lecture Notes in Computer Science

For information about Vols. 1–3687

please contact your bookseller or Springer

Vol. 3735: A. Hoffmann, H. Motoda, T. Scheffer (Eds.), Discovery Science. XVI, 400 pages. 2005. (Subseries LNAI).

Vol. 3734: S. Jain, H.U. Simon, E. Tomita (Eds.), Algorithmic Learning Theory. XII, 490 pages. 2005. (Subseries LNAI).

Vol. 3733: P. Yolum, T. Güngör, F. Gürgen, C. Özturan (Eds.), Computer and Information Sciences - ISCIS 2005. XXI, 973 pages. 2005.

Vol. 3731: F. Wang (Ed.), Formal Techniques for Networked and Distributed Systems - FORTE 2005. XII, 558 pages. 2005.

Vol. 3729: Y. Gil, E. Motta, V. R. Benjamins, M.A. Musen (Eds.), The Semantic Web – ISWC 2005. XXIII, 1073 pages. 2005.

Vol. 3728: V. Paliouras, J. Vounckx, D. Verkest (Eds.), Integrated Circuit and System Design. XV, 753 pages. 2005.

Vol. 3726: L.T. Yang, O.F. Rana, B. Di Martino, J.J. Dongarra (Eds.), High Performance Computing and Communcations. XXVI, 1116 pages. 2005.

Vol. 3725: D. Borrione, W. Paul (Eds.), Correct Hardware Design and Verification Methods. XII, 412 pages. 2005.

Vol. 3724: P. Fraigniaud (Ed.), Distributed Computing. XIV, 520 pages. 2005.

Vol. 3723: W. Zhao, S. Gong, X. Tang (Eds.), Analysis and Modelling of Faces and Gestures. XI, 4234 pages. 2005.

Vol. 3722: D. Van Hung, M. Wirsing (Eds.), Theoretical Aspects of Computing – ICTAC 2005. XIV, 614 pages. 2005.

Vol. 3721: A. Jorge, L. Torgo, P.B. Brazdil, R. Camacho, J. Gama (Eds.), Knowledge Discovery in Databases: PKDD 2005. XXIII, 719 pages. 2005. (Subseries LNAI).

Vol. 3720: J. Gama, R. Camacho, P.B. Brazdil, A. Jorge, L. Torgo (Eds.), Machine Learning: ECML 2005. XXIII, 769 pages. 2005. (Subseries LNAI).

Vol. 3719: M. Hobbs, A.M. Goscinski, W. Zhou (Eds.), Distributed and Parallel Computing. XI, 448 pages. 2005.

Vol. 3718: V.G. Ganzha, E.W. Mayr, E.V. Vorozhtsov (Eds.), Computer Algebra in Scientific Computing. XII, 502 pages. 2005.

Vol. 3717: B. Gramlich (Ed.), Frontiers of Combining Systems. X, 321 pages. 2005. (Subseries LNAI).

Vol. 3716: L. Delcambre, C. Kop, H.C. Mayr, J. Mylopoulos, Ó. Pastor (Eds.), Conceptual Modeling – ER 2005. XVI, 498 pages. 2005.

Vol. 3715: E. Dawson, S. Vaudenay (Eds.), Progress in Cryptology – Mycrypt 2005. XI, 329 pages. 2005.

Vol. 3714: J. H. Obbink, K. Pohl (Eds.), Software Product Lines. XIII, 235 pages. 2005.

Vol. 3713: L.C. Briand, C. Williams (Eds.), Model Driven Engineering Languages and Systems. XV, 722 pages. 2005.

Vol. 3712: R. Reussner, J. Mayer, J.A. Stafford, S. Overhage, S. Becker, P.J. Schroeder (Eds.), Quality of Software Architectures and Software Quality. XIII, 289 pages. 2005.

Vol. 3711: F. Kishino, Y. Kitamura, H. Kato, N. Nagata (Eds.), Entertainment Computing - ICEC 2005. XXIV, 540 pages. 2005.

Vol. 3710: M. Barni, I. Cox, T. Kalker, H.J. Kim (Eds.), Digital Watermarking. XII, 485 pages. 2005.

Vol. 3709: P. van Beek (Ed.), Principles and Practice of Constraint Programming - CP 2005. XX, 887 pages. 2005.

Vol. 3708: J. Blanc-Talon, W. Philips, D.C. Popescu, P. Scheunders (Eds.), Advanced Concepts for Intelligent Vision Systems. XXII, 725 pages. 2005.

Vol. 3707: D.A. Peled, Y.-K. Tsay (Eds.), Automated Technology for Verification and Analysis. XII, 506 pages. 2005.

Vol. 3706: H. Fuks, S. Lukosch, A.C. Salgado (Eds.), Groupware: Design, Implementation, and Use. XII, 378 pages. 2005.

Vol. 3704: M. De Gregorio, V. Di Maio, M. Frucci, C. Musio (Eds.), Brain, Vision, and Artificial Intelligence. XV, 556 pages. 2005.

Vol. 3703: F. Fages, S. Soliman (Eds.), Principles and Practice of Semantic Web Reasoning. VIII, 163 pages. 2005.

Vol. 3702: B. Beckert (Ed.), Automated Reasoning with Analytic Tableaux and Related Methods. XIII, 343 pages. 2005. (Subseries LNAI).

Vol. 3701: M. Coppo, E. Lodi, G. M. Pinna (Eds.), Theoretical Computer Science. XI, 411 pages. 2005.

Vol. 3700: J.F. Peters, A. Skowron (Eds.), Transactions on Rough Sets IV. X, 375 pages. 2005.

Vol. 3699: C.S. Calude, M.J. Dinneen, G. Păun, M. J. Pérez-Jiménez, G. Rozenberg (Eds.), Unconventional Computation. XI, 267 pages. 2005.

Vol. 3698: U. Furbach (Ed.), KI 2005: Advances in Artificial Intelligence. XIII, 409 pages. 2005. (Subseries LNAI).

Vol. 3697: W. Duch, J. Kacprzyk, E. Oja, S. Zadrożny (Eds.), Artificial Neural Networks: Formal Models and Their Applications – ICANN 2005, Part II. XXXII, 1045 pages. 2005.

Vol. 3696: W. Duch, J. Kacprzyk, E. Oja, S. Zadrożny (Eds.), Artificial Neural Networks: Biological Inspirations – ICANN 2005, Part I. XXXI, 703 pages. 2005.

Vol. 3695: M.R. Berthold, R.C. Glen, K. Diederichs, O. Kohlbacher, I. Fischer (Eds.), Computational Life Sciences. XI, 277 pages. 2005. (Subseries LNBI).

Vol. 3694: M. Malek, E. Nett, N. Suri (Eds.), Service Availability. VIII, 213 pages. 2005.

Vol. 3693: A.G. Cohn, D.M. Mark (Eds.), Spatial Information Theory. XII, 493 pages. 2005.

Vol. 3692: R. Casadio, G. Myers (Eds.), Algorithms in Bioinformatics. X, 436 pages. 2005. (Subseries LNBI).

Vol. 3691: A. Gagalowicz, W. Philips (Eds.), Computer Analysis of Images and Patterns. XIX, 865 pages. 2005.

Vol. 3690: M. Pěchouček, P. Petta, L.Z. Varga (Eds.), Multi-Agent Systems and Applications IV. XVII, 667 pages. 2005. (Subseries LNAI).

Vol. 3689: G.G. Lee, A. Yamada, H. Meng, S.H. Myaeng (Eds.), Information Retrieval Technology. XVII, 735 pages. 2005.

Vol. 3688: R. Winther, B.A. Gran, G. Dahll (Eds.), Computer Safety, Reliability, and Security. XI, 405 pages. 2005.